TIME AND LANGUAGE

Time and Language

NEW SINOLOGY AND CHINESE HISTORY

Edited by Ori Sela, Zvi Ben-Dor Benite, and Joshua A. Fogel

University of Hawai'i Press ◆ Honolulu

© 2023 University of Hawaiʻi Press
All rights reserved
Paperback edition 2024
Printed in the United States of America

First printed, 2023

Library of Congress Cataloging-in-Publication Data

Names: Sela, Ori, editor. | Ben-Dor Benite, Zvi, editor. | Fogel, Joshua A., editor.
Title: Time and Language : New Sinology and Chinese History / edited by Ori Sela, Zvi Ben-Dor Benite, Joshua A. Fogel.
Other titles: New Sinology and Chinese History
Description: Honolulu : University of Hawaiʻi Press, [2023] | Includes bibliographical references and index.
Identifiers: LCCN 2022051314 (print) | LCCN 2022051315 (ebook) | ISBN 9780824894078 (hardback) | ISBN 9780824894580 (pdf) | ISBN 9780824894597 (epub) | ISBN 9780824894603 (kindle edition)
Subjects: LCSH: Language and history—China. | China—History. | China—History—Methodology.
Classification: LCC P41 .T48 2023 (print) | LCC P41 (ebook) | DDC 306.442/951—dc23/eng/20221220
LC record available at https://lccn.loc.gov/2022051314
LC ebook record available at https://lccn.loc.gov/2022051315

ISBN 9780824895099 (paperback)

Cover art: Li Jinxi, *Guoyu siqian nian lai bianhua chaoliu tu,* 1926

University of Hawaiʻi Press books are printed on acid-free paper and meet the guidelines for permanence and durability of the Council on Library Resources.

The volume is dedicated to Benjamin Elman,
who for over forty years has demonstrated
how acute and sensible scholarship can break
new ground, making it relevant both for studying
the past and for understanding the present.
His scholarship, ranging from philology and the
examination system, through science and technology,
all the way to Japanese, Chinese, and global history,
has truly made a difference.

CONTENTS

Introduction: Time, Text, and History in China 1
ORI SELA, ZVI BEN-DOR BENITE, AND JOSHUA A. FOGEL

1 Tulišen's *Embassy to Distant Territories:* The Travels of a Text 15
PETER C. PERDUE

2 Struggles over the Historical Memory of a Heterodoxy: Chinese Commentaries on the Nestorian Stele 32
CHU PINGYI

3 How Much Does an Understanding of History Help? Naitō Konan's Reading of "Communism" in China 51
JOSHUA A. FOGEL

4 To "Turn the Historical Clock Back": Past, Text, and the Politics of Yuan Shikai's Monarchy 69
ZVI BEN-DOR BENITE

5 *Wenxue* and New Practices of Writing in Post-1840 China 93
THEODORE HUTERS

6 Cai Yuanpei's Politico-Philosophical Languages 118
PETER ZARROW

7 Vernacular Knowledge in Time: Sinology outside the Archive 141
JOAN JUDGE

8 In Search of a Standard National Language in Republican China 159
JANET Y. CHEN

9 A Guangxu Renaissance? Manchu Language Studies in the Late Qing and Their Republican Afterlife 180
MÅRTEN SÖDERBLOM SAARELA

10 The Textual Time Machine: Truth, Facts, and the *Shuowen,* 1770–1932 204
ORI SELA

11 A Time to Heal or a Time to Kill: Confessions in the Anti-Shaman Campaign at Communist Yan'an, 1944–1945 220
KANG XIAOFEI

Bibliography 241

Contributors 273

Index 275

TIME AND LANGUAGE

INTRODUCTION ◆ ORI SELA, ZVI BEN-DOR BENITE, JOSHUA A. FOGEL

Time, Text, and History in China

Philology's Plight

This collection of essays presents a series of case studies by historians engaging the crossroads of time and text in China's recent past. In paying close attention to text, we call for renewed attention to the utility of a somewhat older apparatus in the historian's tool kit—the philological tradition of textual studies. This apparatus has long been central to indigenous scholarly traditions in East Asia. In China, the practice of "minutia learning" (*xiaoxue* 小學) has been considered for millennia as the principal prerequisite for anyone interested in "big ideas." This field evolved into a significant body of methodology and scholarship during the Qing dynasty (1644–1911), known as "evidence-based learning" (*kaozhengxue* 考證學), wherein philological inquiry reigned in the realms of classical and historical studies. Around that same period, it grew and developed, often in an overlapping manner and through mutual contacts, proving highly influential in Japan and Korea as well. This mode of inquiry has been an essential part of the broad practice of what was known as "learning" (*xue* 學) in China and became the backbone of any serious scholarship in East Asia. As we remind readers below, Chinese philological studies were deeply connected to some of the critical shifts in historical and historiographical practices in China, well into the twentieth century. Such traditions, in fact, went hand in hand with the development of Western Sinology and the gradual emergence of Chinese studies in the West.

In this regard, this book responds to the perceived "plight"—intimately connected to the "crisis in the humanities" and to rising criticisms of "area studies"—of philological studies. In the wake of the rise of newer forms of historical and literary social analysis, philology seems increasingly "irrelevant" for the study of history and society, particularly with regard to the modern period.[1] Practitioners of philology, the scholarship of meticulous reading, or as Sheldon Pollock has defined it, the discipline of making sense of texts, have been reacting lately to this plight with creative reminders of its history and necessity. Sometimes the titles of the books speak for themselves.[2] The most comprehensive among this cluster of studies, *World Philology*, posits that the decline of interest in traditional philology among Western scholars was a product of changing historical interests in the second half of the twentieth century. Still, the arguments against it unfairly characterized this approach as antiquarian or even "reactionary."[3]

We embrace the call for a new form of philology as an important part of the increasingly diversifying tool kit of historians, one that responds to the globalizing trends of the twenty-first century and to new and exciting historical tools in our case—China—while respecting the autonomy of the Chinese classical traditions. Under the name of "world philology," scholars search for comparative angles, intercultural contacts, and linkages between elite and vernacular traditions across Eurasia. We follow this lead and endeavor to enhance it. This book therefore presents a response by historians mindful of philology's value *in* Chinese history and *for* Chinese history, and not just regarding antiquity.[4]

Concretely, understanding that the textual practices in Chinese history are ultimately political, the book advances the view that "classical studies" or a textual/philological approach has the potential to bring new and significant insights into *modern* Chinese history. It allows us to highlight the presence, in modern or twentieth-century historical moments, of past issues and concerns of enduring anxieties and practices that affected or persisted from earlier times. Reading the modern, therefore, in an in-depth and continuous dialogue with the past renders the "new" in a different light; taken as a whole, it creates a new historical narrative of China's modern history, one wherein "ruptures" can exist in tandem with continuities. With the stress on the twentieth century, we aim at putting modern texts in dialogue with their classical predecessors and tracking the lineage of important concepts from imperial to Nationalist eras. This is not just for a twenty-first-century scholar's academic amusement; this dialogue was a virtually constant element for historical actors. By looking at the traces of classical concepts in modern texts, even those written in the vernacular Chinese language, we critique, for example, the stereotypical view of the 1919 May 4th movement—often marked as a critical turning point on China's road to literary modernity—as a radical break with tradition and explore different ways of conceiving of time in modern Chinese history. The new approach maintains the value of immersion in primary texts while also looking for long-term processes of temporal change and connections to areas beyond the Sinophone sphere.[5]

Methodologically, we are arguing that the New Sinology, following Geremie Barmé's term, is not an obsolete "tool of the past," as it is sometimes dubbed. Instead, we show that New Sinology as we understand it—rigorous philological research and *longue durée* perspective in particular—can help us rethink the more recent period in Chinese history and its relationship to the past. To be clear, we are not arguing a thesis of "continuity versus rupture" in modern Chinese history, nor are we making the argument that New Sinology is simply a "bridge" between the present and the past. We are instead claiming that a wide spectrum of textual practices that have been used in past moments in Chinese history remain relevant and sometimes necessary for historical studies of the modern era, that the past has often been present in modern Chinese history. We leave open, however, the question of how far back to look for relevant continuities, which scales of time and space work best for analysis, and which texts in which language will generate greater insight.

Why now? The timing of the intervention this book is making is not coincidental. We write at the moment when China is standing firmly, after a century and a half of marginalization and weakness, at the center of global affairs.[6] As was the case at the beginning of the twentieth century, questions of where China sits on the world-historical clock and its relationship to its own past are once again rising to the surface. However, unlike in previous instances, China's leadership seems frankly boastful when it provides answers to these questions.

Time: A Brief History of China's "3,000/4,000/5,000 Years of History"

As the twentieth century in China recedes ever more in our rearview mirror, questions of time and periodization become increasingly acute. In China, perhaps this question is even more acute. In 2021 the People's Republic of China marked the centenary of the founding of the Chinese Communist Party (CCP); a decade earlier, the Republic of China marked its own centenary. These events of the early twentieth century have been understood as the beginning of the "new China." Placing them on a timeline, from the late Qing forward, it seems as if a linear process, "natural" and perhaps deterministic, pulled "China" from its lowly and backward, nineteenth-century, inferior, and isolated position onto the modern world-historical stage. Twentieth-century historiographies of "how China became modern" often have supported this line of thought. The long nineteenth century, in which the Qing declined, was followed by its inevitable demise in 1911, and then modernity was ushered in, as new China imported modern ways of government and life forms from the West. Traditional China was replaced by modern China. That rupture meant, according to this narrative, that China was joining—in practice and conceptually—world history and global modernity. Indeed, accepting the Gregorian calendar in the first days of the Republic seemed to represent this departure from a Chinese timeline and temporal perception and an acceptance of modern, Western chronology.

A deep sense of inferiority accompanied China's entry into the world-historical time zone a hundred years ago, while the new China claimed to have pulled itself out of a period labeled a "Century of Humiliation" (百年國恥). Coined in 1915 during the protests against Japan's humiliating "Twenty-One Demands," counting the years of "national humiliation" referred to the time that had passed since China's defeat in the First Opium War in 1840. It came to be perceived as a fulfilled prophecy in 1949 with the rise of the People's Republic of China, a little over a century after that war. Today, just over two decades after the return of Hong Kong and Macao to China in the late 1990s, one hears the phrases often in reference to China's place in the world. Not only a matter of foreign affairs, the period of humiliation and the dictum to "never forget" that "century" is a central element of the "politics of historical memory" in China.[7]

Recently, we are perhaps seeing signs that things might be going in a different direction and that in the twenty-first century, China will be the one calibrating—or will attempt to do so—the world-historical clock. One of the ironies in the emerging body of knowledge known as "Xi Jinping's Thought" is the idea that the CCP "is the custodian of a 5,000-year-old civilization."[8] This is ironic, of course, because during most of the twentieth century, no entity more than the CCP—and there were many contenders—tried harder to abandon, if not outright destroy, China's millennia-old legacy and launch something "new." Xi often invokes the phrase "5,000 years" of Chinese civilization, partly, at least, as the basis for China's claim to "take on the leadership of a new global order in a 'post-Western era.'"[9] China's new usage of the "5,000-year-old civilization" phrase is code for, in effect, a new claim to a new place in the global arena and a point of origin on the global calendar. China's past, rejected so many times in the twentieth century, is now the future. And not just China's future—a global future, contesting Western options and visions. This is as well a full-scale attempt at one-upmanship vis-à-vis the West. Since the early twentieth century, such a timescale has been linked to China's place in the world. Almost a century ago, Sun Yat-sen 孫逸仙 (1866–1925) stated that:

> The Chinese people are a very old race. Our recorded history dates back four thousand years, and we have existed at least five or six thousand years. In spite of the many calamities due to natural pressure during these centuries, Heaven not only has not destroyed us but has made us a great people with a growing population and a progressive civilization.[10]

More recently, Xi uses China's millennia-old civilizational "age" to claim a leading position in the world and even to "school" other world leaders. In 2017, during a visit with Donald Trump to the Forbidden City, he reminded the American president that China has "3,000 years with a written language." When Trump countered by mentioning the older ancient Egyptian civilization, Xi remained boastful: "but the only continuous civilization to continue onwards is China."[11] Conversely, Sun used the same trope to lament that China did not have a place in the world:

> What is, then, our position in the world? In numbers, we are the largest national group in the world, and our four thousand years of cultural background may be compared favorably with that of the West. Unfortunately, we lack national unity, and our country, which is weak as well as poor, is being reduced to an inferior position among the nations.[12]

When we compare Sun's and Xi's words, it is striking to realize how the two invocations of a long and continuous past are so similar in that the context for each was in dialogue with the West. At the same time, though, they are conspicuously different, almost opposed in terms of the implied strategic signals. For Sun, the long past meant a moral high ground of sorts vis-à-vis the West; he contended that China had "abandoned" "imperialism and militarism" (a questionable proposition in and of itself, if one looks back on Chinese history). In effect, however, Sun's response signaled frustrated weakness—a frustration, mentioned above, about "being reduced to an inferior position among the nations." Xi, on the other hand, clearly wants to signal strength. This corresponds to the above-mentioned proposition about Xi's and China's claim to global leadership. In short, Sun's concern was what to do with China's ancient past when China was weak and the West was on the rise. Xi's concern, on the other hand, is how to use the same long past when China is on the rise, and the West seems, at least (and it is certainly portrayed that way in China), to be in decline. For Sun, the past was a burden to be converted into some kind of edge. For Xi, the past is one of the most significant advantages. For both, the past was of crucial importance, and that also meant that the past had to be controlled. Sinologically, we may intervene and suggest that, in similar ways, premodern emperors had to come to terms with the past and find ways to try and own it. Today, the possibility that the global clock is transitioning and moving its center from West to East (or that the global clock is "decoupling") is an exciting proposition to consider, but it raises a question: What is the Chinese perception of time and its relationship with history?

When we think of China's perception of its past, nothing can express more the dramatic change between the beginning of the twentieth century and today than the above statements, which use China's continuous past as a code. It is nonetheless precisely this change in the perception of the past, and in particular the sensitivities concerning the *time* within which this past is supposedly embedded, that invites revisiting the long moment of China's transition from a "traditional" empire to a "modern" state with these issues in mind.[13] Indeed, the very debate about whether the modern Chinese state is a "nation-state" or a "civilizational state," as prominent Chinese savants have recently suggested, speaks directly to these diverse, and at times conflicting, notions of time. One way to make sense of these conflicting notions of time in relation to history is through examining language. Discussing the issue of "linguistic change and the history of events" in his *Sediments of Time*, Reinhart Koselleck (1923–2006) maintained:

> A history that has run its course remains as singular as it is past. And if it is held to be memorable, this is mostly because it contains a surprise that humans try to explain. It is only after taking on its linguistic form that we can access all of the reasons that make the singular, often surprising course of a history explainable, evident, and comprehensible. These reasons last longer than the individual, singular events themselves, for otherwise, they would not be justifications. However, in contrast to the events themselves and their consequences, these justifications are solely connected to their linguistic transmission.[14]

Let us see. The tropes of "a hundred years of humiliation" and particularly those of "4,000 [or 5,000] years of civilization" raise questions concerning what François Hartog calls the "regime of historicity"—"a category (without content), which can elucidate our experiences of time."[15] In other words, this dramatic reversal from Sun to Xi, in terms of use and meaning of the same phrase, raises an interesting question: When China "enters" world history, what is the "history," and whose time, does this "entrance" refer to? A century ago, China operated (and continues to operate today) within a complicated time frame:

chronologically, as an idea, as a telos. In the 1910s, literary and institutional revolutions and reforms were declared by prominent Chinese intellectuals such as Hu Shi 胡適 (1891–1962) and Chen Duxiu 陳獨秀 (1879–1942). These movements aimed to rid "New China" of the "old" and open new paths for modernization and revitalization of the newly forming Chinese nation. They also aimed at changing the orientational axis of China and the Chinese, and the temporal reorientation (i.e., the temporal plane of reference and inspiration) was a major part of the revolutions. A key aspect of the reorientation related to language: from language choice (which language and script should be used), through the literary-versus-vernacular debates, and up to specific terminology and linguistic styles, proponents of new temporal orientations or guardians of the old could make their claims. And linguistic challenges and claims were intimately tied to power struggles and competitions, competitions over the shape and identity of the evolving nation, as well as over claims to its temporality (or maybe multiple temporalities). Nonetheless, in all these discussions, controversies, and debates, the linguistic and temporal plane of reference—even when contested—was deeply rooted in the space, time, and languages of the Sinosphere. Protagonists of the era surrounding the Qing's fall did not know that some form of the Republic would emerge triumphantly, nor did those who assembled the first meetings of the CCP know that in 1949 they would declare victory. The teleology that permeates many of the narratives concerning this process is highly problematic.

One cannot even be comfortable with the measure of certainty, at the time, concerning what was seemingly being left behind: the two-millennia-old dynastic history that began with the establishment of the Qin in 221 BCE and ended with the fall of the Qing in 1911. In 1920, the then young, future historian Fu Sinian 傅斯年 (1896–1950) condemned the "autocratic dynasty [that] was the center of Chinese political organization" in the past. When it disappeared, charged Fu, it left a fragmented China with no society, "like a loose sheet of sand."[16] The 2,200 years of dynastic history were replaced with something else, and here things get tricky. In 1902 Liang Qichao 梁啟超 (1873–1929) declared in his famous essay on "New Historiography" ("Xin shixue" 新史學) that the "twenty-four dynastic histories are not history; [they] are nothing but family genealogies" (二十四史非史也, 二十四史姓之家譜而已).[17] But, as Peter Zarrow has shown, even though Liang was responding to modern (read Western) challenges, he was, in fact, reworking an "old myth" about the ancient sage-kings of China into a new history. Liang went back some 5,000 years, to China's mythic times, to resurrect stories about its old kings to establish a new time frame for China's history.[18] One could perhaps argue that Liang's inspiration was the early Han dynasty (202 BCE–9 CE) historian Sima Qian 司馬遷: Michael Nylan claimed that one aspect (the tables) of the *Shiji* 史記 (Records of the Grand Historian) was meant "to impose a measure of significant order on the messy realities of the past," and that Sima Qian was pushing for "the painstaking reaffirmation of the sacred origins, predestined greatness, and the enduring order of the Central States' (Zhongguo 中國) culture."[19] Indeed, Liang even alluded to himself as "the new astrologer" in his work on biographies, directly following Sima Qian ("the astrologer")[20]; "New Historiography" conducted a strategic dialogue with its ancestors.

Liu Shipei 劉師培 (1884–1919) expressed the *longue durée* idea more strongly when he declared, in 1903, that the time had come to start the national "chronology" from the earliest point possible: "[E]very nation cannot but [desire to] trace itself back to its origin" (民族不得不溯其起源). Liu, again echoing Sima Qian, called for going back "4,000 years" to the time of Xuanyuan 軒轅—the Yellow Emperor—who was "the original ancestor of the 400,000,000 people of the Han race."[21] If we, the Chinese, he wrote, "desire to continue the task of the Yellow Emperor, then we should use the birth of the Yellow Emperor as the beginning of our chronology." Liu was indeed speaking about the "nation" (*minzu*) and the "Han race" (*Hanzu*), both seemingly "modern" and European terms, but in effect he was thinking with very old concepts. For instance, he credited the Yellow Emperor with being "the first person who created [Chinese] civilization" (軒轅氏是則黃帝惹乃製造文明之第一人).[22] *Wenming* 文明, translated here uneasily as "civilization," is a term that goes back to the most ancient era of Chinese time. The politically vital *Yijing* 易經 (Classic of changes), for instance, remarked that when the "'dragon appears in the field'—all under Heaven (begins to be) adorned [*wen*] and brightened [*ming*]."[23] Thus *wenming*, either as "civilization" or as the condition of becoming "adorned and brightened," is certainly not "modern" in the popular sense of the word. The Yellow Emperor was not the starting point of the Chinese nation or the father of the "race." If anything, he marked for earlier scholars the starting point of the spread of civilization all over the world, or at least in a place called, at some point, China. And yet there is a seemingly straight—"singular" to use Koselleck's language—line that connects the Yellow Emperor, Sun, and Xi. It was cleverly invented, before Sun and Xi discussed those issues, by the young Liu Shipei.

In 1928, asking "what Chinese historians are doing in their own history," Arthur Hummel (1884–1975) observed that contemporary modern-oriented intellectuals in China were aiming "to reconstruct the past by the methods of literary and historical criticism, it is a very old one, dating back to the so-called school of 'Han Learning' which flourished in the seventeenth and eighteenth centuries." He mentioned that the early modern phase was interrupted "after 1800 by the unmistakable decay of the ruling dynasty, by the ensuing political turmoil, and by the too violent commercial impact of the Occidental powers." But its "modern revival began with the publication in the early [1890s] of K'ang Yuwei's 'The Forged Classics of the Wang Mang Period.'" He proceeded to narrate what he saw as the birth of modern Chinese historiography, mentioning the above-mentioned scholars and others such as Wang Guowei 王國維 (1877–1927) and Gu Jiegang 顧頡剛 (1893–1980). At the same time, he described the great philological enterprise that accompanied this moment[24]—an enterprise that he correctly tied to earlier moments, such as the one in the eighteenth century, even if, as Sela demonstrates in Chapter 10, the philological tradition crossed the 1800 divide.

It is not coincidental that early twentieth-century historians like Wang, Gu, Liang, Fu, and the enigmatic Liu, and many others, were also linguists, scholars of ancient classical texts, each with a prolific portfolio of philological work as well. It would be simplistic to say that ancient texts stood at the cradle of modern China to justify a new Sinological approach to history. We would, however, argue that the task of the historian is to uncover how concepts such as *wenming* were reworked if we wish to make sense of what they meant to the historical actors. Perhaps more importantly, the task of the historian is to expose the many possibilities that the use of such ancient concepts encapsulates and what they might mean for the present. During the dialogue in the Forbidden City, when President Xi responded to Trump's mention of the ancient Egyptians with the statement about China being the "only continuous civilization," he also said: "our people are the original people, black hair, yellow skin, inherited onwards, we call ourselves the descendants of the dragon." With what we just noted about *wenming* and the dragon in the *Yijing*, and the *wenming* that started with the Yellow Emperor, we must ask ourselves: To which was Xi referring? The one that spreads "only" in China, or the one that spreads all over the world?

Chinese History and the World-Historical Clock

Mentioning a Western observation (Hummel) from as early as 1928 reminds us that Western Sinology and Chinese historiography/philology used to be in dialogue with each other. This was the case for the Jesuits and Protestants, working with Chinese and Manchu counterparts, and also for James Legge, mentioned in a note above, whose translations of the Chinese classics were produced through interactions with Chinese, such as Wang Tao (1828–1897); it was certainly the case as well in the twentieth century. A recent study examined in detail the history of the relationship and interaction between "foreign Sinology" and modern Chinese historiography. It shows, or rather reminds us of, the dialogue between the two "sides," Chinese and Western, with Western scholars learning from their Chinese counterparts and vice versa.[25] What Hummel signaled in 1928, regarding China's stance vis-à-vis its past, certainly continued after World War II. In early 1955 Edwin Pulleyblank (1922–2013) gave an "inaugural lecture" on the subject of "Chinese History and World History." It was probably the first direct engagement with a topic that would become much more heatedly debated only a few decades later—the place of China and Chinese history on the world-historical clock. Pulleyblank lamented the fact that "world histories" tend to "dispose" of China and "to treat its history as something entirely external."[26] Pulleyblank, a historian of the Tang period, criticized the position European thinkers gave to China on the global clock, within which "world history" was embedded since the emergence of "scientific," world-historical thinking in the early nineteenth century. He pointed out that, even though the twentieth-century world forces us "out of our parochial attitude to recognize other peoples and cultures from the standpoint of equality," one can still find "authors who are content to assume that such things did not exist east of the Mediterranean lands."[27] Pulleyblank explained what produced the tendency to "dispose" of China: the reason behind "this failure is not merely lack of knowledge [of Chinese history], formidable as this is"; the problem is "the lack of the means of fitting the vast mass of detail of Chinese history into familiar patterns of Western history." This condition meant that:

> [T]o be rendered intelligible to Western readers Chinese history must undergo a process of translation, and not of words alone but of whole concepts and systems of concepts. Further, if it is to be made congruent with Western history, our concepts for dealing with Western history must also come under criticism, and new concepts must be devised which will be adequate to render each culture intelligible in terms of the other.[28]

For Pulleyblank, the question was, first, historiographical: he was, in fact, speaking to historians who he thought were seeking to "widen their historical horizons."[29] Elaborating on his criticisms, Pulleyblank sounded somewhat forgiving regarding historians and other scholars who, to his mind, lacked the proper conceptual tool kit to work with Chinese history.

On second thought, though, we would argue that it should not be surprising that a Tang historian who was also a historical linguist was one of the first to fully articulate the problematic place of China in world history, certainly concerning how it featured in significant strands of European thought. The Tang was the first truly "global" period in Chinese history. Pulleyblank made sure his listeners understood that point when he mentioned Tang connections with the Islamic and Asian worlds; hence, the immediate significance for world history would be clear. Similarly, as a Chinese language historian, he was acutely aware that there *was* history in China—simply put, its language had a palpable, evidential history.[30] In 2003 Pulleyblank remarked on how he embarked on his parallel career as a linguist shortly after writing his first book on Tang history: "I became convinced that, contrary to the prevailing opinion among many teachers of Chinese that, quote: 'Chinese has no grammar,' Chinese both ancient and modern is like every other language in having regular rules of syntax.... This, in turn, led me into the field of historical phonology, which has been my main preoccupation in more recent time."[31]

It is interesting to consider, given the emphasis this volume places on questions of language, the implied parallelism here between the perceived lack of dynamism in China's history and the proposition that Chinese had no grammar or syntax.[32] Pulleyblank's criticisms concerning the location of China on the world-historical clock were coming from the relatively distant past, on the one hand, and from the study of the language on the other. He clearly thought that his experience as a Tang historian and linguist was relevant for discussing China's place in world history in his time. Thus, Pulleyblank deserves his place in this introduction not only because he was among the very first to express the critique sketched above. He also exemplified it in his research.

"We have 3,000 years with a written language," insisted Xi. And, indeed, however one counts China's years and whatever form of "China" they are referring to for this counting, it is language—and the written language in particular—that seems to be the one constant that is always present. It is with this in mind that we bring back China's textual tradition to center stage in research on modern China. We bring it back not to satisfy a mere nostalgic need to burnish an old tool but to function as a means for new understandings of modern China. In so doing, we take our cue from Geremie Barmé's recent manifesto calling for a research agenda that "emphasizes strong scholastic underpinnings in both the classical and modern Chinese language and studies, at the same time as encouraging an ecumenical attitude in relation to a wide variety of approaches and disciplines, whether they be mainly empirical or more theoretically inflected."[33] In other words, we take this as a clarion call for a Sinological intervention of sorts in the history of "modern China," and hence we aim to broaden our temporal boundaries by using the tool kit of New Sinology to take us further into the past—in this book, mainly to the Qing period. As we try to demonstrate, the tool kit of New Sinology helps expose the crucial nexus of time, language, and power, as this Introduction has laid out for consideration. We examine how the historical actors in the following chapters operated in different temporalities and employed in their writings differing topoi, as required by the changes encountered. This is because the actors lived, thought, and worked within and between different timescales, and they envisioned or experienced different horizons of time, with different horizons of meanings embedded within them. We find different temporal planes of orientation and reference at play—from the immediate, daily, or mundane to the deep, long-term, and heavenly. We uncover hidden or pronounced chasms between these temporal planes, and the languages used for navigating these planes are often revealing, also exposing a geography of time. These notions of time and language, at times in competition, also formed a stage upon which authority and power could evolve and assert themselves. The tripartite relationship—of time, language, and power—generated various ways of utilizing the past, often for presentist agendas. These agendas were also concerned with the standardization of time, language, and power, and are thus also part of our inquiry, stressing the nexus of standardization and enforcement, standardization and deviation.

From a variety of diverse angles, we bring together here a collection of essays centered around questions of Chinese perceptions of and engagement with the past—in terms of the scale of time, periodization, and history—mainly during the first half of the twentieth century. We revisit these questions with the present moment in mind, but we also remember that the linkages between China's past and its place in the world are not new. The essays collected in this book engage a variety of questions and issues pertaining to China's history in the past century and a half in a much different yet similar manner to that signaled by Pulleyblank. On the one hand, we view China's recent past with a perspective that considers the more distant past and tries to show how the latter has its bearing on the former. On the other hand, all of our essays revolve around themes about language and China's textual tradition, broadly defined. In this regard, we are again returning to a task that China historians have tried to do beforehand. To quote Edwin Pulleyblank, the essays here render moments in Chinese history "not of words alone but of whole concepts and systems of concepts" intelligible to Western readers through "a process of translation."

The Essays

Our volume consists of eleven chapters, each engaged with a particular case study. Peter Perdue's essay highlights the longer pedigree of "China and world" through an in-depth examination of a Manchu text and its transformation into other languages through the eighteenth and nineteenth centuries. Thus, he also foregrounds the significance of Manchu as a linguistic and identity prism for dealing with the later transformation into modern China. In Chapter 2, Chu Pingyi continues to consider the theme of "China and the world" through an analysis of the famous Nestorian Stele, as a prism to consider the place of Christianity in China's history. He explores how works of exegesis and translation have had a bearing on the ways Chinese intellectuals brought Christian and Western concepts into the fold of the Sinosphere, domesticated and, at times, contested them. Both essays take a long-term approach and diverse linguistic prisms.

In Chapters 3 and 4, Joshua Fogel and Zvi Ben-Dor Benite tackle major political concerns of the early twentieth century from Japanese and Chinese perspectives, respectively. Writing at a time when there were virtually no self-declared communists and no Communist parties as yet in East Asia, Naitō Konan 內藤湖南 (1866–1934), Japan's most famous prewar Sinologist, stated that the principal reason for the failure of the Taiping Rebellion (1851–1864) was its "Communism." What could he have meant by this? Fogel examines the origins of the terms used in Naitō's writings through the 1910s and 1920s in an effort to unpack these lexical items in their proper historical context. Revisiting the short-lived episode of Yuan Shikai's 袁世凱 (1859–1916) monarchy, Ben-Dor Benite exposes the rich classical textual world hiding behind it. Paying attention to this classical backdrop demonstrates how the Yuan monarchy was intimately related to highly relevant political questions that have been debated in critical moments from antiquity to the present.

Theodore Huters and Peter Zarrow, in Chapters 5 and 6, focus on literary thought and literature, and relate these to questions of national identity formation, tradition, and modernity, and they thus unravel notions of time and language from the late Qing into the 1910s and 1920s. Huters problematizes the seemingly straightforward category of *wenxue* 文學, or "literature," from the nineteenth century onward. He demonstrates how this category, and its content, changed during this time, and how these changes became almost dogmatic in the early twentieth century. Nonetheless, even with the rapid changes of the 1900s, the long "traditional" bearing of earlier *wenxue* remained at the core of the new writers. Zarrow's chapter highlights Cai Yuanpei's 蔡元培 (1868–1940) stance vis-à-vis traditionalism and radicalism, and he argues for Cai's complex footing in both realms. Zarrow further discusses Cai's notion of time and his creative views of Darwinism and Confucianism, thereby also emphasizing the links between "old" and "new" that Cai had generated.

Moving to the realm of mass communication, media, and language, Joan Judge and Janet Chen, in Chapters 7 and 8, look at how languages as ways of communicating knowledge have been underwritten by critical interaction with older modes of writing, speaking, and thinking. Judge examines the "epistemologies of the less powerful" through the *wanbao quanshu* 萬寶全書 genre of writing and its supplements. Navigating from Qing to the twentieth (even into the twenty-first) century, Judge shows the "complex interplay between vernacular, mainstream, and scientific knowledge" during that period. Chen follows the trajectory of the attempt at unification or standardization of "the national language" in the early twentieth century. Working on early formal and informal attempts to do so, her research brings to light both the complex relations of language and power, and the ways in which vernacular and classical, local and national, were in constant flux during the formative years of the new nation.

Engaging studies *about* language, Mårten Söderblom Saarela and Ori Sela explore Manchu and Chinese language studies, respectively, from the Qing to the Republican era. Saarela focuses on Manchu and argues that—surprisingly, perhaps—this type of intellectual and academic engagement not only flourished during the last decades of Qing rule, but, in fact, resisted the 1911 marker and continued well into the Republican period. He points out the significance Manchu studies had during these early days of the Republic, and the ways in which, despite all the political, social, and economic upheavals, Manchu, and the academic study of its literature and documents, "remained relevant" and created its own genealogy, one that continues till today, as one of the main pillars of New Sinology. Sela, examining another pillar of Chinese language studies—the *Shuowen jiezi* 說文解字—looks at how elite scholars' concentration on this massive text changed between the mid-Qing and the Republican era, and how this change exemplifies a different notion of time and identity. He further argues that this different notion is closely related to questions of social and political power, and how the past and concepts about the past, on the one hand, persisted across the "tradition"/"modernity" divide, while on the other hand reflecting how time, along with perceptions of antiquity, present, and future, functioned differently for those valorizing the *Shuowen* from Qing to Republican China.

The last essay in the volume, by Kang Xiaofei, takes us in a different and fascinating direction, not as a conclusion but rather as a form of an open-ended invitation for further studies. Probing into the Anti-Shaman Campaign in the central communist base area in Yan'an during the mid-1940s, through propaganda materials, newspapers, and legal sources, Kang demonstrates how the CCP's language at the time shows that the Party did not simply, perhaps simplistically, move against religion, but rather how its engagement with shamanistic phenomena was underpinned by "traditional," even religious, points of departure. Indeed, instead of assuming that the CCP just wanted to sever the new nation's ties with its past, Kang emphasizes the uneasy connections between the new regime and ideology and older, strong and persistent, modes of thought and practice: "time to heal" and "time to kill" were in fact simultaneous.

Taken together, the essays in this volume thus bring different perspectives on time, language, and power, from Qing to Republican China, through the prism of the tool kit of New Sinology. The above does not mean there have not been any such studies to date; rather, we wish to urge a broader and deeper academic pursuit of this line, one that will assist in making better sense of the very idea of "modern China" or "Chinese modernity," grounded in a deep Sinological perspective. We hope this call will go beyond the scholarly practice of experts, and also empower institutions to endorse thorough studies of such tools as classical Chinese and Manchu, thereby fostering the next generations of students.

Notes

1. Pollock, "Future Philology?"
2. For the sake of brevity, we name only the major studies of the past five years. Turner, *Philology;* Lönnroth, *Philology Matters!;* Trüper, *Orientalism, Philology, and the Illegibility of the Modern World.*
3. Pollock, Elman, and Chang, *World Philology.*
4. As scholars usually practicing newer forms of historical and literary sociocultural analysis, we are not expressing here nostalgia for the times when "philology reigned" and, in our case, old-style European Sinology dominated the study of Chinese history. We are mindful of Sinology's connection, sometimes, to projects of Christianization, or to its links to imperialism during the nineteenth and early twentieth centuries. Yet, considering China's own tradition of philological studies, we do argue that the methods and practices employed and presented in each of the ensuing chapters are beneficial and relevant, indeed critical, in revisiting specific questions pertaining to Chinese modernity.
5. We thank Peter Perdue for this elegant articulation of the central task of the book.
6. Carrai, Defraigne, and Wouters, *The Belt and Road Initiative and Global Governance.*
7. Wang, *Never Forget National Humiliation.*
8. Buckley, "Xi Jinping Thought Explained."
9. Kaufman, "China's Discourse of 'Civilization.'" See also Kaufman, "Xi Jinping as Historian."
10. Sun, *San Min Chu I,* p. 11.
11. "Xi Gives Trump a Chinese History Lesson."
12. Sun, *San Min Chu I,* pp. 5–6.
13. Perdue, "Where Do Correct Political Ideas Come From?"
14. Koselleck, *Sediments of Time,* p. 135.
15. Hartog, *Regimes of Historicity,* pp. xvii, 11–17.
16. Cited in Wang, *Fu Ssu-nien,* p. 43. It is no coincidence that Fu established the Institute of History and Philology at Academia Sinica in 1928.
17. Liang Qichao, "Xin shixue" (1902), anthologized in Liang, *Shixue lunzhu sizhong,* p. 241.
18. Zarrow, "Old Myth into New History."
19. See Nylan, "Mapping Time in the Shiji and Hanshu Tables 表"; Nylan, "Sima Qian."
20. See Liu, "Inception, Inheritance and Innovation." The term *taishigong* 太史公 is often translated as "the Grand Historian" or "Grand Scribe" rather than "the astrologer," as Liu has it.
21. Sima Qian promoted the novel idea in his time that the Yellow Emperor was a point of departure of "the Central States' culture," contrary to earlier chronologies (e.g., in the classics).

22. Liu Shipei (Wu Wei), "Huangdi jinian lun" 黃帝紀念論 (Commemorating the Yellow Emperor) (1903), in Luo, ed., *Guomin ribao huipian*. Translation with minor adjustments from Cohen, "Brief Note."

23. This is how James Legge translated this verse. See Legge, trans., *The Chinese Classics*, vol. 2: *The Yi King*, p. 414. Other translations have a somewhat different take, for example: "'Dragon appearing in the field.' Through him the whole world attains beauty and clarity." Wilhelm and Baynes, *The I Ching*, p. 380. On the *Yijing* and politics, see Hon, *The Yijing and Chinese Politics*.

24. Hummel, "What Chinese Historians Are Doing in Their Own History," citation on p. 715.

25. Li, *Yuwai Hanxue yu Zhongguo xiandai shixue*.

26. Pulleyblank, *Chinese History and World History*, p. 6.

27. Pulleyblank, *Chinese History and World History*, pp. 5–6.

28. Pulleyblank, *Chinese History and World History*, p. 7.

29. Pulleyblank, *Chinese History and World History*, p. 6.

30. For a specific discussion of Pulleyblank as a historical linguist and for the full list of his publications as a historian and a linguist, see Chan, "In Memoriam."

31. Cited in Chan, "In Memoriam," p. 258.

32. Other cultures have evinced similar tendencies in relating to their past—for example, Hebrew and Greek. See Gilbert, *Letters to Auntie Fori*.

33. See Geremie R. Barmé, "Towards a New Sinology," p. 4. *Contemporary Chinese Thought* dedicated a recent special issue, "Sinologism and New Sinology: Discussions and Debate on China-West Studies," which is, in part, a response from China to Barmé's call. See the introduction by Gu and Zhou, "Sinology, Sinologism, and New Sinology."

1 ◆ PETER C. PERDUE

Tulišen's Embassy to Distant Territories
The Travels of a Text

The editors of this volume argue for China's having produced in the twentieth century a revival of philology in a new form. Philology, defined as the careful study of words and texts in the primary source language, has been a fundamental style of scholarship in the humanities in both Asia and the West for many centuries. The academic study of Chinese texts by Europeans began in the eighteenth century, after Jesuit missionaries and Russian Sinologists gained access to Beijing and conducted conversations and exchanged texts with Qing literati. This approach to China, focused mainly on the classical texts of philosophy and history, dominated scholarship on China until the twentieth century. After the collapse of the Qing dynasty, Sinologists continued to study the ancient texts, but new forms of historical and literary/social analysis, based on ethnographic studies and social science paradigms, challenged the reign of classical philology. Whatever its value as an investigation of the values of ancient China, philological analysis seemed irrelevant to the understanding of the revolutionary changes in China in the twentieth century. The study of nineteenth-century China pioneered by John K. Fairbank (1907–1991) and others relied on official documents and archival sources instead of prominent cultural products. By the twentieth century, however, social historians shifted attention to the lives of ordinary people instead of literati. Many of the historians who did focus on literati analyzed their social networks and political experience, rather than the content of the texts they wrote.

Sheldon Pollock describes a similar process for the actual discipline of philology. From being the queen of the disciplines in the nineteenth century European university, it has dropped to the bottom of the academic Chain of Being. Fairly or unfairly, philology in all of its versions has lost the unqualified prestige it used to enjoy over a century ago.[1]

The decline of interest in traditional philology among Western scholars, the editors argue, was a product of changing historical interests in the second half of the twentieth century, but the arguments against traditional philology, they believe, unfairly characterized it as antiquarian or reactionary. They call instead for a new form of philology that responds to the globalizing trends of the twenty-first century while also respecting the autonomy of the Chinese classical tradition. Under the name of "world philology," scholars of many cultural traditions have embraced an approach that looks for comparative angles, intercultural contacts, and linkages between elite and vernacular traditions across Eurasia.

What is new about this new philology? In this volume, the stress on the twentieth century marks a new phase, putting modern texts in dialogue with their classical predecessors and tracking the lineage of important concepts from imperial to nationalist eras. By looking at the traces of classical concepts in modern texts, even those written in the vernacular Chinese language, we critique the stereotypical view of May 4th as a radical break with tradition and explore different ways of conceiving of time in modern Chinese history. The new approach maintains the value of immersion in primary texts, while also looking for long-term processes of temporal change and connections to areas beyond the Sinophone sphere. It leaves open, however, the question of how far back to look for relevant continuities, which scales of time and space work best for analysis, and which texts in which languages will generate greater insight.

The Travels of a Text, from the Eighteenth to Twentieth Centuries

Tulišen (1667–1741), a Manchu official sent to Russia on a diplomatic mission, wrote an account in Manchu of his travels in 1723. In this chapter, I track the progress of this text as it was translated into multiple languages from the eighteenth to the twentieth centuries. The reception of the work, the audience for which it was written, the ensemble of other texts with which it was classified, and the effects on perceptions of the Qing dynasty were just as important, if not more important, than the accuracy of the translations themselves. A traditional philologist might focus most of his effort on evaluating the accuracy of each translation, but here I will discuss mainly the context rather than the text itself.

All philology is a form of translation—of either a more or less literal type. Modern literary critics, translators, and philosophers agree that translation does not simply transfer meanings word-by-word from one language to another. Words do not have exact equivalents in other languages, and words do not simply represent objects in the world.[2] The art of the translator is to re-create in his readers some portion of what is contained in the original language, but he will always fail to capture all the implications of one text, and he will add others. In the terms of Reinhart Koselleck, the translator is a linguistic actor whose actions are inevitably penetrated by the social conditions under which he writes.[3] Translations of poetry and philosophy may be exceptionally diverse—one poem by Wang Wei may have more than twenty adequate translations—but even translators of relatively unliterary prose works have to make choices, guided by their own instincts and what they believe their readers need to know. By following multiple translations of the same text into different languages over an extended period of time, we can track not only the influence of one author and his information about one region, but also the changes in contexts of production—the different political motivations, scholarly audiences, and cultural impacts on Chinese and others' knowledge of Central Eurasia.

Why begin with the eighteenth century? Twenty-first-century Chinese writers in search of a global mission for the newly rising Chinese state and economy have invoked many historical parallels, but this period, which we know as the "high Qing," appears to predominate. By the mid-eighteenth century, the Qing, having conquered Manchuria, Mongolia, Taiwan, and Xinjiang, with influence extending into Tibet and parts of Kazakhstan, controlled or influenced a larger territory than any previous dynasty except the Yuan, and they maintained this influence for over 150 years. The much-touted Belt and Road Initiative (BRI) of today invokes the ancient Silk Roads, but in fact the most important period of actual road-building in Central Asia in the imperial period came during the mid-Qing. Qing officials also produced numerous geographical and ethnographical accounts surveying the new dominions under imperial rule. Scholars exiled to Xinjiang wrote poetry and travel accounts displaying the new marvels of imperial rule to readers back in Beijing. At the same time, Manchu officials, for their part, mainly concerned with administering banner territories, took detailed notice of the cultures and natural resources of the frontier regions.[4] Anyone interested in the expansive dimensions of the modern Chinese state cannot ignore the experience of the eighteenth century.

It is also important to stress that the original language of Tulišen's text was Manchu. Even though he may have written the later Chinese translation himself, his first perceptions of Eurasia on his travels came through the eyes and words of a Manchu official. In addressing this question, we need to argue for conceptions of the languages of Qing China that are just as large as its territory. In this sense, "Sinology" is a misleading term if it refers, as most people take it, only to documents in the classical and vernacular Sinitic languages. Modern philologists of China, like scholars during the Qing, must embrace the multiple languages of the empire. Even documents written in Chinese still reflect the influence of terms derived from non-Sinitic languages. Since nationalist Chinese writings, like those of the Qing, included a broad range of ethnic and racial vocabulary that pervaded all prominent discourse, we cannot elucidate the meanings of critical terms in the twentieth century from Chinese sources alone. In addition, the influence of foreign languages beyond the Qing boundaries, especially Japanese and English, was so large that translations either into foreign languages or from foreign languages must also be included in the broad scope of the new Sinology.

Mårten Saarela's chapter in this volume demonstrates that some Chinese continued to maintain interest in the Manchu language into the twentieth century. But the premier tradition of Manchu studies by the 1930s had developed in Japan, part of a lineage of brilliant scholars trained and inspired by Naitō Konan 内藤湖南 (1866–1934). Japanese philological studies of Manchu oriented the study of China in a new direction, away from the insistence on a unitary dynastic tradition centered in the Yellow and Yangzi Rivers, and toward linkages with Central Eurasian cultural traditions informed by multilingual analysis. Because of the rise of this field, Tulišen's text can then take its place among the key Manchu documents that illuminated the early Qing state. The "new Qing history" that is now hotly debated by modern Chinese scholars grounds itself in this early twentieth-century work on Manchu texts, supplemented by Manchu archival materials. Tulišen's text, along with other Manchu texts and scholarship on them, still plays a role in pushing studies of China into increasingly transnational, multilingual, and comparative directions.

Tulišen's Travel Account

In 1712, the Manchu envoy Tulišen 圖麗琛 left Beijing on a mission to Ayuki Khan of the Torghut Mongols.[5] The Torghuts were a branch of the western Mongols who had fled to Russia in the seventeenth century to escape the rising power of the Zunghar Mongol state, eventually settling in the region around the Volga River. Tulišen's goal was to aid in the return of Ayuki's nephew Arabjur from the Qing frontier to the Torghut settlement in Russia. During his journey, Tulišen collected information about places, peoples, and commercial resources of the Russian empire, and the situation of the different Central Eurasian peoples. He met with Ayuki Khan in his pastures near the Volga River, proposing an alliance between the Qing and the Torghut Mongols against the Zunghars. Before he returned to Beijing in 1715, he had begun writing the Manchu text *Lakcaha Jecende Takûraha ejehe bithe* (A book describing the embassy to distant territories), and he submitted a petition to the emperor to allow its publication in 1716. It was published in Manchu in 1723. A Chinese version, entitled *Yiyulu* 異域錄 (A record of alien regions), also appeared in 1723. Although a bilingual version also existed, it is the Chinese edition that became best known in Qing China and in Western Europe.

Western scholars quickly took an interest in this rare account of Central Asian territories. A French translation appeared in 1726, German and Russian translations in the late eighteenth century, and Sir George Staunton's English translation from Chinese appeared in 1821. The text became a very popular source of information for Europeans interested in China, Mongolia, and Central Eurasia, and for Chinese writers on Central Eurasian peoples.[6] But for most of the nineteenth century it vanished from view as an independent textual source. A fully annotated translation from the Manchu text, by the great Japanese Manchu specialist Imanishi Shunjū 今西春秋 (1907–1979), only appeared in the mid-twentieth century.

I have discussed Tulišen's report, along with the contemporaneous travel account of John Bell (1691–1780), a Scottish traveler and diplomat, as part of the story of the Qing campaigns against the Zunghar Mongols.[7] In my book, I relied on the original Manchu text. But the translated versions have their own interest, as each represents a distinct perspective on Eurasia, and each derives from different sources. Instead of using Tulišen's account as a source of information about Central Eurasian diplomacy, we may also view it as a personal account, transmitted through different linguistic media, that affected the perceptions of its audiences in various ways. The Manchu readers of Tulišen's text would respond to it with a different set of expectations than those of the Chinese, English, or Russian readers, who drew on their own linguistic and literary backgrounds. The form of the text, the conditions of its production, and the metatextual material (prefaces, maps, etc.) also shaped the readers' expectations. Each version of the text delivered a different perspective on the Qing and its relationship to Central Eurasia.

A study of *Lakcaha Jecende Takûraha ejehe bithe* contributes several new perspectives to the themes of this volume—time and Sinology, language, and power. First, it expands the meaning of the term "Sinology" to include not just commentaries in English and Chinese, but the relationship between multiple languages and translations. Second, the popularity of this text across Eurasia points to a special "eighteenth-century moment," a time when knowledge production in the West, as well as in Central and East Asia, drew on multiple sources, each viewed as having its own value. European, Chinese, and Manchu scholars drew on personal experience and their acquaintance with other scholarly work to construct their own specific forms of geographical and historical knowledge. For the most part, these separate textual traditions stood on an equal level, each making their own particular contributions to universal knowledge. By the nineteenth century, the relative hierarchy of power in these interchanges had altered fundamentally. The rise of British power, the decline of the Jesuits' access to China, and the increased hostility between China and Western powers raised the status of one language and demeaned the others. For many British traders and officials, in particular, Chinese and Manchu writings lost scholarly value, as their scholars were relegated to sources of policy information or trivial aspects of chinoiserie. Manchu, however, regained importance in the twentieth century for Japanese scholars and policy makers as they intervened in China's frontier territories. The fate of Tulišen's text alerts us to the ways in which changes in the hierarchy of knowledge production guided political transformations. The readings of the text in multiple languages responded to multiple levels of a geopolitical, commercial, and intellectual hierarchy constructed by European and Asian states.

The History of Translations of Tulišen's Account

Each of the Western translations came from a different source. The French translation, done by Father Antoine Gaubil (1689–1759), was a partial translation from the Chinese text, and the German translation was based on the French one. The French and German versions were only "abridged translations of the geographic portions alone," but the Russian translations were the first full translations into a Western language.[8] There are two Russian translations, one by the distinguished Russian Sinologist Ilarion Rossokhin and one by the lesser-known Sinologist Alexei Leontiev. These Russian translations were the only ones made from the original Manchu text until the latter half of the twentieth century. Imanishi Shunjū published thoroughly annotated Manchu and Chinese texts in 1964, accompanied by an interlinear word-for-word Japanese translation. Another translation into vernacular Japanese, based on Imanishi's work, appeared in 1985.

Clearly, we need a full English translation from the original Manchu text, and we need a study of all the available translations in their original form. Now that it is possible to obtain all of them, either online or in libraries, the way is open for a useful research project that would examine the multilingual world of this Central Eurasian traveler. I have so far taken only one step on a 10,000 *li* march.

The Manchu Text and Its Preface

The Manchu text begins with Tulišen's personal preface, which is not included in the Chinese text. (See Appendix.) In it, Tulišen describes growing up in a poor family, obtaining office by imperial favor, and gaining merit in the bureaucracy. He was, however, impeached and dismissed from office in 1705, and then retired to his estate to become a farmer. When the opportunity to travel on an embassy appeared, however, he took up the post with enthusiasm, completed his mission successfully, and returned home. Although the mission itself did not succeed in drawing Ayuki Khan into an alliance with the Qing emperor, it did establish relations with these distant Mongols, laying the groundwork for the later return of many of the Torghuts to the Qing border in the late eighteenth century.

After his return, Tulišen petitioned the emperor for permission to publish his account under imperial sponsorship. In the preface, Tulišen describes his humble life and his immense gratitude at achieving high office. He berates himself for his faults, which led to his dismissal, but he clearly regarded the mission to Ayuki as an opportunity for personal redemption. To support his case, he indulged in extravagant praise of the emperor's merits. Not only had the emperor offered him the grace that redeemed his wretched life; the emperor, he states, offers benevolence and grace (*kesi*) to all of his subjects, grace that extends to the far corners of the earth. We might note echoes here of Sima Qian's 司馬遷 (c. 145– c. 86 BCE) preface to his *Shiji* 史記 (Records of the Grand Historian), in which he, also a disgraced official, who had suffered castration, resolved to leave a written account to his successors, but Tulišen's goal, unlike that of Sima Qian, is to obtain official recognition of his private travel account. One can find, I believe, few precursors in Manchu for this kind of travel writing, unless we include the letters Kangxi wrote to his son during his first Mongolian campaign.[9]

The Russian Translations

Turning from Tulišen's own intentions to those of his translators, we begin with the Russian translators, who worked directly with the Manchu original.[10]

Alexei Leontiev (1716–1786) learned Manchu and Chinese in Moscow, and spent the years 1742 to 1756 in Beijing as translator for the Russian mission. He began work on a history of the Qing upon his return to St. Petersburg, but then went back to Beijing in 1762 as part of a trade mission. He translated many works of Chinese philosophy, along with edicts of the Yongzheng emperor. His biographer describes him as "the most skilled scholar-sinologist of his time."[11]

How Leontiev acquired a copy of Tulišen's text remains unclear, but the printed version in Manchu and Chinese would have been available in Beijing at the time he was there. Leontiev clearly set out to provide a scholarly version for Russian readers, and he added explanatory notes for unfamiliar terms. The terms that he annotated indicate what he expected to be obscure, so they reveal the extent of Russian knowledge about China and Central Asia in the eighteenth century. For example, he explains the title "Shengzu" of the Kangxi emperor, the significance of the Six Boards, and the symbolism of the dragon and other animals.

Some of Leontiev's translations elaborate on the meaning of Tulišen's rather brief account in a revealing way. Where Tulišen, in his preface, says simply "I was by nature foolish and weak [*banitai mentuhun eberhun ofi*]," Leontiev writes, "nature did not provide me with sufficient powers of reason" (*no kak priroda ne nagradila menia dostatochnym razumom*), adding a typically Enlightenment twist to the Manchu text. In general, despite a few errors, Leontiev provides a respectful, careful, and informative version of the text, accessible to Russian readers interested in Central Eurasia and the great empire to their east.

Ilarion Kalinovich Rossokhin (1707–1770) studied Chinese and Manchu in Beijing from 1729 to 1742, and subsequently became known as the most prolific Sinologist-translator in Russia. He published his translation in St. Petersburg in 1764.[12] His version contains many detailed notes on the place names mentioned in Tulišen's text, as well as extensive commentary on Qing institutions and important personages. Rossokhin and Leontiev later coauthored works on the Qing banners, but Rossokhin published more than Leontiev and had a higher reputation. Rossokhin provides more information regarding some details than did Leontiev, and he gives a closer translation in places where Leontiev paraphrased the text loosely. On the other hand, as we shall see below, Rossokhin chose to explicate a critical passage on the moral foundations of the Qing state, whereas Leontiev and other translators looked for a single verbal equivalent. Both translators, however, treated the text as a serious piece of writing on customs, geography, landscape, and institutions, and they produced full translations of the text, including the Manchu preface.

The Chinese Text

Tulišen may well have written the original Chinese translation of his work himself. But he claims to have had only a mediocre education in classical Chinese, so he may have relied on other scholars to revise his draft. Regardless of authorship, the Chinese text claims to be an outstanding contribution to the Chinese classical tradition. It is preceded by nine prefaces praising it as an unprecedented contribution to knowledge of the frontier territories. Tulišen succeeded in gaining recognition from the high-ranking officials and scholars of his day, and the inclusion of his account in the huge imperial compilation, the *Siku quanshu* 四庫全書, was a crowning achievement. It is one of the few texts originally written in Manchu to be included in this collection.

The Chinese version, however, differs significantly from the Manchu text. As Imanishi notes, "Several supplementary notes have been added to the Chinese text, and . . . some incomplete wordings and phrases in the Manchu have been modified in the Chinese. This does not mean, however, that the Chinese text is better than the Manchu. The Chinese version not only omits the important address and the author's preface concerning the origin of the book, but also has many omissions and shortcomings in the text which are [otherwise] necessary for the complete understanding of the context, as well as the historical facts."[13] Most subsequent Chinese readers only saw the Chinese text, and they were not aware that it omitted information that was in the Manchu original. The prefaces and the text's appearance as a *Siku quanshu* edition would have convinced them of the text's importance, but it would not have alerted them to any particular Manchu or Central Eurasia features. It was fully assimilated by these means into the classical Chinese tradition.

European Translations from Chinese

Other European translators relied only on the Chinese edition. Father Antoine Gaubil's French translation appears in a volume of Jesuit reports collected by Étienne Souciet (1671–1744) and published in Paris in 1729 under the title *Observations mathématiques, astronomiques, geographiques, chronologiques, et physiques, tirées des anciens livres chinois; ou faites nouvellement aux Indes et a la Chine*.[14] In presenting this collection to the French king, Souciet stresses the importance of accurate observation for the progress of the sciences of astronomy, geography, and natural history. He notes that certain nations, like the Chinese, have become very advanced in these sciences. In his view, the Chinese study of astronomy "is more advanced than other nations of the world." The Chinese "employ men to make observations day and night of all that occurs in the heavens, and the law punishes by death those who are negligent in their duties." Souciet explains that the Emperor Kangxi himself wanted to learn mathematics, philosophy, astronomy, anatomy, and other European sciences, so Father Gaubil, who knew Chinese and Manchu, was sent to China both to instruct the emperor and his princes and to collect data about eclipses, the motion of planets, and geographical locations. China in the Jesuit view was not merely a passive provider of data; China's long tradition of astronomical observation and travel accounts provided Westerners with an unprecedented source of new information on which they could build the universal science of astronomy and draw more comprehensive maps. The version of Tulišen's text translated by Gaubil, though, reduced the significance of the great Chinese astronomical tradition to a mere shadow.

Souciet's book begins with large numbers of astronomical observations and diagrams, including accounts of eclipses drawn from ancient Chinese texts. These are followed by a series of geographical accounts of places such as Canton, Peking, the Potala in Tibet, and Korea. Gaubil's translation of Tulišen's text is one of these travel accounts, and Gaubil regards its main importance as providing little-known place names of Russia and Central Asia to be entered on global maps. Using the Chinese text, he only translated what was "new and interesting" (*nouveau et curieux*), omitting the prefaces, the instructions from the emperor, and descriptions of the well-known route from Beijing to Chuku Baixing in Mongolia. He recorded the place names in Tulišen's account of the route he followed through Mongolia and Russia, and he added latitude and longitude designations to known places. He told Souciet that he had omitted all of Tulišen's comments on Russian customs, because these only reflected the viewpoint of a person ignorant of Russia, and the information was more accurate in other, non-Chinese sources. Gaubil's account is followed by a long discussion of the difficulties of connecting Chinese versions of Central Asian place names with the local names, including an alphabetic guide to Chinese transcription practices.

For Gaubil, the place names were the only valuable parts of Tulišen's account, and Tulišen's journey served as a source of information about places that were otherwise unknown. He stripped away the literary and cultural context in order to extract raw data for entry in larger enterprises. Still, Gaubil and the Jesuits respected the long continuity and accuracy of the Chinese geographical enterprise, as they used its results in the service of their global cartographic ambitions.

Staunton's English Translation

George Staunton (1781–1859), who as a young man learned Chinese and accompanied Lord Macartney on his mission to Beijing in 1792–1794, translated Tulišen's text from the Chinese version and published it in London in 1821. The full title of his volume was *Narrative of the Chinese Embassy to the Khan of the Tourgouth Tartars in the Years 1712, 13, 14, & 15; by the Chinese Ambassador, and Published, by the Emperor's Authority, at Pekin. Translated from the Chinese, and Accompanied by an Appendix of Miscellaneous Translations, by Sir George Thomas Staunton, Bart. LL.D. & F.R.S.* (London: John Murray, Albemarle Street, 1821).

Staunton regarded the text as a curiosity and nothing more. He opened his preface by saying, "The following translations were the occupation and amusement of a few intervals of leisure, during an occasional residence, of some years, within the Chinese dominions. It is not presumed to offer them to the public as a specimen of Chinese literature; but it is certainly hoped, that the light which they may be found to throw generally on the character and attainments of that extraordinary people, will render them not wholly uninteresting."[15]

Stripping away the exalted status of the Chinese text, which had been supported by the emperor, endorsed by major officials, and incorporated into the massive official compendium of the *Siku quanshu*, Staunton reduced it to a source of disparate information about a people for whom he had low regard. He pronounced, "To that species and degree of civilization, therefore, which necessarily implies a distinct recognition of a law of nations, and of the rights and duties of independent communities, in respect to each other, the Chinese have certainly but little claim." In his view, the Chinese had no interest in foreign nations, had almost never traveled beyond their borders, and left almost no travel accounts.[16] Tulišen's Chinese-language *Yiyulu* stood out for him as "the only one which the translator has met with of any authority, which strictly belongs to this class." He regarded Tulišen's mission as "a singular and remarkable event in

Chinese history." Although he gave credit to the Kangxi emperor, and his Manchu ("Tartar") heritage, for stimulating unusual openness among Chinese ruling elites, he regarded Tulišen's account as "perfectly Chinese, both in its style and its sentiments." In fact, he never mentioned the existence of a Manchu version, nor the fact that the Chinese was a translation from Manchu.

Further trivializing the text, Staunton attached "minor pieces" to the end of his book, including "part of a Chinese novel, some Notices of Chinese Plays, an Extract from a Chinese Herbal, and a Collection of Miscellaneous Official Documents, extracted from the Pekin Gazette [sic]." Staunton does provide, however, a detailed chronology of Tulišen's travels and a map of his itinerary.

Staunton also ruthlessly denigrated the value of the prefaces to the Chinese edition, regarding them as worthless: "The numerous prefaces which precede, as well as postscripts which follow the Narrative, in the original work, the translator has wholly omitted, finding that they contributed little or nothing to the illustration of the text, and that they were written in that higher style of Chinese composition, which is least favorable to efficient translation." Staunton praised Tulišen's own text for being close to vernacular Chinese, making it easier for him to "give a faithful interpretation of the sense of the original."[17] For Staunton, classical Chinese, with all of its allusive and philosophical riches, simply obstructed "efficient" translation, which normally, he thought, was dependent on a purportedly straightforward plain style mimicking everyday speech. As we have seen, Tulišen regarded his own Chinese style as crude, and Chinese scholars of his time prized elegance over "efficiency."

Staunton's views were an extreme example of growing British condescension toward China that had arisen along with the boom in the illegal opium trade in the nineteenth century. The more the British profited from opium, the more they expressed frustration at the obstructions placed in their way by Chinese officials, and the more contemptuous they became of a society that resolutely defended its aesthetic ideals and controls on foreign contact, instead of embracing the "Imperial Lessons" of a drug-peddling Western power.[18] Staunton's views are strikingly extreme for the 1820s, but they gained much more support after the conflict in the Opium War of the 1840s.[19]

In sum, Tulišen's deeply personal account, for which he made great efforts to get imperial approval and official appreciation, one of the few Manchu texts to be enrolled in the great compendium of the Chinese classics, ended up in the British aristocrat's hands as a truncated, mangled remnant, deprived of all majesty and mingled together with other random curiosities of literature and news. Yet this is the only English version of this extraordinary text.

A Table of Virtues

One interesting passage early in Tulišen's text challenged the translators to come up with equivalent meanings for classical Chinese moral ideals. The Kangxi emperor, allowing for the possibility that Tulišen might be summoned for an interview with the Russian tsar, instructed Tulišen on how to respond to questions he might face. Expecting that the tsar would ask about the fundamental values of the empire, the emperor suggested that Tulišen answer by telling him about the five basic virtues of the classical Confucian tradition, which the Manchus endorsed.

[Manchu original]:
Cagan Han be acaha manggi, suweni gurun ai be wesihun obuhabi seme fonjici, damu meni gurun i banjire doro, tondo, hiyoošun, gosin, jurgan, akdun be da obufi, ujeleme dahame yabumbi.[20]

[Staunton translation]:
On the occasion of your interview with the Cha-han-Khan, if you are asked what we principally esteem and reverence in China, you may thus reply: "In our empire fidelity, filial piety, charity, justice, and sincerity are esteemed above all things."[21]

[Leontiev translation]:
Kogda Tsar' ili ego liudi budut vas sprashivat', chto my pochitaem, tak govorite: Pochitaem za osnovanie zhizni nashei, liubov', cpravedlivost', blagochinie, blagorazumie, . . . tverdost', na cem pravitsia gosudarstvo nashe. . . .[22]

The Chinese text reads:
見察罕汗時，如問中國何所尊尚，但言«我國皆以忠孝仁義信為主，崇重尊行».[23]

We can assume that the emperor gave his instructions in Manchu, so the Chinese version was a later interpretation.[24] Each of the translators wrestled with finding equivalents to these five key concepts of the classical tradition. (See Table 1.1.) Tulišen himself was using the most common Manchu versions of the five classical virtues, but even the Manchu language could only approximate their meaning. The Manchu words *tondo* and *akdun* fit their Chinese equivalents (*zhong* 忠 and *xin* 信) fairly closely, but *hiyoošun* was a Chinese loan word from *xiaoshun* (孝順), and *gosin* could mean, in addition to Confucian "benevolence" (*ren* 仁), "Pity, mercy, or love."[25] In Russian, Leontiev also struggled to find equivalents, and even resorted to a note to explain the difficulty of translation. He translated *tondo* (Chinese *zhong* 忠 [loyalty] as "love" [*liubov'*]), *hiyoošun* (*xiao* 孝) as "justice" (*spravedlivost'*), and *akdun* (*xin* 信) as "firmness" (*tverdost'*).

Table 1.1. Terms for Five Virtues in Tulišen's Text and Translations

Staunton	Manchu	Russian (Leontiev)	Chinese
Fidelity	tondo	любовь	忠
Filial piety	hiyoošun	справедливость	孝
Charity	gosin	благочиніе	仁
Justice	jurgan	благоразуміе	義
Sincerity	akdun	твердость	信

Akdun, which in Manchu means "firm, strong, dependable, solid, sturdy," is related to *akdan,* meaning "trust." However, Leontiev's translation as "firmness" is closer to the original Manchu meaning than the Chinese term *xin*. Rossokhin, instead of using a single word, paraphrased each of the five basic virtues as:

> loyalty to our state, consisting of loyalty to the ruler; instructing children in obedience; a clear conscience, consisting of sincerity and truthfulness; and in diligently keeping one's word.

Staunton likewise only approximated the meanings of these concepts. In modern translations, influenced by James Legge, we generally translate *jurgan* (*yi* 義) as "righteousness" instead of "justice" and *akdun* (*xin* 信) as "trustworthiness" rather than "sincerity." We reserve "sincerity" for the Chinese philosophical term *cheng* (誠). The variant usages indicate that the translators could not find exact equivalents of these terms in their own cultural environments, but they made valiant efforts at approximation. The variations confirm modern translators' recognition that there is no perfect equivalence between words in different languages, only a variety of degrees of overlap.

The Recovery of Tulišen in the Twentieth Century

For most of the nineteenth century, Tulišen's Manchu text dropped from sight. His information appeared in many Chinese compendia about Central Asia, but few people even knew of the existence of a Manchu text. In 1943, Professor Imanishi Shunjū (1907–1979) discovered a Manchu copy of Tulišen's text in a bookstore in Beijing. Imanishi is not well known today, even in the Japanese scholarly world. Yet he was one of the most prolific, and arguably most influential, of Japanese scholars studying Manchu in the early twentieth century. In Giovanni Stary's four-volume bibliography of Manchu studies, Imanishi has more citations (forty-seven) than for nearly any other Japanese scholar, including his teachers, Haneda Tōru 羽田亨 (1882–1955) and Naitō Konan.[26] He graduated from Kyoto University's Tōyōshi 東洋史 (East Asian studies) department in 1933, and under the direction of Haneda and Naitō collated materials on Manchuria that are found in the *Ming shilu* 明實錄 (Veritable records of the Ming dynasty). In 1938 he went to China to study and collect Manchu and Mongolian materials. From 1940 to 1945 he taught at Beiping University, as it was then called, and stayed there after the defeat of Japan. He remained at Beijing University after the establishment of the PRC, until in 1951 he was jailed by the Chinese Public Security Bureau for three years. After his release, he returned to Japan as professor at Tenri University, and also taught at Nagoya and Kyoto Universities.

Throughout his scholarly career, Imanishi analyzed and translated essential Manchu texts that revealed the history of the early Qing state. His first major publication, in 1938, was a bilingual translation of the *Manzhou shilu* 滿洲實錄 (Manchu veritable records). He followed the pioneering work of Naitō Konan into deeply based research on the primary sources revealing the early history of the Qing dynasty. Naitō, the founder of Japanese Sinology at Kyoto University, had many scholarly and public interests beyond the Qing, but for an important period of his life, he focused on the early Qing.[27] He taught himself Manchu and Mongolian from 1902 to 1905, when he realized the value of non-Chinese sources for studying the early history of the Qing.

The *Manzhou shilu*, as a published account derived from the Old Manchu Archive, ranks as one of the key sources for studying the early Qing state. Haneda Tōru, in his preface to Imanishi's *Manzhou shilu*, expressed great pride in it as a major achievement of Japanese Sinology. He commented that study of China using non-Chinese sources had until now been nearly exclusively the domain of European Sinologists, but Imanishi's work was literally a "Great Leap Forward" in Japanese Sinology.[28]

Naitō's greatest contribution to early Qing history derived from his discovery of the existence of the Old Manchu Archive (*Manwen laodang* 滿文老檔 [in Japanese, *Manbun rōtō*]) on his travels in China in 1905. These were the only available original Manchu sources on the first Qing rulers during their consolidation of control over Manchuria. (He had the materials photocopied in 1912 for study by his colleagues and students. This study group of six people, headed by Kanda Nobuo 神田信夫 [1921–2003], after decades of work, published the *Manbun rōtō*, a bilingual translation of the entire archive, in six volumes, from 1955 to 1959.)

But Imanishi had already published substantial portions of the *Manwen laodang* in Dalian from 1943 to 1944. He also wrote his first article on Tulišen's text in 1944. After returning to Japan, he collaborated with Tamura Jitsuzō 田村実造 (1904–1999) on a Japanese translation of the great Qing multilingual dictionary, the *Wuti Qingwenjian* 五體清文鑑, published in 1966.

Imanishi, then, was either a pioneer or a collaborator in the Japanese study of all the major Manchu texts discovered by Japanese scholars in the mid-twentieth century. But his adventurous life, which took him to China for nearly twenty years, as student, professor, and prisoner in Beijing, separated him from the mainstream of Japanese scholars of Manchuria, centered at Kyoto and the Tōyō Bunko. Although I cannot provide a general overview of Japanese Manchu studies here, it is clear that Tulišen's text, in Imanishi's view, ranked in importance alongside the other major Manchu materials that he studied: the *Manwen laodang*, the *Manzhou shilu*, and the *Wuti Qingwenjian*. Tulišen's account came from a later period, and it described Central Asia, rather than the internal workings of the Qing state, but it belonged to an important lineage of Manchu-language materials that deserved intensive scholarly scrutiny.

Imanishi's study of Tulišen's text, published in 1964 in its final version, deploys all the highest skills of Japanese philological expertise applied to the other texts. It includes the original Manchu text, the Manchu preface by Tulišen, the multiple Chinese prefaces, and the Chinese text, along with an interlinear word-for-word translation of the romanized Manchu text, a full Japanese translation, and numerous notes commenting on the places and peoples encountered by Tulišen. In Imanishi's skillful hands, Tulišen's text finally received the full-blown scholarly attention that it deserved.

Imanishi considered Tulišen's account to be the most significant source of information about Central Asia published under the Qing. Chinese scholars found no better information about Central Asia until the end of the dynasty. Numerous great compilations of material about Mongolia, Russia, and Central Asia published in the nineteenth century simply copied from Tulišen. Imanishi particularly stressed the accuracy and detail of Tulišen's account. Previous Chinese travel accounts were only "desk works," relying on secondary material or vague aesthetic impressions of landscape, "therefore no accurate information concerning topography and culture could be expected from them." But *Yiyulu*, in his words, "is not only an accurate record of the author's personal experience in traveling over territory previously unknown to any Chinese, but is also a scientific report on the mountains and rivers he passed en route, races, habits, and customs, production, population, armaments in the towns and even the mode of address in foreign regions. This is scientific [*gutaiteki* 具体的, *kagakuteki* 科学的] to a degree rarely seen at that time."[29]

Like the eighteenth-century European philologists, Imanishi admired the text for its factual emphasis. He did not merely extract data from it; instead, he paid meticulous attention to the use of Manchu words and the place names and peoples described in it. His translation is a vital source not only for facts about Central Asia, but for insight into the Manchu language and into Manchu consciousness of the western regions. On the other hand, this scholarly labor of love, published by Tenri University Press, did not receive anything like the public attention of the earlier translations. (After his death, a translation into modern Japanese, based on his 1964 work, appeared in the popular book series of Iwanami Bunko in 1985.) By the mid-twentieth century, information about Central Asia remained valuable, but the dominant languages and academic traditions were Russian, Chinese, and English. Japan retained strong geopolitical interests in Manchuria and Mongolia, but its primary goal had been to collect information of value for the purpose of ruling Manchuria and planning foreign policy. The South Manchuria Railway company sponsored numerous research projects in Manchuria, but nearly all of them focused on Chinese rural society and Manchurian ethnography. Except for a small number of Manchu specialists, this account of eighteenth-century Central Asia once again faded from view.

Coda: Tulišen in the Twenty-First Century

I first read Tulišen's account in Manchu in a graduate seminar with Joseph Fletcher in the 1970s, but I did not use it for my own research until much later. While writing *China Marches West*, I returned to Tulišen's text, focusing on his interview with Ayuki Khan in Russia and its implications for Qing relations with Russia and the Zunghar Mongols.[30] I also realized, as did Staunton, that at nearly the same time John Bell had traveled on a mission for the Russian tsar on a similar journey across Central Eurasia in the opposite direction, from St. Petersburg to Beijing and back. The Russian envoy Unkovskii also visited the Khan at around the same time.[31] Although they did not meet each other, they described the same places and commented on many of the same peoples on the route. Now, in light of the rapidly growing interest in transnational history, border-crossing travelers like these men have aroused attention for what they reveal about intercultural contact in the early modern era.[32] "Entangled history" (*histoire croisée*) is a method of capturing the flows of people, goods, and cultural products across national borders, and it alerts us to the limits of the nation-state and its borders.[33] From this perspective, Tulišen is not just a Qing official, but, like John Bell, one of the bold cosmopolitans who explored distant realms and reported on them from both personal experience and empirical investigation. For philologists, he and others like him direct attention to texts that travel, through translation, copying, interpretation, and diffusion, shifting their implications as they move through time and space. New philology can keep its focus on texts, but also contribute to transnational history while watching the flows that carried them to distant times and places.

Tulišen's text, the first large-scale travel account written by a Manchu author, itself traveled long distances across Eurasia, providing its readers with diverse experiences united by a common interest in the new regions conquered by the Qing dynasty and in its Central Asian frontiers. These readers gave it radically different weights as a source of knowledge, and extracted from it what they found congenial to their own views of China. In the Manchu literary tradition, it stands, alongside Qishiyi's *Xiyu wenjianlu* 西域聞見錄, as one of the few extended personal accounts of Central Asian travel. The Chinese edition entered a much longer tradition of descriptions of distant lands. Contrary to the assertions of Staunton and Imanishi, Chinese writers, including Qing scholars, produced many detailed, empirically based travel accounts of frontier regions.[34] Chinese scholars inserted the text into the vast classical tradition, where Manchu writings survived as a small but necessary leavening for Chinese texts. For the Jesuit translator Gaubil, the text was simply a source of geographic information, but a certain amount of respect for Chinese learning remained. The Russian translators paid serious attention to it as a work of Sinology, using it to explain many aspects of Chinese and Manchu customs and for Qing views of Russian and Central Asian territory. Staunton reduced it to a mere curiosity, of little value except to expose the limitations of the Chinese mind in the face of superior Western civilization. Imanishi and his Japanese colleague revived the study of Manchu in the twentieth century, not only to serve imperial expansion, but to broaden our perspective on the Qing beyond the Nationalist Chinese insistence on the superiority of the Chinese tradition alone. Pamela Crossley has argued that the Qing emperors revealed different facets of their imperial policy to each of the peoples of their empire, by positioning themselves variously as Manchu, Confucian, Mongolian, or Buddhist in different interactions.[35] In similar fashion, Tulišen's work granted each of its audiences a different perspective on the empire that had produced it.

Appendix: Translation of Manchu Preface [Peter C. Perdue]

From my youth, I was by nature weak, and often ill. My parents brought me up with kindness, [which helped me] to gradually come to maturity. Because of a series of generous acts of our benevolent emperor, I obtained office, and received honors. Being foolish and weak, I was impeached and dismissed from my post, so subsequently I retired to my estate to cultivate the fields. I have lived through this brilliant age, thus, fortunately, I once again was offered the opportunity to be sent to the Torghuts, and my deep gratitude caused me to accept the assignment of my humble self as envoy. I traveled for three years and ten thousand miles, completed my mission and returned. As the saying goes, [2a] "men pass on the benefits they have received." Our great emperors, of vast and overflowing virtue, of wonderful merit and great honor, have over thousands of years extended their commands over endless realms and vast spaces. From ancient times until now, the peoples of the Central Kingdom and [even] peoples uncontacted all pour out their yearning for submission. The honors of their times are recorded abundantly, and annals and archives are filled with their deeds. [I 44]

My worm-like self shrinks with awe at the good fortune [derived from] our great emperors, who from ancient times until now have conducted affairs with kings of countries, chieftains, and the common people, [sending envoys] to bear the exceeding virtue and benevolence of our great Lord to them. I know very clearly his majesty and [his majesty's] fame. Because his sacred virtue will be preeminent for ten thousand generations, and his benevolence and grace roll out across the seas, I offer this report up to him, following his command to report affairs in order, recording in Chinese writing the places along the way. After it receives the imperial rescript, may it be transmitted to the Board. If it is so, All under Heaven, in the face of the sacred influence, and all the countries overseas, can follow his benevolence and virtue. Now the people and All under Heaven can know this, extending over ten thousand generations endlessly, making for us an eternal legacy.

Therefore, by connecting everything from my personal experiences from beginning to end and writing it out, I have composed the *Lakcaha Jecen de takûraha babe ejehe bithe* [A book describing the embassy to distant territories]. After the carving and printing were completed, I wrote this preface.

First year of Yongzheng, 11th month, an auspicious day.

Notes

1. Pollock, Elman, and Chang, *World Philology*.
2. Link, "On Translation," pp. 17–30; Weinberger and Paz, *Nineteen Ways of Looking at Wang Wei*.
3. Koselleck, "Social History and Conceptual History," pp. 308–325.
4. Waley-Cohen, *Exile in Mid-Qing China*; Schlesinger, *A World Trimmed with Fur*.
5. I follow the text of *Yiyulu* 異域錄, which gives the characters 圖麗琛. The third character is usually pronounced *chen*, but the Manchu is definitely *šen*. Hummel gives 圖理琛, and others give 圖理珅.

6. For short accounts of Tulišen's life, see Fang, "Tulišen," pp. 784–787; Perdue, "Tulišen," pp. 2, 314–315.
7. Perdue, *China Marches West,* pp. 213–227.
8. Imanishi, *Kōchū Iikiroku; Tulišen's I-Yü-Lu,* p. 38.
9. Okada, *Kōkitei no tegami.*
10. For further discussion of Russian Sinology, see Afinogenov, *Spies and Scholars.*
11. http://lib.pushkinskijdom.ru/Default.aspx?tabid=1100.
12. Rossokhin, *Opisanie puteshestviia koim ezdili Kitaiskie poslanniki v Rossiiu.*
13. Imanishi, *Kōchū Iikiroku,* p. 35.
14. Souciet and Gaubil, *Observations Mathématiques, Astronomiques, Geographiques, Chronologiques, et Physiques.*
15. Staunton, *Narrative of the Chinese Embassy to the Khan of the Tourgouth Tartars,* p. iii.
16. Staunton, *Narrative,* p. vii. On Chinese travel writing, see Strassberg, *Inscribed Landscapes.*
17. Staunton, *Narrative,* pp. xix, xx.
18. Hevia, *English Lessons.*
19. By contrast, the British physician Charles Toogood Downing, who knew no Chinese, had a remarkably sympathetic view of the common people of Canton, even though he resented the arrogance and oppression inflicted on them by the mandarins. Downing, *The Fan-Qui in China.*
20. Imanishi, *Kōchū Iikiroku,* p. 61.
21. Staunton, *Narrative,* p. 13.
22. Leontiev, *Puteshestvie kitaiskogo poslannika k kalmytskomy Ayuke-Khany.*
23. Imanishi, *Kōchū Iikiroku,* p. 376.
24. Incidentally, Staunton, following the Chinese text, uses the term "China" (Zhongguo 中國), but the Russian translators and the Manchu text say "our country." Critics of the new Qing history, who put great stress on the usage of the term *dulimba i gurun* or "Zhongguo," in Manchu texts, should take note of this exception.
25. Norman, Dede, and Branner, *A Comprehensive Manchu-English Dictionary,* p. 148.
26. Stary, *Manchu Studies.*
27. Fogel, *Politics and Sinology.*
28. Imanishi, *Manshū jitsuroku.*
29. Imanishi, *Kōchū Iikiroku,* pp. 7, 31.
30. Perdue, *China Marches West,* pp. 213–227.
31. Bell, *A Journey from St. Petersburg to Peking.*
32. Davis, *Trickster Travels;* Dunn, *The Adventures of Ibn Battuta.*
33. Saunier, *Transnational History.*
34. Teng, *Taiwan's Imagined Geography.*
35. Crossley, *A Translucent Mirror.*

Struggles over the Historical Memory of a Heterodoxy
Chinese Commentaries on the Nestorian Stele

In late imperial China there were three main schools of traditional thought (*sanjiao* 三教), namely Confucianism, Buddhism, and Daoism. The appearance of Christianity in the sixteenth century changed the contours of these teachings. Christians, whether European or Chinese, claimed that Christianity deserved to be treated with the same reverence as Confucianism, while they denounced Buddhism and Daoism as heretical. To persuade their readers, devotees of the new teaching deployed many different strategies, including the crafting of synchronous Chinese and European historical chronologies. Embedded in a universal time line, the Chinese people became part of the great family of mankind, their history part of a universal Christian history.

The French historian Pierre Nora developed the idea of *lieux de mémoire*—literally, memory places—to ground events in material locations. "Our interest in *lieux de mémoire* where memory crystallizes and secretes itself," he wrote, "has occurred at a particular historical moment, a turning point where consciousness of a break with the past is bound up with the sense that memory has been torn—but torn in such a way as to pose the problem of the embodiment of memory in certain sites where a sense of historical continuity persists."[1] The erection of the famous *Da Qin jingjiao liuxing Zhongguo bei* 大秦景教流行中國碑 (Stele commemorating the spread of the luminous teaching from Great Qin [i.e., Rome] to China) instantly endowed its location with a "sense of historical continuity." It amounted to a physical embodiment of various memories of the past. Soon enough, different constituencies projected their different ideologies onto the new structure: a single object acquired a range of irreconcilable significances, each of which supported a different *jiao*. Responding to this monument, commentators anchored themselves at a historical moment when the stele was created to legitimate the status of their *jiao* in the present and project their teachings forward into the future.

The divergent views of Catholics and Protestants regarding the origin of the Chinese people, its history, and its relation to the message of Jesus ensured a complex set of responses to a stele created by heterodox Nestorians. I shall use three commentaries on the stele to sketch the responses of Confucians, Catholics, and Protestants. Through its analysis of these readings, this chapter will contribute to our understanding of the transformation of the concept of *jiao*, including its insertion into the neologism *zongjiao* 宗教, the term adopted to translate *religion,* ubiquitous in the European texts that proliferated after Christianity traveled to China.

The Discovery of the Nestorian Stele

When the Jesuits arrived in China in the late Ming dynasty, God seemed to have bestowed on them a gift. A stele carved in 781 was unearthed in Shaanxi Province in 1623, testimony to the existence of a dynamic Christian community. No longer could mandarins accuse Christianity of being an alien cult. This gift arrived at just the right time.[2] In 1615 the Jesuit mission to China had been promoted to the status of vice province, attached to the Province of Japan. However, since the hopes the missionaries had harbored for the latter were dashed when the Tokugawa shogunate imposed a prohibition on Christianity in 1614, the fate of the Jesuit enterprise in the East came to depend on China. The timely appearance of the ancient stele did much to improve morale.

When Paul Xu (Xu Guangqi 徐光啟, 1562–1633) first heard about the discovery of the monument, he promptly wrote a short essay to affirm the long and persistent history of Christians in China. Employing nearly providential rhetoric, he interpreted the emergence and eclipse of the foreign faith in the Tang and its Ming resurgence in terms of the Mandate of Heaven. For him, the Nestorian monument added glory to the inception of the revered Tang dynasty, was forgotten during a period of chaos, then was rediscovered during the Ming, heralding a time of peace.[3] Later it would become clear that all this was just wishful thinking.

Another famous Chinese Christian, Leo Li (Li Zhizao 李之藻, 1571–1630), expressed similar sentiments after reading a transcription of the stele. He declared that in spite of routine contacts with missionaries during the previous thirty years, scholars had come to suspect that Christianity had only arrived in China very recently and cast doubts on Ricci's teaching. Now that a solid piece of evidence proved that Christianity had been present for a thousand years, scholars could abandon their doubts and embrace the true faith. The stele's appearance, he suggested, was a sign from God warning the people of China to beware of the devil, lest they be barred from entering Paradise. He urged his readers to compare what Christian teachings and the Confucian classics had to say regarding their respective prime movers—God (*shangdi* 上帝) and Heaven (*tian* 天)—so that they might embrace the blessing that the missionaries had brought. If people read the stele carefully, they would be compelled to return to the One Truth (*yizun* 一尊), long contaminated by heterodoxy. Li implied that Confucianism was similar, if not identical, to Christianity.[4] What he did not know was that the Nestorian community whose existence was recorded on this stele had followed a creed condemned by the Holy See.

It is interesting to see how the term *Jingjiao* (景教) became a synonym for Christianity after the discovery of the stele and the diffusion of its text. Quite oblivious to the differences between Catholicism and Nestorianism, scholars made rubbings of the stele, then printed the rubbings in book form. These not only circulated in the Chinese Christian community; copies were sent back to Europe as breaking news from afar. Some converts, impressed by the stele, started to refer to themselves as *Jingjiao houxue* (景教後學), literally "later followers of Nestorianism/Christianity," and they called their churches, which often served as publishing houses, *Jingjiaotang* (景教堂), or "Nestorian/Christian churches."[5] The use of the term was inaccurate, but Chinese Christians had found what they imagined to be their historical roots, and the promise of being recognized as adherents of a "true" religion of long standing must have been exhilarating. The rise of antiquarianism among late-Ming scholars, and the revival of epigraphy, lent tremendous appeal to this physical link with the distant past. History was being reshaped to legitimate the present state of Christianity in China.

The stele itself, beyond its Ming-era interpretations, preserves important information regarding Nestorianism in the Tang dynasty. It first describes the basic *Jingjiao* teachings, so close to Catholicism that they seemed quite familiar to the missionaries and their Chinese converts. The second part of the stele inscription describes the patronage offered by Tang emperors; it concludes by emphasizing the mutual benefits that empire and religion had bestowed on one another throughout the period. The last part of the inscription is an ode summarizing the foregoing passages. In addition, the names of the Nestorian priests active in Chang'an at the time the stele was erected are written in both Syriac and Chinese.

Ever since its discovery, the stele has occupied the center of lively debates. The date, original location, and authenticity of the stele were all contested by Chinese and Western scholars. More than a decade ago, Michael Keevak neatly demonstrated how the monument functioned in the European discourse surrounding a largely imaginary China, revealing far more about the various Western commenters than the Nestorians or the Tang Chinese.[6] Keevak's interesting meta-reflection is a product of the early twenty-first century, a series of reflections that would not have occurred to scholars in the late nineteenth and early twentieth centuries. In that period, over a century ago and almost three centuries after its discovery, the stele had won worldwide attention. European, Japanese, and Chinese scholars devoted considerable energy to deciphering the inscription and reconstructing the history of a Christian cult in an unexpected setting.[7] For these scholars, the stele revealed a great deal about religious interactions during the Tang dynasty.

Most recent research, likewise, has focused on the reconstruction of Nestorian activities during the Tang, yet the efforts of Ming and Qing scholars to make sense of the stele and the inscription, typically in the form of commentaries and essays, has been largely overlooked. Epigraphy, the study of inscriptions, constituted one branch of the Qing *kaozheng* 考證 (evidential) movement, often referred to as "evidential studies." However, late imperial scholars seldom learned foreign languages, and they did little to reconstruct Tang Nestorianism from the stele. Indeed, their goal was different from that of later Sinologists. Most evidential scholars set out to clarify the relations among different *jiao*, a term whose recent use as a stand-in for the English word "religion" has tended to obscure the very different conceptualizations of modes of thought in China and the West.[8]

I focus on three important texts: a late-Ming commentary by a Jesuit missionary named Emmanuel Diaz Jr. (Yang Manuo 陽瑪諾, 1574–1659), a late-Qing commentary by the Protestant Yang Rongzhi 楊榮鋕 (1855–1919), and the abridged edition of Yang's treatise produced by Wang Xianqian 王先謙 (1842–1917), a Confucian scholar. These commentaries on the same text highlight the importance of the concept of *jiao* and how believers in different *jiao* attempted to demarcate the boundaries of the true faith through competing interpretations. Diaz's text was published in 1641, but sank into the darkness of history, and we do not know much about its circulation or readership. Evidential scholars in the seventeenth and eighteenth centuries never cited it, and though they offered many speculations about the stele, not until 1895 did one produce a new commentary. Yang not only summarized the major findings of evidential scholars regarding the stele, he envisioned the significance of the stele anew.

Reconciling Chinese History with Christianity

During the waning of the Ming dynasty, Emmanuel Diaz Jr. served as vice provincial (i.e., the leading Jesuit in the Vice Province of China), making him an appropriate candidate to write a commentary to the Nestorian stele. The work, dated 1641, was titled *Jingjiao liuxing Zhongguo beisong zhengquan* 景教流行中國碑頌正詮 (The text and ode of the stele on the spread of *Jingjiao* in China: An orthodox interpretation). Note that the use of the expression *zhengquan* 正詮 (orthodox interpretation) indicated that Diaz meant to use the stele to refute the belief that Christian teachings had arrived in China quite late, a posture that threatened the canonical status of the three Chinese teachings. In his commentary, Diaz did not mention the Syriac on the stele; nothing he wrote suggests that the inscriptions belonged outside of mainstream Catholicism.

Diaz explained that *Jingjiao*—Christianity—enlightened people by teaching them first the truth of human nature (*xingjiao* 性教) and then the truth about God's grace (*chongjiao* 寵教). Like the light of the rising sun, the word of Christ shone from afar, its truth destined to cover the whole world. Therefore, no one need complain that China was late in experiencing God's grace: so distant is it from the West that it is reasonable that Christianity would arrive there quite a while after its birth in Judea. Still, the newly unearthed stele attested that the people of China had enjoyed God's grace about a thousand years earlier. Therefore, there was no reason to suspect the motivations of the recently arrived missionaries. If Christianity had been in China for a millennium, then the new arrivals were assisting the rebirth of an ancient faith. Diaz declared that he hoped to alleviate any lingering doubts about Christianity through his commentary.[9]

After this prelude, Diaz turned to the character *seng* 僧 (monk), which was the term used on the stele to identify the Nestorian priests. *Seng* typically referred to Buddhist monks. Unfamiliar with the word's implications, the first Jesuits who had entered China applied it to themselves. Assuming that the Tang Christians were Catholic missionaries like those with whom he was familiar, Diaz stated that the Jesuits had referred to themselves as *shi* 士 (gentlemen) or *ru* 儒 (scholars, in this case); he noted that *ru* (Confucian scholars) had been highly regarded by the Chinese. He thus effectively equated Tang and late-Ming Christian missionaries (who were in reality Nestorian priests and Jesuits, respectively), presenting both groups as, especially, respected scholars. If those Christians commemorated on the stele had tried to present their message in Western languages, no Chinese would have understood—they needed to render foreign ideas in the local language. As they distanced themselves from the mundane world and pursued the Way, it was reasonable to call them *seng*, a term that could expand to include others besides Buddhists. *Seng, shi,* or *ru*—all of these nouns could be applied to the respected Christian scholars.[10] They could? One feels a bit uncomfortable with Diaz's free and easy ways with words, something no Confucian would endorse. He distorted the meaning of these terms to legitimate the shaping of the Jesuit identity during the Ming.

In his commentary, Diaz did distinguish the Catholic priest from the Buddhist monk. Yet he was also intent on presenting himself—a Catholic priest—on a footing equal to that of a Confucian scholar. Diaz proceeded through the main text of the stele inscription sentence by sentence and also introduced the European dialectic form into his commentary, creating a sub-commentary layer for apologetic reasons. Implicitly rejecting the philological aspect of this task, Diaz focused on addressing aspects of the Bible that Chinese readers would find particularly puzzling, such as the terrible punishment laid upon Adam, Eve, and all of mankind following the eating of a fruit of the Tree of Knowledge. He even discussed who was responsible for the original sin. Rejecting the orthodox opinions of Augustine and Aquinas, he concluded that it had been Adam's fault, since a man is responsible for his wife's actions.[11] Diaz went on to explain important aspects of Christian beliefs and practices. He concluded this section with an account of the meaning of the term *Jingjiao*. The profound subtlety of the belief in God, Diaz claimed, could not be exhausted by language, and therefore could not be adequately named. However, a name was necessary, and the character *jing* 景 was given to symbolize the belief's far-reaching brightness.[12] Here, Diaz resorted to a piece of solid evidence—the stele, which spoke from the past in order to attest to the truth of the current teachings that he was articulating. At each step, Nestorianism was edged closer to Catholicism.

In the second part of the commentary, Diaz no longer offered readings of individual sentences, skipping the details in order to discuss the "gift exchange" between the Chinese sovereign and the missionaries. Using imperial reign titles as markers, he cataloged the important *Jingjiao* events during the Tang. He was particularly interested in the mutual benefits that the Christians and the emperors could have enjoyed. According to him, the innate corruption of human beings rendered imperial power essential to conveying religious teachings. The unchecked power of the ruler had to be used when humans erred. Only with proper guidance could people be transformed into righteous subjects. The effect would be even greater if the emperor himself was a believer. Diaz used a cosmological analogy, comparing the emperor with the outermost sphere of Heaven (*zongdongtian* 宗動天), a zone conceived by Aristotle as the motive force of the universe (a traditional Aristotelian concept), implying that an emperor who converted to Christianity would possess a similar power to move his people. The Ming emperor could hardly do better than emulate the Tang imperial house, which had acted as a patron to Christians.[13]

But what good could Christianity bring to the empire? A unifying belief system, Diaz answered, which would increase the loyalty of the people to their ruler, shoring up his control.[14] Diaz did not neglect to mention the technical capabilities of the Nestorians: like the Jesuits, they possessed considerable civil engineering and military skills that were put to use in the successful campaigns of the Tang.[15] At the time Diaz wrote, the Ming court had already employed Jesuits to reform the calendar and manufacture cannons. But anti-Christian sentiment was growing, and the Chongzhen emperor had done little to resist it. Diaz seems to have been hinting that the time had come for the court to take a stand and forcefully quash the xenophobic muttering.

Diaz also took the opportunity to attack Buddhism, a cultural and religious force that was despised and feared by missionaries, who saw in it a great foe. Without specifying the event, Diaz insinuated that during the Tang dynasty Confucian scholars had colluded with Buddhists to debase *Jingjiao*.[16] He attributed this to the work of the devil—did he have in mind anti-Christian schemes from his own time?

Superstition was another target to be assailed. If the Lord was so powerful, why did prayers offered to Him seldom work? Why did prayers to local deities seem more efficient? In his answer, Diaz underscored the importance of recognizing one's sinful nature and correcting one's behavior before expecting prayers to be answered. He pointed out that there was only one true God. Even if one successfully fulfilled one's wish by praying to local deities, those lesser figures were answering to God. God's larger plans for mankind often barred him from granting prayers; He hoped that human beings would reflect upon their own misdeeds and pursue the righteous path.[17]

Like a good scholar, Diaz commented on newly unearthed material, even if his main interest clearly lay far from purely scholarly matters. He used the stele to connect the work being done in the present by missionaries like himself to the old Nestorians, thereby rooting modern Catholic beliefs and practices in the historical past. He also exploited the stele to respond to doubts about Catholicism, ward off heretical beliefs, and request court patronage. Chronologically, the focuses of Diaz's commentary took a zigzag path, beginning in the past, traveling further back to dwell on mankind's earliest days, and finally arriving at the present. By depicting the usefulness of Christianity to the Tang empire, Diaz hoped to send a lifeline to the Ming court: if it supported Western learning and Christianity, historical precedent showed, it too would benefit.[18] In sum, Diaz's commentary purposefully relied on a familiar form to bolster the Jesuit agenda, historically lengthen the Christian time line in China, and engage with the ruling power.

Redrawing Religious Boundaries

The Ming fell and the Qing rose. While the eighteenth and nineteenth centuries witnessed many discussions of the relic, it was only near the end of the Qing's grip on power that another commentary on the stele appeared. In 1895 Yang Rongzhi produced his commentarial treatise, identifying himself as a "late learner of the *Jing* school" (*Jingmen houxue* 景門後學); for Yang, the word *Jing* referred to Christianity in general. Nonetheless, as we shall see, Yang was aware of the various denominations of Christianity, knew what made Nestorians distinctive, and disapproved of them.

Yang was baptized by Robert E. Chambers (1870–1932) in 1899 and devoted himself to Christian education and charity. His conversion was accidental. In his early career, he was an erudite scholar specializing in divination and medicine, in addition to the canonical three teachings. Like many of his contemporaries, he also indulged in opium and delighted in leading Christians to tie themselves in logical knots. Not until a downpour drove him to take shelter in a church, where he met the Reverend Ou Fengchi 區鳳墀, was he converted.[19] Yang later became a priest and founded the Shajitang 沙基堂, a church in Guangzhou later renamed Huiaitang 惠愛堂. There he made the acquaintance of Sun Yat-sen 孫逸仙 (1866–1925), who found shelter with Yang on several occasions when pursued by Qing police. Yang promoted the idea that Christianity, which in nineteenth-century China meant Protestantism, should cultivate local priests; he advocated the building of churches by local congregations. The spread of Christianity no longer needed to be entrusted to foreign missionaries.[20]

It is not clear what motivated Yang to write the commentary, but he expressed the desire to map the historical boundaries between China's various religions, and the stele offered a framework for that enterprise. Yang's *Jingjiao beiwen jishi kaozheng* 景教碑文紀事考正 (A critical investigation of documents addressing the Nestorian stele inscription) starts with a complete transcription of the stele itself, including the portion written in Syriac. This is followed by ten reprinted essays on the stele by Qing scholars, whom Yang then assails for religious ignorance, declaring their interpretations nonsense. Some had questioned the authenticity of the stele. Others thought Nestorianism a Central Asian religion. Even the celebrated scholar Qian Daxin 錢大昕 (1728–1804) confused *Jingjiao* with Islam. Like other scholars of the last few centuries, argued Yang, Qian had based his arguments only on Chinese materials and did not even bother—or was unable—to consult the Bible. Qing scholars were unable to understand the meaning of the stele because the transmission of *Jingjiao* had long been interrupted after the Tang. Without evidence there could be no meaningful evidential studies; even sages, if unassisted, were unable to decipher the meaning of *Jingjiao*. Worse than this, some of these writers exhibited a vicious xenophobia. Qian Qianyi 錢謙益 (1582–1664), for instance, suspected that the stele was fabricated by Muslims, or worse, Manichaeans, who were just as refractory as the White Lotus.[21] Later, Qing scholars like Hang Shijun 杭世駿 (1696–1772) and Xia Xie 夏燮 (1800–1875) made similar arguments.[22] Yang further commented that since Heaven must have dictated the survival of the stele, it made no sense to contend that *Jingjiao* was mere barbarism. It had become clear enough that Christian nations could be redoubtable indeed.[23]

Apart from criticizing earlier scholars and praising the stele, Yang was interested in exploring, through the inscription, the progress of human knowledge, which he saw as a means to promote Christianity. He stated that as scholarship advanced, old knowledge became obsolete. Things like fortune-telling, geomancy, the concepts of *yin-yang* and *wuxing* 五行 (five phases) would all eventually be abandoned when knowledge from the West enlightened the Chinese people. There was nothing to be afraid of, Yang insisted; one should simply accept the inevitable. How did he know that with such certainty? Yang explained that the basis for his claims was a deep understanding of the Bible and other religions, and there lay the basis for his claims. Furthermore, even those readers who were fond of ancient ways would benefit from the commentary, as any familiarity with Christianity would lead them closer to an ultimate truth.[24]

Yang's commentary began with a geographical investigation of Da Qin 大秦. While the term was sometimes used to mean the Roman empire, in the case of the stele it meant Syria, a nation whose name sounded, Yang said, like "Qin."[25] In the medieval era, roughly the time of the carving of the stele, Syrians had written in Greek, Arabic, and Syriac. However, the ancient language in that area was Babylonian, and Babylon was where human civilization began. Carried away by a desire to flaunt his familiarity with Syrian culture, Yang implied that Chinese civilization had originated in Mesopotamia. Terms such as *qiankun* 乾坤, *efeng* 閼逢 (*jia* 甲), and *kundun* 困敦 (*zi* 子) could be traced back to Babylon. (Note that these terms refer to the beginning of the universe and of time.) He concluded with a comparison of the chronologies of China and Da Qin, which allowed him to introduce the subject of Christianity.[26]

By and large, Yang equated *Jingjiao* with Christianity. In a chapter entitled "An Investigation of the Origin and Spread of *Jingjiao*," which served as the preface to his commentary, Yang discussed the difficulty of translating "A luo he" 阿羅訶 (Jehovah, the name of God), a term that appeared in the stele. Following a summary of the biblical book of Genesis, he noted that the age of the universe recorded in the Bible was around four thousand years, a figure verified by "scientists" (*gezhi shixue zhujia* 格致實學諸家).[27] He then summarized the remainder of the Bible. Lacing his synopses with quotations from Confucian classics conveyed the impression that ancient Chinese thought mirrored that of the Bible. He treated the Old Testament uncritically as history, as he did the prophecies said by Christians to have predicted the coming of Jesus Christ. Yang recounted the story of Jesus Christ (calling him "the Lord of Jing"—*Jingzun* 景尊) and of Paul. Just like a good evidential scholar, he cited chapter and verse to explain the Bible's supernatural events.

Yang complained that the teachings recorded on the Nestorian stele betrayed the original message of Jesus. He had four criticisms. First, salvation was mistakenly presented as the reward for ritual observances, rather than of a spiritual cultivation guided by divine providence. He had discovered that the Nestorian priests, responsible for interpreting the sacred Christian doctrine, had sometimes encouraged false beliefs. Second, Nestorians confused the "lesser learning" (*xiaoxue* 小學) of the Old Testament, far too focused on ritual, with the "greater learning" (*daxue* 大學), individual and internal, announced in the New Testament. Third, local Eurasian customs and pagan practices had filtered into Nestorianism. Fourth, the physical cross was emphasized at the expense of a deep understanding of the crucifixion by which Jesus had redeemed human sins.

To explain why Nestorianism had disappeared in China (and was on the verge of extinction worldwide in his own day), Yang pointed out that the cult had depended on the patronage of Central Asian kings, whose domains were often shaken by rebellions and invasions. After the rise of Islam, which had conquered the Near East and most of Central Asia, Nestorianism was all but obliterated.[28]

As a Protestant, Yang also criticized Catholicism (*Tianzhujiao* 天主教) for having lost its way. He wondered, rhetorically: Was not the belief in purgatory dangerously close to that of Buddhism? Did not priests sell indulgences to enrich the pope? Was not Mary, the mother of Jesus, worshipped? Was not the cross worn as a superstitious charm? With a positive answer to all, Yang argued that these practices had dragged Catholics toward damnation. Worst of all, the Church forbade believers to read the Bible, to which Yang gave the name *Jingjing* 景經, or "The Classic of Christianity/Nestorianism." By reading only the works of the Church fathers, Catholics lost touch with God's original message. All of these errors had led Martin Luther to challenge the Church, debate Catholic priests, and, most important, to translate the Bible into the vernacular—German—making the message of the Bible available to many who had no Latin, at the expense of his excommunication. Here was a nutshell version of the Protestant case against Catholicism.

Yang described the global distribution of Protestantism, calling it *Yesujiao* 耶穌教 (the teaching of Jesus), and Catholicism, noting that while the leaders of Protestant countries regularly called for peaceful coexistence with Catholics, the reverse was uncommon. To demonstrate his broad knowledge of the branches of Christianity, he briefly mentioned the Russian Orthodox Church, noting that the head of the church was the tsar, and that this denomination was not aggressively evangelical. Protestantism, he ironically concluded, was the "heterodoxy" (*yiduan* 異端) that provoked the pope's most vehement reaction. Was this because Protestants declared the Bible the only religious authority, rejected elaborate rituals, advocated the separation of church and state, and had no interest in intervening in state affairs? Or was it because they eschewed confession, hymns, sacraments, and religious chastity.[29] Yang concluded that it was Protestants who most diligently practiced God's teachings.

After his lengthy discussion of *Jingjiao,* Yang turned to Judaism, Zoroastrianism, Brahmanism (Poluomenjiao 婆羅門教, i.e., Hinduism), Shakyamuni (Buddhism), Muhammad (Islam), and Manichaeism. By presenting these faiths in some detail, he hoped to correct long-standing confusions: eighteenth-century evidential scholars, who were ignorant of foreign languages, had often failed to distinguish Christianity from other faiths. The scope of his investigations covered virtually all foreign religions that had ever existed in China.

There is no question that Yang was determined to prove the superiority of Protestantism to all other contenders. He worked up to this gradually, beginning with a comparison of Judaism and Christianity. He began with the Jews in Kaifeng 開封, "discovered" by Matteo Ricci (1552–1610). Anyone who knew Hebrew, he said, could have immediately read the Ten Commandments written on the wall of the Jewish synagogue in the old Chinese capital. And yet the Jews who arrived in China via the Silk Road had never had the opportunity to hear the good news of the Messiah. The Jewish diaspora was simply God's vehicle to introduce the Old Testament to China, where it had survived for nearly a thousand years. The Jewish Bible that Ricci had found in Kaifeng also proved that the sacred texts of Christianity could not be modern Western forgeries, because Jews had used ancient Hebrew to record the early messages from God.[30] For Yang, the survival of Jewish artifacts and inscriptions in Kaifeng functioned much as did the Nestorian stele, extending the history of Christianity in China; he also suspected that a number of early Chinese terms were based on the language of ancient Babylon (presumably Akkadian). He then offered a remarkable speculation: Could it be that Chinese civilization itself had sprung to life in the Middle East?

Yang's brief introduction to Zoroastrianism begins with the origins of the Persian people, whom he placed in what is now India. The earliest Persian tribes possessed an oral tradition and wonderful customs, which were eventually written down around the time of China's Yellow Emperor. In response to questions about the creation of the universe and the meaning of good and evil a sage named Zoroaster offered an explanation similar to that found in *Yijing* 易經 (The classic of changes) and Neo-Confucianism—except that it posited that spirits were the rulers of the universe. It was only later, when Zoroastrianism declined, that its followers began to worship fire. The cult had gone astray by the Eastern Zhou period, but remnants lingered on, up to the Muslim conquests of Tang times.[31]

As for Brahmanism, Yang first noted that India's civilization was as old as China's. It had thrived during a prehistorical period that corresponded to the era of the mythical Fuxi 伏羲 and Shennong 神農. Brahmanism developed out of the orally transmitted Vedas during the Shang period, according to Yang. He mentioned Hinduism's mythological origin of human beings, which justified a rigid caste system. As a self-proclaimed enlightened Western-style intellectual, Yang denounced the Indian practice of *sati*, the misogynistic demand that widows cast themselves onto their husbands' funeral pyre. After a review of doctrines, rituals, and sects of Brahmanism, Yang surprised his readers by equating the religion with the theory of *li* and *qi* 理氣 that was espoused by Song-era Confucians—both systems of belief held that all material things had come into existence through the action of an agent that lacked human form. The only important difference, according to Yang, was that Brahmanism was idolatrous, leading unwary believers astray.[32]

Comparing Buddhism, Islam, and Christianity, Yang presented Shakyamuni (the Buddha) and Muhammad (the founder of Islam) as human beings fated to grow old and die, unlike the Christian God, who was not bounded by time. Yang pointed out that Shakyamuni had developed his teachings out of Brahmanism. Though the doctrine of emptiness he adopted was wrong, his benevolence made him a great figure. In spite of the many parallels shared by the two religions, Hindus tried to kill Shakyamuni, who survived only because powerful kings had already become patrons of Buddhism. When eventually Shakyamuni did die, Hindus persecuted his followers, who fled to other countries and became idolaters, worshipping Shakyamuni and other Indian deities. Thanks to this diaspora, Buddhism flourished, and past tribulations served as a narrative foil that encouraged the spread of Buddhism.[33] The immigrant proselytizers produced Buddhist sutras, which, in Yang's view, fragmented and tarnished the original teachings of Shakyamuni. Since the founder of the movement was a human being who had died without having written anything, his followers drew on his ideas to compose a great number of texts, which became the sources of the many different schools of Buddhism.

Yang attributed the movement's success to the teaching that affirmed the potential every human being possessed of achieving Buddhahood. However, he also turned a censorious eye on local practices. For instance, the Tibetan custom of sharing a wife among brothers, which he viewed as deeply immoral, he attributed to Buddhist asceticism. He also ridiculed those killed by serpents and tigers because they obeyed the Buddhist injunction to kill no animals.[34]

As with his discussion of other religions, Yang drew up a brief history of Islam as seen through the actions of its founder. He emphasized three points. First, to construct his new faith, Muhammad drew on local Bedouin religions, Judaism, and Christianity. Second, the superiority of monotheism to polytheism enabled Islam to conquer Central Asia. Third, the Uyghur (*Huihe* 回紇) people had nothing to do with Islam, a confusion that had arisen because the Chinese word for "Uyghur" contained the character (*hui* 回) commonly used to refer to Muslims.

Thanks to the rise of Islam, Yang reported, idolatry was largely wiped out in Central Asia and India. For him, this was progress, as his Western masters had conveyed the threat posed by superstition—even Islam was on the side of the angels. After describing the relations between China's imperial lineages and the Muslims who started to arrive in South China during the Tang, Yang declared that all of the world's leading beliefs (*jiao*) had coexisted harmoniously during the heyday of the Mongol empire. Northwest China had been home to many Muslims since then; they had named themselves Hui 回 (literally, "to return"), which meant, Yang showed in an argument that defied all rules of linguistics, "returning to the Lord."[35]

Unlike Islam, Manichaeism had long been extinct in China. Its founder, Mani, had attempted to synthesize Buddhism, Nestorianism, and Catholicism without realizing how ridiculous—and doomed—his project was. "How could it be possible," asked an incredulous Yang, "to integrate a pagan faith, a heterodox faith, and the true faith?" Though the foolhardy synthesist was able to attract a few followers, Manichaeism never became widespread and disappeared shortly after the rise of Islam, at the same moment that Emperor Wuzong 武宗 (814–846) of the Tang dynasty issued an edict banning Buddhism.[36]

After having set out the differences between Christianity and the other major foreign religions in the first section of *Jingjiao beiwen jishi kaozheng*, Yang devoted the two following sections to a comparison of Christianity and Chinese religions. Like Diaz, he worked through the text on the stele sentence by sentence. For critical terms, such as *jing* 景, *jiao* 教, and the like, he even proceeded character by character. Unlike Diaz, who adopted the form of a dialogue to explain away doubts about Christianity, Yang relied on passages from the first comprehensive Chinese translation of the Bible, completed in 1843, to support his theological arguments. His commentary functioned like a companion to the Bible, itself a new and unfamiliar book for Chinese readers.

Yang opened part two of his treatise by affirming that *Jingjiao* was a form of Christianity called Nestorianism, a heterodox sect unknown to previous commenters on the stele. He then set about explaining the use of the character *jing* 景. Yang confirmed Diaz's statement that *jing* referred to brightness, and he also agreed that this was a metaphor for the divine revelation that dispelled the darkness of indigenous Chinese beliefs. Yang cited John 1:4–5 ("In him was life, and that life was the light of all mankind. The light shines in the darkness, and the darkness has not overcome it") and John 8:12 ("I am the light of the world. Whoever follows me will never walk in darkness, but will have the light of life").[37] While Diaz had glossed *Jingjiao* as a single term, Yang defined *jing* and *jiao* separately. He attempted to rebut the definition of *jiao* familiar to his Chinese literati peers: in a famous passage from *Zhongyong* 中庸 (The doctrine of the mean), it was said that *xiudao zhiwei jiao* 修道之謂教 (cultivating the Way is called *jiao*), an idea that even the Chinese Catholics used to explain the relationship between Chinese civilization and Christianity. Here Yang played on the double meaning of *jiao*, which can refer to teaching/cultivation (as in the preceding passage) or a sect/cult (which was the issue under discussion). For the Confucian *jiao*, which the famous Neo-Confucian thinker Zhu Xi 朱熹 (1130–1200) identified as the institution set up by the sages to educate commoners, Yang substituted Christian doctrine. He defined it as God's decrees, miracles, benevolence, His law of rewards and punishments, and the promise of salvation. Perhaps above all, *jiao* was the power of belief to transform people. *Jiao* was thus exclusively reserved for Christianity, a Eurocentric but nonetheless faithful definition of the word "religion" in Western culture.[38]

Turning to a topic investigated by Diaz, Yang offered his own explanation of why the priests whose names appeared on the stele had called themselves *seng*. Here he recapitulated a standard Protestant argument that Martin Luther himself had made: given the declaration in Matthew 19:1–4 that marriage was a sacrament the Lord had set up for human beings, celibacy could not be a requirement for joining the priesthood. Yet Nestorians had demanded that their archbishop abstain from carnal congress. In this passage, Yang went beyond the philology of the character *seng*, justifying Protestantism's policy on marriage and the priesthood by arguing that celibacy ran counter to the will of early apostles, single men who often had to forsake the joys of family life, going into hiding to avoid persecution. Celibacy, and therefore *seng*, was not Christian. By providing an explanation for *seng*, Yang demarcated the boundary not only between Nestorianism (only that church's archbishop was expected to remain celibate), and Chinese Buddhism, but also between Nestorianism and Protestantism (which rejected celibacy).[39]

Examples of this kind of philological-cum-ideological practice frequently occurred in Yang's commentary. For instance, he argued that the terms on the stele that had Buddhist or Daoist associations, such as *changran zhenji* 常然真寂 (unchanged and still) and *yaoran lingxu* 窅然靈虛 (numinous existence), could lead to misunderstandings about the Christian message. They had been used because of the difficulty of translating foreign ideas into the Chinese language, yet while for a Buddhist *changran zhenji* describes emptiness or quietus, this was far from the state of being that sacred Christian texts valued. He cited the occurrences of *changran* in the Chinese translation of Exodus 3:14 ("I am that I am") and 1 Timothy 6:16 ("Who only hath immortality, dwelling in the light which no man can approach unto; whom no man hath seen, nor can see: to whom be honor and power everlasting"), noting that there the meaning of *changran* was *shi* 實, referring to God as "the immortal being who is always there." The idiom *yaoran lingxu*, meaning roughly a state of "profound spiritual sublimity," sounded Buddhist or Daoist, yet the passages Yang quoted from Job, Psalms, and Romans showed that it referred in fact to the unpredictability and omnipresence of the Lord of Heaven.[40]

Like Diaz, Yang took every opportunity to explain the basic doctrine of Christianity, but unlike his predecessor, Yang knew that the ideas recorded on the stele were heterodox, a form of Christianity that had been corrupted by ancient customs and pagan doctrines. For instance, he criticized Nestorian thinking about the cross on which Christ was crucified: Ancient Egyptian superstitious beliefs had corrupted the true meaning of the cross by treating it as a magical object. He also annotated the phrase *gu yuanfeng er sheng erqi* 鼓元風而生二氣 (agitating the primordial wind and producing the two modes of *qi*), which Yang understood as an indirect reference to *Yijing*, which discussed the Great Ultimate (*taiji* 太極) and its Two Modes (*liangyi* 兩儀, i.e., *yin* and *yang*). For Yang, this was a result of the corruption of the Chinese language, which in his mind had deviated from the timeless Christian truths that lay at the very origins of Chinese civilization. Whatever Christianity might be, it did not possess the Chinese idea of the binary opposition of *yin* and *yang*.[41] Thinking about how earlier readers of the stele might have reacted to *gu yuanfeng er sheng erqi*, Yang argued that everything depended on the standpoint of the interpreter. A Confucian sympathetic to Christianity, for instance, would respond to loan words that seemed to echo such texts as *Zhongyong* by deciding that *Jingjiao* resembled Confucianism, while a hostile reader might accuse Christians of plagiarizing Confucian teachings. Yang believed that Jingjing 景淨, the author of the inscription, had drawn inspiration from the description of the creation of the world in Genesis to contrive the couplet 判十字以定四方, 鼓元風而生二氣 *panshizi yi ding sifang, gu yuanfeng er sheng erqi*, which he rendered as "The cross pacifies the four directions"—a straightforward reading of the first seven characters—"and God creates light and darkness." The reading offered of the second half of the couplet was fanciful. Yet Yang cried out, "Isn't that a great achievement!" Given the difficulty of translation in the Tang period, when Christianity and China had just met, perhaps more imagination than usual is required in deciphering the inscription. In any case, the heterodox nature of Nestorianism in the Tang still needed to be exposed. The so-called *erqi*, though a great rendering in Chinese, deviated from the original meaning in the Bible.[42]

Yang's discussion of Satan, the source of all evil, is interesting. He argued that Satan was manipulated by God, who humiliated him to demonstrate the subtlety of His omnipotence. God, creator of all, had by definition created all of the evils that had plagued mankind through history. For instance, the father, stepmother, and stepbrother of Shun 舜, the famous sage-king, were all vicious persons. God created them as foils to render Shun, by contrast, a great model of filial piety and fraternity.[43] According to Yang, then, Satan had been created by God as the means to an end. Satan spawned other ills, including heterodox sects, local cults, Buddhism, and the belief in *yinyang* and *wuxing*, all of which Yang considered imports from Mesopotamia during the Shang period. For Yang, nothing was worse than superstition, "a vice that runs counter to religion through sheer excess—it's not because it offers more opportunities to worship the divine than true religion, but because it offers those opportunities either to those unfit to receive them or in the wrong manner." Yang referred to pagan cults as *wangdao* 妄禱 and inappropriate worship as *xiedao* 邪禱. He cited developments in the new science of chemistry to argue against the ordinary Chinese worship of objects, including mountains and rivers; we now knew that such things were simply combinations of different elements, created by God but containing no gods. He claimed that natural phenomena could be comprehended by "fathoming their principles" (*qiongli* 窮理); there was no need to resort to supernatural powers to explain them.[44] In addition to absurd beliefs passed on from one person to another, the desire each human being possessed from birth led to inappropriate worship and to the longing to satisfy unfulfillable appetites; false gods were nothing but reflections of false consciousness.[45] After a lengthy discussion of the problem of evil, Yang concluded that it was a test of the strength of one's faith. Faith in God brought salvation; indulgence in vice brought eternal damnation.[46]

In his third and last section, Yang clarified the meaning of more loan terms from Buddhism, words like *zihang* 慈航 (the ferry of compassion), which was used in the synopsis the stele offered of the story of Noah.[47] Diaz had offered a completely different interpretation, hazarding that *zihang* referred to Jesus Christ's resurrection, an event that would convey sages to Paradise. In any case, both denied that *zihang* had any Buddhist connotations. Yang also criticized Nestorian rituals, fasts, and a number of other practices that he considered sacrilegious.[48] But China's moral decline had begun far earlier, during the time of Houyi 后羿 in the Xia dynasty, when Satan instigated chaos, wars, depravity, and the spread of the cult of ghosts and spirits. Yang even complained that the corruption found in the examination and judicial systems—he was presumably thinking of the late Qing—was caused by Satan. Thanks to their belief in the Messiah, Chinese Christians in his day clung to a slim hope that they might avoid tumbling into the depths of Hell.[49]

Yang took for granted that Nestorianism was a heterodox sect; he recognized only Protestantism as the orthodoxy. What sometimes looks like simple commentary was both descriptive and prescriptive, explaining what a religion was and what it should be. He devoted more space to attacking Catholics and Chinese local cults than to elucidating Nestorianism. In the end, what Yang did was to demarcate the chronological boundaries of various religions across Chinese history, each of which functioned to prefigure some aspect of the true faith.

It is important to note that Yang had a better understanding of Nestorianism than any previous Chinese scholar; he was also the first non-Western scholar to deal with the Syriac inscription. To break the language barrier, he had turned to *Liuhe congtan* 六合叢談 (Collected stories from the world), a missionary journal compiled by Alexander Wylie (1815–1887) and published in Shanghai. There he seized upon the works of Justin Perkins (1805–1869), an American Presbyterian priest and linguist who worked in a Nestorian community in Urmia, northwestern Persia, today's Iran.[50] Among Perkins' fellow missionaries was a physician named Asahel Grant (1807–1844), who considered the Nestorians one of the ten lost tribes of Israel.[51] According to Yang, from the time Perkins started his "civilizing mission in Urmia in 1835, he collected ancient Syriac books and manuscripts, including Bibles, which he translated into modern Syrian and published."[52] Yang rewrote their story translated and collected in the *Liuhe congtan*. Perkins and Grant were witnesses attesting to the existence of a living Nestorian culture; though they may never have learned of the existence of the stele, their testimony permitted Yang to prove previous scholars wrong. Though in many ways his was a traditional commentary, Yang's text showed the influence of newly imported knowledge about natural sciences, theology, and new forms of communication introduced by Protestant missionaries. It represented a new kind of scholarship, informed by but going beyond traditional scholarship such as evidential research and Neo-Confucianism.

The afterlife of Yang's study shows that his approach resonated. Indeed, his erudition was promptly recognized by one of the most renowned evidential scholars of the day, Wang Xianqian, who republished the first *juan* of Yang's commentary in 1901, adding a preface and a postscript. Presumably Wang was attracted by Yang's comparisons of different religions and his historically informed approach to texts; he showed no interest in the second and third *juan*. In his preface, Wang stated that Yang had helped readers grasp the differences between Nestorianism and Zoroastrianism; the book also provided useful geographic information. But the tendentious nature of the commentary, written only to advance Christian interests, rendered it useless.[53] Wang's postscript went further, arguing that every element of the biblical creation mentioned in Yang's book had precedents in Chinese texts. Reversing Yang, Wang implied that all the foreign religions mentioned in Yang's book had originated in China.

At the end of his piece, Wang returned to the famous *Zhongyong* phrase discussed by Yang—*xiudao zhiwei jiao*. Certainly this referred not to a covenant between God and man, but to the fact that Confucianism was the only true teaching.[54] At the turn of the twentieth century, Yang and Wang occupied two sharply divergent positions on the nature of religion, orthodoxy, and Chinese civilization, in spite of some superficial agreements about the Nestorian stele.

In the previous pages I have investigated how Emmanuel Diaz Jr. and Yang Rongzhi used the Nestorian stele to create different histories of Christianity in China; each scholar—and this is true of Wang Xianqian too—applied the inscription to his own enterprise, while demarcating the boundaries of various *jiao*. We can see the modern concepts of religion and religious studies beginning to emerge, dialectically, from exegeses driven by different intellectual positions. The Nestorian stele conveyed a great cargo of historical implications, enabling Diaz and Yang to anchor themselves in the intersection of Christian history and the glorious Tang, send a longboat back to Creation, and from there, take sextant readings for human beings' future salvation. More importantly, these historical agents distinguished their religious positions from other belief systems by building their arguments around a concrete site of memory, a stone stele.

For missionaries arriving in China in the late sixteenth century, the stele served a variety of functions, providing a reason to discourse upon the word of God while simultaneously justifying their own appearance in a foreign land. Diaz revived long-dormant memories of Christianity in China, attacked local religions, suggested that Christianity could be of use in governing, and appealed to the emperor for support. Turning back the clock helped him both duck and parry all sorts of problems facing his fellow missionaries in the late Ming, while creating an identity for the converts.

Yang's commentary produced similar effects. The problem for him, however, was somewhat different. As the Qing dynasty ran out of steam, seeking imperial patronage was no longer the first priority for a Protestant priest. Rather than dwell on Christianity's Tang moment, he placed his hope in the present, advocating modern reforms. Politically, Yang supported Sun Yat-sen's revolution. Culturally, he promoted Protestantism and attacked the various alternatives found in China. Moreover, his experience showed that the information being transmitted around the world by Protestant priests opened the door to a new type of scholarship, inspiring him to imagine a Babylonian origin for Chinese civilization. In the eyes of many Chinese scholars—like Wang—Yang was a true traitor to orthodox Confucianism.

For both Diaz and Yang, the discovery of the stele meant that Christianity was in China for good, even though they had different interpretations of what that meant. Each had a different concept of his connection to historical time. While Diaz attempted to associate the Jesuit mission with Chinese history, he took a series of detours from the present to the Tang, moving on to the birth of mankind, only to circle back to the present, where he argued for the legitimate presence of Catholicism at the time of the Ming–Qing transition. Yang, as a Protestant, had little use for such a roundabout approach, examining instead human progress over time. He assailed the inadequate scholarship on the Nestorian stele that had been produced in the eighteenth century. Writing during the downfall of the Qing and the advent of the Republican era, he advocated jettisoning superstition (those ubiquitous Chinese beliefs) and embraced the theory that Chinese civilization had come from the West. He hoped that this would help reform the nation and save Chinese culture. Much as the Nestorian stele evoked memories of errant Christians, the Chinese past was an embarrassment: the time had come to overthrow the Qing and advance to a new era.

Wang Xianqian used Yang's first *juan* against Yang, subverting his Christian message by pressing for a return to Confucianism's golden age. He believed Confucianism would prevail—no matter how times had changed—even though he already sensed the imminent collapse of the Qing. The ancient sages had created Confucianism as a *jiao* to cultivate human minds—its value was eternal and would not be replaced by a foreign religion, according to Wang. Here was a thinker who had not embraced "progress"; for him, time continued to move in cycles, meaning Confucianism might soon gain the upper hand once more. Christianity's moment in the sun was, in his eyes, an aberration in an otherwise much longer temporal space.

None of the three men was able to define *jiao* in any sort of comprehensive way. Between them, though, they triangulated the important issues faced by the *jiao* (in its broadest sense) of their times. Each proposed a different way of drawing the boundaries among "religions," but it was the political power of the Republican government that would determine what constituted a legitimate religion, as it endorsed a neologism that would replace *jiao* and reshape how the people of China imagined their relation to the world and time.

Notes

1. Nora, "Between Memory and History," pp. 7–24. The quotation appears on p. 7.

2. The stele was unearthed in either 1623 or 1625. Most Western scholars use the latter date, while Chinese scholars prefer the former. Since Western scholars largely rely on European sources, and the Jesuits did not see the stele until some years after it was discovered, they have been led to use 1625. But according to Paul Xu and Emmanuel Diaz Jr. (see below), two contemporary witnesses, the date was 1623. For a summary of this debate see Zhu, *Zhongguo Jingjiao*, pp. 73–81; Lin, *Tangdai Jingjiao zaiyanjiu*, pp. 3–26; Standaert, *Handbook of Christianity in China*, vol. 1: *635–1800*, pp. 10–38.

3. Xu, "Jingjiaotang beiji."

4. Li, "Du Jingjiaobei shuhou," pp. 9a–16a.

5. For instance, Wu You 吳佑, Xu Ji 徐驥, and Feng Wenchang 馮文昌 all identified themselves as *Jingjiao houxue*. See Aleni, *Tianzhu jiangsheng yinyi*, title page. That work may be found in Archivum Romanum Societas Iesu, Rome, shelf: Jap. Sin. I, 77. Churches in Zhejiang and Fujian bore the name *Jingjiaotang*. See Aleni, *Shengmeng ge*, p. 334.

6. Keevak, *The Story of a Stele*.
7. Zhu, *Zhongguo Jingjiao*, pp. 73–87.
8. Chen, "'Zongjiao,'" pp. 37–66.
9. Diaz, *Jingjiao liuxing Zhongguo beisong zhengquan*, pp. 1a–3b.
10. Diaz, *Jingjiao liuxing Zhongguo beisong zhengquan*, pp. 2b–3a.
11. Diaz, *Jingjiao liuxing Zhongguo beisong zhengquan*, pp. 10b–12b.
12. Diaz, *Jingjiao liuxing Zhongguo beisong zhengquan*, p. 42b.
13. Diaz, *Jingjiao liuxing Zhongguo beisong zhengquan*, pp. 42b–43a.
14. Diaz, *Jingjiao liuxing Zhongguo beisong zhengquan*, pp. 43a–43b.
15. Diaz, *Jingjiao liuxing Zhongguo beisong zhengquan*, pp. 48b–49a.
16. Diaz, *Jingjiao liuxing Zhongguo beisong zhengquan*, pp. 44b–45a.
17. Diaz, *Jingjiao liuxing Zhongguo beisong zhengquan*, pp. 47b–48b.
18. Diaz, *Jingjiao liuxing Zhongguo beisong zhengquan*, p. 49b.
19. Feng, "Xingzhonghui shiqi zhi geming tongzhi," p. 33.
20. For a short biography of Yang Rongzhi, see Wu Chang-shing, "Jianjie" 簡介 (Brief introduction), in *Da Qin Jingjiao liuxing Zhongguo bei*, pp. 336–337.
21. Yang, *Jingjiao beiwen jishi kaozheng* (hereafter, *Kaozheng*), pp. 365–366.
22. Yang, *Kaozheng*, pp. 356–359, 362–364.
23. Yang, *Kaozheng*, pp. 365–366.
24. Yang, *Kaozheng*, p. 366.
25. Yang, *Kaozheng*, p. 368.
26. Yang, *Kaozheng*, pp. 369–372.
27. Yang, *Kaozheng*, p. 373. It was during this time that scientists in the West started to suspect that the earth was far older than calculations based on the Bible.
28. Yang, *Kaozheng*, pp. 392–393.
29. Yang, *Kaozheng*, pp. 395–397.
30. Yang, *Kaozheng*, pp. 398–400.
31. Yang, *Kaozheng*, pp. 401–402.
32. Yang, *Kaozheng*, pp. 402–406.
33. Yang, *Kaozheng*, pp. 406–409.
34. Yang, *Kaozheng*, pp. 409–412.
35. Yang, *Kaozheng*, pp. 413–418.
36. Yang, *Kaozheng*, pp. 418–419.
37. Yang, *Kaozheng*, pp. 420–421.
38. Yang, *Kaozheng*, pp. 421–422.
39. Yang, *Kaozheng*, pp. 423–424.
40. Yang, *Kaozheng*, pp. 426–427.
41. Yang, *Kaozheng*, p. 447.
42. Yang, *Kaozheng*, pp. 445–448.
43. Yang, *Kaozheng*, p. 452.
44. Yang, *Kaozheng*, pp. 465–466.
45. Yang, *Kaozheng*, pp. 466–467.
46. Yang, *Kaozheng*, pp. 494–495.

47. Yang, *Kaozheng*, pp. 533–534.
48. Yang, *Kaozheng*, pp. 546–557.
49. Yang, *Kaozheng*, p. 531.
50. "A Report of Nestorians 景教記事," pp. 11b–13b. See also Perkins, *A Residence of Eight Years in Persia*.
51. Grant, *The Nestorians*; Ben-Dor Benite, *The Ten Lost Tribes*, p. 101.
52. Yang, *Kaozheng*, pp. 393–394.
53. Wang, "Xu," pp. 1a–2a.
54. Wang, "Houxu," pp. 3a–4a.

3 ◆ JOSHUA A. FOGEL

How Much Does an Understanding of History Help?
Naitō Konan's Reading of "Communism" in China

In 1911, as the Qing dynasty verged on collapse, ultimately succumbing to the revolution in October of that year, Japan's famed Sinologist Naitō Konan 內藤湖南 (1866–1934) tried to explain how it was that, not only was the Qing *kaput* but China's entire dynastic form of government was doomed—a position not at all widespread among scholars. In the process, he traced events back to the earliest years of the dynasty, more than two and a half centuries previous, and sought to locate longer-term trends that rang the death knell not just for the Qing, as it turned out, but for what he dubbed "monarchical autocracy" (*kunshu dokusai* 君主獨裁), the entrenched power of the dynastic authorities and their proxies, the examination officialdom. He would, most famously, identify "monarchical autocracy" as one of the two essential features of *kinsei* 近世 (the modern era) that emerged out of the destruction of China's medieval aristocracy in the late Tang, Five Dynasties, and early Northern Song periods. The logical result, as he saw it, could only be republicanism based in constitutionalism, which was (in his understanding) the natural outcome of modernity (everywhere). Perhaps even more importantly, such a conclusion could not be reached in a journalist's or political scientist's manner of addressing the immediate issue at hand on the basis solely of proximate causes, but it had to be seen over *la longue durée*. That things did not turn out as neatly as he hoped and predicted, despite the better intentions of Sun Yat-sen 孫逸仙 (1866–1925) and his colleagues, was something that Naitō would address many times over the last two decades of his life.

In 1911, Naitō had two decades as a journalist under his belt and half a decade as a professor at Kyoto University. He was hired when the latter launched its East Asian history department in 1906, but unlike so many of his contemporaries, he retained at least one eye focused on the contemporary scene while also teaching earlier periods of Chinese history. And, to be sure, the lion's share of his numerous journalistic articles were well informed by a scholar's knowledge of China's (and Japan's) history. That dual attention served him well in essaying an explanation with deep historical roots for the fall of the Qing dynasty.[1]

In the process of connecting the dots to the demise of the Qing, Naitō drew a straight line from the Taiping rebels to the Wuchang rebels. How so? He

51

offered plaudits and kudos to men such as Zeng Guofan 曾國藩 (1811–1872) and Hu Linyi 胡林翼 (1812–1861) for their tactics in defeating the Taipings, but then he went on to offer an internal assessment, as presented orally in May 1911 and published the next month, still four to five months before the final uprising that would force the Qing emperor to abdicate:

> Furthermore, although communism was implemented [by the Taipings] at that time, it ended in defeat. When the Taiping rebels took Nanjing, which they made their capital for over ten years, they at first summoned the men of the city. Not allowing the men to return to their families, they built male compounds to house them. They believed there would be divine punishment if these men returned home and had contact with women. The Taipings were followers of a strange Christianity and were completely wrapped up in their God. Several days later they decided to build special dormitories for the women to live in as well. The men and women were completely segregated, and even when husbands and wives saw one another or mothers and sons met, they could not exchange words. They were treated virtually as prisoners. A perusal of the records of the Taiping Loyal King Li Xiucheng 李秀成 [1823–1864] will reveal that these orders were strictly kept and that people complied with them.[2]

(それから又共產主義の實行のあつたのも其の時であるが, 是は失敗に終つた. 南京を十數ケ年間首府にして居つた長髮賊が南京を取つた時に, 初めは城内の男子だけを呼出して, 家に歸ることを許さずに, 南館と云ふ者を立てゝ, そこへ打込んで仕舞つた. 家へ歸つて婦女に接すると天罰があるといふのである. これは長髮賊は一種の變つた天主教徒で, 何事でも天主を振廻す為である. 數日の後には女も一定の居場所を造つてそこへ置くことにした, 之を女館と云うた. それで男と女をマルで分けて仕舞つて, 夫婦が顏を合しても, 母子が出合うても, 語を交すことも出來ぬ. 恰も監獄のやうな扱ひである. 長髮賊の巨魁忠王李秀成の記錄を見ると, 其の時の號令が嚴々整々で, 人民が佩服したと書いてある.)

He goes on to describe various Taiping institutions in detail, based on sources available at the time, and then concludes:

> No country in the world could do all these things and hope for success. Communism was temporarily put into effect by the Taipings, but without giving rise to any results; it has not lasted until now in either custom or thought. Li Xiucheng was an extraordinary man among the Taipings, and there are some people who occasionally pay homage to him today, but no one goes so far as to refer to the system put into effect by the Taipings as good. I think that among the phenomena that have existed in China for a time, this [communism] will certainly have no bearing on China's future constitutionalism.[3]

(何處の國でもそんな事をやつて成功するものはない. 此の共產主義も長髮賊が一時行つて居つたが, 何の結果も來さずに, 實際の習慣としても, 思想としても, 今日は殘つて居らぬ. 長髮賊の中に居つた李秀成などは餘程の人物で, 之を崇拜する者も近頃往々あるが, 併し其の長髮賊が行つた制度までを良いと云ふ人はない. 是れは一時支那にあつた現象でも, 其の立憲政治には將來關係を及ぼすことはあるまいと思ふ.)

Imagine my surprise when I read those lines some forty years ago as a young graduate student, with the Cultural Revolution winding down and the chairman in his waning years. I kept wondering: Didn't Marx have a rather different assessment of the Taipings? Isn't China now putatively a communist country a century or so after the demise of the Taiping Rebellion? What could Naitō have been thinking, I wondered many years ago, when he made these assessments?

Naitō was not through, though, describing the "communist" institutions these Christian rebels established. He went on to explain their textile factory, the *paiweiguan* 牌尾館 (Tag Tail Halls) and *paimian* 牌面 (Tag Faces),[4] various military-like brigades to attend to their occupational needs, and how the literate among them were selected and taught to transcribe a variety of pronouncements coming from their commanders in wartime. He drew his information from the work of Wang Tao 王韜 (1828–1897), who, as is well known, had considerable contact with the Taipings and accordingly had to escape from Qing China.[5] Drawing on Wang's writings and whatever else may have been known from other sources in 1911, Naitō gave as full a description of the social and economic institutions of the Taipings as one might find outside of China at the time. He focused on the perverse separation of the sexes, periodic conjugal visits, and strict monogamy enforced on all followers except for Jesus' younger brother and his extended and fictive male family members who had their own mini-harems. "Women who expressed displeasure with their marriages were punished by having their hands or feet severed. That was how business was actually carried out in the walled city of Nanjing" (結婚を嫌ふ女があると、手足を斫つて懲らしめにした. かう云ふやうに南京城の中では實際に施行して居つた). Whether or not this was actually true, Naitō would have obtained such information from Wang Tao's work; that is, he would not have based such a statement on gossip. In a summary sentence, though not at the end of his description, Naitō stated: "In the walled city of Nanjing over 100,000 people operated within this communistic system [or: with these communist institutions]" (南京城の中では十何萬人と云ふ人が共産主義の制度でやつて居つた).[6]

How does the Taiping Rebellion foreshadow the decline and death of the form of government against which it had actually fought for fourteen years? If Sun Yat-sen could style himself a latter-day Hong Xiuquan 洪秀全 (1814–1864), how could the revolution he putatively was leading ultimately betoken the end of political and social institutions inimical to republicanism? It all seems very complicated and confusing, requiring some unpacking.

"Communism" (*kyōsanshugi* 共産主義)

First, what would the term *kyōsanshugi* (*gongchanzhuyi* in Chinese) have meant in 1911 when Naitō first employed it? Indeed, what *could* it have meant? There was no Communist Party anywhere in East Asia then, nor would there be for another decade or more. The Bolshevik Revolution was still over six years away, and its future leaders were in exile or prison. So I turn first to the major multivolume dictionaries. It is telling that Morohashi Tetsuji's 諸轍徹次 *Dai Kan-Wa jiten* 大漢和辭典 (Great Sino-Japanese dictionary) and the *Hanyu da cidian* 漢語大詞典 (Great dictionary of Chinese) are both useless for etymologies here. Both do indeed have entries for the four-character term, but neither has an etymology. This is a strong clue that the term is not of Chinese origin, as both of these works are, first and foremost, dictionaries of the Chinese language. Had there been a Chinese *locus classicus,* it would surely have been there.

The *Nihon kokugo dai jiten* 日本国語大辞典 (Great dictionary of the Japanese language) fills the gap nicely.[7] For the term *kyōsanshugi* it cites three sources from mid- to late Meiji times. The first, dating to 1886, is the *Futsu-Wa hōritsu jii* 佛和法律字彙 (French-Japanese legal vocabulary) of Fujibayashi Tadayoshi 藤林忠良 and Kabuto Kuninori 加太邦憲 (1849–1929), which states simply: "COMMUNISME. 共産主義." If this is, in fact, the *locus classicus,* then it would indicate that the term entered Japanese (and later Chinese from Japanese) via French. But what sort of influence would France or the French language have had on Japanese in the early or mid-Meiji? Slight, at best. Perhaps there was a tie with the Paris Commune, only fifteen years before this dictionary appeared in print, but there appears to be no lexical relationship. The Japanese term for the "Paris Commune" (*La Commune de Paris, Pari komyūn*) パリ・コミューン is unrelated in any fashion to the term *kyōsanshugi* and thus offers us no help. In fact, it now seems the French *Communisme* was merely a translation of the term, not an etymological hint of any sort. Strike one.

Let us turn to the next source given in the *Nihon kokugo dai jiten,* this one dating to 1893: the novelist and journalist Matsubara Iwagorō's 松原岩五郎 (1866–1935) *Saiankoku no Tōkyō* 最暗黒之東京 (In darkest Tokyo), part 9: "Seeing items covetously acquired being distributed to both sides of the wall and watering the land uniformly, this is the implementation of a society just like communism (*kyōsanshugi*)" (其貪り獲たる物品は、直ちに兩鄰合壁へ向つて散じ、萬遍なく其土地の霑澤となるを見るは、殆んど類似たる共産主義（ケウサンシュギ）の斯の社會に行はれ居るが故なり). This is a fairly primitive explanation of the basic principles of communism. It does vaguely suggest that the idea was sufficiently current by 1893 that one could make the connection between such a description and the name for such a system. One factor militating against this argument, though, is the simple fact that the term had to be glossed (or at least provided with a reading in *kana*) for readers. Ball, just outside; maybe a foul tip.

The third instance dates to 1904, roughly a decade after Matsubara's piece: the Christian socialist Kinoshita Naoe's 木下尚江 (1869–1937) *Hi no hashira* 火の柱 (Pillar of fire), section 2.2: "Is not a home whose doors are not shut tight prime evidence of the professor's communism?" (戸締なき家と云ふことが、先生の共産主義の立派な證據じゃないか). Taken out of context, it is not entirely clear whether this is supporting or denigrating the idea, but ultimately that is less important than the fact that this was the general view—irrespective of one's perspective on it—at the end of the Meiji period in the early years of the twentieth century. Naitō was writing only few years later. Home run.

The *Communist Manifesto* in Japan

The relatively new language of "communism" might have come to Naitō's attention via another route: translations and discussions of the *Communist Manifesto* of Karl Marx and Friedrich Engels. Although Naitō was frequently painted as a dyed-in-the-wool conservative (even an imperialist), in recent years assessments of this sort have receded before the facts. More to the point, his colleague in the Economics Department at Kyoto University, Kawakami Hajime 河上肇 (1879–1946), one of the founders of Japanese Marxism, began teaching to packed classes in 1908, and Naitō was a frequent auditor of his early lectures on *Das Kapital*.[8] Naitō knew no foreign languages other than (various lects of) Chinese, and the first Chinese translations of the *Communist Manifesto* were apparently based on the first Japanese ones.

The initial Japanese translation (minus the third section of the text, which concerned theories of socialism and communism) appeared in the weekly *Heimin shinbun* 平民新聞 (The commoners' newspaper) on November 13, 1904, a joint effort by Kōtoku Shūsui 幸徳秋水 (1871–1911) and Sakai Toshihiko 堺利彦 (1871–1933). This was not a direct translation from the German original, but a retranslation from the English version of Samuel Moore (1823–1899). The Japanese text was banned by government officials on the very day that it appeared in print. Kōtoku and Sakai were promptly indicted for violating the government's newspaper regulations and both were assessed a fine.

On March 15, 1906, the journal *Shakaishugi kenkyū* 社會主義研究 (Studies of socialism) commenced publication, and Sakai produced for its initial number a full translation of the *Manifesto* (including that earlier missing third section). It included a number of corrections to the *Heimin shinbun* edition, but it was substantially the same—and this time it was printed and circulated legally. Soon thereafter, though, the Akahata Incident of June 1908 transpired, in which an anarchist activist was released from prison and was greeted by a group waving "red flags" (*akahata* 赤旗) and shouting slogans such as "anarcho-communism" (*museifu kyōsan* 無政府共產); they were, of course, broken up and arrested by the police. Then the Great Treason Incident of 1910—as a result of which Kōtoku was executed along with ten others—transpired, which led to repression of whatever was deemed "dangerous thought." As a consequence, virtually all writings associated with socialism were placed on the index.

With the Russian Revolution of 1917 and the famous Rice Riots the next year, the brief era known as Taishō Democracy ensued, and an equally short period in which socialism enjoyed a mini-renaissance circa 1920. The Peace Preservation Laws of 1925 pulled the curtain down on this intellectual respite, and it would continue through the end of the Pacific War. Interestingly, in 1919 the Home Ministry's Police Affairs Bureau produced its own translation of the text—though not for popular consumption.[9]

Some fifteen years after the 1906 publication of the full *Manifesto,* in 1921 Sakai brought a much-revised translation. For the first time, this was a direct translation from the German original. Both Kawakami Hajime and Kushida Tamizō

櫛田民藏 (1885–1934), another early Japanese Marxist economist, worked on the German text to come up with a translation, and Sakai made use of their work. Also, the earlier translations were effectively written in an elite literary style, while the 1921 version was more vernacular in tone. The translators' names were given as Sakai and Kōtoku, but inasmuch as Kōtoku had already paid the ultimate price a decade previous, this was probably the work largely of Sakai.[10]

In any event, it would be more than safe to assume that Naitō probably did not see the 1904 translation, which scarcely circulated, but did see either the 1906 version or the reverberations from it in the scholarly press. And if activists had popularized slogans by 1908, including phrases such as *kyōsan* 共產, then these terms were already in the air. That would have been sufficient for him to gain an introductory socialist-communist vocabulary.

"Communism" and the Taipings

At the most general level, then, this understanding of *kyōsanshugi* roughly corresponds, it would seem, to what Naitō had in mind when assessing the Taiping Rebellion. We also need to remember that the Taipings were only finally defeated two years before he was born, making it an event somewhat comparable to what World War II was for some of us, or perhaps what the American war in Vietnam is for others, or the Six Day War for many younger Israelis—namely, a recently fought war we talk about and even use in comparisons, despite the fact that we never personally experienced it. "Communism" entailed, often in the utopian sense, the sharing of possessions and real estate, and it forbade the holding of private property. These characteristics would fit most depoliticized definitions (assuming that is possible) of communism even nowadays. In Naitō's day, it did not as yet have a hyper-politicized connotation.

Naitō, though, had much more in mind, one level deeper, in his analysis of local Chinese society, and this was profoundly tied to his larger claims about the "modern" development of China in all regards. At the time of the Taiping Rebellion, Japanese intellectuals who were trying to assess what was happening in China may have hailed the effort to topple the Qing as they dismissed or even scorned its Christian underpinnings.[11] For his part, Naitō had nothing to offer pro or con about Christianity. He was arguing that the Taipings, with their idiosyncratic institutions and their assault on the very fabric of Confucian society, completely failed to appreciate the essence of local society in China—which spelled their ultimate doom. Perhaps they understood all too well—a concession he was not prepared to make—and simply were out to destroy it; certainly, the Taipings had an entirely different vision of what the social order should look like, albeit rather fuzzy around the edges. He called the reorganization they attempted to effect "communism" (*kyōsanshugi* 共產主義)—his term, not theirs—and that system, he opined, was utterly inimical to the core fabric of local society. What, then, was the quintessential core of Chinese society in his view?

Naitō was, of course, aware of the fact that local conditions varied greatly over Chinese space and time, but he nonetheless went for the (much) bigger picture. Using a familiar image, but not specifically mentioned, local Chinese society seemed to live as if "heaven was [very] high and the emperor [very] far away" (*tiangao diyuan* 天高帝遠). At the village level it was, if not an egalitarian world, then its perceived longevity was the result of a fair and balanced distribution of resources. The entity he notes many times as the virtual quantum unit of Chinese society was the *xiangtuan* 鄉團 (*kyōdan* in Japanese).[12] At the head of these *xiangtuan* were village elders (*fulao* 父老 [J. *furō*]). They all worked collectively to protect local society from invasion and to facilitate the smooth operation of local affairs with the periodic appearance of centrally appointed bureaucrats who would have known little or nothing about their communities. Zeng Guofan and his colleagues understood this basic fact and worked through local leaders to build their *tuanlian* 團練 system,[13] which posited local "braves" as protectors of their local communities—rather than the utterly ineffective standing armies of the Qing.

Thus, as of 1911, Naitō appears to have understood "communism"—actually, *kyōsanshugi*—to refer to all things not intrinsic to Chinese society. While not a direct critique of China's "distinctive" brand of Christianity, his analysis did point to aliens invading the Chinese social and economic body and attempting to establish institutions to which that body was allergic—though allergic in such a way that the body itself would not die but would fight off and destroy the invader. One can play with these metaphors only so far, but Naitō elsewhere frequently used the metaphor of the life of an organism to portray historical developments.

The Rise of Anti-Japanese Sentiment and "Communism" in China

In the years immediately following his 1911 essays on the decline and fall of the Qing dynasty, Naitō continued to contemplate how China had reached such a state of affairs. As a consequence of that period of reflection, in 1914 he published what may constitute his most influential work: *Shina ron* 支那論 (On China). In it he offers his famous thesis that understanding the collapse of dynastic China (not just the Qing but the form of government it embraced) requires looking back to the onset of modernity in the Song dynasty.[14] He actually welcomed the revolutionaries' promise of republicanism, which he saw as the natural historical development for China (and, eventually, elsewhere), and he regarded Yuan Shikai 袁世凱 (1859–1916) as an opportunistic villain, but he could see by 1913 that the revolutionaries had greatly miscalculated:

> We have expressed our sympathies for the revolutionaries who have failed. Because the revolutionaries themselves did not understand the national character of the Chinese people, they reduced the fruits of their labors to naught. The national character of the Chinese is to seek peace at any sacrifice.

> (我々は今以て失敗したる革命黨の人々に同情を表する．革命黨の人々は，自から支那の國民性を了解せなかつたので，其の限りなき辛苦の效果を水泡に歸せしめてしまつたのである．支那の國民性は何物を犠牲にしても平和を求める．)[15]

Outmoded notions such as "national character" notwithstanding, what is important here is Naitō's recurrent claim that the political actors in China did not comprehend their own people's essence. When discussing the Taipings, it was they who failed in this regard, while Zeng Guofan, Li Hongzhang 李鴻章 (1823–1901), and others did understand and were thus able to defeat the rebels. With the passage of time, Naitō might retain sympathy for the Chinese revolutionaries in 1911 (Sun Yat-sen and his colleagues) but pity their ignorance and thus their failures. As time would continue, the same claim reappears, but his mood would change.

Shina ron is a profoundly scholarly work, with the political ramifications of his conclusions cropping up here and there. It makes no mention of radical students or "communism." Ten years later, he would return to many similar themes, but the tone had now changed considerably—and what a difference a decade, this decade, makes! Between 1914 and 1924, we get the following: the Russian Revolution had successfully brought the Bolsheviks to power in China's immense neighbor Russia; the Chinese labor movement had grown remarkably; the China Communist Party had been founded; the Great Kantō Earthquake and subsequent devastating fire had destroyed large swaths of Tokyo; anti-foreign sentiment in general and anti-Japanese sentiment in particular were on the rise in China; the May 4th and New Culture Movements emerged full-blown; and the extraordinary explosion of Chinese nationalism (especially after the Twenty-One Demands of 1915) seemed to target Japan.

Although his 1924 work would provide a fuller treatment of the topic, readers did not have to wait a full ten years to see him use a new term for this idea. In a New Year's Day article in 1921 for *Ōsaka mainichi shinbun* 大阪毎日新聞, he described in highly condensed form many of the trends in modern history that he had outlined in far greater detail earlier, but with an acute concern for the imminent pitfalls confronting China and the dangers of the radical and anti-Japanese movements getting stronger:

> Many people have recently discussed the issue of whether or not China will go communist. The group which at present shows the most likely communist inclination is the military. In the Shanghai area right now, the most radical group in China is trying to proselytize communism to the military. The extent to which soldiers along the Yangzi River who have either risen up recently or have tried to do so have indicated a desire to move in a communist direction is unclear, but nonpayment of salaries and fluctuations in the value of silver have provided ample reasons for the soldiers to go communist. In particular, the peasants living in the surrounding area have sufficient wealth to be able to satisfy themselves by plundering by the soldiers, and this enhances all the more the possibility of communism. However, at the same time that it enhances the possibility of communism on the part of the military, the wealth of the peasantry also should give them greater capacity for self-defense.

(近來屢ゝ支那が赤化するか否やの問題を論ずる人がある。今の所で先づ赤化すべき傾きを有するものは兵隊である。又現に上海邊の支那一流の過激派なども先づ兵隊に赤化宣傳を行はんとしてゐる。近頃或は勃發し或は勃發せんとする狀態の存する長江沿岸の兵隊等が、何れだけ赤化せるかを示すことは明かではないけれども、給料の不渡とか、銀貨の變動とかの事からして兵隊の赤化すべき原因は多く具備してゐる。殊に其の周圍に居る農民が兵隊の掠奪を飽足らすべきだけの富裕の狀態にある所から、益ゝ赤化の可能性を増すのである。しかし兵隊の赤化の可能性を増すと同時に、又農民の富裕は農民の自衛の實力をも増すべき筈である。)[16]

As can be readily seen, he does not use *kyōsanshugi* here for the seven times the word translated as "communist" or "communism" appears, but instead a parallel, possibly newer, term for communism: *sekka* 赤化 (*chihua* in Chinese, literally, "becoming, or turning red").

The New Year's Day article compares the present situation in China to that facing the peasantry at the time of the Taipings—using the Qing-era government term *Changfazei* 長髮賊 (long-haired bandits)—and positing the capacity again in the early 1920s for the peasantry to form local self-defense units to defeat those who would radically transform the social order. We shall return below to why he chose at this point to switch to *chihua* from *kyōsanshugi* as the preferred term for "communism." Suffice it here to note that what he meant by either term at this point, when no Communist Party in China or anywhere else in East Asia as yet existed, needs to be addressed as well. Several years later, when there were Communist parties throughout the region, *sekka* appears to have acquired a decidedly negative connotation. It was associated with any sort of leftist or left-of-center, anti-government, liberal-socialist, and, of course, communist thought. The notorious 1924 incident involving Kawai Seiichirō 川井清一郎 (1894–1930), who used a textbook not designated for use by the state in his elementary school class at the Matsumoto Women's Normal School, sent shivers throughout the educational establishment: it marked a severe attack on freedom of thought in the late Taishō period (1912–1926). At this point, the language of *sekka shisō* 赤化思想 (communist thought) and *sekka seinen* 赤化青年 (communist youth) came into wider circulation.[17]

In the year 1924, Hakubundō 博文堂 published Naitō's much shorter work, *Shin Shina ron* 新支那論 (On the new China), the immediate stimulus for which was, he says, the startling rise of anti-Japanese incidents in China.[18] He announces from the start that anything resembling Chinese patriotism in the anti-Japanese movement is pure fiction; the cause (just as he saw Yuan Shikai a few years earlier manipulate Chinese public opinion) was agitators, if only because the Chinese had little or no concept of a nation or nation-state. Then why worry about it? The problem was that it might at any moment explode once again and cause serious damage. He had absolutely no faith in Chinese politicians to grasp the problems facing their country, in either domestic or foreign affairs, as they lacked the earnest spirit of reform that the previous generation had embodied. Having a lack of commitment to anything but lining their own pockets, they were, in his opinion, "Just like wildly drunk people, and if bystanders don't stand in their way as an obstruction, they take that to be success" (まるで醉狂人の如く狂ひ廻つて, 見物人が妨害さへしなければそれを成功だと心得てゐる).[19]

With more than enough blame for China's quagmire to spread around among domestic and foreign parties—and no small share was placed at the door of Japan—Naitō went on to assert that those (Chinese and Japanese) who considered that Japan would be solely at fault should China collapse and break apart were entertaining an utterly absurd idea. Why? Because they "have no knowledge whatsoever of the foundation of the Chinese nation and the history of Chinese societal organization" (支那の國家の成立, 支那の社會組織の歷史を全く知らぬ). What in particular did they fail to understand? The national condition of China was like that of a planarian worm: Sever one part and the rest survives, as the Chinese people and their culture have done for centuries. Chinese society possesses, he claimed, a firm sense of security (*anzensei* 安全性), a kind of self-defense mechanism, and later in this piece he claims that the "Chinese national character" is to be "content with one's lot" (*anbun* 安分). And that is the reason, he states unequivocally, for the utter lack of success, despite repeated efforts over the most recent few years, of communist propaganda: China's "immunity" (*men'ekisei* 免疫性) to it.[20]

We return to the alternative word for *kyōsanshugi* (communism), namely *sekka*. Why he adopted it is unclear, though the two may have possessed altogether different connotations in his mind, and indeed he may simply have identified *kyōsanshugi* solely with the Taipings at this point. In 1924 *sekka* was still in its terminological infancy, dating back less than a decade and clearly pointing to the radical developments in the world that Naitō found so worrisome. Its literal meaning of "becoming red" reflected the increasingly omnipresent "red banners" that marked the emergence of communists (and, now, Communist parties) everywhere. On the sense of the word "communist," a 1921 volume by Kobayashi Kamin 小林花眠, entitled *Atarashiki yōgo no izumi* 新しき用語の泉 (The source of new terms), reads as follows:

> *Sekka* bears the meaning of becoming radical [extremist]. As red carries the meaning of the radicals [extremists], "to become red" implies a saturation with its principles. In the United States the subjugation of radicals is called the "red hunt" [or "red scare"].
> (赤化 (セキカ) 過激化の意. 赤は過激派を意味するので, 其の主義に浸潤することを「赤化する」といふ. 米國では過激派退治のことを「赤狩 (あかがり)」と呼んでゐる.)

Writing just a few years later (1926), reporter Ubukata Toshirō 生方敏郎 (1882–1969) noted in his *Meiji Taishō kenbun shi* 明治大正見聞史 (Things seen and heard in the Meiji and Taishō eras) in a chapter on student life in the Meiji period: "From about Taishō 6 or 7 [1917–1918], . . . the term *sekka* newly emerged" (大正六七年頃から新に . . . 赤化だのと云ふ言葉が出來て).[21]

The dating here speaks volumes, as this early reference places the term in the immediate context of the Bolshevik Revolution and the rapid spread of radical thought around the world in its aftermath (the repression that followed). Fearing its further spread eastward, Japan at that time sent troops to join the Siberian

Expedition in an attempt to smother the Bolsheviks in the crib—a colossal failure. The Japanese government in the 1920s spread its anti-*sekka* net further and pulled in communists, anarchists, socialists, and labor activists, and in several notorious cases these people never re-emerged. There was a long-standing fear of Russia in Japan, even predating the Russo-Japanese War of 1904–1905, and Naitō appears to have shared it to a certain extent, but much more was at work here.

He was now dealing with self-avowed (capital "C") "Communists," and his fears were that the reform movement in China might veer off in a radical direction and find China forging some sort of rapprochement with Soviet Russia. Lenin was offering China bait in the early post-Revolution years, as the Karakhan Declaration made clear, and Naitō was also well aware of the fact that the most outspoken anti-Japanese elements in China were the Chinese Communists. Like the Taipings before them, the pre-1927 Chinese Communists were focused on urban labor and worker-peasant organizations intent on thoroughly destroying the fabric of Chinese society, which was to be replaced by something utterly inimical to it.

There is another interesting and early Chinese reference to *chihua* (as mentioned above, it is the Chinese way of pronouncing the two characters for *sekka*) from the Chinese press. Writing under the pen name Shuanglin 雙林, Qu Qiubai 瞿秋白 (1899–1935) penned an essay in 1925 entitled "Diguozhuyi de yongpu yu Zhongguo pingmin" 帝國主義的傭僕與中國平民 (Servants of imperialism and the common Chinese people). Qu asks (rhetorically, to be sure) in this piece (and using our term in a highly positive manner):

> What is *chihua*? *Chihua* is revolution—the revolution of the Chinese people; it is also the struggle for China's liberation and independence and so that the foreign capitalists are not able to enslave the Chinese people. In the eyes of the foreign imperialists and their running dogs, [such revolution] is utterly reprehensible and [thus] *chihua*.
> (什麼是赤化?赤化便是革命:中國的民族革命,便是爭中國的解放獨立,使外國資本家不能奴隸中國人。這在外國帝國主義及其走狗的眼裡看來,便算是罪大惡極,便算是赤化。)[22]

In *Shin Shina ron*, Naitō goes on to say that the Communists' propaganda was not panning out, largely because the forces of Chinese society were more powerful. The Communists "advocate the destruction of the family system" (家族破壞論を主張する) in China and see its Confucian underpinning as the "morality of slavery" (奴隸主義の道德). That their efforts were going nowhere was "due to the fact that China's social organization is an advanced communal family system" (支那の社會組織が進步した共產的の家族制度から成立つて居るがため). Note that the last term, translated as "communal," was *kyōsanteki* 共產的. In the context of his earlier writing on the Taipings, this may either be a slip of the brush or just an indication of terminological anarchy.

As this unusual essay nears its end, Naitō explicitly mentions the New Culture Movement and the Literary Revolution, both still reverberating at the time of composition. Some critics, he argues, claim that advocates of the destruction of China's "old morality"—meaning Confucianism—have "completely adopted individualism, socialism, and communism, newly arrived from the West, while others say that they have adopted old ideas from Mozi and Laozi" (全く西洋から新らしく來た個人主義とか, 社會主義とか, 共產主義とかを採用せんとし, 或る者は舊い墨子, 老子などの主義を採用せんとして居る).[23] Here we have *kyōsanshugi* for "communism" in a vaguely negative sense, but the overarching point in this essay—as in virtually all of his writings—is that without a firm grasp of history, no accurate assessment of the present and future is possible. Of course, there are at least as many assessments of history as there are observers, but Naitō here, as elsewhere, claims to have not just a firm understanding but one that goes back several thousand years and clearly points to trends over time.

Back to the Real China! Further Thoughts on "Communism"

Naitō returned one last time to the topic of "communism" in China in a somewhat notorious article of 1926. Entitled "Shina ni kaere" 支那に還れ (Go back to China!), it was a long piece, printed over six consecutive days (May 25–30), again in the *Ōsaka mainichi shinbun*.[24] The year 1926 was his retirement year, and he began a host of scholarly projects, but, as always, he also kept a close eye on current events, and the press solicited his historically informed opinion on those events. By 1926 Naitō had witnessed the early failures of the CCP to score victories among the peasantry; Mao Zedong's 毛澤東 (1893–1976) "Report on an investigation of the peasant movement in Hunan" (Hunan nongmin yundong kaocha baogao 湖南農民運動考察報告) would not be published until the following year.

As the title of this 1926 essay indicates, Naitō was arguing strongly for China and the Chinese (government, people, everything) to stay the course—the long historical course—and not get caught up in the heady events he now consistently identified as *sekka* 赤化 (communism); *kyōsanshugi*, though, will later re-emerge from the dead—zombie-like. Why he chose this term now over *kyōsanshugi* is not immediately obvious, though. Despite passages like that quoted above, from Qu Qiubai's 1925 writing (Qu being one of the principal leaders of the Chinese Communist Party), *chihua* would never really catch on in China.

What, then, did Naitō actually have to say in the essay? His first paragraph reads:

> The recent disruptions in China have turned startlingly volatile, battles fought repeatedly, with centers of power moving each and every time. The changes we are seeing, however, are merely superficial, with no appreciable links to the fundamental ideas of the Chinese people. Genuine change in China has nothing to do with such things as the vicissitudes of the warlord regimes but rather lies in the basic notions of how to reform China. In this regard the Chinese have in recent years abruptly demonstrated a communist [*sekka*] inclination, to which intellectuals inside and outside China have responded either with concern or interest.

(支那近年の變動は實に目まぐるしいほどに激しく，屢屢戰爭を繰かへし，勢力の中心もその度每に移動してゐるが，しかしこれは單に外形にあらはれた變化で，支那の國民の根本の思想には大した關係がないものである．真の支那の變化はむしろかくの如き軍閥などの勢力の消長にはあらずして，支那を如何に改革すべきかといふことに關する根本思想にある．近年支那人が急激に赤化してゐる傾きをあらはし來つたので，支那の內外における有識は，その點において非常に憂慮もし或は興味をももつに至つた．)[25]

The "recent disruptions" of his first sentence may point to the May Thirtieth Movement, which had been violently crushed only months before. More likely, though, he was referring to the warlord fighting taking place in northern China especially, and in his next paragraph (see below) he will explicitly mention the Fengtian 奉天 and Zhili 直隸 cliques. As was frequently his wont, he cautioned against jumping to an uninformed conclusion that the most immediate thing before your eyes is the most important. No, he averred in a fashion not dissimilar from his earlier dismissal of the Taipings, these are all entirely epiphenomenal, but they have given rise to something that is highly important. For, he was essentially saying here, warlords come and go, they win one day and lose the next, but this new radical trend is far more haunting: it is the specter of Communism.

In his next paragraph he proceeded directly to the point:

If a country such as China, the most populous in the entire world, goes Communist and assumes the same attitude and changes to the same social organization as Russia, this will constitute a problem of utmost gravity for the entire world. Advocates of communism in China plan, of course, to create a new China on this basis to resist the oppression of all the capitalist countries, beginning with Japan. Japan and England [i.e., their interests in China] have already been attacked. Even the United States, which has until now professed to be China's friend, is beginning to be worried about how to ward off an attack in the future. The Nationalist Army [of Feng Yuxiang 馮玉祥 (1882–1948) et al.], considered the center of Communist power in recent years, may have collapsed, and the Fengtian and Zhili [warlord] cliques regained prominence, but this is still superficial. For Communism, embraced in the ideology of "young China," has not as yet completely collapsed.

(支那の如き，全世界の中，最も多數の人口を有する國が赤化してロシアと同一態度をとり，同一社會組織にかはるといふことになれば，たしかに全世界にとつてゆゝしい問題であらねばならぬ．支那における赤化論者は，勿論これを以て新支那を形作り，日本を初めあらゆる資本主義の國々の壓迫に對抗しようと企てたので，すでに日英兩國はそのために打擊を被り，今までは支那の友人をもつて任じてゐた米國の如きも，將來における打擊を如何にして防がうかといふことに苦心しはじめるに至つた．最近赤化の中心勢力と呼ばれてゐる國民軍が衰へ，奉直二派が勢力を盛返したといつても，それは矢張り外形上のことであつて，いわゆる「青年支那」の思想に含まれてゐる赤化主義は未だ全く衰へたといふことを得ない有樣である．)[26]

As this quotation reveals, there was a brief time in the mid- to late 1920s when the foreign press, and many others as well, believed that certain warlord groups and even the army of the Guomindang 國民黨, which was about to launch the Northern Expedition, was allied with the "Communists." That would cease to be the case in April 1927, when the United Front (then in operation in 1926, and possibly another reason for believing the Communists were behind warlord military machinations) came to a cataclysmic end. Otherwise, Naitō's read on the Communists' plans strikes this reader ninety years later as spot on. Whatever confusion there may have been about Chinese communism at this stage of its infancy and warlordism, Naitō clearly noted that warlords were as irrelevant to fundamental change in China as the Communists may have been relevant.

It might be tempting to dismiss him as a cranky old anti-communist or a nationalist Japanese angry at rising anti-Japanese sentiment in China—or both. But this was not the Cold War era, and the international alliances and divisions were altogether different at that time. Thus, his views about the new movement on the mainland deserve a much closer look. He goes on to note the concern among Chinese youth for a possible future for communism in China and credits a renovation effort on their part with the phrase that he took for the title of this essay, "Go back to China!" It is not clear about whom he is speaking here, but it is definitely not the Communists; rather, it is those who want to reform and unify their country and who are significantly shying away from Communism. But there is a big problem. In addition to the fact that this group had no meaningful base of power and remained unorganized, "they may have hit on the idea of the need to return to China, but they have no hard knowledge of where to start or in what form to build a renewed new China" (支那に還ることの必要を思ひついても，如何なる點から着手してよいか，如何なる形式で新々支那を形作るべきかといふことについては確實な智識をも持たず).[27]

In essence, this is a critique Naitō had been leveling at commentators from many different countries for decades, but now with a much more forceful and stark tone than before. In this incarnation, he seems to refer to the fact that, in the wake of the New Culture Movement and a decade of Chinese repeatedly trashing their own culture, those wishing to build something rooted fundamentally in knowledge of Chinese historical sources were thoroughly lost at sea. It was, then, the Communists who were continuing to play the ferocious anti-traditional chord, while this vague, unorganized group who, he claimed, went by the name "New New China" was grasping at straws to rebuild something genuinely Chinese—perhaps the motley crew of Chinese liberals. He was just as withering in his critique of contemporary Japanese views of China:

> Views concerning the China issue have been undergoing considerable change in recent years in Japan too. As the further dissemination of knowledge about contemporary China has accompanied proportionately a decline in the depth [of our knowledge], often criticism of China has become entangled with the Chinese authorities and lost its level-headed spirit. All the measures with which the Japanese have actually been involved in changing the state of affairs in China, though, have ended in failure.

(日本においても，近年支那問題に關する議論には大分變化を來たしては居る．最近支那に關する智識が多少普及すると反比例に，その深さは寧ろ減じて來た為に，支那に關する批評についてはかへつて當局の支那人に卷込まれ，冷靜な批評の精神を失ふことが多くなつて來た．しかし支那の變局に對して，日本人が實際に關係したあらゆる方策がすべて失敗に歸して)[28]

In short, nobody has gotten it right.

Later, in his essay "Shina ni kaere," Naitō takes a few wild last swings at the danger he sees on the horizon. While the world appears to be ready to accept China's autonomy, as the Washington and Paris Peace Conferences effectively indicated was to be the new move toward self-determination, radical elements in China were moving in an anti-Japanese direction, and:

> At the same time the influence of Russia's [the Soviet state's] organizations of laborers and peasants has become marked. Socialist and communist viewpoints in Japan have been extensively imported [to China], indicating a shift toward destroying the entire old structure of China and fashioning a new one. This has led to the sudden development of Communism.
> (それと同時にロシアの勞農組織の影響が著るしくなり，日本における社會主義，共產主義の議論が盛んに輸入されるところから，あらゆる支那の舊組織を破壞して新組織を作り出さうといふ傾きになり，赤化主義が急激な發展を來した．)[29]

As if to make the terminology more complicated than need be, Naitō actually used both terms for "Communism" in this short passage, and the term *rōnō* 勞農 (especially when preceded by "Russia") was fairly transparent code for the Soviet Union and the Bolsheviks.

His point here, which is clearly implied by the title, is that the Chinese need to examine their past to ascertain strengths and weaknesses on which to build a program of reform that will last beyond the immediate present. That required a solid knowledge of Chinese history, and he had no faith that the political actors on the scene in China had such. Wealth and power make for a nice mantra, but without due consideration of Chinese culture, it will all be a waste of time and perhaps a tragic one. England made a mad rush for wealth and power, which the Industrial Revolution provided, but all that effort and all the concomitant results have left England with a poorly developed culture, he claimed. This is a fairly specious argument, especially as Naitō knew no European languages, and thus was ignorant of the greatest writers in the English language (Dickens, Eliot, Austen, et al.).

"Communism" in China, Nineteenth- and Twentieth-Century Varieties

The question, then: Is Naitō's understanding of *sekka* linked to his earlier discussion of *kyōsanshugi*, or are the two just coincidentally related by our English translation of both as "communism"? Put another way, does he ever attempt to use *sekka* to explain why the Taipings failed, as he earlier used *kyōsanshugi*, or is there ever for that matter a clear differentiation of the two technical terms? It is hard to say for certain. Some years ago, I posited that *kyōsanshugi* might indicate (small "c") communism—namely, a newish theory on the radical redistribution of property, of which Naitō saw earlier resonances in the Taiping movement and well before there were any (capital "C") Communist parties in the world. Later, when he was criticizing the ignorance of the student movement in contemporary China, he switched to *sekka*, at a time when there were a handful of Communist parties, including a small one in China. Later still, however, he began using the terms almost interchangeably, although the distinction still basically holds. It does seem clear that, during the Taishō period of politics and society, *sekka* bore a derogatory connotation, similar to the use of "red" later, at the height of the Cold War. It should also be noted that *aka* アカ (literally, "red"; usually written in *katakana* but occasionally the graph 赤) would soon enter the lists in a determinedly negative sense. (This two-syllable term can easily be confused with an identical expression, short for *akademikku* [academic], and not always used in a positive sense.)

Bigger question: Does the kind of extraordinary knowledge of the depth and breadth of Chinese history and culture as possessed by someone like Naitō Konan help in correctly addressing a contemporary issue, such as the rise of Communism in China? Do the textually based Sinological methods Naitō used give us greater clarity when applied to contemporary concerns? I would like to say, definitively, yes, but I remain doubtful—or, at least, open to doubts. Why?

Naitō was clearly wrong about an eventual failure of the Communists, though by the time of his death in 1934, the CCP was on its last legs and about to launch the greatest escape from the jaws of death in world history (better known as the Long March). The Communists not only came to power after epic battles with the armies of Japan and the Guomindang. It then followed its 1949 establishment of a Communist government by implementing land policies theoretically not that dissimilar from those of the Taipings a century earlier. Were they successful? Does this prove Naitō wrong and Mao and his colleagues right? One need not jump to conclusions in answering these questions.

If the answers to these last questions are "yes," then there would seemingly have been no need for the wholesale reform movement launched in 1978 by Deng Xiaoping 鄧小平 (1904–1997). As we all know, the reforms have utterly undone most of the "communistic" policies of the Mao period—except, of course, the stranglehold of the CCP over politics in China—and turned China into the world's largest capitalist country. But the failure of the commune system, historically unprecedented mass starvations, and a whole host of horrifying policies might, in the minds of some, indicate that Naitō just may have been onto something. Perhaps his incomparable knowledge of Chinese history, society, and culture enabled him to foresee that the radical changes effected over the years from the late 1940s through the late 1970s were, indeed, ephemeral, if also just as disastrous in the resultant human carnage. China has now lived longer (1978–present) with post-Communist rural policies than it did under state-imposed land redistribution policies, and it is prospering on the whole like no other country in the world.

Understanding of History | 67

I do believe it incontrovertible that Naitō's sense of history provided him with at least something of a map to understand the present and a tentative guide to the future. Far from Naitō's own innovation, this is a hallmark of traditional Chinese historical studies: the past as a mirror for reflection on things to come. It is also a fundamental tenet of the New Sinology, and that alone should make us attentive to what Naitō had to say nearly a century ago.

Notes

1. I treat this issue on some depth in *Politics and Sinology*.
2. Naitō, "Shinkoku no rikken seiji," p. 429.
3. Naitō, "Shinkoku no rikken seiji," pp. 430–431.
4. See Ono, *Chinese Women in a Century of Revolution*, p. 207. (Kathryn Bernhardt translated this specific chapter.)
5. See Cohen, *Between Tradition and Modernity*, pp. 32–34.
6. Naitō, "Shinkoku no rikken seiji," p. 430.
7. "Kyōsanshugi," in *Nihon kokugo daijiten*, vol. 4, pp. 435–436.
8. See Mitamura, *Naitō Konan*. It may be worth mentioning, though not overstressing, that in his youth Naitō (writing under the pen name "Gayūsei" 臥遊生) published an essay entitled "Shakaishugi o tore." The essay was in the mold of state socialism—namely, the best way to protect the poor was to build a strong state. On Kawakami, see Bernstein, *Japanese Marxist*.
9. Ōmura, "Kōtoku Shūsui Sakai Toshihiko yaku *Kyōsantō sengen* no seiritsu denshō to Chūgokugo yaku e no eikyō," pp. 1–13; Tamaoka, "*Kyōsantō sengen* hōyaku shi ni okeru Kōtoku Shūsui Sakai Toshihiko yaku (1904, 1906 nen) no ichi," pp. 14–26; Tamaoka, "*Kyōsantō sengen* hōyaku shi." Mention should be made of the most extraordinarily detailed analysis of Japanese vocabulary used in the various *Communist Manifesto* translations since 1906: Miyajima, "*Kyōsantō sengen* no yakugo," pp. 425–517.
10. These details and more may be found in Tamaoka, "*Kyōsantō sengen* hōyaku shi," pp. 142–144. In his longer article, Tamaoka actually compares these early translations with the German original and Moore's English translation: "*Kyōsantō sengen* hōyaku shi," pp. 15–25.
11. I have addressed this in *Maiden Voyage*, pp. 102–117, and elsewhere. There is a great deal more that could be said about this interesting topic.
12. Not to be confused at all with the same term used in the Sui and Tang and translated by Hucker as "township militia." See Hucker, *A Dictionary of Official Titles in Imperial China*, p. 234 (no. 2364). Hucker identifies it as a Sui institution; Baidu 百度 states its time frame as "Sui-Tang" (http://baike.baidu.com/view/651232.htm).
13. Described most famously by Philip A. Kuhn in his *Rebellion and Its Enemies in Late Imperial China*.
14. Dictated in October and December 1913 and published by Bunkaidō shoten 文會堂書店 in March 1914; Naitō, "Shinkoku no rikken seiji," pp. 291–408.
15. Naitō, "Shinkoku no rikken seiji," p. 296.
16. Naitō, "Shina no chūkokusha," p. 143.
17. Wasaki, "Taishō jiyū kyōiku to 'sekka shisō,'" pp. 753–770.
18. Naitō, *Shin Shina ron*. In early 1978 I interviewed the late Professor Ikeda Makoto 池田誠 (1922–2008), who had published a number of fine studies of Naitō's writings. He confessed to me that he simply could not make complete sense of *Shin Shina ron*.
19. Naitō, *Shin Shina ron*, p. 493.
20. Naitō, *Shin Shina ron*, pp. 499–501, 531 (quotation, p. 499).

21. "Sekka," in *Nihon kokugo dai jiten,* vol. 7, p. 1365.
22. Qu, *Qu Qiubai wenji,* February 26, 1925; *Hanyu da cidian,* vol. 9, p. 1158.
23. Naitō, *Shin Shina ron,* p. 540–541.
24. Naitō, "Shina ni kaere," pp. 171–181. It was reprinted as part of his collection *Tōyō bunka shi kenkyū.*
25. Naitō, "Shina ni kaere," p. 171.
26. Naitō, "Shina ni kaere," p. 171.
27. Naitō, "Shina ni kaere," p. 172.
28. Naitō, "Shina ni kaere," pp. 172–173.
29. Naitō, "Shina ni kaere," p. 177.

To "Turn the Historical Clock Back"
Past, Text, and the Politics of Yuan Shikai's Monarchy

Yuan Shikai on the Historical Clock

The year 1915 is remembered for plenty of significant events in Chinese history, not least of all the bizarre attempt of Yuan Shikai 袁世凱 (1859–1916) to re-establish the monarchy. It was short-lived, between November 1915 and Yuan's death in June 1916. Officially, it was an emperorship of only eighty-three days—from January 1 to March 23, 1916. Such a short period certainly supports the notion that the whole episode was simply a slight deviation from the course of history in twentieth-century China—a trajectory that began with the demise of the last monarchy, the Qing, followed by the rise of the Republic and later the People's Republic. The attempt to restore the monarchy is therefore a very short-lived detour from this trajectory. Because it failed within a few months, there is hardly any reason to revisit it. Yuan Shikai himself went down in history, at least in this regard, as an unlucky usurper, a "restoration maniac," or as someone who "turned back the historical clock" (*kai lishi daoche* 開歷史倒車).[1] A recent biography of Yuan, still considering the whole episode an "adventure," addresses it in a short chapter detailing the political goings-on on the surface during those few months. As it narrates the story, the short-lived adventure was not a one-man whim. Various forces wanted to see the monarchy restored, and they were the ones that suddenly pushed Yuan, in power as president since 1913, to embrace the idea of monarchy. A recent Japanese assessment of Yuan also ignores that episode in a biography that declares him the "starting point" (*shuppatsu* 出発) of "modern China."[2] Therefore, the short-lived episode of the monarchy remains an almost unexplained anomaly. This kind of treatment is not entirely without reason. Peter Zarrow, in a book dedicated to the "conceptual transformation" that China underwent during the transition from empire to Republic, shows how the idea of the monarchy gradually gave way after 1911. Looking at several attempts to restore the monarchy, of which Yuan's was the most significant, Zarrow examines the discourses around each and shows how they waned. As he correctly observes, the "last emperors of China were deposed by military force," but "in each case, military power was not the determining factor. Rather, the popular imagination, or at least mainstream elite imagination, no longer conceived of the state as based on an emperor."[3]

Here we shall revisit the episode but take a different tack with regard to contextualizing it within an identified historical trajectory. Instead of looking at it in retrospect—that is, writing with awareness of later history—I am asking what role the Chinese past, even the distant past, played in this episode. To put it differently, if Yuan was "reversing the historical clock," I ask where the dial in this clock was at the moment of "reversing" without, crucially, assuming that we know where it was going. I ask from where was it coming and to which past was the dial pointing? This essay therefore is less concerned with reappraising the political significance of Yuan Shikai's move in terms of what followed. Rather, it exposes and discusses echoes from China's past that were at play at the time.

Minguo and *Diguo* as "Regimes of Historicity"

General Yuan Shikai, president of the Republic of China, had been preparing to declare the founding of a new dynasty and the restoration of the monarchy perhaps since 1913.[4] As the orchestrator of the last Qing emperor's abdication, Yuan had already forced Sun Yat-sen (1866–1925) to relinquish the presidency and became provisional president shortly after the 1911 Revolution. In 1915, he was planning to restore the traditional dynastic state and declare himself emperor.[5] On December 12, 1915, having completed his preparations and proclaimed himself to have been "appointed by Heaven," Yuan declared the founding of the Empire of China (*Zhonghua diguo* 中華帝國) and himself, the "Hongxian" 洪憲 ("Vastly Constitutional") Emperor. The title Yuan picked for his new polity, *Zhonghua diguo* (literally, *Empire* of Central Florescence) was meant to replace *Zhonghua Minguo* 中華民國 (*Republic* of Central Florescence). The year 1916 would, therefore, be named "Hongxian year 1" (*Hongxian yuannian* 洪憲元年). This deserves some attention. Right after the 1911 Revolution, Sun Yat-sen, the provisional president and founder of the Republic, announced that the thirteenth day of eleventh month of the 4,609th year of the Yellow Emperor's reign (January 1, 1912) would be the first year of the Republic of China—"Minguo 1." Seemingly, by this Sun meant to follow the old imperial practice of counting the years according to a particular emperor's reign. But he wanted to indicate that with the new calendar China was entering into a new ("modern") era. Sun wanted only to adopt the Gregorian calendar, but the *minguo* numbering—a counting that resembled, in structure only, the traditional counting, was put in place simply because the Chinese public had already begun using it.

But now, Yuan would change all that and reform the calendar by declaring the Hongxian reign era. The practice of naming a new reign era, or *jianyuan* 建元 (establishing the year of origin), is a term heavily loaded with political and theological significance. Literally meaning "establishing the [new] beginning," it set the systematic point of origin for year one of a new reign.

The move to "establish the year of origin" for a new reign was the culmination of dynastic changeover and the clearest public indication of its pretensions. What concerns us here are Yuan Shikai's preparations. Acutely aware of the significance of what he was doing, Yuan spent much of 1915 secretly preparing for such a move and staging it with provincial leaders and other potentates. The plot finally became public when "letters of support" and "letters of nomination" calling for Yuan's appointment as emperor began coming from the provinces in early October. The letters—written or dictated by Yuan himself—ostensibly aimed to show that Yuan enjoyed the people's support. However, not everyone supported the action. Liang Qichao 梁啟超 (1873–1929), perhaps the person most responsible for the conceptual transformation China underwent on its way from monarchy to republic, and a former member of Yuan's government, was outraged. He published a bilingual English-Chinese pamphlet against Yuan as soon as the nature of the letters was exposed. Liang's pamphlet presented and analyzed the so-called letters of support. His reaction may be characterized as an anxious attempt to call upon the Chinese people as well as the international community to stop Yuan Shikai.[6] Liang identified in those letters a critical sentence—what he said were "the 45 [incriminating] characters"—that reads in part as follows: "calling to respectfully nominate the present President Yuan Shikai as emperor of the Chinese Empire [*Zongtong Yuan Shikai wei Zhonghua diguo huangdi* 總統袁世凱 為中華帝國皇帝]. . . . He is appointed by Heaven to ascend the Throne and to transmit it to his heirs for ten thousand generations [*chengtian jianji zhuan zhi wanshi* 承天建機傳之萬世]."[7] Focusing on the mention of Heaven in this passage, Liang furiously cried, "[I]s this the will of the people, the will of the officials, or the will of the would-be emperor? I leave my readers to answer."[8] The will of Heaven, in Liang's mind, was indeed not the will of the people. Liang perceived Yuan's political move as a moment of danger for both China and himself as "a citizen of China and as a member of the human race." That is why he felt he must call for action: "I am not unaware of the duty of respect I owe the Chief Magistrate of the Nation, but why should I hesitate to denounce one who is no longer the constitutional head of the state, but a cowardly usurper."[9]

Liang's outrage is understandable. The phrase "appointed by Heaven" that he juxtaposes with the "will of the people" is but one glaring clue. Another phrase, "Emperor of the Chinese empire" (*Zhonghua diguo huangdi* 中華帝國皇帝), which we should juxtapose with *minguo* 民國 (Republic), is also a blatant indicator. In the same manner, we should pay attention to the term *huangdi* 皇帝 (emperor) that Yuan's self-serving public relations letter itself juxtaposes with *zongtong* 總統 (president). Yuan, as the language of the letters revealed, was not only getting rid of the young Republic. He was also, seemingly, bringing back the old political vocabulary that sustained the imperial institution itself even as discrete royal dynasties rose and fell for more than 2,000 years.

The 1911 Revolution indeed had failed to attain certain national goals, but it did effectively deal a blow to the idea that a falling dynasty ought to be replaced by a rising one—something that had kept the imperial monarchy going since the founding of the first empire of the Qin dynasty in 221 BCE.[10] Moreover, in choosing to go from the modern term *zongtong* (president) to the imperial title *huangdi* (August Thearch), Yuan was making a most significant move. *Huangdi* is a loaded term: It came about when King Zheng 政 of the pre-imperial state of

Qin 秦 (259–210 BCE) assumed the imperial throne in the aftermath of the successful conquest of the last of the rival Warring States. The title he created for himself was carefully crafted: "Di" 帝 was the title of the supreme deity since the times of the first historical Chinese state, the Shang (1600–1046 BCE); it was also the title posthumously given to the deified Shang kings. In later periods, Di acquired additional meanings, all associated with very powerful deities or with mythical thearchs of the past.[11]

One can say that all of Yuan's actions suggest his attempt to restore monarchic rule as previous dynastic founders had done before him. But the polity he was trying to create was still different from earlier dynasties. The term *diguo* 帝國, literally meaning "state led by the Thearch," is usually thought of as "empire." But *diguo* is much more than just that. As "empire," *diguo* seems to convey the structural/spatial dimensions of the state. These spatial dimensions, ironically, are not necessarily too different from those of the modern, twentieth-century Chinese states and their structures. Finally, we tend now to think of *diguo* as "empire" mostly because of the term *diguozhuyi* 帝國主義, "imperialism," a misnomer of sorts in the sense that it does not speak to the nature of the polity itself. For instance, a 1903 encyclopedic dictionary attached the term to *minzuzhuyi* 民族主義, "nationalism," (*minzudiguozhuyi* 民族帝國主義).[12] Indeed, other early Chinese uses of *diguozhuyi* tended to emphasize the "expansionist" dimension of the term in various configurations.[13] A 1904 text explained that *diguozhuyi* was "unmatched violence" exercised by various countries in the contemporary global international arena (*jinri diqiu zhuguo, suowei lingli wuqian zhe, diguozhuyi ye* 今日地球諸國, 所謂陵厲無前者, 帝國主義也). The author of the text contrasted the term *diguozhuyi* with *minzuzhuyi*, defining the latter as "universal right" and "justice on earth" (*gu minzuzhuyi zhe, shengren zhi gongli ye, tianxia zhi Zhengyi ye* 故民族主義者, 生人之公理也, 天下之正義也).[14] All of this suggests that the fact that *diguozhuyi* came to mean "imperialism," does not mean that *diguo* means "empire."

Missing from the understanding of *diguo* as "empire" are its profound temporal and politico-theological dimensions. Wang Hui has explained that the term *diguo* carries meanings on three levels. First, "*diguo* exists alongside such concepts as enfeoffment (*fengjian* 封建) and centralized administrative structure (*junxian* 郡縣), all of which refer to a political community with specific values and forms." Second, "*diguo* is a political form that is placed on a historical sequence that runs from the mythical Three August Rulers and Five Emperors of antiquity (*sanhuang wudi* 三皇五帝), through the Zhou kings, the hegemons of the Spring and Autumn period, and the contending powers of the Warring States period." That is, *diguo* "represents a political form and ethical direction from the era of the Five Emperors that is characterized by 'virtue' and distinguished from those states founded by usurpers, hegemons, and kings and their associated political forms." Third, "the concept of *diguo* represents a disavowal of those political systems whose constant struggles for power resulted in an endless series of political plots and military conflict."[15]

Wang's discussion of *diguo* and its meanings represents a historical anachronism of sorts. As Yuri Pines reminds us, Gu Jiegang famously established the fact that the legends about the ancient kings were "introduced," for political reasons of course, into Chinese history centuries, if not millennia, after their supposed times. As he puts it, "the earlier the legendary sage was, the later he was introduced into intellectual discourse."[16] At this point, however, I am less interested in their historicality. Rather, let us examine their role as "anchors" of a "regime of historicity" centered on the concept of the *diguo*. Of the three meanings of *diguo* presented by Wang Hui, the second and third are crucial for us. The first one speaks of *diguo* as an empire in the common spatial/structural meaning of the term. But the other two relate to the *temporal* dimensions of *diguo* and at the same time place greater importance on the sense of rulership. The sovereign is not just a ruler but, ideally, he is a sage whose rise to power is based on virtue. Virtue is, presumably, what enabled him to rise above, and put an end to, the constant series of political plots and military conflict and unify the realm under one rule. So not only geography (the ordering of vast areas) is at stake here, but importantly also time and political virtue. They play a more crucial role inasmuch as the size of the realm can, as it often did, change. The Republic tried to hang on to the *space* it inherited from its immediate predecessor, the Qing empire. But it left the question of the ruler's political virtue unanswered. At the same time, the *minguo* insisted on breaking away from the ethic imbued in the whole time frame of the *diguo*. Wang Hui's words about *diguo* as "a historical sequence," suggest that *diguo* time carries much meaning: The idea of it stretched all the way back to the mythological era of the Five Thearchs, beginning with the Yellow Thearch (Huangdi 黃帝), and then through Zhuanxu 顓頊 and Ku 嚳 to the idealized moral paragons, Yao 堯 and Shun 舜.[17] Indeed, as Peter Zarrow shows, the legendary figure of the Yellow Emperor was very much on people's minds at the time, and his image was used mostly to further the cults of the Han "race" and the Han "nation"—first as an anti-Manchu trope, and later as a unifying symbol for the Republic.[18]

But *diguo* itself, particularly as a code for "5,000 years" of continuous history, was itself a modern construct that was quite "young," certainly not 5,000 or even 2,000 years old. There are only eighteen instances in the huge imperial manuscript collectanea of literature titled *Complete Writings of the Four Treasuries* (*Siku quanshu* 四庫全書) where the term *diguo* appears.[19] A glance at these instances, originating in various far-flung moments in different periods, shows that all refer to the realm as it existed at the time the phrase was used or, at best, the time since the extant dynasty was founded.[20] Thus, even though the term *diguo* existed in the Chinese vocabulary in premodern times, it was quite insignificant, almost never used. More importantly, "China" in premodern times was identified by the name of the dynasty that ruled the realm and possessed the Mandate of Heaven. In its modern incarnation, the word entered the Chinese political language when the Japanese took up its usage (J. *teikoku*) after the 1868 Meiji Restoration, during which time Japan the nation was renamed *Dai Nippon Teikoku*

大日本帝國 (Empire of Great Japan).[21] But that story is not so simple. It is worth remembering that what mattered most in the Japanese phrase was the branding of Japan after 1868 as "Great Japan" (*Dai Nippon*). The "greatness" (大) of the state is the key word here. Timothy Brook has recently drawn our attention to the importance of the term Great State (as in 大元, 大明, 大清) in Inner and East Asian political history since Chinggis Khan. The Great State was "a state under the supreme sovereignty of the Great Khan, but it was also a form of dominion in which other sovereigns could coexist with him as subordinate rulers." A "dominant political form of this phase of Inner and East Asian history," the Great State was "adopted by Chinese, Oirat (western Mongol), and Manchu rulers in naming, if not crafting, their subsequent imperial projects. It corresponds most closely to the European concept of 'empire.'"[22] Crucially, the term *diguo* does not appear in any of these formulations. Change comes only after 1868. It is after that moment that *diguo*, now charged with the notion "imperial," made its way into Korean and Chinese political vocabularies. In 1897, the last Joseon monarch Gojong (1852–1919) proclaimed the *Daehan Jeguk* 大韓帝國 (Great State of Korea). In 1905, a press in Shanghai published a map of China with title *Da Qing diguo quantu* (Complete map of the great Qing state).[23] Thus, it is quite clear that only after the Meiji Restoration paired the terms *da* and *diguo*, the latter came to mean "empire" in Chinese. In 1906, one of the reformed Qing legal codes, published under the Guangxu emperor, carried the title *Da Qing diguo xinbian fadian* 大清帝國新編法典 (New legal code of the great Qing state). The phrase *Da Qing diguo* occurred only in the title and nowhere else in the text.[24] A quick survey of contemporary Chinese press shows that the term was used very minimally, mostly in the context of the aforementioned map. Tellingly, the one outlier came in 1932, when a newspaper reported on "Japan's great conspiracy to reinstate the Qing Diguo."[25] That was in the context of the creation of Manchukuo, and that episode was certainly not an empire. In short, *diguo* as "empire" had a very brief history in China, and it did not necessarily mean empire. Most importantly, the term was itself modern. Thus, in 1911, the *minguo* "departed" from something that was almost as new as it was. In declaring himself the *Zhonghua diguo huangdi* in 1916, Yuan Shikai was, paradoxically, the *first* and only man in Chinese history who declared the founding of a *diguo*. In a way, he "turned history back" on a clock that he helped to invent.

The relationship between *diguo* and time, its temporal scope, and its meaning as a "historical sequence" as Wang Hui puts it, were thus also a modern development. The creation of the Republic did not just do away with the last dynasty and with 2,100 years of dynastic rule. It rendered all of China's past up to that point—the "5,000 years"—into a past now defined by the supposed *diguo* nature of the Chinese state. What made it modern was its claim to have a link to the (newly created) past of 5,000 years. In this regard, *diguo* did not refer to real time. Rather it was a code for "5,000 years of history." As such it was what François Hartog would call a "regime of historicity"—"an artificial construct whose value lies in its heuristic potential."[26] Hartog is inspired here by Reinhart Koselleck, who asked how, "in a given present, are the temporal dimensions of past and future related?"[27] Following Koselleck, Hartog theorizes historicity as "the primary experience of estrangement, of distance between self and self, to which the categories of past, present, and future give order and meaning, enabling it to be grasped and expressed."[28] In this regard, the present that the *minguo* represented created a new past that was in turn defined as *diguo*.

To "Arouse the National Spirit"

The third meaning of *diguo* as discussed by Wang Hui refers to the role of the "emperor" as a unifier of the land and a political pacifier. Such a man clearly represents the sage ruler who brings unity after times of chaos and political disunity at the end of a dynasty and restores order, dynastic rule, and the *diguo* per se. Thus, despite the fact that the term was new, modern in fact, Yuan's use of it signaled the "return" of the Chinese state to its long continuous time: a sequence that ostensibly went back thousands of years to when the Yellow Emperor held sway as an ideal emperor and unifier of China.[29] As mentioned above, the Yellow Emperor was on people's minds, and his image was used to cultivate the Han "race" and the "nation" as important notions. Yuan's move was, therefore, far more complicated than merely restoring a familiar type of monarchy. Instead, it was a "restoration" of a time line (and therefore a regime of historicity) from which the Chinese Republic had seemingly departed and the dynastic regimes since the Qin had apparently distorted. At the same time, he was "reviving" a direct monarchic link to mythical Chinese times. Liu Shipei 劉師培 (1884–1919) was critical in creating that link. Liu, who began his political and intellectual career as an anti-Manchu nationalist, flirted for a while with anarchism, and turned into a champion of the "national essence" project, was appointed in 1915 to the National Assembly. From this position, he became one of the leading supporters of the movement to restore the monarchy.[30] There should be no doubt that Liu, a conservative nationalist intellectual, a historian of the Han period, and a prolific philologist, played a key role during the transition from the *minguo* to the *diguo*. His scholarly skills were most crucial for Yuan. Between late 1914 and late 1915 Yuan issued several official announcements appointing Liu to various offices and naming him in charge of several ceremonies. In many of these messages Yuan referred to Liu as a "classics scholar" and a "man of prodigious learning" (*jingxue tongru* 經學通儒).[31] Some evidence presented below will show that Yuan and Liu were closely engaged in direct conversation about monarchical rulership and the (textual) ways it is legitimated. But at the same time, it is more important to look at what Liu wrote for wider audiences.

Liu expressed his support for Yuan's project in an essay titled "On Monarchic Government and the Restoration of Antiquity" (Junzheng fugu lun 君政復古論) that Peter Zarrow aptly characterized as a "highly abstruse" text riddled with "archaic language." There, he insisted that the restoration of antiquity was necessary because the Republic did not work properly.[32] The link between a "monarchic government" headed by a virtuous ruler (*junzheng* 君政) and a restoration of antiquity (*fugu* 復古) that Liu proposed is worth noting. No one, perhaps, worked harder to invent "antiquity" and make it relevant for early twentieth-century Chinese politics than Liu Shipei. He was certainly very creative concerning the need for a new time line for China based on a newly invented antiquity. In 1903 Liu published a call to reset the Chinese historical clock according to a chronology whose starting point was the Yellow Emperor. Some scholars at the time tried to calculate the years of the Yellow Emperor, but not for national purposes as Liu did. His "On the Yellow Emperor Chronology" (Huangdi jinian lun 黃帝紀念論) hit this point right from the start: "[E]very nation cannot but [desire to] trace itself back to its origin" (*minzu budebu su qi qiyuan* 民族不得不溯其起源). Liu identified the origin with a man "named Xuanyuan," namely, the Yellow Emperor, who was the "original ancestor of the 400,000,000 people of the Han race." He was "the first person who created [Chinese] civilization (*wenming* 文明) and the one who initiated [our] 4,000 years of [historical] development." Although "our northern enemies" used "every opportunity" to "trample on and rule China," the Han nation never changed, Liu declared. Now (in 1903) was the moment to express that idea: "If we desire to continue the task of the Yellow Emperor, then we should use the birth of the Yellow Emperor as the beginning of our chronology."[33]

Establishing and using this chronology had two important meanings and goals. The first was to recalibrate Chinese history and turn all "the reign periods of the rulers" (*junwang zhi nianhao* 君王之年號) into "just empty terms" (*kongwen* 空文). This way, the "argument for the nobility of the rulers [would fall] apart by itself without being attacked." The second meaning was "displaying a national awareness of the Han Nation" (*fa hanzu minzu zhi ganjue* 發漢族民族之感覺).[34] No wonder Liu ended thus: "How great is the merit of the Yellow Emperor! How exquisite are the people of the Han Nation!" That was in 1903. In his new essay from 1915, Liu seemed to have transformed the "desire" to "trace the nation back to its origin" into a desire to "restore antiquity" with the creation of a monarchy. Not just a monarchy, but a new model charged with the consciousness of Han continuity. This new monarchy was not going to be simply another version of previous dynasties and rulers. Rather, it was supposed to be conscious of the "national" past of the Han people. Liu doubted the ability of the *minguo*—the Republic—to be the embodiment of this national past. In 1915, he opened with a grim declaration about the current state of affairs in China: "This nation does not distinguish between strong and weak; and when we observe its politics, the politics do not distinguish between good or bad" (*fuguo wu qiangruo, shihu qizheng, zheng wu liangyu* 夫國無強弱視乎其政政無良窳).[35] Furthermore, he explained that the Republic "lacked vitality" (*buzhen* 不振) and could not "display the awareness of the Han Nation." These, then, were the main problems of the *minguo,* and as we shall see, the term *zhen* 振 (vitality) was something that Liu Shipei was keen on bringing back from the deep past to restore the country.

The monarchy, in the sense of *junzheng*, or virtue-based rulership, and restoration of antiquity (through monarchy) were the remedy. This makes sense. Liu tended to be quite "utopian" in the powers he assigned to the restoration of antiquity through different, mostly linguistic, means and strategies.[36] But was Yuan Shikai the ruler Liu Shipei longed for? In trying to answer this question we enter the tricky terrain that exists between political power and intellectual authority, between the ruler and the scholar-official facing him, when the latter is forced to produce clever formulations that would fall nicely on the former's ears without straying too much from the moral-political ideal the intellectual is trying to promote.

In his 1915 essay, Liu was careful not to mention Yuan Shikai as the chosen monarch. Instead, he planted clues pointing to a very significant historical precedent that probably was shaping his thinking. A key phrase in Liu's essay expresses hope that the "grace of the awe-inspiring [monarchic] spirit would revitalize national destiny" (*xing meng weiling sui zhen guoming* 幸蒙威靈, 遂振國命). This phrase, containing the key words *zhen* and *guoming*, corresponds nicely with Liu's general complaint that the Republic "lacked vitality," and therefore merits attention. It is taken from a memorial to the throne by a noted figure from antiquity—Huangfu Gui 皇甫規 (104–174 CE), not a terribly well-known Later Han general, statesman, and a prolific and learned writer. Liu specifically mentions Huangfu in his essay, but the phrase in question appears later in the text.[37]

Liu's bringing in a Later Han figure was carefully measured. We find the phrase, which Liu sees as "promoting the state's destiny," in a memorial to the throne by Huangfu that is included in his biography in the *Hou Han shu* 後漢書 (History of the Later Han). The phrase he quotes never appears in later texts or contexts, except when reused in numerous collections of the writings and/or biographies of famous early officials.[38] We know that at the time of writing, Liu was immersed in the classical heritage of the Later Han period. In fact, a study that he produced on the subject mentions Huangfu Gui several times. He was probably the only modern scholar who was even aware of the Han general and his work.[39] Liu Shipei was, therefore, the first, and probably only, writer to focus on the words *meng weiling sui zhen guoming*, which more literally should be translated as "to be graced/covered by [His Majesty's] awesome spirit/animus, and subsequently revitalize the state's destiny," and to give it a modern twist, borrowing on the presence of the emperor's own spirit. Liu strongly wished that said spirit would flow into a new nation, to "arouse the national spirit," if we allow ourselves to hear Liu deviating from a strictly literal translation.

Why Liu did what he did has a lot to do with the very meaning, that is, the moral lesson, of Huangfu Gui's whole career. Let us look: A native of Anding 安定 (today's Ningxia), Huangfu entered the service of the Han state after proving himself valuable by volunteering to respond to a military threat posed by the northwestern Qiang 羌 tribes in 141 CE.[40] He rose through the military ranks and became a general and was considered one of the three military leaders who saved China at its western and northwestern frontiers. When he became involved with court figures in Luoyang, however, things did not go well. His career took severe swings and suffered political strife. His biography in the *Hou Han shu* lists his endless quarrels with corrupt officials; it states that he was "hated inside and outside the court." Huangfu, an upright and vocally critical general, "utterly loathed the eunuchs," several of whom publicly impeached him. More than once he exposed the eunuchs' incompetence and corruption in the court. Crucially, in 162, having again successfully pacified the Qiang, he turned around and impeached other generals who he thought were cruel or corrupt. Emperor Huan 漢桓帝 (r. 147–168) of the Han, whom Huangfu had supported earlier during his accession to the throne, reprimanded him for these actions. In response, Huangfu Gui sent up in 162 the abovementioned memorial as a proactive political apologia.

The text is masterfully crafted. Huangfu Gui tells the emperor that he had not reported on his most recent military success, per se, merely because he was "ashamed to mention [such a] tiny achievement." But now that he was facing reprimand, he wanted to report on it, but he prefaced everything by giving all the credit to the emperor—a usual sort of trope: "[Y]our majesty's wise command, believing that I was neither stupid nor feeble, sent me urgently to lead troops and to take the road." All success in the battlefield, he asserts, was thanks to the spirit of the imperial majesty, bringing us once more to that specific phrase, here underscored and translated literally: "I, through sheer fortune, have come under [His Majesty's] awesome spirit/animus, and subsequently [have been able] to promote the state's destiny; and the various Qiang [tribes], great and small, kowtowed in submission."[41] This success was not so tiny given the state of affairs at the time and Huangfu's assessment of events in the kingdom. In this same memorial, he laments the corruption of the officials on the borders, which leads to military despair and defeat. One can see the troops set out to fight, he tells the emperor, but the "sound of the orderly return of a victorious army is not heard" (*buwen zhenlü zhi sheng* 不聞振旅之聲).[42]

The rest of Huangfu's memorial narrates certain significant gains for the court that occurred because of Huangfu's diplomatic and military skills. What is important for us here, though, is the almost explicit desire that Huangfu Gui expresses in the letter, namely, that the emperor can animate (*zhen*) the spirit of the state so that its destiny (*guoming*) is promoted and the sound of the orderly return of a victorious army (*zhenlü*) is heard again.

We can now see better why Liu Shipei was attracted to Huangfu Gui, a general with a fine record of defeating non-Han enemies from across the borders. Liu himself liked to combat the barbarians by expunging non-Han peoples from China's history. He understood very well that non-Han peoples played an important role in Chinese history. But he also strongly believed that after the Han period the Chinese had lost the "assimilative powers" they possessed in ancient times, because they "welcomed too many non-Chinese into their midst." Not only were the true assimilative powers lost, but also the "non-Chinese became militarily superior."[43] The Han period was therefore the last time in history in which we can locate the Chinese people in a position of cultural, political, and military superiority over non-Chinese peoples. Within that period, according to Liu's logic, Huangfu Gui's successful wars against the Qiang "barbarians" were probably the last expression of that true essence of Han superiority before it was lost for millennia. Small wonder, then, why Liu returns to that moment in history.

But Huangfu Gui was more than just a good general. He was also a competent official and prolific writer, famous for upright criticism and for being off on a limb by himself. Yet the inclusion of Huangfu's image in an essay that defended Yuan Shikai's declaration of a new monarchy still requires further thinking. If Liu was trying to draw an analogy between Huangfu Gui and Yuan Shikai, only some things work. Above all, Huangfu and Yuan differ in that while both were military men and officials, and both handled difficult power transitions at the Han and Qing courts (respectively) in times of dynastic trauma, Huangfu was not trying to become emperor! We should, therefore, conclude that Liu saw Yuan more as a tool in the creation of the monarchy rather than its goal. Like Huangfu Gui, Yuan's job was to respond to the crisis and help to set things in order by creating and supporting the notion, or the institutional levers, of monarchy.

This insight might offer us a glimpse into Liu Shipei's political vision. Recall that in the 1903 essay Liu wanted to tear apart "all arguments for the nobility of rulers." What he wanted was a monarchy whose rulership was based not on nobility (dynastic bloodline) but on virtue. Coming to 1915, instead of a monarchy centered on dynasty, that is, the Yuan family, Liu wants to see the creation of a monarchy that would appoint virtuous rulers as monarchs. Yuan was merely supposed to be the tool. Thus, more than wishing Yuan to become emperor, Liu wanted to see the monarchy restored at that moment. For him, it seems, Yuan Shikai was merely playing a transitional role, like Huangfu Gui in his time, who could knock off invaders from the north and west but could not get a place in the real political battles in the capital. The preceding assertion must be examined by looking more closely at the phrases cited by Liu. I would suggest that the sentence from Huangfu Gui's biography speaks at once and more directly about the power of imperial majesty to "promote the state's destiny," or to "arouse the national spirit." He also makes an implicit statement about Yuan Shikai—merely the subsidiary minister of the great officers—who now holds in his grasp those same orders of the state.

Shanrang: Yuan Shikai and Cao Pi

The specter of the Later Han dynasty's twilight days, hardly concealed beneath Liu Shipei's words, was not incidental. Let us first review some dates on Yuan Shikai's road to declaring the *diguo*. On December 22, 1914, winter solstice day, he visited the Temple of Heaven in Beijing and presided over extraordinarily elaborate sacrificial rites to Heaven, as the Qing emperors had done in the near past. In September 1915 the National Congress of Representatives, 1,993 delegates, voted unanimously to install Yuan as emperor. This move was followed by calls from the provinces, in the forms of the pre-imperial promotional letters, mentioned above, to aid his becoming emperor. On December 11 the Council of State voted to make him emperor. In that final session, the members of the council made their call three times, and Yuan refused three times. He only agreed upon the fourth call.[44] The assembly went on to perform the *sanyi sanrang* 三揖三讓, a ceremony detailed in the ancient *Zhou li* 周禮 (Rites of Zhou)—bowing toward Yuan Shikai with their hands clasped three times.[45] Some interpret this repetitive asking and declining (to accept the emperorship) as a sign of Yuan's "reluctance" to become emperor and part of the scheme designed by him and the monarchists to "create the impression that he felt compelled to accept the monarchy."[46] But this interpretation misses the whole point. A careful look at the scene and the day on which it happened matter a great deal. We shall return to the meaning of the scene at that ceremony shortly. But for now, it is important to note that more than Yuan's being attentive to politesse, it suggests careful attention to ancient, vaunted Chinese rituals surrounding political legitimacy—always a paramount political concern.

Some rituals, like the worshipping in the Temple of Heaven, are easy to understand. But the scene at the Council of State has greater significance. Yuan refused to be emperor three times and agreed upon the fourth; it may seem to us an act of false humility that sovereigns sometimes make.[47] Declining three times the Council's invitation to ascend the throne is a very important action. It asks us to view what happened in the Council as the principal stage, in fact a principal ritual in an accession process marking the transfer of power, coming even before the rites that symbolize the emplacement of royal authority. The ritual of the Council was, I would suggest, modeled on a myth concerning a well-known political moment related to Yao and Shun, the "paragons of political virtue," and the last of the aforementioned five sage-kings. As the legend goes, when Emperor Yao realized that his sons were all evil, he picked the commoner Shun to take his seat. Shun declined three times and then agreed to take the throne after Yao abdicated. Shun did the same when his time was up and transferred the power to Yu. There are several versions of the abdication legend, and we know that it was attached to the figures of Yao and Shun long after they first appeared in ancient Chinese text.[48] Here, however, I am focusing on its political uses as "the most cited model for proper, nonviolent abdication."[49]

Moreover, I am interested in how the legend is used as the epitome of the "rule by virtue" model. Both Yao and Shun supposedly came to the throne when their virtue was recognized, and both abdicated voluntarily. They did not pass power to their offspring but to someone of great virtue, establishing and affirming the principle, as stated by Howard Wechsler, that "the empire belonged to the most virtuous" (*tianxia weigong* 天下為公).[50] Yao and Shun make a nice and oft-quoted "pair" because the rule-by-virtue model ended with them. (Yu the Great 大禹, the founder of the Xia dynasty, sat on the throne after Shun abdicated in his favor, but his dynasty initiated the principle of rule by hereditary right.) Wechsler identifies two models of taking rulership that had a long impact on the accession ceremonies that follow. The first "voluntary yielding" (*shanrang* 禪讓) occurs when the ruler voluntary abdicates and someone else takes the throne. The second was accession by "conquest of arms" (*fangfa* 放伐): "the forceful chastising of tyrannical rulers and the seizing of their power."[51] One does not have to know a lot about Chinese history to learn that *fangfa* was the way in which most regimes actually assumed power in China. As Wechsler notes, most regimes in Chinese history were founded through force and violence. Indeed, there are very few similar instances, when the political strongman of the time orchestrated a "peaceful" transfer of the Mandate of Heaven from an existing legitimate ruler to the strongman or his people. I am interested here in these instances and particularly in the accession ceremony that abused the ritualized *shanrang* element in the Yao-Shun legend.[52]

A quick count of *shanrang* instances in China's long history shows that aside from the two mythical cases of *shanrang*—from Yao to Shun and Shun to Yu—there were twenty-five such events, most of them in the first millennium. Of those, there are five instances of "internal" (*nei* 內) *shanrang*, when one emperor abdicates and gives the throne to a member of his family. The case of the Qianlong 乾隆 emperor (r. 1736–1796) ceding the throne in 1796 to his son the Jiaqing 嘉慶 emperor (r. 1796–1820) is the most famous.[53] It is important to mention here that, even though it was referred to sometimes as *shanrang*, the abdication of Pu-yi in 1912 was not understood as a "classical" *shanrang* because power was not transferred to another monarch. A newspaper article at the time even bothered to explain that it was not a *shanrang* but a "surrender of power."[54] Indeed, the significant, and the majority of *shanrang* cases are the ones involving a transfer of power from one dynasty to another. Excluding that of Wang Mang 王莽 (c. 45 BCE–23 CE), the first such case, and the most crucial, was the *shanrang* story of the Han-Wei transition in 220 CE.[55]

The long-lived and glorious Han dynasty (206 BCE–221 CE) ended after a long decline. Its practical end was already on the horizon in about 180, when eunuchs dominated the court and struggled for power against various generals leading their own troops, and against many scholar-officials who led separate, dedicated factions. The only question that remained was who would deal the dynasty the final blow and claim the Mandate of Heaven for someone outside of the dynastic line. Emperor Xian of Han 漢獻帝 (r. 189–220, d. 234) sat on the throne of the Son of Heaven for over thirty years until Cao Pi 曹丕 (187–226, r. 220–226), son of the famous general and chancellor Cao Cao 曹操 (156–220), caused him to abdicate. Thereupon, Cao Pi proclaimed the Wei dynasty. This was a crucial moment in the history of the Three Kingdoms period, which was chronicled already in the third century by Chen Shou 陳壽 (233–297), then expanded upon by a skilled historian in the early fifth century, and ultimately immortalized in a vastly influential novel, *The Romance of the Three Kingdoms* (三國演義). Well before 220, Cao Cao had emerged as China's strongman and spent most of his career trying to reunify the crumbling empire and secure his power. He received honorifics naming him the king of his Wei state, hierarchically and theoretically a subject of the Han emperor and his court; but he never declared himself emperor of Han or founded a new dynasty. Famously, as we learn from the Chen Shou and other historians, China as any semblance of a unified empire was being drawn and quartered among three rival forces—two other states besides Cao Cao's Wei. Cao Cao all this time in fact kept protecting the royal Han family. When he died on March 15, 220, his son and successor to the throne of the Wei state, Cao Pi, decided to make the expected move. The political situation was unprecedented and peculiar—the Son of Heaven, Han Xiandi, sat at court as the sacred dynastic representative while a member of a powerful, non-dynastic family and ruler of the rising Wei state planned this emperor's abdication. The decision to end the Han's Mandate of Heaven to rule China was not driven solely by military contingencies, emergencies, or general chaos and rebellion. It was also the result of a long, calculated decision by Cao Pi. He took time to prepare the required critical symbols, gestures, and rhetoric. Although he was, upon his father's death, the most potent political figure in China, Cao Pi was fully aware that his power was somewhat limited, and his legitimacy was still questionable. Therefore, the transfer of the Mandate required a great deal of negotiation. Cao Pi held true political power, but timing was everything. And this brings us to the issue of the dragon.

From March 15, 220, to the winter solstice in December of that year, Cao Pi prepared for the proclamation that would correctly indicate the transfer to him of the Mandate of Heaven. This tactic was, as Wechsler points out, in such instances "essential to demonstrate that a dynastic founder had rightfully inherited the Mandate."[56] Howard Goodman's meticulous, day-by-day account of the process shows how assiduously the Cao-Wei court employed numerous officials to effect a correct notion of legitimacy, as sorely needed by Cao Pi. Above all, it shows how important ritual, divination (especially portentology), and the *Yijing* were in this process, as we discuss next. Cao Pi had time to prepare; thus he could carefully pick the right moment. For that, he needed portents, and as timing was key, much hinged on the *Yijing*. On November 21, 220, one Xu Zhi 許芝, a low-ranking astrologer, memorialized: "The *Yi Zhuan* [*Yijing*] states, 'When the sage receives the mandate to become a king, a yellow dragon will be seen.... On the fourth day ... of the seventh lunar month, a yellow dragon was seen. This is a most shining manifestation of [our] lord king's receipt of the mandate.'"[57] And now comes the dragon! As Goodman shows, reports of sightings of dragons were quite frequent that year and began already several weeks after Cao Cao's death. The November 21 memorial delivered by Cao Pi was an almost open expression of his intentions. He wanted to be emperor and wanted a dragon to appear. On December 3 he asked again if he indeed was the potential ruler that Heaven had been indicating. His question cited the *Yijing*: "[B]ut if you are not the right man, the *tao* [*dao*] will not manifest itself to you." His officials gave him a "*Yijing* pep talk," in Goodman's words, which utilized various places in that multilayered text. They reassured him: he was the one.[58] Again, the presence of the *Yijing* in this story should not surprise us. The book was one of the most critical and influential pedagogical, political, and scholarly texts and remained so at least until the last days of Qing. Long before that time, the hexagrams had already acquired names and brief explanations concerning the hexagrams' qualities and properties. In short, the classic was fully invested with the language for explaining the cosmic powers and patterns of the workings of the universe.[59]

Finally, on December 11, 220, eleven days before the winter solstice, the Han Emperor Xiandi issued a decree declaring his abdication and asking Cao Pi to inherit the Mandate of Heaven.[60] On that same day, Cao accepted the imperial jade seal and tassels and went before the altar and performed the necessary ceremonies to become emperor. (The altar had already been prepared on November 25.)[61] Here again, the political ritual of three refusals before accepting was employed. The Han emperor, acting on specific orders coming from the Cao ducal court, of course, asked to abdicate four times. The first three requests were declined, and Cao Pi accepted the fourth. This was a major part of the accession ceremony. Cao Pi indicated his hope to be able to refuse three times already a week previously.[62] In short, Han Xiandi was made to play the role of Yao; Cao Pi played that of Shun.

Concerning the politics of *shanrang* in general, Howard Wechsler notes that because of "its association with sage-rulers, *shan-jang* [*shanrang*] became in Chinese eyes a sacred political instrument by which power was transferred, and, simultaneously, legitimated." However, he adds, beginning "with the Ts'ao-Wei [Cao-Wei] regime in the third century, whose founder made it appear as if he had assumed power by means of *shan-jang*, it became a much-abused practice empty of all significance."[63] Indeed, many dynastic founders during the centuries between the Cao-Wei and the Tang dynasties practiced *shanrang* as they assumed the Mandate of Heaven, especially during the sequence of the Southern Dynasties (420–589). During this period *shanrang* developed into a ritual, but a turning point came when the Tang founder, Li Yuan 李淵 (598–649), refused to participate in this sham gesture toward the Yao–Shun legend. He was honest enough to admit that his accession was about power and military force (*fang-fa*). Moreover, he recognized how many of his predecessors had abused *shanrang*, thereby emptying the ritual of its political significance. On December 20, 617, just before victory was to be proclaimed for the new Tang dynasty, the last Sui ruler offered to perform the *shanrang* ritual and cede the throne to Li Yuan. Li, who at that moment was already in control of the Sui government, refused to participate in it. A few days later he made clear his opinion about *shanrang* precedents: "Whenever I read past history and encounter such examples, I always clap my hands and laugh." In fact, at some point, he even "vowed not to follow the examples . . . of the founders of the Ts'ao-Wei and Chin [Jin] dynasties who had . . . falsely fabricated *shan-jang* rites." He would be, he insisted, "ashamed one day to be included in the same chapter of history as they!"[64] Small wonder, then, that in the second millennium CE and all through the late imperial period we see no instances of *shanrang*.

Yuan Shikai was the first "founder" since the Tang to attempt a transition of power from one polity to another framed as a *shanrang*. And he did so in a way that brings Cao Pi to mind. Citing Yuan's daughter, Patrick Shan mentions with some mischievousness, that "like all of his ancestors" Yuan was "superstitious." The poor man "believed in *fengshui* and sought out diviners to cast prophesies."[65] Yuan's daughter tells us that when Yuan was considering the emperorship, "*fengshui* masters had told him that his ancestral tombs had shown a blessed sign favouring imperial rule."[66] (Maybe these masters were giving him a sort of a *fengshui* "pep talk," because like Cao Pi he badly needed one.) We have no clear evidence that Yuan was using the *Yijing* or consulting *Yijing* masters, and I doubt we shall find any as this is something one might wish to hide. But absence of evidence is sometimes not evidence of absence, and more importantly, if we recall the sequence of events before the declaration, we see clues that cannot be the result of mere coincidence. The train of events sketched above should provoke the reader's suspicions about Yuan's moves in November and December 1915: the letters of request from the provinces, the ritual of refusing three times before agreeing to take the throne, the ceremonies at the altar, and the date of December 11–12. The dates fit, and why wouldn't they? It was not the intense pace of political developments that shaped his course of action, but human calculations concerning timing and historical precedent. We should pay close attention to the chain of events because of one fundamental affinity between Cao Pi and Yuan Shikai—both men found themselves in the same peculiar situation of having all the political power while someone else was still sitting on the throne. Yuan was the first person after a long hiatus of many centuries of Chinese history who found himself in a situation similar to Cao Pi's—he already had the power, as president of the Republic since 1912, and only needed to orchestrate his peaceful accession to power; and he had time to do it. There was one big difference, of course—whereas in Cao Pi's story the Han emperor needed to abdicate, in Yuan's case the "abdicating" side was the entire Republic—the *minguo*.

Was Yuan thinking about the Yao-Shun *shanrang* model? In January 1912, when he was busy orchestrating the transfer of power from the Qing to the Republic and arranging the abdication of the last emperor Aisin Gioro Pu-yi 溥儀 (1906–1967), Yuan told his ministers: "[The abdication would be] like the resignation of Yao and Shun, who simply followed the people's wishes, and it should not be compared to the loss of the state in the previous dynasties."[67] A few days before the ceremony in the Temple of Heaven, *Shuntian shibao* 順天時報, a Japanese-owned newspaper heavily involved with Yuan Keding 袁克定 (1878–1958), Yuan Shikai's son and a driving force behind the whole episode, published an article on the subject of *shanrang*. In it, none other than Liu Shipei discussed the differences between the "shanrang of Yao and Shun" and the Republican political system.[68] Finally, the official acceptance announcement that Yuan issued on December 12, 1915, which opens with the famous line "the rise and fall of the realm concerns even the commoners" (*tianxia xingwang pifu youze* 天下興亡匹夫有責), makes a clear reference to *shanrang*, stating that the "declaration" (*chenshu* 陳述) "strictly follows the old [practice] of *shanrang* (*benfei gu wei shanrang* 本非故為禪讓).[69]

The story would not be complete without reviewing how China's anthem was tortured during those few months. In May 1915—recall, this is just when Yuan was secretly preparing to declare himself emperor—the Ministry of Ritual published a new national anthem entitled "China Bravely Stands in the World" (中華雄立宇宙間). One of the lines goes as follows: "The rivers and lakes are vast and mighty and the mountains never-ending. Five races under the republic open the Yao age, which will last forever and ever" (江湖浩蕩山綿連, 共和五族開堯天, 億萬年). The phrase *Yao tian* 堯天 was an allusion to a term coined during the Song period: *Yao tian shun ri* 堯天舜日 (literally, days of Yao and Shun), which by extension means "the Golden Age." However, another version of the anthem was issued on December 19, a week after Yuan had his day in the Council. It reads almost the same, but the word "Republic" (共和) disappeared and the line about unity of the Five Races leading to the Golden Age was altered: "The Majestic and the Brilliant [Yao and Shun] open the Yao age, which will last forever and ever" (勳華揖讓開堯天, 億萬年).

As we shall see immediately below, the revised stanza in the anthem contains two references to Yao and Shun, not just the one that was before (*Yao tian*), and this is not a "redundancy." To better appreciate the meaning of the alteration, one must begin with the four characters that were omitted, *gonghe wuzu* 共和五族: the unity (under the Republic) of the Five Races—the Han, Manchu, Mongol, Tibetan, and Muslim (Turkic)—was one of the most central ideas; it was seen as crucial for the preservation of the former imperial borders and territories of the Republic.[70] It was also an important source of legitimacy for the new state, symbolized in numerous ways but most notably in the five-color flag of the Republic.[71] Thus, the phrase *gonghe wuzu* became a ubiquitous slogan, appearing on posters and bills. The first Chinese national anthem, used by the provisional government during the first year of the Republic (1912–1913), was in fact entitled "Song of Five Races under One Union" (*Wuzu gonghe ge* 五族共和歌).[72] Therefore, omitting the *wuzu gonghe* slogan from the anthem was significant, yet the idea behind the phrase that replaced it, *Xun Hua yirang*, is even more important. One cannot do justice to the clever use of the characters in this phrase. The first pair, *Xun Hua*, is code for the combined name of Yao (whose given name allegedly was Fangxun 放勳) and Shun (whose given name was Chonghua 重華). The second pair, *yirang* 揖讓, synonymous with *shanrang*, points most strongly to the event Yuan wanted to highlight—the abdication of Yao to Shun.

Digging deeper, we find the phrase *Xun Hua yirang* in Kong Yingda's 孔穎達 (574–648) commentary on the *Shujing* 書經—the ancient classic containing the earliest material on the mechanics of statecraft. Speaking of the book's structure, Kong compares two types of state's orders created through two radically different processes of political assumptions of power. The first is rule achieved by voluntary yielding (to a morally superior person). As he elaborates: "[T]he voluntary yielding of Yao and Shun gave rise to the Canons [of Yao and Shun] and to the Counsels [of Yu and Gao Yao]" (*Xun Hua yirang er dian mo qi* 勳華揖讓而典謨起).[73] The second part of the phrase presents an alternative way of dynastic change, namely through forceful replacement of an inadequate ruler: "[T]he revolts of Tang and Wu gave rise to harangues and declarations" (*Tang Wu geming er shi gaoxing* 湯武革命而誓誥興).[74] Here, Kong refers to the revolts (*geming*) of Kings Tang 湯 (c. 1600 BCE) and Wu 武 (c. 1046 BCE) against the last rulers of the Xia and Shang dynasties, respectively. Their violent acts—we can call them *fangfa* accessions—did not produce great canons like those in the *Shujing* that became associated with Yao, Shun, and Yu. Instead, they produced royal harangues for going to war (*shi* 誓) or announcements that the ruler makes to his people (*gao* 誥).[75] The term *yirang* therefore stands for *shanrang*, and very specifically refers to the abdications of Yao and Shun, not just to any *shanrang*. More importantly, Kong Yingda has made things very clear— while both sets of state's orders are legitimate, the former is superior. Kong repeats this idea again later in his discussion of the Canon of Yao.[76] We can therefore say that *yirang* also serves to express an essential source of legitimacy for the newly created Hongxian monarchy—more so than the *gonghe wuzu* slogan.

We can now appreciate the second version of the anthem, the one that makes verbatim use of Kong Yingda's phrase. Evidently, it tries to "sell" the new polity (the words now softened by removal of the phrase "Five Races under union"), as born from an act of voluntary yielding—*shanrang*. The latter then gives way to a Golden Age in which state's orders would enjoy the esteemed status of the canons of Yao, Shun, and Yu (*dian* 典; *mo* 謨). This also explains better the name chosen for the new monarchy—Hongxian (Vastly Constitutional). By invoking Kong Yingda's apposite use of voluntary yielding and the production of wise statecraft canons (*shanrang/dian mo*) on the one hand, and violent revolts and autocratic orders (*geming* 革命/*shi* 誓; *gao* 誥) on the other, Yuan Shikai also signals what kind of rule he was offering. It would be a rule of virtue, producing state orders that would enjoy great accordance and esteem by the people.

Finally, we have evidence that Liu Shipei and Yuan Shikai met on December 10, 1915, a day before Yuan Shikai had the crucial ceremony at the Temple of Heaven. In the meeting Liu presented (*cheng* 呈) Yuan with a study he prepared on "the Han [period] Confucian Scholar Jia Kui's scholarship, moral conduct, and outstanding scholarship" (*Jia Kui xue xing zhuojue* 漢儒賈逵學行卓絕).[77] The topic of meeting seems strange, given how busy Yuan have been at that moment, but the protagonist of their conversation, Jia Kui 賈逵, tells us why they met. Jia Kui (30–101 CE) was a famous and very prolific scholar-official during the Latter (Eastern) Han period serving mostly under the dynamic and able rulers Ming 漢明帝 (r. 57–75), and Zhang of Han 漢章帝 (75–88). This period, known as the Rule of Ming and Zhang (*mingzhang zhi zhi* 明章之治), is considered a "golden age" of sorts in history of the Latter Han. It was a time when China regained control over the northwestern and Central Asian territories it lost before and had several successful campaigns against the Xiongnu "barbarians" there.[78] (One can see why Liu Shipei was interested in this period.) It was a period of major debates about China's past and its meaning. Like many of his peers at the time, Jia Kui was highly involved in palace intrigue and political wars centered around text, particularly the *Zuozhuan* 左傳. He is most famous for one particular episode. When Emperor Zhang ascended to the throne in 75 CE, he asked Jia to establish the *Zuozhuan*'s superiority over other texts of historical value. Jia, a known commentator of classical text, did that and more. He "demonstrated" that the *Zuozhuan,* an ancient text of enormous value, was "proof" that the apocryphal prophetic/mystical texts (*chenwei* 讖緯) linked the House of Liu, rulers of Han Dynasty, with the legendary emperor Yao.[79] Apocryphal "divinations" and prophetic texts that "suggested" that the founder of the Han dynasty was the descendant and true successor of Yao were prevalent during the early Eastern Han period, a time when the dynasty was struggling to regain legitimacy and prestige. The Rule of Ming and Zhang period was a time when scholars such Jia Kui tried hard, under imperial sponsorship, to reconcile these apocryphal prophecies with the Confucian classics. Jia Kui's projects within that context were probably the most outstanding.[80]

Let us return, for the final time, from the Han Dynasty to 1915 and to the meeting between Liu Shipei and Yuan Shikai. One cannot do enough justice here to the writings of Jia Kui or to Liu Shipei's serious interest in him. But it seems to me that it is quite clear why Yuan was interested in Liu's study of Jia at that critical moment. Liu Shipei's new study provided additional strategies for legitimacy using the Han dynasty precedent, and furnished Yuan with yet another carefully crafted link to the legendary Yao. Tellingly, this link also invoked the trope of mystical prophecy. If you will, the meeting between Liu and Yuan on December 10, 1915, was the "pep talk" the latter needed before making his move toward founding of the new dynasty.[81]

The various messages that the Yuan court was signaling were clear to many Chinese at the time. Educated elites got the message but did not really appreciate the messenger and his mentor. The most active critic was Liu Chengyu 劉成禺 (1876–1953), a 1911 revolutionary and a member of the Southern Society (Nanshe 南社, founded in 1909), the largest and one of the most influential literary societies of the time.[82] In a beautiful essay entitled "The Voluntary Yielding of the 'Hongxian Emperor'" ("'Hongxian Huangdi' de yirang" 洪憲的揖讓), Liu reminded his readers that the whole *yirang* business was produced by "Liu Shipei and other teachers of the emperor" (*dishi* 帝師), who claimed: "the ancients used [the tool of] voluntary yielding in order to rule the country, Yao yielded to Shun, Shun yielded to Yu" (*guzhe yi yirang er you tianxia, Yao rang yu Shun, Shun rang yu Yu* 古者以揖讓而天下堯讓於舜舜讓於禹).[83] Liu Chengyu was in fact being sarcastic.[84] He summarized Liu Shipei's elaborations on the *yirang* ceremony and its meaning only to show that what took place at the Assembly was a farce. His conclusion: "The Hongxian [emperor's] officials are putting up a front, they pretend to search for antiquity, but in reality, they indulge in fantasies" (洪憲臣子, 为裝点门面计, 忽思搜及古董, 真可谓想入非非).[85] Soon after, the fantasy was over. By way of lending further support for the centrality of the Yao–Shun *shanrang* imagery in Yuan's attempts to legitimate his moves, let us look at the next version of the much-abused national anthem. After Yuan Shikai's death it was rewritten again, this time with all the allusions to Yao and Shun removed. The key phrase now read: "Various industries are prosperous, and the nation is solid. Peaceful and tranquil time within four seas. Ten thousand years!"[86] This symbolic removal signaled one message: all links to the great past that Liu Shipei worked hard to establish were swept away.

Does It All Matter?

About ten years after this episode, in his prefaces to his monumental *Gushi bian* 古史辨 (Debates on ancient history), Gu Jiegang referred to the Yuan Shikai episode as one of the critical moments in the development of his historiographical thinking. He was fed up with the way in which contemporary Chinese intellectuals were uncritically using ancient Chinese terms.[87] In a manner like that Liu Chengyu in 1916, he made a mocking reference to the "atmosphere of restoration of antiquity" (復古的空氣) that Yuan and his "old fogies" (遺老們) were creating at the time.[88] One can be almost certain that he was referring to Liu Shipei and his above discussed essay on the restorations of antiquity. Gu proceeded to dedicate much of his hundred-page preface to debunking the myths related to Yao and Shun. Considering the above, it should be clear that he was not just engaging in textual criticism, but also in concrete political and social criticism.[89] If that is true, though, one can say the same about the maneuvers of Liu Shipei and others a decade before. They also were using ancient texts for the sake of contemporary political moves. Thus, the multilayered, masterfully crafted remaking of the past that Liu Shipei produced for Yuan Shikai seemed to intellectuals such as Liu Chengyu and Gu Jiegang as its abuse. At least for Gu, it was the reason why he decided to dedicate his life to writing a Chinese history that would prevent such abuse.

Aside from novel meanings to historiography, the Yuan monarchy episode teaches us a lesson in politics and history. The 1915 invocation of the *shanrang* model, of the Yao and Shun imagined past, and of the ideal of virtuous monarchy about which Liu Shipei was fantasizing speaks precisely to that possibility—a China that was not "democratic," but was not a hereditary monarchy either. Perhaps Yuan, or better yet his learned advisor Liu Shipei, thought that the clever use of *yirang*, as opposed to just *shanrang*, separated him from all other would-be dynastic founders and linked him directly to Yao and Shun. He would tell us, I would argue, that Yuan was only emulating the rites that had developed as elaborations on the Yao–Shun *shanrang* story because he found himself in a similar situation. In essence, he would say that *his shanrang* was produced via a direct and real link to antiquity that he had talked about, as we have seen, since the last days of the Qing dynasty. This is crucial, because it means, I would argue, that the Yuan monarchy was not turning the historical clock back to the past that had just ended with the Qing. Rather, it was resetting its main wheel altogether. Yuan's Hongxian monarchy transcended the 2,000 years of dynastic rule and was going to fulfill the promise of history encapsulated in the story of Yao and Shun, going back 5,000 years. Maybe Yuan was to be succeeded by a truly virtuous monarch and not by his son.

A political narrative of Yuan Shikai's gambit of eighty-three days, even if one seeks to reappraise Yuan's entire career, leaves the *Hongxian diguo* episode more or less as the hardly meaningful anecdote we often find in modern Chinese history books. But I would argue that a cultural intellectual history as drawn above reveals a richly textured past, pregnant with potential political meanings, hiding beneath this very same episode. More than just an exercise in Sinology, it brings to the fore questions of tremendous political importance such as the peaceful transfer of power—not only from one dynasty to another, but also from one form of rule to another. It also brings to the fore more forcefully the possibility of Chinese political models and ideals that are not derived from Western, modern experience, on the one hand (republic), and not from the late imperial Chinese past that preceded the founding of the Republic (imperial dynasty). That is to say, the *diguo* that Yuan Shikai declared was another political possibility that history presented for China after the fall of the last dynasty. Like the Republic, it was just as modern.

Notes

1. Patrick Fuliang Shan provides a list of such terminology with regard to Yuan in his *Yuan Shikai*, p. 209; a quick unscientific survey I have done online suggests that "turning the historical clock back" is the favorite term for Yuan. This is how he is remembered on the anniversary of his death, for example, at https://kknews.cc/zh-cn/history/j6bmy3y.html (accessed October 12, 2020).
2. Shan, *Yuan Shikai*, pp. 210–216; Okamoto, *En Seigai*.
3. Zarrow, *After Empire*, p. 270.
4. For a general account see Young, *The Presidency of Yuan Shih-k'ai*. See also the new edition of Ma Zhendong's chronicle of Yuan's actions from the Wuchang Uprising in 1911 till his death in 1916, which came out initially in 1932. Ma, *Yuan Shikai Dangguo shi*, pp. 259–286. Below I am also using the complete writings of Yuan Shikai, in thirty-six volumes. See Yuan, *Yuan Shikai quanji*.
5. Zarrow, *After Empire*, pp. 242–249.
6. Liang, *The So-Called People's Will*.
7. Liang, *The So-Called People's Will*, p. 6. The Chinese original is on page 4 of the Chinese section. A slightly better translation should read, "[This] respectfully nominates the present President Yuan Shikai as august emperor of the Chinese Empire. . . . He has been appointed by Heaven to ascend the Throne."
8. Liang, *The So-Called People's Will*, p. 6.
9. Liang, *The So-Called People's Will*, p. 16.
10. For a nuanced account and analysis of the above, see Zarrow, *After Empire*, pp. 212–241. On the imperial idea in Chinese history, see Pines, *The Everlasting Empire*.
11. Chen, "From God's Chinese Names to a Cross-Cultural Universal God."
12. Spira, *A Conceptual History of Chinese -Isms*, 130–131.
13. Karl, *Staging the World*, 15, 64, 84, 146–148.
14. Cited in Jin and Liu, *Guannian shi yanjiu*, 52.
15. Wang, *China from Empire to Nation-State*, p. 33.
16. Pines, "Disputers of Abdication," p. 254. Gu Jiegang discussed their historicality during the 1920s in his correspondence with the linguist Qian Xuantong 錢玄同 (1887–1939) and extensively in the preface to his *Gushi bian* in 1926. See Gu, *Gushi bian zixu*, pp. 1–9, 16, 113.
17. Sun, "Continuity and Discontinuity"; Zhang, "From Myth to History."
18. Zarrow, *After Empire*, pp. 169–173. 179–180.

19. Wang, *China from Empire to Nation-State,* p. 30.
20. This is my analysis of the sources, rereading Wang Hui's counting.
21. Yanabu, "The Tennō System as the Symbol of the Culture of Translation."
22. Brook, van Praag, and Boltjes, *Sacred Mandates,* pp. 17–18l; Brook, *Great State.*
23. *Da Qing diguo quantu.*
24. *Da Qing diguo xinbian fadian.*
25. "Ben Kong" (pseud.), "Riben yinmou Da Qing diguo."
26. Hartog, *Regimes of Historicity,* p. xvi.
27. Koselleck, *Futures Past,* pp. 2–3.
28. Hartog, *Regimes of Historicity,* p. xvi.
29. Leibold, "Competing Narratives of Racial Unity in Republican China."
30. Bernal, "Liu Shih-p'ei and National Essence."
31. Yuan, *Yuan Shikai quanji,* vol. 29, pp. 9, 185.
32. Zarrow, *After Empire,* p. 245. Zarrow translates the first part of this essay as "Imperial Government." I prefer "monarchic" given the emphasis Liu places in the essay on the question of rule by virtue of the monarch. Liu, "Junzheng fugu lun."
33. Liu Shipei (Wu Wei), "Huangdi jinian lun" (1903), in Luo, *Guomin ribao huipian, pian 2, ji* 1–2.
34. Liu, "Huangdi jinian lun."
35. Liu, "Junzheng fugu lun," shang, 1a, p. 1954. Note the play on words: *qiangruo* 強弱 (strong/weak) and *liangyu* 良窳 (good/bad). Liu Shipei clearly enjoyed writing this essay. One suspects he thought Yuan could not understand a word.
36. Yu, "The Vision of New China Suggested by the Politics of Language."
37. Liu, "Junzheng fugu lun," shang, 3a. The quotation from Huangfu's memorial is from *Hou Han shu, juan* 65, p. 2134.
38. Liu, "Junzheng fugu lun," shang, 3a, p. 1955. Huangfu Gui's *Hou Han shu* memorial also appears in collections such as Zhu, Cai, and Jiang, eds., *Lidai mingchen zhuan,* vol. 8, pp. 25a–25b.
39. Liu, *Zhongguo zhonggu wenxue shi Han Wei Liuchao zhuan jiawen yanjiu.*
40. For a modern biography of Huangfu Gui, see de Crespigny, *A Biographical Dictionary of Later Han to the Three Kingdoms,* pp. 352–354. Much of my précis of Huangfu's life is derived from de Crespigny's skilled summary. See also Tse, *The Collapse of China's Later Han Dynasty,* pp. 55–136.
41. *Hou Han shu,* p. 2134. See also a summary of the event in de Crespigny, *A Biographical Dictionary,* p. 353.
42. *Hou Han shu,* p. 2129.
43. Schneider, *Nation and Ethnicity,* p. 268; see the entire chapter on Liu and this specific question (pp. 211–269).
44. Zarrow, *After Empire,* p. 243.
45. Ma, *Yuan Shikai dangguo shi,* p. 282. Perhaps because the overall political maneuver was outrageous, this small anecdote concerning the *Sanyi sanrang* was overlooked by observers. This specific ceremony at the Assembly was described and effectively ridiculed by Liu Chengyu 劉成禺, a keen observer and a learned critic of Yuan Shikai and the intellectuals supporting him. See Liu, "'Hongxian Huangdi' de yirang," p. 218. I shall return to Liu Chengyu's critique below.
46. Shan, *Yuan Shikai,* p. 216.
47. As Peter Zarrow writes, Yuan "gracefully" agreed; *After Empire,* p. 243.
48. On the origins and political significance and twists and turns in the legend, see Allan, *Buried Ideas,* pp. 9–24 *passim.* For a discussion of *shanrang* in the pre-Qin context (when the concept emerged) see Pines, "Disputers of Abdication," pp. 243–300.

49. Goodman, *Ts'ao P'i Transcendent*, p. 21.
50. Wechsler, *Offerings of Jade and Silk*, p. 85.
51. Wechsler, *Offerings of Jade and Silk*, p. 81.
52. For a comprehensive study of *shanrang* tales, see Yang, "Zai lun Yao-Shun 'shanrang' chuanshuo: Zhongguo gushi yanjiu fangfa lunlie." See also Martin, "Des faux qui ne trompent personne." For a summary of the Yao–Shun legend in the classical sources that defines the *shanrang* "system" as "primitive democracy," see Yang, "Lun Yao Shun Yu shanrang de zhengzhi yuanze yu lishi xiangtai."
53. This brings to mind the case of Zhu Di 朱棣, the Yongle 明永樂 emperor (1402–1424) of the Ming, who in 1402 murdered his nephew and took the throne. He then invoked the famous precedent of the Duke of Zhou 周公 (r. 1042–1035 BCE), who ruled as regent, placing his boy-nephew on the throne as King Cheng of Zhou 周成王 (r. 1042–1021 BCE). See Elman, "'Where Is King Ch'eng?'"
54. "Tuizheng wu shanrang Ziyang," p. 319.
55. Wang Mang (r. 9–23) attempted to force a *shanrang* in 9 CE, but his maneuver was made in haste, inelegantly, and in any case was very short-lived.
56. Wechsler, *Offerings of Jade and Silk*, p. 84.
57. Goodman, *Ts'ao P'i Transcendent*, p. 101. Cao Pi was the not the only one about whom dragon sightings came into play. His rival Liu Bei 劉備 (161–223) in the state of Shu had had the same experience some years before, and he also used the *Yijing*; Goodman, *Ts'ao P'i Transcendent*, p. 43.
58. Goodman, *Ts'ao P'i Transcendent*, pp. 151–152.
59. Smith, *The I Ching*, p. 9.
60. The December 11 date was not incidental. As Goodman shows, solstitial calculations played a crucial role during the months leading to Cao Pi's proclamation of the new Wei; Goodman, *Ts'ao P'i Transcendent*, pp. 150–151, 178–179. This practice goes back to pre-Zhou times; see Pankenier, "The Cosmo-Political Background of Heaven's Mandate."
61. Goodman *Ts'ao P'i Transcendent*, pp. 167–169.
62. Goodman, *Ts'ao P'i Transcendent*, p. 152. On December 7, responding to an earlier request, he still refused: "how then could I possibly bring such disgrace to the entire world. . . . I do not dare to obey the mandate." Goodman, *Ts'ao P'i Transcendent*, pp. 163–164.
63. Wechsler, *Offerings of Jade and Silk*, pp. 80–81.
64. Cited in Wechsler, *Offerings of Jade and Silk*, p. 93.
65. Shan, *Yuan Shikai*, p. 15.
66. Shan, *Yuan Shikai*, p. 211.
67. Yuan Shikai, cited in Ma, "From Constitutional Monarchy to Republic," pp. 26–27.
68. Liu, "Lun Tang-Yu shanrang yu Minguo zhidu butong," p. 239.
69. Ma, *Yuan Shikai dangguo shi*, p. 283.
70. Leibold, *Reconfiguring Chinese Nationalism*, pp. 2–3, 66–67.
71. Fitzgerald, *Awakening China*, pp. 180–182.
72. In fact, even the Japanese puppet state of Manchukuo made use of this idea with a slightly different slogan: *Wuzu xiehe* 五族協和 (J. *Gozoku kyōwa*): "the Five Races in Harmony Together."
73. Kong Yingda, "Shangshu zhengyi xu" 尚書正義序 (Introduction to the rectified interpretation of the *Shangshu*), in Ma and Li, *Shisanjing zhushu (biao dian ben)*, vol. 2, p. 2.
74. Kong, "Shang Shu Zhengyi xu," pp. 2–3.
75. Martin Kern, "The 'Harangues' (*Shi* 誓) in the *Shangshu*," pp. 281–319.
76. Kong Yingda, "Yao dian diyi" 堯典第一 (Code of Yao, first part), in Ma and Li, *Shisanjing zhushu: Shang shu*, p. 19.

77. Yuan, *Yuan Shikai quanji,* vol. 33, p. 566.
78. De Crespigny, *A Biographical Dictionary,* pp. 366–368.
79. Zhao, *Great Peace,* pp. 213–215.
80. Qiu, "Jia Kui yu shixue," pp. 70–72.
81. Yuan, *Yuan Shikai quanji,* vol. 33, p. 566.
82. For an edition of most of the society's literary work, see the collection edited by its founder Liu Yazi 柳亞子 (1887–1958), *Nanshe congke.*
83. Liu, "'Hongxian Huangdi' de yirang," pp. 217–219 (quotation on p. 217).
84. Liu Chengyu's sarcasm did not end there. In 1918 he published a "narrative poem" (*jishi shi* 紀事詩) recording the history of the Hongxian dynasty. The poem was modeled after two poetic texts critiquing the histories of the Southern Song, "Nan Song zashi shi" 南宋雜事詩 (A poem on Southern Song trivialities), and the Ming, "Mingshi zayong" 明史雜詠 (Ming history in narrated verse). See Liu, "Hongxian jishi shi." Liu kept publishing increasingly elaborate versions of the poem until the whole narrative made up several volumes. See Liu, *Hongxian jishi shi benshi buzhu 4 juan.* This book in fact is one of the authoritative histories of the Hongxian episode. See the recent edition, *Yuan Shikai dangguo.*
85. Liu, "'Hongxian Huangdi' de yirang," p. 219. This article was one in a series of essays he wrote in response to the goings-on in Beijing.
86. See all nineteenth- and twentieth-century anthems listed, with dates of publishing, at http://sunchateau.com/zl/china.htm (accessed December 18, 2018).
87. Gu, *Gushi bian zixu,* pp. 37–38.
88. Gu, *Gushi bian zixu,* p. 46.
89. Schneider, "From Textual Criticism to Social Criticism."

5 ◆ THEODORE HUTERS

Wenxue *and New Practices of Writing in Post-1840 China*

Of all the features of the "modern" that transformed Chinese intellectual life, the new notion of literature that began to take shape in the last years of the Qing has been among the most consequential. Its most evident trace was the reconfiguration of the term *wenxue* 文學, a shift that, while universally recognized, has occasioned surprisingly little scholarly comment. It changed in a fairly short period from being a term used to refer to a variety of things having to do with writing or the humanities in general to being quite specific in following recent Japanese usage in being essentially a translation of the European sense of "literature." It came to denote specifically creative writing with an aesthetic purpose, set off from other types of discursive or theoretical writing. One of the effects, as Qian Zhongshu 錢鍾書 (1910–1998) pointed out in the early 1930s,[1] was that the new concept of *wenxue* gathered under its umbrella a set of various genres that had before the late Qing generally been more autonomous. The new portmanteau term also enabled the elevation of the category of fiction, or *xiaoshuo,* onto a plane of equality with other, previously more privileged genres, something unprecedented in Chinese letters, and something of profound consequence for subsequent literary writing. One effect of this new sense of the term is plainly contradictory: on the one hand it broadens the scope of what can be discussed within a common lexicon of terms grouped under the new rubric of literature, but on the other hand it opens the door to limiting what had been a highly diverse stylistic horizon that had more often than not been spread over most genres of writing, to a more restricted range of those genres specifically delimited as belonging to *wenxue*. Since this new definition bore implications one way or the other for all Chinese writing, the transformed term inevitably signaled a significant reconfiguration of Chinese literary thinking and, more broadly, of intellectual life in general. This essay will attempt to delineate how this change played itself out against the background of the development of the term itself and literary thinking in general in the two generations before the new understanding of the term became established, at first a bit tentatively, but eventually with an almost legislative force.

Before delving into the specifics of how the meaning of the term *wenxue* developed over the course of the past two centuries, one must set aside for the moment the almost infinite number of glosses and commentaries on the origins, meaning, and significance of the graph *wen* 文 that have accrued over the millennia and look at the most influential, if not the earliest, appearance of the binomial in recent years most frequently attached to it. This famously occurs in the Confucian *Analects* XI.2, where 「文學」 (culture and learning) is listed along with *dexing* 德行 (virtuous conduct), *yanyu* 言語 (speech), and *zhengshi* 政事 (government)—all the translations are those of D. C. Lau—as the final of four evaluative categories by which Confucius grouped his favorite disciples.[2] Given our modern familiarity with the word *wenxue*, it no doubt strikes us as being the most specific and tangible of these "four departments" (*si ke* 四科), as they were subsequently called. It has, however, over the centuries since its first appearance in the canon, taken on a broad variety of meanings, coming variously to indicate men of textual learning, the learned texts themselves, or refined writing, although over subsequent centuries, for all its distinguished provenance, it seems not to have been used as much as other binomials containing *wen* or just the single character on its own. In the late Qing, for instance, it is even rather rarely used to refer to embellished writing itself, with the terms *wenzhang* 文章, *cizhang* 詞章 (辭章), and *shiwen* 詩文 being much the more frequently occurring.

It is also notable that of the nine broad definitions of the binomial in the encyclopedic dictionary, *Hanyu da xidian* 漢語大辭典, the gloss that most closely matches our present understanding of the term—"the art of reflecting reality through the creation of linguistic images" (以語言塑造形象來反映現實的藝術)—is, appropriately enough in terms of its historical sequence, placed in the final position, with the only usage examples given being two twentieth-century writers, Lu Xun 魯迅 (1881–1936) and Guo Moruo 郭沫若 (1892–1978). This accords with the conventional understanding that this sense of the term was a late Qing import from Japan, where it had come to stand as a translation for the English term "literature" during the Meiji reform. One of the early statements of this origin of the revised meaning of the term in China is from a 1934 essay by Lu Xun: "The resumes of ancient speech written in such difficult characters used to be called *wen*, what we today call *wenxue*. This term comes to us not from *The Analects* of Confucius, but from Japan, where it was a translation of the English word 'literature.'"[3] It is significant that, while the term "literature" in English can still be used in one of its older senses of "writing in general" (one example being the term "literature review" used in scholarship to signify prior writing on a given topic),[4] the term *wenxue* in post–May 4th Chinese has no such extended use and is more strictly confined to the sense of writing with an aesthetic intent. In other words, for all the multiple understandings of the word in the past, in the most recent century, the sense of *wenxue* has come to center specifically around the aesthetic patterning of language within a fairly short list of approved genres—poetry, the prose essay, the novel, and drama.

In seeking to determine the ways in which the term was understood in the late Qing, just before the most recent sense of the word became dominant, we find a variety of usages, in spite of the relative paucity of its occurrence. Before going into them, it would be well to set out a couple of ground rules. The first is temporal: since 1949, the Chinese academy has generally followed an official periodization of two eras of the "modern": the *jindai* 近代 and the *xiandai* 現代, the former beginning in 1840 and lasting until 1919, and the latter dating from 1919 to 1949. The entire *jindai* period, moreover, is taken as an epoch of ever-deepening crisis, being seen as a time when the old imperial order had finally sunk into palpable collapse, with possible solutions, if discerned at all, visible only hazily and with great uncertainty. For all the extensive use of this periodization, however, there has been skepticism about its validity in recent Chinese scholarship. For instance, Yuan Jin 袁進 astutely makes the point that the literary and intellectual trends generally said to characterize the *jindai* period can actually be traced out through the entirety of the nineteenth century, if not the late eighteenth. That Gong Zizhen 龔自珍 (1792–1842) obviously did almost all of his writing before 1840 bears this insight out. The historian Zheng Dahua 鄭大華 makes a similar argument, additionally pointing out that to use the Opium War of 1840 as the demarcation line pushed historical periodization outside of indigenous developments in China.[5] In other words, the *jindai* demarcation should more accurately be seen as an indicator of a certain state of mind rather than as an actual temporal marker. Accordingly, the figures picked out for scrutiny by most intellectual and literary historians are those that register the keenest awareness of the crisis, which in much literary scholarship means taking Gong Zizhen and Wei Yuan 魏源 (1794–1857) as foundational figures in the literary thinking of the period. They are almost universally portrayed as men uniquely aware of the predicament of Chinese civilization that marks the period, as well as having original and provocative things to say about it.

It would be easy to see this as a function of the Whiggish historicism characteristic of the post-1949 Marxist regime and its social Darwinist orientation. The singling out of these two thinkers as uniquely influential, however, can be traced back at least to Liang Qichao 梁啟超 (1873–1927) in his often ungenerous 1921 book, *Qingdai xuexu gailun* 清代學術概論 (Intellectual trends in the Qing period). After criticizing Gong for his shallowness, for instance, Liang does allow that "he did in fact contribute to the liberation of thought in the late Qing period, and most of what are called the 'scholars of the new learning' in the Guangxu (1875–1908) era went through a period in which they worshipped him."[6] Liang also points out that both Gong and Wei were the effective progenitors of the intensely activist late Qing New Text school (*jinwen pai* 今文派), a group whose radical reinterpretations of texts arguably had a good deal of influence on the methods by which literature has been read and understood in subsequent years. So these two figures, and others who followed in their wake, while certainly not the only important theorists of writing in the late Qing, can still be said to have been particularly influential in the literary history that has come to have so much influence on our understanding of the period. They are thus worthy of our attention not just for their ideas themselves, but for the influence they have had on subsequent scholarship and the way writing came to be understood.

The second issue is the question of didacticism in literature, or, in less highly charged terminology, the place of morality in writing. While it is impossible to deny that virtually all aesthetic writing in every place and in every time has concerned itself in one way or another with moral issues, this matter is particularly fraught in China, as one of the major concerns of the May 4th literary reform was to diminish the role of the didactic in literature—however much efforts in that direction were in essence reversed by the general politicization of writing from the late 1920s on—as it was encapsulated in the Song dynasty phrase "Writing is meant to convey the *dao*" (*wen yi zai dao* 文以載道). This effort was best summed up by Zhou Zuoren 周作人 (1885–1967) in his highly influential 1932 lectures subsequently published as *Zhongguo xin wenue de yuanliu* 中國新文學的源流 (The origins of the new Chinese literature), where he attempted to make a stark and frankly invidious distinction between writing meant to convey the *dao*, and that of self-expression.[7] Rather than following this extreme example, the issues of writing to be dealt with below may be more profitably evaluated with more specific metrics such as what is the nature of the morality expressed, what are the modalities of its expression, how central is it to the particular writing or theorizing at hand, and who is the agent behind the moral agenda being advanced? Among other advantages of this more precise approach is that it enables modern and premodern writing to be evaluated on the same discursive plane.

A Synthesis of Learning and Fine Writing?

In looking at some of the ideas that surrounded writing in the nineteenth century, there is evidently a substantial amount of overlap with prior notions about writing in China. While this fact might seem to argue for nothing more than a general continuity within Chinese literary thinking, many of these ideas either received particular emphasis in the late Qing or were given a new twist and thus arguably left a greater imprint as a result.[8] In addition, because these ideas were part and parcel of the early reform movement in the late Qing, the stress they received in these years rendered them more impingent upon the generation of literary thinkers that followed, paradoxically, perhaps, including those who were most intent upon departing from the tradition. The following is an example of one such nineteenth-century change: As I have argued elsewhere, the early nineteenth century saw an upsurge in concern for and advocacy of a newly empowered *wenzhang*, a movement set in motion by Yao Nai 姚鼐 (1732–1815), the effective founder of the Tongcheng 桐城 school of prose.[9] In an attempt to assuage the contention between the advocates of evidential learning (*kaozheng* 考證 or *kaoju* 考據), or what has come to be known familiarly as "Han learning," and those intent upon being faithful to the interpretations of Zhu Xi (1130–1200, summed up as adherence to *yili* 義理, or principle), and thus known as "Song learning," Yao had suggested adding a third term, *wenzhang*, or a refined writing that would do justice to both. Thus, a literary writing that could balance both at least the spirit of evidential research and Zhu-ist morality came to be increasingly advocated by the middle of the nineteenth century. When taking the measure of this added stress on the quality of writing, it is important to note that virtually all writing that was to be taken seriously was regarded as requiring what we would think of as aesthetic deliberation in the process of its composition. The fairly common lumping together of such seemingly disparate genres as the prose essay and the examination response is one result of this, as is a persistent ambiguity about what can be considered *wenxue* and what cannot.

As Mei Zengliang 梅曾亮 (1786–1856), perhaps the most "literary" of his generation of Tongcheng disciples of Yao Nai and his tireless efforts in the cause of promoting ancient style prose (*guwen* 古文), said of the ability to combine learning and poetry:

> At the beginning of the dynasty, Wang Shizhen 王士禛 (1634–1711) and Shi Runzhang 施閏章 (1619–1683) were famous for their poetry, but neither of them was learned in evidentiary studies. Of those who were learned in the latter, such as Yan Ruoju 閻若璩 (1636–1704), Hui Dong 惠棟 (1697–1758), and He Zhuo 何焯 (1661–1722), each had their strengths in scholarship, but were not much good at poetry. Only Gu Yanwu 顧炎武 (1613–1682) and Zhu Yizun 朱彝尊 (1629–1709) were good at both. Gu[, however,] did not think of himself as a poet, and as for Zhu's relationship to poetry, he worked at the craft and achieved much, but while he had a good deal in his poetry that was successful, there was little he was satisfied with. This may well have been because his poetry was encumbered by his learning. It is often said that "Poets cannot be without learning," but it is a rule for those who write poetry that they must set their minds in a distant and empty expanse. All the many miscellaneous names, things, and manifestations must be cleared of their dross. Only in this way can my learning be of assistance to my poetry in the expression of my intent and not encumber me; only then can I write poetry.[10]

In this passage, Mei gives expression to what he evidently regards as a new synthesis of poetry and learning, an idea clearly following in the footsteps of Yao Nai's invigorated sense of the power of writing. The extent to which he envisions this as something new is testified to by the fact that even Gu Yanwu and Zhu Yizun, celebrated by others as having been able to infuse their poetry with learning, are damned with faint praise here, imparting the sense that only we of the present generation are really bringing learning and poetry together into an unprecedented unity (at least in the post-Tang age). That Mei might be particularly sensitive to seeing the difficulty and novelty of this fusion between learning and letters is suggested by the rather complacent view of his slightly younger contemporary, Lin Changyi 林昌彝 (1803–1876), that this fusion had been quite common throughout the Qing: "It is now generally said that those who explicate the Classics cannot write poetry, taking evidentiary scholarship and belles lettres as mutually exclusive, but I do not think this is the case. Classical scholarship has flourished in the current era, and there is a profusion of those adept at both Classical scholarship and belles lettres." After presenting a long list of names, Lin concludes with: "Who can [thus] say that explicators of the Classics cannot achieve prominence through poetry?"[11]

As for the term *wenxue* itself, I have found a number of different, albeit almost always ambiguous uses. The following examples capture some of its variety of meanings. For instance, in his *Haiguo tuzhi* 海國圖志 (Illustrated gazetteer of the maritime nations), Wei Yuan has a passage in which the term seems to correspond with the sense of "embellished writing," broadly defined:

> After three years, in the time of the Emperor Xiao Ai 孝哀 of the Han [6–1 BCE], Jesus was born in Judea. Thus were the origins of Rome. Its techniques of *wenxue* had yet to be established, and it was only practiced in military matters and agriculture. By the time it had conquered Greece, and had gained all of its wonders, it subsequently caused all the countries of Asia to submit to it, gaining all their hoarded reserves. The cultural cream of all these countries flowed into Rome. With foreign enemies having been pacified, they then devoted themselves to the cultivation of *wenxue*. They would frequently place men of great talent in high position, with no scarcity of outstanding men composing prose and poetry.[12]

Setting aside the alarmingly Christianist misunderstanding of Roman origins in this passage, the term *wenxue* poses some difficulties here. In the first instance, juxtaposed as it is with military matters and agriculture, it would seem to refer very broadly to something between humane letters and the humanities in general, while the second usage, juxtaposed to poetry and prose, would seem to suggest more strictly writing, or even "literary" writing, in itself. There is, however, plenty of ambiguity, at least from our modern perspective, where taxonomies of learning have become more strictly drawn. In the eleventh essay of his "On Learning" (學篇十一) series, Wei Yuan also wrote: "So those who labor with their minds do not labor physically, and those who value the military do not cultivate writing. *Wenxue* is always insufficient for statecraft, while statecraft is mostly inadequate to *wenxue*. Only with well-developed fundamentals can one from time to time arrange things to the utmost, so the gentleman works at these fundamentals, devotes all his energies to virtue, and does not wander outside it, for fear that it will divide one's efforts toward virtue and result in a double loss."[13] The term *wenxue* as used here seems pretty clearly to refer to embellished writing, although, given the renewed emphasis on writing as cultivation in the nineteenth century,[14] not to mention the rhetoric employed by Wei in his statement, mere "embellished writing" would not seem to be an adequate translation, with something like "the essence of humane letters" perhaps more apposite.

If Wei Yuan's notion of *wenxue*'s meaning is overly broad, the definition provided by the great statesman Zeng Guofan 曾國藩 (1811–1872) is correspondingly narrow. In defining his sense of the four terms *yili, kaoju, cizhang* 辭章, and *jingji* 經濟 (statecraft) (the first three being the divisions of learning first popularized by Yao Nai, with the final term added by Zeng himself to emphasize his sense of the importance of statecraft to learning), Zeng wrote: "*Yili* is the 'virtuous conduct' of the Confucian tradition, which we now view as Song learning. *Kaoju* is the 'culture and learning' of that tradition, which we now view as

Han learning. *Cizhang* is the 'speech' of the tradition, stretching from ancient writings to the modern examination essay, including poetry and rhyme-prose. *Jingji* is 'government' in the Confucian tradition, with the ceremonies of prior ages, political writings as well as contemporary historical records all included in this."15 For Zeng, then, *wenxue* is not embellished writing, but rather empirical research, a sense that does not seem to have caught on, despite Zeng's extraordinary influence as both actor and thinker in the period in which he flourished. His idiosyncratic definition, however, does go to show how fluid the sense of the term was over the course of the nineteenth century. It is interesting that his "*cizhang*" includes both the utilitarian examination essay as well as "poetry and rhyme prose," which we would certainly think of as "literature."

Finally, there is Mei Zengliang's careful account of what his idea of what the general enterprise of *wenxue* should be. In 1834 Mei wrote of *wenxue* thus:

> As for writing (*wenzhang*), if one does not favor it, then leave it be. If one does favor it, then one must become close to the ancients and seek one's craft there. If one does not do this, then there is only a nominal difference between ancient style prose on the one hand and examination prose on the other. Is this enough to satisfy one? No. If one were now to take oneself as a man of letters and simply make efforts to copy the techniques of the ancients, that is the equivalent of copying bronze inscriptions to write an examination paper: it just will not sell. To work at letters and not meet their requirements is unacceptable. And to meet their requirements, will not the practitioner be able at once to accord with the ancients and to have a satisfied mind? If the result is not sufficient to satisfy the mind, then the practitioner inhibits contentment, and writing that disappoints expectation is no different from an official ledger.16

In this important passage, Mei sharply delimits literary writing from other forms of it, with aesthetic satisfaction being the major criterion for judging what proper writing must be. It is notable here that he uses *wenzhang* 文章 and *wenci* 文詞 to refer to the actual writing itself, while *wenxue* is reserved for the overarching calling. He also draws a sharp line between capturing the spirit of the ancients and mere imitation of their technique, a disposition he shares with many of his fellow theorists of writing in this period. Particularly noteworthy as well is Mei's stress on the writer being able to find contentment in the process of creating his own work.

In a letter written a dozen years later, Mei, while not using the term *wenxue*, does expand upon his sense of the difference between aesthetic and other types of writing:

> In the past the Confucian school had those who excelled at virtuous conduct and those who excelled at speech, and from then on [it was seen] that the great worthies could not do both. It cannot be said that speech is unrelated to virtuous conduct, but it equally cannot be said that those who excel at speaking of virtuous conduct also excel at speech. What is the relationship between virtuous conduct and *Zhuangzi*, Lie Yukou [*Liezi*] and the *Stratagems of the*

Warring States? But who can say that their language is not skilled? And the Song and Ming men who composed colloquies: they of course cannot be spoken in terms of the art of language, so there are those of virtuous deportment who do not excel at speech.[17]

While the modern scholar Huang Lin argues that Mei here is ultimately defending the status of *guwen*, he does allow that the Tongcheng writer is also effectively advocating a real notion of literary autonomy.[18] Huang is surely at least partially correct here, with Mei's emphasis on the singularity of letters seeming to create a unique space for literary autonomy. Of all the definitions presented here, this one seeing literary writing as unique and not to be confused with other types of writing seems closet to our contemporary sense of the aesthetic nature of "literature." It is important to note, however, that, perhaps because of the close links between writing and personal cultivation, the aesthetic satisfaction Mei describes seems to be as much located within the writer's sense of personal satisfaction through successful moral cultivation as in pleasing an audience. As China moved into the twentieth century, the question of the status of the audience for writing that lies just below the surface in Mei's argument was to loom ever larger and become much more complicated.

For all the resonance regarding *wenxue* that Mei brings to bear, the sense of the term as simply referring to embellished writing in general remained pervasive in the late Qing. Even as late as 1914, for instance—long after *wenxue* had been all but universally accepted in its current sense—the inertial force of the old understanding can be seen in the title of a book by the late Tongcheng writer Yao Yongpu 姚永樸 (1862–1939): *Wenxue yanjiu fa* 文學研究法 (The method of studying writing). As Huang Lin notes: "the 'writing' it refers to is ancient style prose, including apologia, prefaces and afterwords, imperial edicts, memorials, exegeses, admonitions, biographies, funeral inscriptions, and eulogies, and excluding all novels and plays"[19] (所指 '文學' 也就是包括論辯, 序跋, 詔令, 奏議, 書說, 箴銘, 傳狀, 碑誌, 讚頌等在內的古文辭, 將小說戲曲等一概排斥於外). In general, however, the fluid nature of the pre-1890 sense of *wenxue* renders the term ultimately elusive, with an understanding of the word that limits it to specific sets of aesthetic writing only having become current in the past 120 years or so. There seems to have been little general agreement, or even concern, about an exact definition of the term. Aside from Zeng Guofan's eccentric understanding of the word, however, all the definitions one finds in nineteenth-century discussions of the term seem to include the notion that good *wenxue* or *wenzhang* include an aesthetic consciousness on the part of the writer as part of what it should be. In other words, English usages like "the literature on environmental protection" would have had to have been expressed with a term other than *wenxue*. Given the inclusiveness of Yao Yongpu's usage of the word, however, the question of where to draw the line between what is *wenxue* and what is not remains moot.

For those few who have pursued the question of *wenxue*'s definition, however, most have ignored the fact that the use of the term "literature" in English in many ways mirrors the historical uncertainty in China, if preceding it by a bit more than a century. According to Raymond Williams in his important lexical study *Keywords*, "literature" in English usage only took on its contemporary sense sometime during the course of the eighteenth century, or barely more than a hundred years before that usage became predominant in China. This development from a broader sense that included all writing or as a marker of learning was gradual and did not wholly displace earlier meanings as our eventually dominant understanding of the word became current. That this evolution of meaning was generally considered to be inconsequential, as well as lacking in dramatic milestones, at least as concerned literary practice, probably accounts for why it has received so little notice in Western literary scholarship. A point relevant to China is that Williams notes that the term in its current sense was linked to the notion of a "national literature," with the English usage following the German, Italian, and French in this.[20] He also points out that prior to the particular sense of literature as "art, aesthetic, creative and imaginative," the general term for such writing was "poetry," before that term became specific to metrical composition, and that once that change came to pass, "literature" took its place as the marker for aesthetic writing.[21]

Needless to say, China certainly had a long tradition of aesthetic writing, as well as a rich critical tradition that both categorized it and evaluated the texts produced. Perhaps the nineteenth-century term that comes closest to our sense of literature and was in most common usage was the term *shiwen* 詩文, used, for example, throughout Fang Dongshu's 方東樹 (1772–1851)—another student of Yao Nai—influential colloquy on poetry (*shihua* 詩話), *Zhaomei zhanyan* 昭昧詹言 (Tidbits on discerning right from wrong) (preface dated 1839). The following excerpt gives a good sense of how Fang understood *shiwen*: "There is a sort of implement that has form but no spirit, and although such things have a function, *shiwen* cannot be included among them. *Shiwen* is marked by its vitality. If[, however,] one covers a paper with things cut, pasted, and engraved, but lacking vitality, then one ends up with merely examination and official prose that has nothing to do with authorship."[22] While this assertion certainly emphasizes the aesthetic qualities of writing that make it literature, it also, as Huang Lin and many others have pointed out, effectually leaves out all vernacular writing, as well as fictional narrative and drama.

A Renewed Emphasis on Utility

If there had long been a highly developed sense of the aesthetics of writing in the realm of Chinese letters, as the nineteenth century drew on—for all the emphasis on aesthetics of those like Mei Zengliang—the utilitarian note that had also always been there as well grew stronger, in part, at least, in response to the sense of national crisis that grew apace in those years. As Huang Lin notes: "It is generally recognized by literary historians that an important feature of writings about literature by Chinese writers of the *jindai* period was to emphasize the utilitarianism of literature, to the point of exaggerating it and going to extremes."[23] Zeng Guofan's aforementioned addition of "statecraft" to Yao Nai's triumvirate of *yili, kaoju,* and *wenzhang* is perhaps the clearest emblem of this, but an earlier statement by Wei Yuan more hyperbolically demonstrates the expansively utilitarian role he envisioned for letters:

> [The function of writing] is to develop one's internal temperament and externally to regulate things according to the imperial order; there is a primary way of gathering it up, an order in the way it is set forth, leading in the end to a capacity to shift heaven and earth as well as to move ghosts and spirits. There is no *dao* outside writing, and no order either. Writing that has the ability to set the world straight begins with writing that is curious and punctilious in its learning: there is no learning outside of writing, and no teachings either. Grasping this in seeking for writing that will run through the contemporary world and cause it to take notice will result in: Writing (*wen*)! Writing![24]

For all the didacticism in Wei Yuan's proclamation about writing, it would seem unable to carry his intended force without it also containing a powerful admixture of expressive capacity. The sense of a renewed power of writing similar to that announced by Mei Zengliang in his discussion of the relationship between poetry and learning quoted above is also very much in evidence here. In general, the didactic and expressive aspects of writing were seen as complementary in the nineteenth-century discussions of writing, something at complete odds with dominant twentieth-century theories as represented by Zhou Zuoren. If, as Huang Lin maintains,[25] Wei is primarily associated with writing as advancing statecraft, Gong Zizhen is more often characterized as emphasizing the individual voice, although they were not seen as contradictory positions. Gong's stress on the expressive is illustrated by the following statement:

> Speech exists only by necessity. If there in nothing in your breast that you wish to say, your talents will not reach to words, and if you force the words and become lost in ignorance as to what you are saying, then there will be no help for ending up imitating the words of others, and if you imitate the various words of others, you really will not know what you are saying. In thus looting, forcing errors and omissions, copying, getting things upside down, it is like speaking when drunk or asleep, and when the speech is done I do not know what I've said.[26]

This note of writing independently of others—and predecessors in particular—is frequently voiced by nineteenth-century writers, although nowhere more forcefully than here. Given such a high degree of investment in one's work, this way of thinking leads directly into a sense of identification between the author and the work, as evinced thus by Gong: "People gain a name through their poetry, while poetry particularly gains its name from people. The great Tang poets like Li Bai, Du Fu, and Han Yu . . . who combine poetry and person into one; there is no poetry without the person and no person without the poetry, and their appearance is the same."[27] This identification between author and work is a feature that suffuses twentieth-century criticism, whether politically motivated or not. While Wei and Gong overlap in their stress on the resonance and importance of the individual poetic voice, it seems apparent that Wei places more emphasis on function while Gong devotes himself more to promotion of the individual voice, and while these two notions were seen as complementary at the time, in the twentieth century they became, at least in theory, resolutely opposite poles around which literary thought revolved.

If both of these thinkers were emphatic on the importance of individual voice, the problematic question of the relationship between that voice and the written tradition was still very much at the forefront of literary thought in the period, a question that evidently needed a substantial amount of finesse to deal with. Yao Ying 姚瑩 (1785–1853), another of Yao Nai's principal disciples and someone who enjoyed a distinguished official career, at least until being sent into exile in the 1840s, wrote of the relationship of writing to the Classics in a letter to one Wu Zifang 吳子方:

> When I was young I favored the study of *guwen* and poetry. This was not because I sought to leave a name for myself to posterity, but because I thought writing was the means to convey the *dao* through its being able to perceive the mind of heaven and earth, to reach sympathy with the myriad things, to make clear *yili,* and to lend support to the Six Classics, and thus something not lacking substance. I disdained the study of the commonplace letters of the world, which even if worked at would not yield good results. I wished to dive into the purport of the Classics and to go over the ideas in the Hundred Schools over and over again. To study these with great care one must cause the spirit and subtlety of the ancients to completely penetrate one's mind until one molds it into one's authorial persona, and when one wields one's writing brush, the resulting work will not be haphazard. The role of poetry in the creation of the *dao* is also like this: the *Classic of Poetry* does not go against the purpose of stimulating the imagination, showing one's breeding, and giving expression to complaint and is thus sufficient for the ages. . . .[28] Were the [poets] listed here made the way they were just because of their talent and learning? It was also because their spirit of loyalty and filiality was superior to that of others. If poets of any generation do not seek the roots and only pay attention to wording and metrics, it will be a shallow pursuit. Moreover, the words and meters they put together will not be worth looking at.[29]

Yao Ying's pursuit here of what we might call the higher didacticism is adamant in its anti-formalism. Like Gong Zizhen, he sets any copying beyond the pale, but Yao goes beyond Gong in even seeming to rule out any formal approach to learning how to write. Beyond immersion in the canon and the enduring values permeating these texts, he seems to have no particular method to recommend to those who would produce writing worth reading. In a letter to a Mr. Yang, Yao continues in the same vein:

> So, if one wishes to ameliorate matters, one must encompass knowledge ancient and modern, be widely conversant with the Classics, Histories, Thinkers,

and Collected Writings and penetrate their meaning. One must visit all the famous mountains and great rivers and become familiar with them, and use an expansive spirit to work at this, after which what you [write] can be passed down within the realm. Will later generations really value only talent at rhyme and mere skill at composition? . . . It is said that those good at learning get the *dao*, but those not good at learning only capture the words. But I think if one fails to get the *dao*, then how can one get [even] the words? Writing (*wen*) is to clarify understanding of the mind of heaven and earth and to explain the pattern of things. . . . Writing is not done only through talent and energy, but the *dao* must be within, and only if one gets this *dao* will one share the breath of the creator and fill up heaven and earth. The Six Classics are the ocean and one will have great talent only if one sees this in the Classics. Literature (*shiwen*) is an art; one knows the good through the *dao,* and if art and the *dao* become one, then one's energy will flourish. Writing and the Classics are not different *dao*s, and neither are poetry and prose.[30]

The scope of writing has been impressively expanded here, perhaps inspired by the dictates of the statecraft school to become involved in governance of the realm. But for Yao Ying, good writing continues to be explicitly separated from "mere" technique. As he saw it, a reliance on only technique has had the following deleterious consequences: "Scholars of the present generation merely take their metrics and wording and assume they can just proclaim to people that 'I have achieved fame through poetry.' Is this not far from the way the ancients considered themselves? Since the Song and Yuan those who have worked at poetry number at least in the hundreds and thousands, but there are very few who have struck their generation with awe, something worth pondering."[31] In other words, the reason there are so few notable post-Song poets is due to the excessive reliance on the study of technique, which has made true creativity impossible.

For all Yao Ying's stress on the social and moral function of proper writing, however, he at the same time advances the apparent paradox of not favoring discursive argument in such writing:

> What literature is most intent upon avoiding is discursive argument, which has been particularly the case since the Song. Men of the Han and Tang were not like this: they would set things out evenly and at the point of rendering judgment they would make clear the rights and wrongs and advantages and disadvantages in a word or two, with an infinite purport to their emotional incantations. This provides support for the depth of the writing. Those who are not good at discursive argument absolutely cannot create the "splendor" that Su Dongpo referred to. [Yao Nai]'s writing did not lightly present discursive argument, but his intent was profound, and this is what I am referring to: that readers would seek [his intent] beyond the words.[32]

There seems to be a subtle line being drawn here: while it may have been done in the Han and the Tang, discursive argument is no longer suitable for aesthetic writing, but the power of good writing itself is now being called upon to at least deliver the purport of such argument through a "meaning beyond words." This somewhat paradoxical statement is also congruent with the growing emphasis on esoteric interpretation that was, as outlined below, so much a part of New Text advocacy. Zeng Guofan is even clearer on the point of the need to avoid discursive argument in *guwen,* stating that "I often say that there is no place where one may not apply the *dao* of archaic prose, but it cannot be used for discursive argument."[33] Since Zeng believed that *dao* and writing were inseparable—"The *dao* and writing cannot be separated into two"[34]—the absence of discursive argument emphatically does not mean that good writing be without intellectual and moral significance. It is clear enough here, once again, that the line between expressing the *dao* and not indulging in discursive argument is a fine one, and one that was to prove highly vexatious as the sense of national crisis grew more impingent and the role of the writer more highly fraught.

The power these writers imputed to writing properly done lent it to being invested in meanings that went beyond what was displayed on the surface, something quite explicit in the Yao Ying statement quoted above; Huang Lin asserts this idea to be of long standing in Confucian thinking about writing.[35] While not denying this to be true, this tendency to look beneath the surface of texts was also given new force by the interpretive practices of the New Text school. As Wei Yuan wrote in his "Shi bi xing jian xu jian" 詩比興箋序) (Preface to Comments on analogy and stimulus in poetry)":

> Poetry cannot be direct, but must distort to get its meaning across. Feelings cannot be intense, but must be illustrated by analogy. The writing of the *Li Sao* uses poetry to entice, with good birds and fragrant plants matching loyal officials, while malevolent beasts and foul objects [stand in] for slanderers and toadies.... When Xun Qing describes silkworms, he is not [actually] writing of silkworms, and when he describes clouds, he is not actually describing clouds. In declaiming poetry that speaks of the world, knowing about people and explaining their secrets, and how one's intentions anticipate one's will, only then will one realize that all the poems in the *Classic of Poetry* are the determined creations of sages and worthies, and not simply flowery description and empty vehicles.[36]

In his preface to a work entitled *Shi guwei* 詩古微 (The esoterica of ancient poetry), Wei Yuan writes that the name of the work is derived from its "elaborating the esoteric meanings of [these] poems," and he brings to his comments the same method he applies to his New Text studies, with the phrase *weiyan dayi* 微言大意 (subtle meaning) also being a hallmark of the goals of pursuing hidden meanings in textual investigations of that sort. Wei sets out his method this way:

> So the *dao* of the *Classic of Poetry* must begin with being clear about rites and music and end with being clear about *The Spring and Autumn Annals*. And

after that the mentality of the ancient sages in being anxious about ages to come will not have ended in the realm.... When these [methods] are collected over time, the unity of all the Classics will be clear. When friends have passed and eras are gone, it will be clear as a window and as if publicly announced. This is the merit of eagerness and of being anxious to explain, of showing one corner and tumbling to the other three.[37] The way of learning cannot be of shallow encounters, but should be of profound meetings.[38]

Writing, in other words, must be of profound subtlety, or, in the words of Confucius, "the lesson will not be worth repeating." While Huang Lin objects to such thinking as permitting "subjective conjecture and far-fetched interpretations" (主觀臆測, 穿鑿附會),[39] it is equally possible as seeing the notion of writing containing esoteric meanings that will yield themselves only to particularly finely honed interpretive practices as accounting for much of the power attributed to writing as the dynasty neared its end, while also being a major factor behind the surpassing role that literature has played in modern Chinese intellectual and political life.

Given the difficulties and mysteries involved in writing prose or poetry that would pass muster, it should come as no surprise that not everyone could aspire to these rarefied heights, whether in composition, interpretation, or appreciation. As early as 1821, in his preface to the writings of Yao Ying, Fang Dongshu, someone who was certainly wedded to the notion of the political utility of letters, noted that "in 1819 I visited Guangdong. At the time Yao Ying was serving in Zhangzhou in Fujian, as magistrate of Pinghe County. Those who were traveling through all conveyed stories of his extraordinary skill in administration, but no one brought up his writing."[40] In other words, for all that the Tongcheng epigones strove to further the practice and position of letters, Fang laments the apparent lack of the sort of enlightened comprehension they hoped for. It should also be noted that, while laments for the undeserved obscurity of men of hidden talent are common in the history of Chinese letters, this lament is for Yao's obscurity as a writer only, even as it acknowledges his conspicuous success and fame as an official. In a preface written in 1842, Mei Zengliang wrote of the isolation and singularity of the man of letters: "To be content to follow a lonely way and not regret it, this is Xifu's 熙甫 [Gui Youguang 歸有光, 1507–1571] preference to set himself as the odd-man-out position of the man of letters, not wishing to place himself among the mediocrities seeking fame and fortune."[41] As Huang Lin notes, this willingness to see literature and its creators as part of an independent sphere is something that had theretofore been rare in Chinese literary history.[42]

As the years went on, and the awareness of crisis grew more acute, this sense of the alienation of the writer could only become more powerful, as the prodigious writer of *shihua* of a later generation, Chen Yan 陳衍 (1858–1938), gave voice to in a much-cited essay:

Quiet things can be done by a single person, and can be held constant, but things that are cried out are the opposite. I have therefore said that the path of poetry is a desolate and cold one, with no recompense in wealth or career, and those willing to participate in it must be virtuous. But subsequently one knows this is not wholly the case. It is like a poem: if one does not write it or even if written it can be something that cannot persist; but if it is written, one is fearful only that it will not please people, and even if it pleases people, then one fears one has not been careful enough, so many people are needed for this enterprise. Internally, it shakes one's mood, while externally it gathers condemnation. Why is this? A scene or a feeling may not be perceived by others, and only perceived by oneself. Some see something one way while others do not. Some are like this, while others are not. This is because of the [difference between being] quiet and crying out.[43]

Written just after the dynastic collapse, the sense of isolation here has become all-encompassing. If decades previous to this Mei Zengliang had seemed to find ultimate satisfaction in writing for his own satisfaction, in the new era the utilitarian undercurrent seems to have come to the fore, and the presence of an audience has become all too pressing on Chen, for all that he addresses the individuality and loneliness of the poet. It is to this new and more fraught literary arena that we now turn.

Wenxue as Literature

In the summer of 1898, Wu Rulun 吳汝綸 (1840–1903), generally regarded as the last influential writer of the Tongcheng school, wrote a preface to Yan Fu's translation/adaptation of Thomas Huxley's *Evolution and Ethics,* in which he appraised the current state of Chinese writing, something he thought took on particular importance now that translations from foreign languages were beginning to appear on the scene: "I thus think that just now, as Western books are flowing into our country it happens to be a time when our *wenxue* is at a nadir: our gentry who pride themselves on being scholars can only [write] examination prose, official documents, and novels, and aside from these three, there is almost nothing they can write. But these three are hardly worthy of being considered *wenxue.*"[44] Overall, Wu seems to continue to use an older and broader notion of *wenxue* here—that is, as referring to writing in general, since examination prose and official documents would hardly fit within the more restricted definition of *wenxue* as creative writing or writing working within specific genres for a strictly aesthetic goal. On the other hand, he also seems to be moving toward a narrower definition: in ruling out the three genres he dislikes from within the scope of *wenxue,* he seems to be giving it a specific aesthetic and by implication a formal dimension that he deems it by definition to require. In other words, his first and second usages of the word within this same short passage at least potentially represent the two different understandings of the term, and we may well be seeing him move from the older meaning to the newer within the same paragraph.

At the same time as he moves toward a narrower and more specific sense of *wenxue,* Wu follows his illustrious predecessors in continuing their firm determination to exclude *yili,* or moral reasoning, from being a suitable component of literature:

> The learning of the Song Confucians was the clan discipline of prior generations in our county [of Tongcheng], so how would I dare not wholeheartedly accommodate myself to it? But to be determined to apply notions of *yili* in belles lettres poses great difficulties. For someone not good at writing to then further encounter obstacles in reasoning, and given that the learning of Zhu Xi and the Cheng brothers cannot even completely satisfy the mass mind now, how much less so will it be able to do so for our descendants? In his learning [the early Tongcheng eminence] Fang Bao 方苞 (1668-1749) practiced the teachings of Zhu and Cheng, but in his writing it was Han Yu and Ouyang Xiu. These were two separate matters, and if one would like to combine them into the one path of belles lettres, although the ambition is noble, it is not easy to attain. This is something I have heard directly from sensible people, so I share it now all around so as to establish it as a directive for belles lettres, and in the hope that people will not follow a different path.[45]

In another letter, Wu is even firmer: "It is not easy to make fine writing out of explicating the *dao* and the Classics. The *dao* is the province of normalizing, while writing attains success through the extraordinary. [Writing on] the Classics includes the smooth expression of the commentaries, the often trivial detail of philology, and the erudition of empiricism, all of which impede literary form. So those who excel at writing take particular care in observing this."[46]

As Huang Lin adds (and as noted above), this notion of excluding moral reasoning from literary writing is something that can be found in embryo in Mei Zengliang's writing, and much more directly in the arguments of Yao Ying and Zeng Guofan. This determination on the part of Wu Rulun on this point is much firmer, however, and signals a definitive departure from Fang Bao and particularly Yao Nai's efforts to combine *yili,* empiricism, and belles lettres into one. The nineteenth-century tendency to separate out literary writing from other forms that can be seen both in Yao Nai's disciples and efforts like Ruan Yuan's 阮元 (1764-1849) move to separate an aesthetically grounded *wen* from a utilitarian *bi* 筆[47] has perhaps combined with the "reimported" idea of *wenxue* to create a much stronger sense of the autonomy of literature. The extent to which these new ideas were potentiated by concepts attributed, often on not very firm ground, to Western literary history can be seen in a short essay, "Wo zhi gailiang wenxue guan" 我之改良文學觀 (My views on literary reform) by the young Fang Xiaoyue 方孝岳 (1897-1973), published in *Xin qiannian* 新青年 (*La Jeunesse*) in early 1917.

Fang, a young man intent upon marking his Tongcheng origins and membership in the distinguished Fang Bao lineage—he inserted the word "Tongcheng" after his name at the head of the article—begins by characterizing what he sees as several key differences between Western and Chinese literature, one of which is "Chinese literature is understood broadly, while Western literature is narrowly conceived." Ignoring the various nineteenth-century attempts to delimit belles lettres and keep them separate from prosaic writing, Fang goes on to say that "right down to Zeng Guofan and Wu Rulun, the Classics, histories, and the pre-Qin thinkers were all included in literature," whereas "European literary history is all the history of the novel and poetry, with no other works like commentaries and applied writing included." Another distinction Fang makes is that "Chinese literature is a literature of the mandarins, while European literature is that of the common people," about which he presents the following background: "The learning of Confucius is to learn to become a court official, which became a principle from the Han dynasty on. There was thus no trace of the common people in literature or scholarship."[48] This determination to link Chinese writing to an elite circle seeking court favor, when combined with the accusation that the same writing is too inclusive in the genres it encompasses is another manifestation of the May 4th paradox that at the same time seeks to limit the range of what literature might include even as it attempts to expand its audience. And both notions are based on what can charitably only be called a highly partial impression of European literary history, which conveniently serves as a foil to reveal all that the author believes is lacking in traditional Chinese views of literature.

Writing just a few years after Wu Rulun's death, the wunderkind Wang Guowei 王國維 (1877–1927) moved this notion of literary autonomy and what it could include to new extremes. He had managed at quite a young age to give himself an excellent grounding in Western learning, and under this influence he wrote one of the earliest and certainly most peremptory statements of how the new understanding of *wenxue* was to be differentiated from the broader category represented by Wu's first usage in his Yan Fu preface. In his "Wenxue xiaoyan" 文學小言 (Desultory remarks on literature), Wang says:

> When Sima Qian praised the resplendence of learning in the age of Han Wudi [r. 140–87 BCE], he assumed it was the promise of emolument that rendered it so. I would say that if all learning can be spurred by the promise of emolument, only philosophy and literature are exceptions. Why is this? Since all matters scientific are either directly or indirectly concerned with securing livelihood, they never run athwart the interests of politics and society. When a new worldview or outlook on life surfaces, however, there will invariably be incompatibilities with social and political interests. If philosophers take political and social interests as their own, and disregard truth, then [what they produce] will certainly not be true philosophy.[49]

Wang treats *wenxue* and philosophy in a similar fashion, concluding that "literature for 'eat and drink'—that is, that undertaken for pecuniary motives—cannot be literature."[50] Wang thus places *wenxue*, along with philosophy, in a different realm from practical writing, its defining characteristic being that there is no place in this form of writing for personal gain, in this case plainly referring to writing within the official or even the newly expanding public realm. He then goes on, however, to further define the particular characteristics of literature, as distinct from philosophy: "Literature is a matter of amusement.

When the force of human competition for survival is afforded some surplus, it expresses itself through amusement.... Therefore, unless a national culture has reached a certain level, it cannot have literature; individual hankering for survival clearly does not provide the qualifications for being a practitioner of literature."[51] It must be said that this view of literature in general as originating in a quest for amusement is something quite new in the Chinese literary tradition.

This differentiation of *wenxue* from ordinary written language plainly resonates with the thinking of many of the nineteenth-century epigones of the Tongcheng school, but perhaps more immediately with the distinction between *wen* (ornamented prose) and *bi* (plain prose) that had originated with Ruan Yuan and was now being advocated by the so-called *Wenxuan* 文選 school, which was just then enjoying a revival led by such figures as Liu Shipei 劉師培 (1884–1919).[52] As defined here by Wang, however, *wenxue* becomes not only more rarefied than the *Wenxuan* followers' use of *wen*, but even more esoteric than Wang's sense of philosophy: not only is there no space within it for writing for personal advancement, but neither can it have any real purpose, a radical break with the notions of the need for writing to encompass morality implicit in the oft-quoted platitude, "*wen yi zai dao*," or, "the purpose of writing is to transmit the *dao*." While Wang Guowei was later to claim that he was never able to completely understand Kant, this formulation is unmistakably Kantian in origin. It is worth noting that, as Tony Pinkney has pointed out, the response to this Kantian notion of literary autonomy in Europe was "euphoric liberation in the first instance, [but] autonomy soon condemns art to a social impotence which is progressively internalized in the artifact itself."[53] For the most part, then, while Wang Guowei's notion of a *wenxue* beyond the realm of practical concern is at complete odds with the earlier Qing notion that writing, while difficult and refined, at the end of the day still was in the service of utility.[54] He went even further than this, however: "Ornamented literature cannot be considered true literature; it is the same as literature for 'eat and drink.'... Therefore, derivative literature is the sign of ornamented literature and the literature of 'eat and drink.'"[55] So for all his radical departures from earlier literary thought, Wang ends up sounding the same note in opposition to imitative writing that had very much been the norm two generations earlier.

Once the more determinate definition of *wenxue* became established, however, it was seized upon by some as a powerful tool in coping with the national crisis (much as Williams noted was the case in Europe) and moved resolutely back toward a utilitarian function much more overt than anything seen in the theorizing of even Zeng Guofan. For instance, in 1907 the critic Tao Zengyou 陶曾佑 wrote an essay entitled "Zhongguo wenxue zhi gaikuang" 中國文學之概況 (The status of Chinese literature) that encapsulated the attraction that literature held out to writer, reader, and nation alike:

> I have heard that to establish a country on this globe requires a particular spirit.... And for it to be strong for eternity, it requires a natural endowment for strength.... Ah! What is this particular spirit? What is this natural

endowment? It is literature! "When letters receive their proper treatment, the world will know a wave of reform." Countrymen! Countrymen! Do you not know that this literature is superior to other branches of learning? That it truly possesses the greatest of power? That it should enjoy the most beautiful of names? That it contains limitless significance? And that it alone should occupy the highest position in the world?[56]

Although written in a vastly cruder register, echoes of the enthusiasm and hopes for embellished writing expressed by Wei Yuan and Mei Zengliang are clearly apparent here, even if amplified almost out of recognition. Moreover, in another article in the same series, Tao sets the preponderance of this power in the vernacular novel:

Oh! There is a great monster at the heart of the twentieth century. It walks without legs, flies without wings, sounds without speaking; it stimulates the mind, surprises the eye, opens one's mental horizons, and increases the intelligence; it can by turns be solemn, facetious, lyrical, lachrymose, angry, hortatory, satirical, or mocking. . . . It has immense strength and attraction as well as unimaginable force; in the realm of literature it casts a particular brilliance and indicates a special quality. What is this thing? It is the novel. . . . The novel! It truly is the most noble vehicle in world literature.[57]

Based on the research of Chen Guoqiu 陳國球, the musings of the likes of Tao Zengyou were much closer to mainstream thinking about writing in the final decade of the Qing than was Wang Guowei's notion of a pure realm of aestheticized *wenxue*. For most thinkers, the sense of national crisis had rendered the utility of learning (*zhiyong* 致用) the major intellectual concern of the age. In Chen's discussion of the various draft curricula for the new *Jingshi daxuetang* 京師大學堂 (Capital University, the original name of Peking University), for instance, we learn that even a reformer like Liang Qichao was quite open in his negative assessment of the position of literature in the new institution: "Literary writing cannot be considered a branch of learning"[58] (詞章不能謂之學也). After carefully examining the various recommendations about *wenxue* for the curriculum, Chen concludes: "this conception of 'literature' is nothing other than a set of rules and standards for putting words together to create prose, using traditional models as its basis . . . to establish individual ability to write essays. . . . Clearly any effort to do anything intellectually beyond this yields to the goal of instruction in applied writing."[59]

While I believe that Chen somewhat overstates his case here, ironically, it turns out that the more conservative Zhang Zhidong 張之洞 (1837–1909) was the one responsible for advocating a more prominent position for *wenxue*, but as Chen notes, it is for quite a different purpose than that advocated by Wang Guowei. Showing again the fluidity of the term, it also bears a completely different definition, here being a throwback to its old sense of being virtually equivalent to the current notion of "the humanities": "In the 'Imperially Sanctioned Regulations for Capital University,' there were seven divisions within the university and the '*wenxue*' division included the following subdivisions: the Classics, History, Confucian Philosophy, Pre-Han Thinkers, Historical Anecdotes, Letters, and Foreign Languages. Aside from the final subdivision of 'Foreign Languages,' all the others seem to constitute the sum of 'Chinese learning,' or that which can be said to be traditional learning that could not be absorbed into the divisions of the 'Western learning' of a modern academic system."[60] In other words, in keeping with his conviction of "Chinese learning as essence, Western learning for function" (*Zhongxue wei ti, Xixue wei yong* 中學為體, 西學為用), Zhang places all Chinese learning in a zone apart, with the clear danger of its becoming reduced to irrelevance in an age desperately engaged in the pursuit of "the modern," and perilously close to what Joseph Levenson called "museumification."[61] To the extent that *wenxue* came to be seen as the core discipline of the traditional categories of learning, categories that had been relegated to a subsidiary place in the new curriculum, its range of authority was correspondingly limited. If Wang Guowei's understanding of literature cut it off from the utility had always been at least part of it, Zhang Zhidong's bracketing it off as a rubric for the "old" learning threatened it with another form of irrelevance, namely rendering literature unable to be part of the new "modern" order reformers were intent upon creating for China.

In the early theoretical essays of Lu Xun, this paradox of the purpose of writing, as well as its links to statecraft, is powerfully elucidated. These concerns are embedded in his famous peroration to his 1908 "Maluo shi li shuo" 摩羅詩力說 (On the power of Mara poetry):

> Where are the warriors of the spirit in today's China? Is there a voice to speak forth sincerely and truthfully the words that will lead our people to goodness, beauty, strength, and vigor? Is there a voice of warmth and compassion ready to assist our people to exit the frozen wastes? Our nation is barren, but we are without a Jeremiah to compose a dirge for us to the world and to future generations.... Although the past decade and more has seen a constant stream of introductions from abroad, an examination of what has been brought back reveals little other than cake recipes and the techniques of operating a prison system. China thus is perpetuating her own desolation for eternity.[62]

Aside from lamenting the lack of powerful writers able to move the national spirit, Lu Xun's imperious dismissal of those who have offered solutions to China's problems as having done no more than bring to bear "cake recipes and the techniques of operating a prison system" suggests that, at least for Lu Xun, the easy commerce between good writing (however difficult that was to create) and its promotion of social melioration had become problematic in ways that men like Zeng Guofan of an earlier generation could not have imagined. The isolation of the writer suggested first by Fang Dongshu and amplified by Chen Yan takes on a new dimension here: it is now explicitly linked, however abstractly, to the larger crisis of the Chinese polity and the means of addressing it.

Finally, the difficult question of audience, which had not been a primary concern when writing and theorizing about it, was generally directed at the social and intellectual peers of the author. Wu Rulun hints at this when he lets slip that "our gentry who pride themselves on being scholars" were now given to writing novels, something that simply had not been an issue for prior generations of Tongcheng writers. With the full-throated encouragement given to the novel form by such prominent popularizers as Liang Qichao, particularly in his 1902 hortatory article "Xiaoshuo yu quanzhi shi guanxi" 小說與群治之關係 (On the relationship between fiction and public governance), the form and stylistics of this genre came up for debate. While there were important exceptions, fiction did not have the long tradition of discussion about how best to write it that we have seen was such an important feature of nineteenth-century elite *shiwen* discourse (and even with these exceptions, critics of the novel were generally regarded as eccentric, leaving them with a smaller and self-selected audience, enthusiastic as it might have been). The novel itself provides the perfect vehicle both to address a new audience and to accommodate elements that traditional theories of writing had no place for, since it was, at least according to Liang Qichao in his pivotal 1898 essay, "Preface to Translating and Publishing Political Novels" (譯印政治小說序), a blank space: as vital a conduit for imparting important information as the novel was, the actually existing Chinese novel was to be completely discarded in favor of following Western models.[63] This stands in marked contrast to his much more conservative advocacy vis-à-vis the "revolution in poetry" (*shijie geming* 詩界革命), where, in addition to asking for "new imaginative realms" (*xin yijing* 新意境) and "new diction" (*xin yuju* 新語句), he still maintains the "need to include the style of the ancients" (须以古人之風格入之).

As Hu Shi 胡適 (1891–1962) noted in the early 1920s, writers now had to face writing for the considerably less educated cultural other rather than their peers alone.[64] What, then, to do? Liu Shipei early on suggested two types of writing, one for the educated to write for one another, and the other, principally fiction, for the masses.[65] The issue here is given added weight when one takes into account Mei Zengliang's suggestion that one writes to satisfy oneself, that it is perhaps more than anything else an aesthetic and moral satisfaction *for the writer*, so he writes not just for others like himself, but also for himself. Thus, when the time comes for the conscientious author to write to persuade others not like himself (i.e., the "people"), this is perhaps where a new and under-theorized genre might (although not inevitably) provide fertile ground for this difficult task. The novel suits this demand perfectly, but then also the resort to the vernacular, justified as a reaching out, is also a place where one can write without doing damage to the spirit that Mei describes, as Liu Shipei suggested. This is perhaps why someone like Lu Xun, for all his fulminating against the classical language, continued to write his personal poetry in the traditional classical: his poetic writing is simply a different order of things, an expression of a private realm with deep roots in Chinese literary thought, now rendered more private than ever, if not at times downright illicit. And the new category of *wenxue* provides a newly enlarged space, large enough to allow all these issues to, if not coexist, then to jockey uneasily for position within the same discursive rubric.

Given that the new sense of *wenxue* as "literature" came to the fore simultaneously with the unprecedented determination to create writing for a broader and less educated audience, to a certain extent this sense of "literature" was to become attached to a modern public function, particularly after about 1920, when the term "new literature" (*xin wenxue* 新文學) came into vogue. Thus, writing bifurcates, with someone like Lu Xun apparently quite comfortable writing poetry in the traditional classical style for himself and his friends, even as he attempted to master a new vernacular in his published writing meant for a wider audience. Roland Barthes' famed distinction between "readerly" texts (those defined as works in which the reading of them is already determined for the reader and allows only one path of interpretation) and the "writerly" (those texts of a more indeterminate nature, where the reader is called on to synthesize meaning for him or herself)[66] originally was confined to fiction and draws a sharp distinction between nineteenth-century novels as "readerly" and modernist fiction of the twentieth century as "writerly." While it thus does not fit itself very precisely onto the pattern of Chinese literature over the past two hundred years, it would seem fair to say that the emphasis on communicating with a mass audience in the New Literature put overwhelming pressure on it to write in a distinctly "readerly" fashion. The newly defined *wenxue*, then, could be emptied of all the specific ideas and practices that had gathered around traditional ideas about writing, or even about *shiwen,* to be set on a utopian course at the beck and call of society's most powerful voices. This new version of writing was still in effect, however, a palimpsest, and under the new surface older versions of literature subsisted and often exerted their influence, however indistinctly and uncertainly.

Notes

1. See Huters, *Qian Zhongshu*, pp. 15–16.

2. D. C. Lau, trans., *Confucius: "The Analects,"* p. 106.

3. Lu, "Menwai wentan," in *Lu Xun quanji*, vol. 6, pp. 95–96; Lu, "A Layman's Remarks on Writing," p. 111. Kiyama, "'Wenxue fugu' yu 'wenxue geming,'" pp. 209–210, notes that Lu Xun was reluctant to use the newly redefined concept of *wenxue* long after other writers had naturalized it into the modern Chinese lexicon.

4. In other words, the word "literature" in English usage still maintains the sense that the term *wenxian* 文獻 (documentation) carries in Chinese. In this context, it is interesting that in his memoir of 1916, *Forty-Five Years in China,* Timothy Richard throughout uses the terms "literature" and "literary" to refer to any published material or publishing in general, as in "Besides publishing our own literature, I was asked to aid in the production and publication of literature for the purpose of creating a public opinion against the evils of footbinding." The society responsible for publishing the renowned late Qing missionary-sponsored journal *Wanguo gongbao* 萬國公報 (Review of the times), originally called the Society for the Diffusion of Christian and General Knowledge, sometime before 1905 changed its name to the Christian Literature Society. See Richard, *Forty-Five Years in China*, pp. 227, 223.

5. Yuan, *Cong chuantong dao xianzai,* p. 7. Zheng, *Wan-Qing xixiang shi,* pp. 4–5.

6. Liang, *Qingdai xueshu gailun,* p. 75. The English translation follows that of Immanuel C. Y. Hsü, p. 89.

7. Zhou, *Zhongguo xin wenxuede yuanliu.*

8. In his magisterial work on late Qing literary criticism, the Fudan scholar Huang Lin 黃霖 is obliged to admit that none of the literary ideas set forth by the "progressive" thinkers of the period is really new, although he attempts to recuperate both the thinkers and their ideas by declaring them to have more flexible inclinations, or that they are more in tune with the political needs of the times, rather than simply echoing eternal Confucian themes. See Huang, *Jindai wenxue piping shi,* pp. 41, 70, 80.

9. I developed this argument in my "From Writing to Literature," pp. 51–96.

10. Mei, "Liu Chuzhen shi xu" 劉楚楨詩序 (Preface to the poems of Liu Chuzhen), in *Baijian shanfang wenji,* p. 152.

11. Lin Changyi 林昌彝, *Sheying lou shihua* 射鷹樓詩話 (Eagle-shooting pavilion poetry colloquy), *juan* 7, in Du, *Qing chu shihua fanyi chubian,* cited in Huang, *Jindai wenxue piping shi,* p. 103.

12. Wei, *Haiguo tuzhi, juan* 37, p. 1112.

13. Wei, "Mogu, shang" 默觚上 (The silent tablet, part one), "Xuepian shiyi" 學篇十一 (On learning, number thirteen), in *Wei Yuan ji,* shang, p. 27.

14. See my "From Writing to Literature," *passim.*

15. Zeng Guofan 曾國藩, "Quanxue pian shi zhili shizi" 勸學篇示直隸士子 (Exhortation to learning shown to the scholars of Zhili), in *Zeng Guofan quanji,* p. 348, cited in Huang, *Jindai wenxue piping shi,* p. 183.

16. Mei, "Fu Zou Songyou shu" 復鄒松友書 (Letter in response to Zou Songyou), in *Baijian shanfang wenji,* p. 34.

17. Mei, "Da Wu Zishu" 答吳子叔 (Response to Wu Zishu) (1848), in *Baijian shanfang wenji,* p. 41.

18. Huang, *Jindai wenxue piping shi,* pp. 143–144: "If we say that Yao Nai had based himself as a writer of ancient-style prose on artfully raising the banner of claiming that *yili,* empirical research and embellished writing were of equal stature and thus expanded his influence and established himself, then his student Mei Zengliang actually stressed that the three could not be combined, but that one must rather emphasis one, thus promoting the independence of literature so as to raise the status of writers of ancient-style prose" (假如說姚鼐曾經立足在古文家的基礎上巧妙地打出了義理,考證,文章三者並重的旗號以擴大聲勢,奠定基礎的話,那麼他的弟子梅曾亮卻又強調這三者似乎不能得兼而必須專其一,通過鼓吹文學的獨立性來提高古文家的地位).

19. Huang, *Jindai wenxue piping shi,* pp. 212–213.

20. Williams, *Keywords,* pp. 134–138.

21. On the early nineteenth-century discussion on the differences between "elaborated" *wen* 文 and "plain" *bi* 筆 prose, see my "From Writing to Literature," pp. 83–92.

22. Fang, *Zhaomei zhanyan,* p. 25.

23. Huang, *Jindai wenxue piping shi,* pp. 6–7.

24. Wei, "Mogu, shang," "Xuepian er" 學篇二 (On learning, number two), in *Wei Yuan ji,* shang, p. 8.

25. Huang, *Jindai wenxue piping shi,* p. 37.

26. Gong Zizhen, "Shu si gu zi yi" 述思古子議 (Disputations on thinking of the discourses of the ancients), cited in Huang, *Jindai wenxue piping shi,* p. 29.

27. Gong Zizhen, "Shu Tang Haiqiu shiji hou" 書湯海秋詩集後 (Afterword to the collected poetry of Tang Haiqiu), cited in Huang, *Jindai wenxue piping shi,* p. 31.

28. These purposes for poetry are from the Confucian *Analects* 17.9. See Lau, trans., *Confucius: "The Analects,"* p. 145.

29. Yao, "Fu Wu Zifang shu," *juan* 1, p. 8a.
30. Yao, "Fu Yang Jun lun shiwen shu," pp. 7a–b.
31. Yao, "Huang Xiangshi shi xu," *juan* 2, p. 6a.
32. In Yao, "Shi xiao lu," p. 2b.
33. Zeng Guofan, "Yu Liu Xiaxian" 與劉霞仙 (To Liu Xiaxian), *Zeng Guofan quanji*, "shudu" 書牘 (letters), p. 893, cited in Huang, *Jindai wenxue piping shi*, p. 187.
34. Zeng, "Yu Liu Xiaxian."
35. Huang, *Jindai wenxue piping shi*, p. 41.
36. Wei, "Shi bi xing jian xu" 詩比興箋序 (Preface to notes on analogy and stimulus in poetry), in *Wei Yuan ji*, shang, p. 232.
37. Wei here quotes *The Analects*, book 8, "Shu er" 述而: "The Master said, 'I do not open the truth to one who is not eager to get knowledge, nor help out any one who is not anxious to explain himself. When I have presented one corner of a subject to any one, and he cannot from it learn the other three, I do not repeat my lesson'" (子曰：不憤不啟, 不悱不發, 舉一隅, 不以三隅反, 則不復也). Legge, trans., *Confucian Analects*, p. 197.
38. Wei, "Shi guwei xu," in *Wei Yuan ji*, shang, p. 120; see also Wei Yuan's "Shu guwei xu" 書古微序 (On esoterica in the Book of Documents), in *Wei Yuan ji*, shang, pp. 109–110.
39. Huang, *Jindai wenxue piping shi*, p. 40.
40. Fang, "*Dongming wenji* xu," *juan* 1:1b.
41. Mei, "Zeng Wang Xieyuan xu" 贈汪寫園序 (Preface presented to Wang Xieyuan) (1842), in *Baijian shanfang wenji*, p. 62.
42. Huang, *Jindai wenxue piping shi*, p. 143.
43. Chen, "He xin yu shi xu," pp. 1056–1057. For analysis of this passage, see Wu, *Modern Archaics*, pp. 239–245.
44. Wu, "*Tianyan lun* xu," vol. 5, p. 1318.
45. Wu, "Da Yao Shujie" 答姚叔節 (In reply to Yao Shujie), cited in Huang, *Jindai wenxue piping shi*, p. 200.
46. Wu, "Yu Yao Zhongshi," p. 307.
47. On Ruan Yuan's theorizing about writing, see my "From Writing to Literature," pp. 83–92.
48. Fang, "Wode gailiang wenxue guan." Fang Xiaoyue was the father of Fang Guide 方珪德 (1922–2009), better known by his penname of Shu Wu 舒蕪.
49. Wang, "Wenxue xiaoyan," vol. 4, p. 378.
50. "Eat and drink" (*buzhuo* 餔啜) is a reference to Mencius 4A.25, in Legge, trans., *The Chinese Classics*, vol. 2, p. 312.
51. Wang, "Wenxue xiaoyan," vol. 4, p. 378.
52. On the *Wenxuan* school, see Huters, *Bringing the World Home*, pp. 87–93.
53. Tony Pinkney, "Introduction," in Williams, *The Politics of Modernism*, p. 17.
54. For instance, for all his determination to separate artistic prose from moral reasoning, Zeng Guofan ultimately saw belles lettres as being in the service of expressing morality: "*Yili* learning is of primary importance, and once it is made manifest, then one's personal practice has its essentials and statecraft has a base; the learning of belles lettres is also intent upon expressing *yili*" (義理之學最大, 義理明, 則躬行有要, 而經濟有本, 詞章之學, 亦所以發揮義理者也). Quoted in Huang, *Jindai wenxue piping shi*, p 183. Writing is thus in the end instrumentalized. So although Huang Lin maintains that Zeng lays great stress on the specific characteristics of literature, it is clear also that Zeng sees the need for attention to writing as being a means to better express the *dao*: "If we discard the animal spirits there is no way to see the mind, and we also know that if we discard writing, there is no way to glimpse the *dao* of the sages" (捨血氣無以見心裡, 則知捨文字無以窺聖人之道矣). In Huang, *Jindai wenxue piping shi* p.186.

55. In Guo and Wang, eds., *Zhongguo lidai wenlun xuan,* vol. 4, p. 379.

56. Tao Zengyou, "Zhongguo wenxue zhi gaikuang" 中國文學之概況 (The status of Chinese literature), in Guo and Wang, *Zhongguo jindai wenlun xuan,* vol. 1, p. 241.

57. Tao Zengyou, "Lun xiaoshuo zhi shili jiqi yingxiang" 論小說之勢力及其影響 (On the power and influence of the novel), in Guo and Wang, *Zhongguo jindai wenlun xuan,* vol. 1, p. 251.

58. Chen, *Wenxue shi shuxie xingtai yu wenhua zhengzhi,* p. 7.

59. Chen, *Wenxue shi shuxie xingtai yu wenhua zhengzhi,* p. 20.

60. Chen, *Wenxue shi shuxie xingtai yu wenhua zhengzhi,* p. 19.

61. For Levenson's explanation of this, see *Confucian China and Its Modern Fate,* vol. 3, pp. 113–115.

62. Lu, *Lu Xun quanji,* vol. 1, p. 100.

63. Liang, "Yi yin zhengzhi xiaoshuo xu" 譯印政治小說序 (Preface to translating and publishing political novels), in Guo and Wang, *Zhongguo jindai wenlun xuan,* vol. 4, pp. 205–206.

64. Hu, *Wushi nian lai zhi Zhongguo wenxue,* p. 144.

65. Liu, *Lun wen zaji,* pp. 109–110.

66. Barthes, *S/Z.*

6 ❖ PETER ZARROW

Cai Yuanpei's Politico-Philosophical Languages

Cai Yuanpei 蔡元培 (1868–1940) was a self-proclaimed Kantian whose central idea of the self seems to have been shaped by an unacknowledged Buddhism.[1] He was fluent in German and had good reading knowledge of Japanese and English, but key to this chapter is his comfort in operating in China's own classical hermeneutic tradition stretching back to the Warring States era (c. fourth century BCE). Cai was not an ivory tower philosopher who produced monographs working out his ideas (nor did most Chinese intellectuals and scholars of the period). He produced a major work on the history of Chinese ethics, but his numerous essays and lectures also spoke to issues of education and aesthetics. Cai is best known as the liberal-minded president of Peking University during the New Culture and May 4th movements of the 1910s and early 1920s, and as an anti-communist "elder" of the Guomindang in the 1930s. He helped shape China's educational system through the Republican era and contributed to political discussions. His was an important voice from the turn of the twentieth century through the 1930s, though he never dominated public opinion as Liang Qichao 梁啓超 (1873–1929) and Hu Shi 胡適 (1891–1962) did.

The following examination of Cai's thought challenges the notion that a "new China" emerged in 1912, or 1919, or 1949. The importance of the events associated with those dates is real, but they tend to be used to mark a politicized myth-history. The misdirection stems not from sheer overemphasis on the new—or renewal, renovation, and revolution—but on a misinterpretation of the new as a teleology rather than as an ordinary, natural process of development shaped by immediate needs. Of course, under conditions of imperialism, invasion, revolution, state collapse, and economic stress, Chinese naturally came to sense that time was compressed and that the arrow of time was moving at a great pace. What historians can do, armed with Sinological tools, is to decompress time, add nuance to the stories of "national becoming" that dominate historical memory, and highlight the dialectic between cultural and national identities.

Forging a Pedagogical Language (1912)

Born to a comfortable Shaoxing merchant family, Cai was a bright student who was trained for the prestigious civil service examinations. He attained the highest, or *jinshi*, degree in 1890 and was appointed to the celebrated Hanlin Academy at the young age of twenty-six. He was thus all set for a conventional official career. He remained aloof from the reform movement of the late 1890s, but lamented the reformers' failure in 1898. He joined the anti-Qing revolutionary movement in the wake of the Boxer disaster after 1901. Cai participated in secret revolutionary activities in Shanghai, but as revolutionary energies waned he traveled to Germany under official Qing auspices at the beginning of 1907, staying through 1911 and studying philosophy, history, and psychology at Leipzig University.[2]

Cai returned to China to become the new Republic's first minister of education in 1912. He sought to reform the system of state schools that the Qing had begun to build after 1904. The immediate target for Cai's 1912 essay "Some Opinions on the Direction of Education" was professional educators and bureaucrats, but the essay dealt with matters far outside of ordinary school concerns.[3] Citing Kant, Cai advocated aesthetics education as the ultimate goal of teaching, on the grounds that it offered a way to bridge the conventional, temporal, or "phenomenal world" (*xianshi* 現世) and the world of fundamental reality, or "noumenal world" (*shiti* 實體). With the knowledge of the essential unity of these two aspects of the universe, Cai said, the illusionary distinction between self and other may be destroyed. What then opens up, presumably, is a kind of path toward ever-improving social consciousness and higher personal consciousness as well. This view of the possibilities of the transformation of the sense of the self led Cai to an ambivalent view of the realm of the political.

Cai began his essay by distinguishing between political education and education that transcended the political. First he equated "political education" with autocracy: he found that it stemmed from China's era of autocracies, when educators simply followed the government's directions.[4] This is in contrast to education now, during the Republican era, when educators should base their standards on the position of the people—that is, in Cai's view, going beyond the political. Cai acknowledged the importance of "political education" in the sense of fostering Republican citizenship, though he regarded this ideally as teaching a depoliticized form of ethics. It is worth noting that even as an anti-Qing revolutionary in the years before 1911, Cai had contributed to the Qing government's new school system by writing a fat textbook on ethics for middle schools.[5] Now, in 1912, "loyalty"—a fundamental value in that earlier textbook—remained a virtue, but it was transferred from the emperor to the nation. This was to shift the ethical anchor of the nation from the autocratic ruler to a truly "public" entity.

Second, Cai found a role for "militant citizenship" in the new school system. He noted that educational reforms of the late Qing period had started with the goal of fostering a militant citizenry. In Cai's view, this goal in more advanced countries was now being superseded by socialism, but it was still necessary for self-defense in the case of a China under assault by stronger powers. Cai suggested as well that only a militant citizenry could now, as of 1912, in the wake of what he regarded as a military revolution, prevent an officer caste from coming to power. That is, a disciplined people would not only form the basis of a strong state, but would form the basis of a democratic one.

Third, Cai held that practical or vocational education was also necessary in a world of competing nation-states, because military power basically stemmed from economic might (this was Cai's third modification of late-Qing educational goals). Other countries were emphasizing vocational education, and thus Cai felt that China—mired in poverty, its industries immature, and its resources undeveloped—could not ignore it either. From the viewpoint of the people's livelihood, vocational education was necessary to teach skills and crafts in order to bring China's material conditions closer to those of the advanced Western countries.

A militant citizenry and vocational education, Cai concluded, represented the ideology of "strong army–wealthy country." But a strong military had the potential of committing aggression, and a wealthy country might bring an increase in the gap between rich and poor and end in a tragic struggle between capitalists and workers. Cai therefore emphasized the importance of "civic morality" (*gongmin daode* 公民道德). Civic education was needed to tame, in effect, the dangers that stem from strength and wealth. But what did Cai mean by civic education? He explained it was nothing less than the "liberty" (*ziyou* 自由), "equality" (*pingdeng* 平等), and "fraternity" (literally, "intimacy," *qin'ai* 親愛) proclaimed in the course of the French Revolution. Cai was using modern political terminology that had become widespread among revolutionary circles in the last years of the Qing, a terminology that had given them a new language with which to attack autocracy. This was not a language necessarily clear to many ordinary teachers in China itself, nor necessarily accepted by them. For some conservatives, for example, equality and liberty simply meant the horrifying prospect that sons rejected their fathers.[6] Cai used this new language to describe radical educational goals appropriate for a new republic, while at the same time he wanted to demonstrate its links to, or even rootedness in, traditional ideals.

Cai thus chose to explain liberty, equality, and fraternity through quotations from the Confucian classics. Many of Cai's readers, especially the conservatives he was trying to appeal to, would have memorized the classics. Thus a brief phrase from a classical text would conjure up the original context of that phrase in the reader's mind. But Cai's reader was simultaneously forced to consider how the notions associated with that phrase apply to China's—and the world's—new circumstances. The long tradition of Confucian hermeneutics recontextualized texts in precisely this way, and indeed the examination system that had been abolished only in 1905 tested precisely a kind of double vision of ancient meaning and contemporary use. Confucianism's capacity for reinvention relied on an expansion of vocabulary. At the same time, a rough historical precedent for what Cai was doing is seen in the partial incorporation of Neo-Daoist and Buddhist concepts into the Confucian tradition starting in the Six Dynasties period.[7] Cai was a practiced code switcher.

Cai Yuanpei may not have thought of himself as working in the Confucian tradition, but he was certainly appealing to it. According to Cai, the following represented *liberty*, which he said the Confucians had called "righteousness" (*yi* 義):

- Confucius—"The will of even a common man cannot be taken from him."[8]
- Mencius—"Great men are those whom riches and honors cannot taint, poverty and lowly station cannot shift, majesty and power cannot bend."[9]

Likewise, according to Cai, *equality* was what the Confucians had called "reciprocity" (*shu* 恕):

- Confucius—"What you would not have done unto yourself, do not do unto others."[10]
- Zigong—"What I do not wish men to do to me, I also wish not to do to men."[11]
- "Great Learning" chapter of the *Liji*—"What he hates in those who are before him, let him not therewith precede those who are behind him; what he hates in those who are behind him, let him not bestow on the left; what he hates to receive on the left, let him not bestow on the right...."[12]

Here Cai commented that individual liberty was subjective, but, with respect for the liberty of others, it becomes objective. Equality was objective, but it becomes subjective as a matter of treating others equally and insisting on equal treatment for oneself. In other words, liberty and equality govern the morality of human relationships, and are not qualities attached to individuals. The two values complement one another, Cai insisted, and need to be treated as "positive morality" rather than negative prohibitions. Finally, the following notions, according to Cai, represent *fraternity,* which the Confucians called "benevolence" or "humaneness" (*ren* 仁):

- Mencius—"Four classes of indigents, who had no one to speak for them, were officially recognized: the elderly man with no wife, the elderly woman with no husband, the elderly who had no children to support them, and the young who had no parents."[13]
- Zhang Zai—"All under Heaven who are tired, crippled, exhausted, sick, brotherless, childless, widows, or widowers—all are my siblings who are helpless and have no one else to appeal to."[14]
- Confucius—"The man of perfect benevolence, wishing to be established himself, seeks also to establish others; wishing to be enlarged himself, he seeks also to enlarge others."[15]

Cai further found worthy exemplars of this principle in the ancient (mythical) sage-kings. Yu said that if anyone in the kingdom drowned, it was as if he had drowned them; and Ji said that if anyone in the kingdom went hungry, it was as if he starved them; and the minister Yi Yin thought that among all the people of the kingdom, even the common folk, if there were any who could not enjoy such benefits as Yao and Shun conferred, it was as if he, Yi Yin, had pushed them into a ditch.[16]

For Cai's audience, the terms *yi, shu,* and *ren* possessed extraordinarily rich sets of connotations. Now we may ask if Cai's search for terminological equivalency was justified, and even if he was really making a claim of terminological equivalency in the first place. He was not claiming that ancient philosophers of China had foreshadowed liberty/*yi*, equality/*shu,* and fraternity/*ren.* That is, he did not argue that these Western ideals were derived from earlier Chinese discoveries, as the familiar theory of "Chinese origins" (*Xixue Zhongyuan* 西學中源) proclaimed. This approach to Western concepts, seen often in the late Qing (and later), was largely a form of special pleading, though also a tool that reformers used to legitimate their stance against conservative opposition.[17] Rather, Cai was saying that Western political ideals can be understood and explained by Confucian writings. Then we may ask, if Cai's set of equivalencies is precise, what is the need for the newer vocabulary and the French Revolution—why not keep to the Confucian vocabulary? If it is not precise, then what is Cai up to? It is entirely plausible, given his background in both Chinese and Western philosophy, that Cai simply saw real parallels while not claiming precise equivalency. In this sense, the two traditions of Confucian morality and the civic consciousness of the French Revolution overlapped and enriched each other. It may also be, considering his audience of less cosmopolitan and more conservative Chinese educators, that Cai simply thought the Confucian terms helped explain and familiarize, not translate, key concepts.

We can distinguish between claims to an equivalency that is already in place, on the one hand, and translation through a process that necessarily involves giving existing terms new meanings, on the other. To translate "equality" with the originally Confucian *shu* seems no less arbitrary on the face of it than with the originally Buddhist *pingdeng* 平等, which came to be the standard translation. But to claim that the Western concept of equality was exactly what Confucians had long called *shu* is another matter. The latter claim is manifestly absurd. Nonetheless, Cai's examples, while hardly showing equivalency, did offer examples of behavior that could be regarded as exemplifying the principle in question. The stories associated with Cai's classical citations—that is, the contexts of which his audience would have been aware—illustrate certain patterns of moral principles and behaviors. The Chinese examples, in my view, do approximate utopian visions of equality and fraternity, but not liberty. This is to define equality as simply the basic notion that people should be treated the same, and fraternity as empathy, mutual support, and intersubjectivity. Liberty is more difficult to derive from traditional Chinese ethical or political thought.

Whether or not this is the case, we can read liberty/*yi*, equality/*shu*, and fraternity/*ren* as a case of cross-cultural hermeneutics—conscious or not on Cai's part—that expands the three sets of concepts. Let us return to "liberty." Liberty is a highly moral concept when seen through a Confucian lens. It refers to the individual will, quite specifically the will to hold steadfast to the good. To adopt Isaiah Berlin's famous distinction, Cai believed in "positive liberty" (self-fulfillment and agency), and he was not speaking here of "negative liberties" (freedom from external restraints).[18] Insofar as equality rests on respect for others, or an acknowledgment of their humanity on a par with one's own, it serves as a check on liberty in the sense of negative liberties. Fraternity, in this Confucian perspective, represents a kind of extension of equality, but rooted in a clearer sense of common humanity, especially empathy for the disadvantaged and oppressed. Fraternity is a moral demand to take responsibility for others' suffering. Liberty for Cai, then, refers to the capacity to make ethical decisions.

We can see better what Cai was doing if we return to 1906, when the Qing's Education Ministry had announced five central goals for its new school system. These were: fostering loyalty to the emperor, honoring Confucius (*zun Kong* 尊孔), public-spiritedness, militant citizens, and practical learning. While accepting, up to a point, the last three goals, Cai explicitly rejected the first two.[19] Loyalty to the emperor obviously had no place in a republic. Confucianism was a more complex issue for Cai. He was careful not to reject Confucius or Confucianism, but he pointed out that "honoring Confucius" violated the tenets of religious freedom. In his 1912 plans for a new, republican school system, he wished to abolish the late Qing's heavy emphasis on Confucian texts, but also to continue to teach many of those texts in such classes as literature and history. At first glance, this might suggest a tension between Cai's views of the usefulness of Confucian ethics in understanding (Western) civic morality on the one hand, and his desire to decenter Confucianism on the other. But he was really just distinguishing between the texts as reservoirs of ancient wisdom and cultural heritage on the one hand, and the texts as sacred objects of reverence on the other.

Much of what the Qing had called public-spiritedness, Cai called "civic morality," though as defined by liberty, equality, and fraternity, as we have seen. However, returning to the distinction between political education and education that transcends the political, Cai emphasized the limits of civic education.

In civic morality it may seem that education reaches its final goal, but this was not the case for Chen. Education in civic morality is still unable to go beyond the political, and even what is called the best politics (republicanism) limits its goal to the achievement of the greatest happiness for the greatest number. Now, the greatest number is made up of the accumulation of individuals. The happiness of an individual stems from having good clothing and food, and avoiding disaster and hardship, but this is simply the happiness of the phenomenal world. When the happiness of individuals accrues to form the happiness of the greatest number, its goal is reached. The discussions of the legislature, the actions of the executive, and the safeguards of the judiciary are simply this as well. And even if we progress to the point that we can approach the public spirit of the Datong (大同) of the "Liyun," the golden age of the future of the socialists, and "from each according to their abilities and to each according to their needs," this is still essentially no more than the happiness of the phenomenal world.[20]

Aesthetics Education and the "Noumenal World"

Cai did not believe there was anything wrong with the phenomenal world; indeed, adequate material wealth is a necessity, and, as we have seen, he supported the goal of strengthening China. But the phenomenal world is not sufficient.

To argue that something more was needed than the achievement of a good life, Cai turned to Kant's notion of the noumenal world. Cai's views of the noumenal were in all probability influenced by Buddhist notions, but he himself gives no indication of this. If indeed inspired by Kant, Cai believed, unlike Kant, that there were ways to understand or enter into the noumenal world, and it was not simply a logical inference about ontology.[21] First, in highlighting the limits of the phenomenal world, Cai pointed out that happiness (in the phenomenal world) is inevitably extinguished upon death. That rule applies to nations and the whole world as well as to individuals, so, Cai asked, what is its value? Happiness and material good cannot be made into ultimate goals. They are the goals that are the realm of politicians, not educators. Cai's second step, then, was to argue that education must go on to show people and institutions how to see beyond their immediate interests.

What, then, should be the ultimate concern of educators? For Cai, it was the noumenal world. More precisely, he began by claiming that there were not in fact two distinct worlds but only one—phenomenal and noumenal are like two sides of a sheet of paper. There is no contradiction between them, and it is not necessary to reject one in order to achieve the other. It is possible that Cai conceived of the phenomenal world as the site where the political goal of happiness was properly pursued, and the noumenal world as the site where people experienced higher truths. He was thus not rejecting the phenomenal world. Indeed, education should promote happiness in the phenomenal world and precisely on that basis seek the noumenal world. The usual subjects—geography, math, reading—equip students for the phenomenal world. How, then, could students be equipped for the noumenal world? Before answering that question, we need to note that Cai believed this was a task religion had shown itself incapable of fulfilling. There was another way.

In spite of his emphasis on the unity of the phenomenal and the noumenal, Cai clearly felt that the noumenal was the higher, superior realm. He thus tended to discuss the phenomenal and the noumenal as separate, though compatible worlds: the world of phenomena, or ordinary reality, is "relative," and the noumenal world is "absolute"—the former regulated by cause and effect, the latter transcending cause and effect; the former inextricably bound by space and time, the latter free of space and time; and the former subject to experience, the latter felt intuitively. And the noumenal world was ineffable, though as a kind of concept it has to have some kind of name. Cai found examples from China as well as the West: *dao,* Supreme Ultimate (*taiji* 太極), God (*shen* 神), "dark consciousness," and "unconscious will." Cai seems to have meant these as approximations rather than exact equivalents (if only because the concept behind them was ineffable), but they show his belief in the universality of the concept across historical cultures.

At this point, we might note some of the connotations or at least the penumbra of the terms Cai chose to render "phenomenal world" and "noumenal world." The term *xianshi* (現世) is derived from Buddhism, where it distinguishes this life from past and future lives. But it also was used in secular contexts simply to refer to this world, or the present-day world. In Cai's use, *xianshi* did not refer to any specific text or doctrine outside of Kantianism, though of course the echoes with Buddhist doctrine are striking. As for *shiti* (實體), although the term had appeared occasionally in Buddhism, as well as in Confucian metaphysical speculation, by and large it had no particular weight. Perhaps, indeed, *dao* and Supreme Ultimate were better equivalences though worse translations. In any case, it is not the choice of terminology that reflected Cai's use of traditional cultural resources, but his citations.

Again, for Cai, the phenomenal world and the noumenal world were in principle ultimately the same. Why, then, did some people see them in contradiction to one another? In answering this question, Cai proposed to teach the noumenal through "worldview education" and aesthetics. In his 1912 article on the direction of education, Cai cited Kant on how to reach the noumenal but did not refer to Confucianism or Buddhism, as the following extended quotation shows:

> There are simply two forms of consciousness that block the noumenal world from within the phenomenal world. First, distinguishing between self and other. Second, seeking happiness. Because the strength of everyone differs, there are the strong and the weak; and because the survival skills of everyone differ, there are the rich and the poor. These differences give rise to the distinction between self and others. The weak and the poor suffer from the insufficiency of happiness and so arises the consciousness of seeking it. Thus amid phenomena multifarious boundaries divide the self from others, contrary to the noumenal world. When the seeking of happiness fails, the suffering is endless; when it succeeds, too much searching circles through phenomena, and becomes divided from the noumenal world. If balance can be achieved and biological needs satisfied according to nature, then the seeking in the realm of consciousness is extinguished and the view of self and others transformed. When all the consciousnesses of the phenomenal world are blended together, then they can coincide with the noumenal world. Therefore it cannot be doubted that the happiness of the phenomenal world is a kind of function enabling unhappy humanity to approach the noumenal world....
>
> What are the methods of promoting the concept of the noumenal? The negative method is to approach the phenomenal world with neither denial nor with attachment. The positive method is to wish for the noumenal world and gradually become enlightened. Following the universal precedent of freedom of thought and freedom of speech and avoiding the shackles of a single school or sect, our goal is an unbounded and infinite worldview. I cannot name this kind of education, but it might be called "worldview education."
>
> However, worldview education cannot [lead to the noumenal] just by incessant chatter. Furthermore, the relationship [of the noumenal] to the phenomenal is not such that it can simply be captured in a few tired phrases. How, then, can it be achieved? The answer is: through education in aesthetics. Aesthetic feeling encapsulates both beauty and awe [the sublime], and it

forms a bridge across the divide of the phenomenal and noumenal worlds. This was created by Kant, and no philosopher since has differed from him. In the phenomenal world mortals all experience feelings of like and dislike, surprise and fear, delight and anger, sadness and happiness, and then the phenomena of separation and unity, life and death, and disaster and good fortune are handed down. As for art, it takes these phenomena as its raw material and allows the viewers to experience no notions other than aesthetic pleasure. For example, gathering lotuses and cooking beans are a question of eating, but once they are in a poem they become of interest. Volcanic fires and storm-tossed boats are terrifying sights, but once they are in a painting they become exciting.[22]

Cai argued that aesthetics education was the ultimate goal of true pedagogy because it inculcated a kind of partial detachment from this familiar phenomenal world: it could give students a sense of their place in a larger whole—what Cai called being "friends with the Creator"—without removing them from this world.

Thus Cai laid out a vision of education that claimed certain continuities with late Qing goals and the entire Confucian tradition but also staked out new ground. The five areas that Cai wanted schools to emphasize—military, utilitarian, ethical, worldview, and aesthetic—would, taken together, produce good citizens who also understood the existence of something beyond everyday life.[23] Cai cited ancient Chinese precedents from the mixing of moral and aesthetic education under King Yu to the six arts of the Zhou, which included archery and charioteering (militant citizenry), writing and mathematics (vocational education), ritual (morality), and music (aesthetics).[24] And from the Greeks, physical training and art. And from the West today, the aesthetics education of the Herbartians and the vocational education of the Deweyans.

Arguably, Cai took his examples from wherever he could get them. Yet in his numerous discussions of aesthetics in the following decades, he seldom referred to Chinese examples of art or literature. What did Cai think of Chinese art? He never quite said, but in a talk to an art students' club at Peking University, Cai urged the students to spend more time drawing from nature, which he attributed to the Western tradition, and to copy masterworks, the Chinese tradition, less. At least, he said, in an age of cultural interchange, as Westerners had learned something of the Chinese tradition, Chinese should be free to adopt Western techniques.[25] Cai also criticized the lack of beautiful things in China, especially in public spaces, dismissing traditional paintings and calligraphy as private luxuries.[26] Cai was essentially celebrating all the arts as part of a global culture that offered the potential of civilizational transformation.

Aesthetics, Politics, Society

Cai cared about both aesthetics education and the role aesthetics could play in improving society.[27] Through the 1910s, he distinguished "desirous beauty" (*yumei* 慾美) from "true beauty."[28] This was to distinguish the beautiful from the "sublime" (literally, "lofty," *gao* 高). Beauty lay in the pleasure that derived from imagery that captured the true spirit of things, such as the light of the moon and sun, the clarity of clouds, and the beauties of other natural phenomena, but the world also contained terrifying phenomena, such as steering a ship through tumultuous seas and volcanic explosions—phenomena that become appealing if they are in a film or painting. This sublime, or true beauty, was a kind of strength or power. But in his later writings, Cai was not much concerned with the distinction between the beautiful and the sublime.

Given the enormous power of beauty and the sublime, Cai believed that art should provide some of the functions traditionally performed by religion. Cai argued as much in 1917, in an essay titled "Replacing Religion with Aesthetics," noting again that "pure aesthetics" could eliminate the distinction between self and other, but focusing on social utility.[29] He began with a standard New Culture critique of religion, dismissing contemporary religious practice as merely a relic of habit. Science was solving old religious questions, and religion itself had nothing to offer China today, whether in the form of Christianity or Confucianism. Nonetheless, in "primitive times" religion had met three spiritual needs: knowledge, will, and sentiment. It had answered basic questions like the origins of the universe: through knowledge. It had helped end a period of pure exploitation with doctrines of altruism: through the will. And it had fostered music, dance, and art: through sentiment. However, the progress of knowledge demonstrated that religious answers were partial at best. Also, people came to realize that supposed mandates of the gods did not provide a sound basis for morality. Rather, numerous factors depending on time and place formed moral beliefs. In time, then, the religious functions of knowledge and will decayed. Cai believed that the aesthetic spirit of religion continued longer. But the evolution of aesthetics had also moved beyond its religious origins. Tang poetry and Renaissance art were more secular than earlier styles, and today, Cai said, the secular achievements of architecture are seen in schools, theaters, and museums.

In particular, Cai felt, links between religion and autocracy made religious aesthetics inappropriate for a republic. Religion also aroused the emotions in ways that could become pathological. Aesthetic education, on the contrary, could do what religions may have sometimes glimpsed but largely failed to accomplish.

> Through molding the sentiments of the people with pure aesthetics, noble and pure habits will be fostered, and the view of self and other that seeks to benefit self at the expense of others will be gradually eliminated. And as beauty becomes universal, the view of the distinction between self and others will have no entry point. The food I personally eat cannot feed others, and the clothes I personally wear cannot warm others: this is because they are not universal. But beauty is not like this. For example, I have traveled in the hills west of Beijing, and others have also traveled in them: we have not inflicted any losses on one another.[30]

Cai claimed that beauty had been helping to extinguish the distinction between self and others for thousands of years, as people experienced aesthetic pleasures together. In ancient times, Egyptian pyramids and Greek temples; today, public museums, concerts, and theater. Not merely a cheerleader from the sidelines, Cai did a great deal to promote public exhibitions of all kinds.

Most important for Cai was the notion that beauty—and perhaps especially the sublime—provides a universal experience, as Kant had said. Cai could not derive from Kant the notion that the sublime actually erases the boundaries between self and other, but he seems to have had confidence that the noumenal world may be reached through the kind of self-forgetfulness that art could induce. The noumenal world for Cai thus seems tinged with a mystical aura: it could be sensed, even practiced, but while the means to "bridge" it could be analyzed and perhaps its effects analyzed, it itself could not be analyzed. Cai's conviction that the boundaries defining selfhood were in some ways illusory gave his self-avowed Kantianism a strong Buddhist flavor.

Distinguishing the realm of aesthetics from the realms of science and morality, Cai borrowed a Buddhist term to explain Kantian aesthetics.[31] However, it is not entirely clear what Cai meant by concluding that the concept of "self" (*woxiang* 我相) is the "thing-in-itself" (*benti* 本體) of the unimaginably powerful sublime. Perhaps this was a reference to the neo-Kantian view that experience of the sublime leads to self-forgetfulness as the self is overmastered by an outside force.[32] But Cai also believed at least in some sense that the concept of the self is a delusion, blocking realization of the unity of self and other, and that aesthetics, particularly the sublime, was a kind of route into the noumenal that in some sense erases the self (or the consciousness of self). In Buddhism, selfhood—at least the reification of the self as opposed to self-nature—is an obstacle to enlightenment. The term that Cai used here, *woxiang*, is central to both the *Diamond Sutra* and the *Sutra of Perfect Enlightenment*. The *Diamond Sutra* was an early Sanskrit text (*Vajracchedikā prajñāpāramitā sūtra*) first translated into Chinese (*Jingang bore poluomiduo jing* 金剛般若波羅蜜多經) at the beginning of the fifth century. In it, the "concept of self" is the first of four concepts or "marks" or "perceptions" that enlightened beings and Buddhas know do not exist, along with the concepts of others, sentient beings, and life.[33] Buddhas are rare, but do exist, conveying this knowledge. The tone in the *Sutra of Perfect Enlightenment* (*Yuanjue jing* 圓覺經), probably an early eighth-century Chinese work, is slightly different. It notes that the "concept of self" is the first of four delusions that prevent one from achieving enlightenment: "from beginningless time all sentient beings deludedly conceive and attach to the existence of 'self,' 'person,' 'sentient being,' and 'life span.'"[34]

For Cai, at any rate, it is not meditation or some other explicitly spiritual discipline that leads one to abandon selfhood; rather, it is aesthetic experience that leads one to transcend selfhood.[35] What Cai seemed to be driving at was the sense that when the ego is overpowered by an aesthetic experience, it feels its oneness with the cosmos. Cai began by referring to Kant's definition of aesthetics in terms of four categories: transcendence, or complete disinterestedness; universalism, or that which is common to all persons; patterns, or the entirely intrinsic purpose; and necessity, or that which is inherent in humanity. Now, Cai said, the need to develop humanism is widely acknowledged, but it is blocked by the "ego" (*zhuanjixing* 專己性). But the transcendent and universal can cure the ego. For aesthetics refers not merely to the delicately beautiful but to the "beauty of the overmastering" (or the sublime). When one encounters that which is great beyond any calculation and strong beyond any resistance, one does not at first feel aesthetic appreciation, but one intuitively and even unconsciously comes to realize in the face of its power how tiny and weak is one's small self.

Cai had written his only direct evocation of Buddhism earlier, in 1900 as the Boxer Uprising was reaching its climax and he was beginning to question his loyalty to the Qing throne. Cai looked to Buddhism to "protect the nation."[36] He seemed to argue that the true and original democratic impulse of Confucianism had long been lost and corrupted by an irredeemable autocratic system. Historical Buddhism was also corrupted, but it might be revived (presumably unlike Confucianism). As Chaohua Wang points out, Cai's views owed something to the arguments of the 1898 reformers, especially Tan Sitong 譚嗣同 (1865–1898), though Cai's contempt for and hatred of Christianity set him apart.[37] Cai had begun at this point to think his way through Chinese and Western traditions, and looked to the Shinshū sect of Pure Land Buddhism and the Japanese reformer and philosopher Inoue Enryō 井上円了 (1858–1919), who sought to make Buddhism compatible with modern science and even looked to it for the "protection of the state." The point here, however, is that while Cai, too, wanted to rid Buddhism of its superstitious elements and turn it into a modern educational tool, he ended his essay with a utopian view of evolution that would turn humans into literally spiritual beings.

This is to say that several years before his encounter with Kant, Cai was searching for a formula for transcendence. In his early call to revive Buddhism, Cai not only called for vegetarianism, but he predicted that science would progress to the point where we could abstain from eating even plants, and even the microfauna found in a drop of water. Cai called for abstaining from marriage. He predicted that, as Herbert Spencer supposedly showed, evolution will progress beyond the material.

> One day in the future when evolution reaches its highest point, people will be able to couple in a purely spiritual fashion, without bodily contact. When they have become physically eternal, without birth or death, there will be nothing to be gained by intercourse between male and female, and the custom of marriage will naturally disappear.[38]

In other words, Cai moved beyond his first argument that Buddhism might protect the state to a vision of the elimination of the boundaries between all living forms. As we have seen, he would restate this vision in later years in Kantian rather than Buddhist terminology.

In 1913, a year after he explained his notions on education as discussed above, and notwithstanding political defeats and dangers, Cai remained cautiously optimistic that people could bring the phenomenal and noumenal worlds together.[39] Writing from an evolutionary point of view, Cai insisted that while as individuals human beings were limited entities that could not transcend their particular times and places, precisely as elements in a larger world people could use their "consciousness" (*yishi* 意識) to touch other elements of the world. It is the "will" (*yizhi* 意志), Cai claimed, that might recognize the shared nature of all the elements making up the world. However, if the will aims at specific targets, it descends into the phenomenal world, the world of individual wills. In the noumenal world, the will has no target. Cai was not saying, in my reading, that humans should live in the noumenal world, but that in recognition of the fundamental identity of all the elements of the world, they can live in both the phenomenal and noumenal worlds simultaneously. Cai rejected what he saw as the promise of religion to jump into the noumenal. Rather, the progress of human consciousness is leading in this direction. Inorganic matter developed into plants and animals; animals developed relationships of kinship and friendship. The human species developed ever-increasing forms of mutual relationships marking its growing "interconnectedness" (*tong* 通) and "undifferentiatedness" (*tong* 同). Cai emphasized material abundance brought about by the division of labor, and especially the growth of all fields of knowledge. Humans had come to recognize their common humanity, and even the commonalities they shared with animals. Harkening back to his earlier essay on Buddhism, Cai pointed to vegetarianism as an example of consciousness that transcended previous distinctions.

In the following years—exile again, triumphant return to head up Peking University, stalwart supporter of the Guomindang, founder of Academia Sinica, and disillusioned liberal—Cai frequently spoke of the importance of art and of aesthetics education in shaping the moral individual and the good society. Not as often, but sometimes, he still referred to the power of aesthetics to break down the "bias" of the self–other distinction. Writing at the end of 1919 to again warn students against extremism in their "culture movement," Cai began by pointing out the complexity of culture.[40] In effect, he urged students to use science to understand the nature of culture and to use aesthetics to learn how to "practice" it.[41] Aesthetics education was necessary "to raise interest in transcending personal interests, unify the partial perception of the division of self and others, and maintain a sense of perpetual harmony," whereas joining in trendy "cultural [political] movements" led to self-righteousness, self-indulgence, and discouragement. Arguably, then, the notion of transcending the distinction between self and other could be used for purposes either of liberation or of restraint—Cai was urging self-restraint on students at this time, though he may have seen no tension between the two. In the tumultuous year of 1919, he saw the need to commit to a long process of building up China's educational institutions; in addition to the sciences, Cai foresaw schools and graduate schools devoted to art, art history, music, acting, crafts, and so forth. Next would come a whole world of public museums that displayed pieces lent from private collections and those purchased with state funds, as well as public concerts and plays. People would live on streets lined with trees and flowers, with public plazas, fountains, and sculptures. Cities would have parks to preserve natural environments. Capable artists would produce not only beautiful public and private architecture, but utensils, printing, and even advertisements.

Cai's faith in enlightenment through aesthetics was limitless. First, his notion of the beautification of public space: this creates not just a more pleasant world but a world in which, living amid beauty, everyone would experience lively and uplifting sentiments. This was a purely secular view or, as Cai might have put it, leading toward perfection of the phenomenal world. By the late nineteenth century, a global reformist discourse had emerged on the topic of urban planning. Better social organization and technology were to transform the diseased, polluted, and poverty-stricken cities created by the Industrial Revolution.[42]

But, second, Cai's notion that aesthetics could dissolve the distinction between self and others represented a kind of spiritual enlightenment, or his view of the noumenal. Cai occasionally revisited this idea throughout the 1930s.[43] His notion of replacing religion with aesthetics was based on his understandings of human psychology and social utility. Although Cai clearly did not derive his contempt for religion from Kant, the notion that aesthetics or art might replace religion was in the air as German Romanticism developed in the nineteenth century and idealist philosophy spread to the Anglo-American world. Given belief in the transcendent powers of art, and disbelief in old religious stories, it was thus a logical possibility that aesthetics should be reconceived in religious terms.[44] Schiller, Goethe, and especially Schopenhauer can be seen, in Cai's view, as heading in this direction.[45] Through Cai, China was participating in a global discourse; in Britain, for example, the nineteenth-century crisis of faith had led to a new interest in the German idealists.[46] This was the world—or one of the contemporaneous worlds—in which Cai operated. The question for many thinkers then became: Where could meaning be discovered if not in religion? To Chinese intellectuals like Cai, perhaps one of the appeals of Kropotkin's theory of mutual aid was that it seemed to temper the meaninglessness of Darwinian selection with a kind of morality.[47] And perhaps one of the appeals of the Kantian notion of the noumenal or thing-in-itself was that it seemed to temper the harshness of a purely material, atomistic world with the promise of higher meaning.

That the urban reformer Patrick Geddes and the philosopher Schopenhauer both acknowledged "Oriental" influences on their thought suggests the importance of global circulations of knowledge by the nineteenth century. In a somewhat unfocused talk to students in March 1919, Cai considered the advantages of "scientific personal cultivation," referring to both Chinese and Western moral sources.[48] By cultivation, Cai meant a kind of training to learn how to make instant decisions as to right and wrong. Normally, there is time to consider what one should do, but sometimes one must decide immediately. In that case, one has to follow rules. Cai pointed out that all societies provide such rules, and they necessarily evolve over time. The Neo-Confucians of the Song and Ming had devoted a great deal of thought to appropriate methods of self-cultivation, but they had not succeeded in making everyone good. The people of today cannot simply follow such ancient rules, nor is retreat from the world practical. Yet—Cai gloomily observed—modern pressures and responsibilities leave little time for spiritual cultivation. Presumably, Cai found some hope in the prospect of a scientific approach, but he seemed less than confident. He did not have much faith that people were prepared to engage in scientific personal cultivation.

No one, even the most antiquarian-minded, has any choice but to live in their present. Cai Yuanpei's "time," therefore, was not some eternal Confucian land where the sun never set on the classics, nor on Kant's enlightenment. It was a kaleidoscopic moment of extreme and convincing claims to civilization made by people practicing extreme violence and exploitation. Similarly, we might understand the thrust of Cai's thought without reference to the dusty texts of Kant, Confucius, or the Buddha. But that would reduce Cai's thought to some airless ideas about aesthetic education lacking context and reason. Willy-nilly, Cai framed his ideas in an unusually wide variety of intellectual systems. In the end, he was able to use several languages of politics and psychology to make a coherent case for the role of aesthetic education in creating *communitas,* as well as for the importance of beauty in reforming society.

Let us re-pose the question: What time did Cai Yuanpei live in? Of course, Cai lived in his "own" time, which spanned the late Qing and almost the entire Republican period. But these political labels do little justice to the range of his thought. To make sense of this question, we can turn to the perhaps crude notion of "levels." On one level, then, Cai lived in a revolutionary period and identified as a revolutionary. On another level, he lived in a hermeneutic tradition stretching back to the Warring States era, a tradition in which he was thoroughly comfortable and capable of mining for his own purposes (which is the point of hermeneutic traditions). On yet another level, he was an explorer in the realms of Kant and the later neo-Kantians and other idealistic philosophers. If Cai did not exactly produce a finely tuned synthesis, he certainly produced an intellectual melting pot.

Politically, Cai can be seen as a radical promoting fundamental change during the late Qing, but he clearly had a traditionalistic side. He self-consciously operated in the Chinese classical or Confucian tradition and in the traditions of the European Enlightenment. Put another way, these were both languages he was comfortable with. Arguably, Cai became more politically cautious and indeed conservative over the course of the 1920s.[49] "Radical" and "traditional" are etic categories that distort that actual coherence of Cai's worldview. They can be convenient labels for us to grasp Cai's purposes, yet in no sense did they represent for Cai contradictory tendencies. Rather, we see that Cai explicitly and implicitly constructed a forward-looking ideological synthesis. Cai's anarchist inclinations helped shape his sharp critique of contemporary society. And his cosmopolitanism encompassed his familiarity with past thought as well as new thought, in addition to his ability to work with the resources of distinct cultures.

As is well known, a sense of history as marked by linear and progressive time had emerged by the late Qing period. Cai took for granted that the linear view of history challenged the certain commitments to tradition but did not constitute a totalistic rejection of tradition. That is to say, tradition could no longer be effectively promoted merely on the grounds of ancestral practice or particular cosmological principles, for this was to argue tautologically. However, it could be defended in particular aspects and incorporated as part of a larger ideological program on the grounds of its utility and truth.

The power of social Darwinism—expressed above all in the slogan "survival of the fittest"—held enormous explanatory force among several generations of educated Chinese. It followed that civilizations, societies, countries, and races could be measured according to a linear scale. This implied that the temporal dimension was of greater significance than the spatial. In other words, what mattered was the new–old binary, not an East–West binary. However, it should be noted that Cai resisted the amorality of Darwinism. He preferred the ethical attitudes of Confucianism and, as an account of evolution, Kropotkin's emphasis on the role of mutual aid. He agreed with the social Darwinists that China had to become strong if it were going to survive. In other words, while cultures could be judged according to various standards such as morality (however defined), as well as wealth, religious or cosmological discourse, and the like, they also had to be judged according to their overall fitness in the realpolitik world of Western imperialism and global competition. Nonetheless, Cai did not think that the nation-state represented anything like the final point of history.

For all our rejection of the reductionism inherent in the binary of "traditional" versus "modern," we still have to explain the revolutionary transformations that murdered the ancient regime and gave rise to Chinese modernity. In that sense, Cai belonged to a transitional generation of intellectuals. He was thoroughly grounded in traditional Chinese thought and was among the first Chinese to achieve real familiarity with Western thought. What does it mean to label Cai a transitional figure? In focusing on the period from 1895 into the 1920s as a time of transition, Hao Chang emphasizes not merely the intellectual changes of the period, but also new media including daily newspapers, journals, new schools, and study associations, giving rise to a new type of intellectual class.[50] The new conditions facing China and intellectuals' new familiarity with Western learning led this generation to new problems and ideals that were informed by the interaction between two traditions. By the end of this transitional period, much of the Chinese tradition was lost. This is not to say that traditional ideas disappeared, but many were rendered meaningless or were diminished: the inner dynamics of the tradition, some of the problems that its various schools dealt with, and the role that it played in shaping society. Yet a well-known problem with the notion of "transition" is that it seems to downplay the importance, even the reality, of the period in question. It serves the teleological function of getting from state A to state B, and somehow the period is not fully a state itself in this sense. But another, better way to look at any period that appears transitional is to see it as a moment of creation. To call Cai a transitional figure, then, is to acknowledge him as one of the builders of Chinese modernity.

Cai also appears "transitional" in an entirely different sense, if the New Culture movement is regarded teleologically. That is, if the iconoclasts of the 1910s and the Marxists of the 1920s are regarded as somehow on the right road of history, then Cai looks old-fashioned and at best a precursor, not a representative of Chinese modernity. But this is absurd, and not merely because of today's Confucian revival. History does not move along neat roadways. Cai Yuanpei was more concerned with being right than being new, but even more concerned with the future than the past. He was not motivated by any need to forget, reject, or deny the past, but neither was he much concerned with preserving it. He was happy to use it when it seemed convenient to do so. Cai's approach was effectively hermeneutical in the sense that he did remain in dialogue with Confucianism and Buddhism. His thought does not fit into teleological myths, but displays a sensitive reaction to tumultuous times.

While Cai Yuanpei's radicalism was dissipating by the 1920s, he never became a cultural conservative or traditionalist. Neither did he reject Chinese culture in toto; rather, he continued to make use of its resources for new ends. His vision was not that of the Three Dynasties golden age of old, but rather lay in what amounted to an inner spiritual search. Only, as a modern, Cai could not call it spiritual. He called it "the Learning of Beauty" and promoted aesthetics education. Cai accepted modernity's rupture with the past, but he saw little reason to celebrate it. The rupture, for Cai, required immersion in the New Learning—in its deepest foundations—but it did not require denunciations of the old. It may be that as a student of German philosophy in particular, Cai accepted that every cultural unit possessed a spirit of its own, not in isolation but in ways that made total displacement impossible. He resisted any vision of time as consisting of different regions of the world all hurtling toward a uniform modernity, albeit at different rates.

If Cai's epistemology was reflected in his pedagogical vision, as I think it must have been, he accepted the dissolution of "classical learning" as a distinct discipline. However, individual classics should still be taught in literature, history, philosophy, and geography. They therefore remained living texts. It may be that in China today, knowledge of Kantianism (broadly defined as Enlightenment thought) runs deeper than knowledge of Confucianism. This may not be the case, but if we do accept that notion in the spirit of intellectual speculation, then Kantian metaphysics in China has to be understood also as a continuation of certain strands of Buddhist metaphysics and Confucian ethics. If this is indeed the case, Cai Yuanpei played a major role in making it so. And if, on the contrary, we assume Confucianism (loosely defined) remains a key mode, if not the dominant mode of thought in China, then Cai Yuanpei also played a major role in repositioning it in the modern world.

Notes

1. For Cai's explicit appreciation of Buddhism at an early stage of his career, see Gildow, "Cai Yuanpei (1868–1940), Religion, and His Plan to Save China through Buddhism," pp. 107–148. In my view, although in his later years Cai said relatively little about Buddhism and was critical of religion, his metaphysical views (though not his social thought) continued to owe much to Buddhism.
2. Overviews of Cai's life and thought include Duiker, *Ts'ai Yüan-p'ei*; Wang, "Cai Yuanpei and the Origins of the May Fourth Movement"; and Cai, *Cai Yuanpei yu jindai Zhongguo*.
3. Cai, "Duiyu jiaoyu fangzhen zhi yijian" 對於教育方針之意見 (Some opinions on the direction of education), in Cai, *Cai Yuanpei xiansheng yiwen leichao* (hereafter CYPXYL), pp. 77–84.
4. In an echo of recent debates and burnishing his strict republicanism, Cai dismissed even constitutional monarchies as in essence autocracies.
5. Cai, *Zhongxue xiushen jiaokeshu*.
6. Liu, *Tuixiangzhai riji*, pp. 138, 153, 158.
7. Chow, Ng, and Henderson, eds., *Imagining Boundaries*.
8. In context:

   > The Master said, "The commander of the forces of a large state may be carried off, but the will (*zhi* 志) of even a common man cannot be taken from him."

   Analects 9:25; Legge, trans., *The Four Books*, p. 241. More prosaically:

   > The Master said, You may rob the Three Armies of the commander-in-chief, but you cannot deprive the humblest peasant of his opinion.

   Waley, *The Analects of Confucius*, p. 144.
9. In context:

   > Jing Chun said to Mencius, "What great men are Gongsun Yan and Zhang Yi. When they are aroused, the princes tremble, but when they are at ease, the whole world is quiet." Mencius replied, "When did they become great men? Have you, sir, never learned the Rites? . . . But he who properly might be called a great man is one who dwells in the broad mansion of the world, takes his place in its seat of rectitude, pursues the Great Way of the world, who, gaining his ambition, shares it with the common people, but who, failing to gain his ambition pursues his principles in solitude. He is one whom riches and honors cannot taint, poverty and lowly station cannot shift, majesty and power cannot bend. Such a one I call a great man."

   Mencius 3B2; Dobson, trans., *Mencius*, pp. 124–125.
10. In context:

    > Zhong Gong asked about perfect virtue. The Master said, "It is, when you go abroad, to behave to every one as if you were receiving a great guest; to employ the people as if you were assisting at a great sacrifice; not to do to others as you would not wish done to yourself; to have no murmuring against you in the country, and none in the family." Zhong Gong said, "Though I am deficient in intelligence and vigor, I will make it my business to practice this lesson."

    Analects 12:2; Legge, trans., *The Four Books*, pp. 279–280.
11. To which Confucius replied that Zigong was not able to do that yet. *Analects* 5:11.

12. In context:

> What is meant by "The making of the whole kingdom peaceful and happy depends on the government of his state," is this: When the sovereign behaves to the aged of his own family as the aged should be behaved to, the people become filial; when the sovereign behaves to the elders of his own fmaily as the elders should be behaved to, the people learn brotherly submission; when the sovereign treats compassionately the young and fatherless, the people do the same. Thus the ruler has a principle with which, as with a measuring square, he may regulate his conduct. What a man dislikes in his superiors, let him not display in the treatment of his inferiors; what he dislikes in inferiors, let him not display in the service of his superiors. What one hates in those who are ahead of one, one should not practice on those who are behind; what one hates in those who are on the right, one should not practice on those who are on the left; what one hates in those on the left, one should not practice on the right: this is what is called "The principle with which, as with a measuring square, to regulate one's conduct." In the *Book of Poetry* it is said, "How much to be rejoiced in are these princes, the parents of the people!" When a prince loves what the people love, and hates what the people hate, then is he what is called the parent of the people. In the *Book of Poetry* it is said, "Lofty is that southern hill, with its rugged masses of rocks! Greatly distinguished are you, O grand-teacher Yin, the people all look up to you." Rulers of states may not neglect to be careful. If they fall into selfishness, they will be a disgrace to the empire.

Legge, trans., *The Four Books,* pp. 27–29 (modified). In much traditional scholarship, this text was attributed to Confucius.

13. In context:

> Mencius replied, "In antiquity, when King Wen governed at Qi, the people farmed one-ninth of the land for the king, and the officials enjoyed hereditary tenure. At the state borders, merchandise was inspected but not taxed. No prohibitions were placed on the use of marshes and bridges. The families of criminals were not punished along with the criminal. Four classes of indigents, who had no one to speak for them, were officially recognized: the elderly man with no wife, the elderly woman with no husband, the elderly who had no children to support them, and the young who had no parents.... In King Wen's ordinances and in his Humanity, these four classes received prior attention.

Mencius 1B5; Dobson, trans., *Mencius,* p. 19 (modified).

14. In context:

> Yang is the father; yin is the mother. And I, this tiny thing, dwell enfolded in Them. Hence, what fills Heaven and Earth is my body, and what rules Heaven and Earth is my nature. The people are my siblings, and all living things are my companions. My Ruler is the eldest son of my parents, and his ministers are his retainers. To respect those great in years is the way to "treat the elderly as elderly should be treated." To be kind to the orphaned and the weak is the way to "treat the young as young should be treated." The sage harmonizes with Their Virtue; the worthy receive what is most excellent from Them. All under Heaven who are tired, crippled, exhausted, sick, brotherless, childless, widows or widowers—all are my siblings who are helpless and have no one else to appeal to. To care for them at such times is the practice of a good son. To be delighted and without care, because trusting Them, is the purest filial piety.

Zhang, "Ximing."

15. In context:

Zi Gong said, "If someone extensively conferred benefits on the people, acting to save all of them, what would you say of him? Might he be called perfectly virtuous?" The Master said, "Not just perfect virtue, true sageliness. Even Yao and Shun couldn't criticize him. Now the man of perfect virtue, wishing to be established himself, seeks also to establish others; wishing to be enlarged himself, he seeks also to enlarge others. In fact, the ability to take one's own feelings as a guide—this may be called in the direction of perfect virtue."

Analects 6:28; Legge, trans., *The Four Books,* p. 199; Waley, trans., *The Analects of Confucius,* p. 122.

16. The referents are from *Mencius.* In context:
Yu and Ji:

Yu and Ji happened upon quiet times. Three times they passed the gates of their own homes but did not go in. Confucius thought them worthy for this. Yanzi happened upon troubled times. He lived in a mean street, on a handful of rice and a gourdful of water a day. Others could not have endured such distress, but his happiness remained unchanged. Confucius thought him worthy too. Mencius said, "Yu, Ji, and Yan Hui pursued identical paths. Yu thought that if one man drowned it was as though he himself were drowned. Ji thought that if one man starved it was as though he himself starved. And so it was that they took matters with such seriousness. Had the circumstances of Yu, Ji, and Yanzi been reversed, they would have acted no differently."

Mencius 4B.29; Dobson, trans., *Mencius,* pp. 183–184.
Yi Yin:

Wan Zhang said, "It is said that Yi Yin first met King Tang through his knowledge of cooking. Was this so?" Mencius replied, "No. That was not the case. Yi Yin was farming some land in the territory of the Ruler of Xin. He learned to appreciate the Way of Yao and Shun there. Had he been offered the salary of the ruler of the world, he would have disregarded the offer if it involved anything contrary to the teaching and just principles of Yao and Shun. . . . Three times, Tang sent messengers to entreat him. His air of indifference then changed. He said, 'If they allow me to remain among my fields, I can appreciate the Way of Yao and Shun, but perhaps I might be able to make this king a Yao or a Shun, and make his people a people after the order of Yao and Shun's people. Perhaps I might see this done with my own eyes. When Heaven begat our people (Heaven ordained that) those who already know should teach those who are yet to know, and that those who are already taught should apprise those who have yet to be taught. I am one from among Heaven's people who has already been taught. I will teach these people the Way of Yao and Shun, for if I do not do so, then who will?' He was concerned that while among the common people, both men and women, if there were those who had never felt the life-giving beneficence of Yao and Shun, it was as though he himself had pushed them into a ditch. In this way, he took upon himself the heavy burden of the world. He went to King Tang as a result, proposing that Tang attack the Xia and rescue the common people."

Mencius 5A.7; Dobson, trans., *Mencius,* p. 61.

17. There is an extensive scholarly literature that touches on this seemingly weird view. For a convincing and bracing appraisal, see Jenco, "Histories of Thought and Comparative Political Theory," pp. 658–681.

18. Berlin, *Four Essays on Liberty.*

19. Cai, "Duiyu jiaoyu fangzhen zhi yijian," p. 84.

20. Cai, "Duiyu jiaoyu fangzhen zhi yijian," pp. 78–79. Again, Cai's rhetorical strategy depended on mixing classical references such as the *datong* and modern socialist doctrine, and claiming their essential equivalence. Unlike Cai's glosses for liberty, equality, and fraternity, the term *datong* was not only a classical reference to something like a perfect social order; it had also been associated with Western utopias for a generation by the time Cai was writing. As Cai references, the term *datong* is found in the *Record of the Rites* (*Liji* 禮記), in the chapter "Movement of the Rites" (*Liyun* 禮運). The passage describes the sadness of Confucius, who lamented that he had missed the age of Datong, when the "empire belonged to all" (*tianxia wei gong* 天下為公), wealth was shared, people were not concerned with private profit and did not love only their own kin, and charity was extended to young and old, widow and widower, and orphans and cripples. This text periodically emerged as central to Confucian idealism. For general discussions, see Elman and Kern, eds., *Statecraft and Classical Learning,* and Nylan, *The Five "Confucian" Classics*. By the 1890s, Western missionaries had used *datong* to introduce the concept of the Christian millennium, and Chinese writers used it in discussions of socialist and sometimes anarchist reforms; arguably, this modern usage culminated in the *Datongshu* 大同書 ("Great Commonweal," 1902) of Kang Youwei 康有為 (1858–1927).

21. For Cai's Kantianism, see Li, "Cai Yuanpei sixiang zhong de Deguo ziyuan," pp. 199–229.

22. Cai, "Duiyu jiaoyu fangzhen zhi yijian," pp. 80–81.

23. Cai concluded his essay with reflections on how these five goals—or spheres—of education mutually supported one another while contributing to the standard school subjects. For example, mathematics was first a vocational or practical branch of learning, but if we follow Pythagoras in thinking of numbers as the source of all things, math is also an aspect of worldview, while geometry also concerned aesthetics. History and geography are primarily utilitarian, but heroic figures of the past can represent the ideal of the militant citizenry, while stories of artists speak to aesthetics, and of course these subjects touch on morality and worldview as well. This final section of the essay may have helped Cai's audience of educators to understand how to apply his theory, but it need not detain us here. Cai, "Duiyu jiaoyu fangzhen zhi yijian," pp. 82–84.

24. Cai, "Duiyu jiaoyu fangzhen zhi yijian," p. 82. Cai's interest in the traditional "six arts" is noted in Chen, *Touches of History,* p. 205.

25. Cai, "Zai Beijing daxue huafa yanjiuhui shang de yanshuoci" 在北京大學畫法研究會上的演說詞 (Lecture to the Society for the Study of Painting Technique at Peking University, 1918), in *Cai Yuanpei wenji* (hereafter, CYPWJ), *meiyu* 美育 (aesthetics education), pp. 85–87.

26. Cai, "Wenhua yundong buyao wangle meiyu" 文化運動不要忘了美育 (The culture movement should not forget aesthetic education), CYPWJ, *meiyu,* p. 92.

27. For discussions of Cai's views on aesthetics, see Duiker, "The Aesthetics Philosophy of Ts'ai Yuan-p'ei," pp. 385–401; Li, "Cai Yuanpei sixiang zhong de Deguo ziyuan," pp. 199–229; Lu, *Zhongguo jindai meixue sixiang shi,* pp. 504–549.

28. Cai, "Meishu zhi zuoyong" 美術之作用 (The uses of art, 1916), CYPWJ, *meiyu,* pp. 57–59.

29. Cai, "Yi meiyu dai zongjiao shuo" 以美育代宗教說 (Replacing religion with aesthetics education), CYPXYL, pp. 229–232. This essay, Cai's first on the subject, was originally given as a lecture and has been translated into English by Andrews as "Replacing Religion with Aesthetic Education," pp. 182–189.

30. Cai, "Yi meiyu dai zongjiao shuo," p. 232.

31. Cai, "Meixue guannian" 美學觀念 (The concept of aesthetics), CYPWJ, *meiyu,* pp. 22–24.

32. Brooks, *The Menace of the Sublime to the Individual Self.* Conversely, perhaps Cai was wrenching *woxiang* out of its Buddhist context to refer to what neo-Kantians sometimes called the noumenal self (but this does not seem likely to me).

33. The third chapter of the *Diamond Sutra* explains:

The Buddha said to him, "Subhuti, those who would now set forth on the bodhisattva path should thus give birth to this thought: 'However many beings there are in whatever realms of being might exist, whether they are born from an egg or born from a womb, born from the water or born from the air, whether they have form or no form, whether they have perception or no perception or neither perception nor no perception, in whatever conceivable realm of being one might conceive of beings, in the realm of complete nirvana I shall liberate them all. And though I thus liberate countless beings, not a single being is liberated.' And why not? Subhuti, a bodhisattva who creates the perception of being cannot be called a 'bodhisattva.' Any why not? Subhuti, no one can be called a bodhisattva who creates the *perception of a self* or who creates the perception of a being, a life, or a soul."

Red Pine, *The Diamond Sutra,* pp. 2–3. In Chinese: 佛告須菩提:「諸菩薩摩訶薩, 應如是降伏其心:所有一切眾生之類—若卵生, 若胎生, 若濕生, 若化生;若有色, 若無色;若有想, 若無想;若非有想非無想, 我皆令入無餘涅槃而滅度之。如是滅度無量無數無邊眾生, 實無眾生得滅度者。何以故?須菩提!若菩薩有我相, 人相, 眾生相, 壽者相, 即非菩薩。

34. Muller, comp. and trans., *The Sutra of Perfect Enlightenment,* pp. 202–205:

Good sons, what is the "trace of self" (*woxiang*)? It is that which is witnessed by the mind of sentient beings. Good sons, when you are in good health you naturally forget about your body. But when the body becomes sick, and you make an effort to correct the infirmity, with the slightest application of moxibustion and acupuncture you are immediately aware of your existence as a self. Thus, it is only in reference to this "witnessing" that you perceive and grasp to an apparent self-essence. Good sons, every kind of witnessing from this level up to the Tathāgata's perfect perception of pure nirvana, is all the "trace of self."

35. Cai, "Meixue guannian," p. 22.
36. Cai, "Fojiao huguolun" 佛教護國論 (On protecting the nation with Buddhism), CYPWJ, pp. 58–62; this essay is excellently translated in Gildow, "Cai Yuanpei (1868–1940), Religion," pp. 139–149.
37. Wang, "Cai Yuanpei and the Origins of the May Fourth Movement," p. 234; see also Gildow, "Cai Yuanpei (1868–1940), Religion," pp. 127–128.
38. Cai, "Fojiao huguolun," p. 61; cf. Gildow, "Cai Yuanpei (1868–1940), Religion," p. 147; Wang, "Cai Yuanpei and the Origins of the May Fourth Movement," pp. 235–236.
39. Cai, "Shijieguan yu renshengguan" 世界觀與人生觀 (Worldview and life-view, 1913), CYPXYL, pp. 16–20.
40. Cai, "Wenhua yundong buyao wangle meiyu," pp. 91–92. Cai was referring to the antigovernment and anti-imperialist political demonstrations that started with students in Beijing and spread across China's major cities. As head of Peking University, Cai found himself in an awkward position.
41. Cai used the terms "art" (*meishu* 美術) and "art education" (*meishu de jiaoyu* 美術教育) here, but he meant what he generally termed aesthetics, that is, the study and appreciation of art.
42. Not the least of such visions was Edward Bellamy's *Looking Backward,* which, along with several novels of Jules Verne, helped shaped Chinese views of the future. Other significant ideas that linked planning and social progress were found in Ebenezer Howard, whose *To-Morrow: A Peaceful Path to Real Reform* was published in 1898, launching the garden city movement in Britain, and Patrick Geddes, who published his *Cities in Evolution* in 1915.
43. Cai, "Meiyu yu rensheng" 美育與人生 (Aesthetics education and life), CYPWJ, *meiyu,* pp. 373–375.

44. Gregory, "Philosophy and Religion," pp. 102–114; Krimmer and Simpson, eds., *Religion, Reason, and Culture in the Age of Goethe*.

45. See also Li, "Cai Yuanpei sixiang zhong de Deguo ziyuan," pp. 199–229.

46. Allard, "Idealism in Britain and the United States," pp. 43–59. See also Carroll, "Beauty contra God," pp. 206–223.

47. For social Darwinists, Darwinian selection had a kind of meaning insofar as it produced superior species and races, but this was hardly a moral principle.

48. Cai, "Kexue zhi xiuyang" 科學之修養 (The cultivation of science), in CYPXYL, pp. 474–477.

49. Of Cai's anti-communism there is no doubt; but if he became more dubious of mass action, he maintained his commitments to progressive reform, egalitarianism, and human rights through the 1920s and '30s. See Duiker, *Ts'ai Yuan-p'ei*, chapter 7.

50. Zhang, "Zhongguo jindai sixiang shi de zhuanxing shidai," pp. 29–39; Chang, *Liang Ch'i-ch'ao and Intellectual Transition in China, 1890–1907*, esp. pp. 1–4; and see Wang et al., *Zhongguo jindai sixiang shi de zhuanxing shidai*.

7 ◆ JOAN JUDGE

Vernacular Knowledge in Time
Sinology outside the Archive

The archives of modern Chinese history, like all archives, privilege and preserve particular genres of texts that are associated with distinct historical narratives. This chapter applies Sinological methods generally used in the study of archival documents—deep contextualization, close reading, and edition studies—to materials that are largely "extra-archival," crudely produced compendia of vernacular knowledge. The resulting examination offers a new perspective on the relationships among temporality, politics, and the epistemological status of bodies of knowledge.

Vernacular texts have followed a different trajectory from texts that are better aligned with received narratives of modern Chinese history. The latter foreground the Time of Foreign Aggression—periodizing this history according to events such as the Opium War, the anti-foreign Boxer Rebellion, and the first and second Sino-Japanese Wars. They analyze the political and cultural fallout of these Sino-foreign interactions: the establishment of treaty ports, the influx of foreign experts, and the outflow of indemnities and students. While far from immune to such national upheavals and the reality of the foreign presence on Chinese soil, vernacular texts are not solely driven by them. "Emic" rather than "etic," they have emerged more directly from within Chinese culture, rather than from entanglements with various outside influences.[1]

Late Qing (1890–1911) and Republican (1912–1949) cultural authorities who were obsessed with leaving weighty elements of the Chinese past behind in order to join the global present dismissed much of vernacular knowledge, including the texts that emerged from it, as coarse and ignorant. A nexus of the material, semiotic, and experiential worlds, this vernacular knowledge is usable and practical, but also intriguing and wondrous. Most importantly, it is not merely a product of the unidirectional "popularization" of intellectual theories from above, but a complex assemblage of diverse knowledges and an artifact in its own right.[2] Scholars in our own day who tend to study what is most immediately legible to them—high intellectual traditions, translation practices, the Sino-Western epistemic encounter—have generally focused on new, Western-inspired genres of texts, leaving largely unexamined the vernacular materials that were published in their midst.

The present essay argues that neglected vernacular materials are, nonetheless, critical to understanding time and knowledge in modern China. They offer access to certain as yet largely unexplored corners of China's knowledge culture, the epistemologies of the less powerful. They serve as an entry point into the lives of the most repeatedly invoked and objectified target of Chinese reformist and radical politics from the late nineteenth through the mid-twentieth centuries: the common people (*yiban renmin* 一般人民, *pingmin* 平民, *minzhong* 民眾).[3] They offer glimpses of the little-understood preoccupations of the Chinese common readers who would have flipped through their pages in search of a particular nugget of information, and of less literate members of their communities with whom these common readers would have shared their knowledge.[4] And finally, they bring important nuance to the received narratives of the radical ruptures in late Qing and early Republican culture.[5]

This essay is inspired by agnotology, or the study of what has been dismissed as ignorance, a recently established field of scholarly inquiry. It uses the tools of New Sinology to explore two neglected facets of Chinese vernacular knowledge in the late Qing and early Republic.[6]

The first object of inquiry is the genre known as *wanbao quanshu* 萬寶全書 (comprehensive compendia of myriad treasures, which for convenience I will refer to as *myriad treasures*). It emerged late in the Ming dynasty (1368–1644) and continued to be published through the first decades of the twentieth century. As the genre's name suggests, such compilations textualized myriad practical and sometimes fanciful knowledge that was distinct from traditional learning (*xueshu* 學術). They also sought to engage common readers, a demographic that was largely separate from the office-seeking literati.[7] A variety of books in the *myriad treasures* genre continued to be published with minor internal changes through the Qing dynasty. By the end of the nineteenth century, one particular edition, Mao Huanwen's 毛煥文 *Zengbu wanbao quanshu* 增補萬寶全書 (Expanded complete compendia of myriad treasures), was the most commonly reprinted. From the mid-1890s, which marked a high tide in new foreign learning, it was revitalized and expanded in unprecedented ways.[8] Editors of the renewed editions of Mao's work shifted media from woodblock print to lithography and, most importantly, enlarged the compendia by adding four supplementary *juan* in 1894 and an additional two *juan* in the early twentieth century. The longevity of the *myriad treasures* genre and its revitalization at one of the key moments in the shift from late imperial time to the new Imperialist Time of foreign encounter makes these string-bound, lithographed texts an excellent source for examining questions of vernacular epistemic shifts in modern China.

The second facet of vernacular knowledge that the present essay probes is the specific content of one of the supplements added to the *myriad treasures* in 1894. While most of the material in the supplements was drawn from nineteenth-century practical manuals and directly or indirectly addressed foreign topics, I focus my discussion on material excerpted from a seventeenth-century text, Chen Haozi's 陳淏子 (Chen Fuyao 陳扶搖, Xihu huayinweng 西湖花隱翁, b. 1612 [1615]) *Huajing* 花镜 (Mirror of flowers), which appeared in the fourth supplement. As we see below, the historical trajectory of Chen's text from the early Qing through the early twenty-first century by way of its inclusion in expanded editions of the *myriad treasures* highlights the complex interplay between vernacular, mainstream, and scientific knowledge over time.

Myriad Treasures in the Marketplace and the Archive

IN THE MARKETPLACE

Scholarship to date has failed to analyze the prominent place of expanded editions of *myriad treasures* in the late Qing and early Republican marketplace.[9] The most extensive studies of the genre itself, conducted by scholars from Japan and Taiwan, have focused intensively on Ming dynasty editions. While a number of these scholars have made important arguments about the genre, they have generally focused on one particular kind of information within these texts—legal or medical, for example—rather than on their place within a broader history of books and knowledge.[10] There has been even less Sinological interest in *wanbao quanshu* dating from the late nineteenth and twentieth centuries. Wu Huifang 吳蕙芳, who has produced the most extensive bibliographic study on the history of the genre, does not analyze changes in the last generation of editions.[11]

The dramatic revival of *myriad treasures* from the mid-1890s, and its ramifications for an understanding of modern Chinese print and knowledge culture, have thus been unexplored for reasons that are directly related to the triumph of Imperialist Time. The compendia revival took place at precisely the moment when the print marketplace began to be inundated with various forms of "new knowledge" published in the new media of the time: periodicals, Japanese translations of Western-derived encyclopedias, and compendia of Western learning.[12] The revival was manifest in the unprecedented addition of supplements to the body of *myriad treasures* texts: for the first time in the genre's three-hundred-year-plus history, during which information had been added and deleted from *within* the compendia's existing categories, publishers appended a series of additional *juan* to the core texts. In keeping with the simultaneously practical and fanciful nature of the core *juan*, the supplements include an eclectic range of material: useful information on foreign coins, flags, and trade treaties for merchants; proto-scientific instructions on magic tricks, and cultivating plants for moments of leisure; a canonical method of prognostication dating to at least the Tang dynasty; and tested cures for urgent health crises including opium addiction and cholera.

The supplements in all of their seemingly chaotic diversity are integral rather than auxiliary to an understanding of China's turn of the twentieth century knowledge culture. They signal that the editors of these materials perceived a lack in the compendia that could be added to.[13] Rather than jettison the entire epistemic structure and abandon the notion of *wanbao* for *baike* 百科—the longstanding "myriad treasures" for the recently imported "one-hundred branches of new learning"—they considered it possible to "fill in" what was missing. This was a rational commercial decision based on knowledge of the print market and a careful cultural calculus: publishers seem to have understood that regular users of *myriad treasures* would also be interested in the particular kinds of knowledge they included in the supplements. The accuracy of this market calculus is evident in the number of both editions and reprints of expanded *myriad treasures* in this period. Over twenty nearly identical editions of these supplemented texts were repeatedly put out by various commercial publishers well into the Republic.[14]

The very pervasiveness of these texts is perhaps one of the reasons they have received so little attention from scholars and archivists. Similar to almanacs (*lao huangli* 老皇曆), *myriad treasures* could be found in most households in the late imperial and early Republican periods. Part of the invisible substrate of knowledge, they were so widespread that they neither elicited scrutiny nor required commentary. Ubiquitous and ragged from use, of little aesthetic value and so frequently reprinted that the characters were often barely legible, they were more likely to be disposed of rather than preserved.[15]

This ubiquity and ordinariness posed a challenge to publishers who struggled to replace the *myriad treasures* with new genres of daily-use compendia on household bookshelves and in the early twentieth-century marketplace. Editors of these competing works trumpeted the innovativeness and distinctiveness of their collections by explicitly or implicitly condemning *myriad treasures*. Their disparagement masked the extent to which their own new daily-use works were lineal descendants of the *myriad treasures*. They too were often published by small, commercial (*minjian* 民間) lithographic presses, they targeted common readers, were relatively inexpensive, and like the *myriad treasures,* were produced in the mode of traditional *leishu*—category books compiled from (unattributed) preexisting works. The preexisting works these competitors drew on, as I will demonstrate below, included the *myriad treasures* themselves.

Editors of these "new-style" daily-use texts presented their publications as superior alternatives to the crude and inferior works sold in bookstalls on the streets.[16] The preface to the 1919 *Guomin baoku quanshu* 國民寶庫全書 (Complete treasury for citizens) specifically identified *myriad treasures* as among the inferior works it was superseding: "Formerly there were block-printed editions [*fangben* 坊本] such as *Wanbao quanshu* and *Liuqingji* 留青集," the preface notes. These texts "neglected important source materials, used outmoded methods, and were based on flawed ideas." Clearly, they are not appropriate to the times: using them today would be "like trying to put a square peg in a round hole."[17]

The "Introduction" to the 1929 *Riyong wanshi baoku choushi bixu* 日用萬事寶庫 酬世必需 (Treasure house of all daily things necessary for social relations)—a text that reproduced content that was also found in the *myriad treasures*—offers a similar critique. Without directly naming the *wanbao quanshu,* the author states that there were countless, low-quality, commercially produced daily-use books—enough to "make a packhorse sweat or fill a house to the rafters" (*hechi hanniu chongdong* 何啻汗牛充棟) in the familiar idiom. They were essentially useless, however, filled with platitudes and excessively narrow. The *Treasure House,* in contrast, offers "new and original sources" that respond to society's needs. Moreover, it was technically superior, so well organized that readers could find the information they needed *at a glance* (*yilan liaoran* 一覽瞭然).[18] This rhetoric of user-friendliness echoes the very rhetoric that was used to promote expanded editions of *myriad treasures*. The slightly revised preface of editions of the *myriad treasures* published from 1912 makes a nearly identical claim for ease of use. "With one glance," readers are assured, "you will have about all that you need" (*yilan dagai yi ju* 一覽大概已具).[19]

The greater challenge to the epistemological status and market share of *myriad treasures* was posed, however, by a new genre of Western-inspired Japanese encyclopedia, *baike quanshu* 百科全書 (J. *hyakka zensho*).[20] Whereas Edo-period (1600–1868) Japanese intellectuals had avidly sought out Chinese editions of *myriad treasures* as sources of valuable information, the flow of encyclopedic knowledge was reversed in the late nineteenth century.[21] This reversal was a barometer of the broader shift in the Sino-Japanese balance of power and knowledge at this time. Manifest in Japan's resounding victory over China in the first Sino-Japanese War (1894–1895), this shift was grounded in the Meiji government's (1868–1912) pivot toward Western political, legal, and pedagogical models, which had itself fueled a veritable Japanese encyclopedia frenzy between the years 1873 and 1915.[22] Rather than turn to *myriad treasures* for information about Chinese daily life as their Tokugawa forebears had done, Meiji officials and intellectuals consulted *Chambers's Information for the People* (first edition 1833–1835) and the *Encyclopaedia Britannica* for Western knowledge on new topics including science and parliamentary government.[23] When the Chinese themselves began to publish compendia under the new title *baike quanshu* from 1903, all were translations of Japanese works.[24]

It was at precisely this moment when Japan's encyclopedia frenzy was at its peak—from the 1890s through the early twentieth century—that compilers began to update and expand the *myriad treasures*. While several scholars have closely examined the phenomena of the rise of the *baike quanshu* in early twentieth-century China, none have studied the concurrent expansion and revision of *myriad treasures*.[25] This enduring emphasis on new genres and neglect of vernacular texts has determined the latter's place in the Chinese cultural imaginary and in the East Asian historical archive.[26]

Lu Xun 魯迅 (1881–1936), prominent intellectual, Japanophile, and acerbic critic of many aspects of both the Chinese cultural tradition and Chinese vernacular culture, offers some insight into the place of *myriad treasures* in the elite Chinese cultural imaginary. In his commentary on Li Ruzhen's 李汝珍 (c. 1763–c. 1830) "novel of erudition," *Jinghua yuan* 鏡花緣 (Flowers in the mirror), Lu Xun described it as a veritable "nexus of learning" and "storehouse of art." This was not, in Lu Xun's mind, a compliment. With its extravagant display of eclectic knowledge—of flowers and birds, calligraphy, painting, lyre playing, chess, medicine, fortune-telling, astrology, phonology and mathematics, riddles, drinking games, ball games, and games of dice and cards (all topics included in *myriad treasures*)—he derisively concluded that Li's work was ultimately "more like a *myriad treasures* than a novel" (*ran yi yu wanbao quanshu wei lin bi yi* 然亦與《萬寶全書》为鄰比矣).[27]

Another indication of the status of the genre is the use of the term *wanbao quanshu* in satirical writing in the 1930s and 1940s to describe know-it-all braggarts. It continues to be used today to describe someone who is "a jack of all trades and a master of none."[28]

IN THE ARCHIVE

The lowly place of the *myriad treasures* in elite culture, together with their ubiquity on household bookshelves and in street-side bookstalls, had a direct bearing on their status in the East Asian historical archive. While the compendia are more widely and carefully preserved in Japan (where scholars have assembled massive reprint editions of late Ming *myriad treasures*), only disparate copies can be found in major Chinese libraries. Slightly greater numbers are held by minor libraries such as the Shoudu tushuguan 首都圖書館 (Capital Library) in Beijing and in unofficial collections. They can also still be found in secondhand bookstores, particularly in Taipei.

The copies of late Qing and Republican *myriad treasures* that are available in major East Asian libraries were not acquired through careful collection practices but through more serendipitous routes. This is the case for the Kansai University Library, which acquired Qing and Republican editions of *myriad treasures* when it was bequeathed the idiosyncratic personal collection of Masuda Wataru 增田涉 (1903–1977). A scholar of modern Chinese fiction with eclectic tastes, Masuda apparently appreciated the extent to which vernacular texts could nurture an understanding of Chinese culture.[29]

A similar appreciation for vernacular culture informed the collecting practices of Gu Tinglong 顧廷龍 (1904–1998), the first director of the Shanghai Library in the early People's Republic of China (PRC). Gu saved great quantities of daily-use texts from historical oblivion, in one instance literally rescuing them from a recycling dump.[30] When he heard in the fall of 1955 that a papermaking plant in Shanghai had purchased about 20,000 piculs (1.2 million kilograms) of waste paper from Suian 遂安 County in Zhejiang Province, he immediately conjectured that this "waste paper" would include valuable string-bound books. His inspection of the lot confirmed his supposition. He returned the next day with six associates to help him sift through the material and determine which works to include in the library collection. Over a period of eleven days, the group selected 1,000 kilograms of texts.[31]

Gu recounts that his attentiveness to such materials and his collection practices had been inspired by Gu Jiegang 顧頡剛 (1893–1980), the renowned historian and folklorist who considered the culture of "the people" to be a vital and creative counterpoint to the increasingly sterile culture of the educated classes.[32] In a little-known work, *Gouqiu Zhongguo tushu jihua shu* 購求中國圖書計畫書 (Program for seeking out and purchasing Chinese books), Gu Jiegang described the difficulty—and value—of collecting books that did not fall under the orthodox classification of Classics (*jing* 經), History (*shi* 史), Philosophy (*zi* 子), and Belles Lettres (*ji* 集).[33] Gu Tinglong relied on this text in determining which works to salvage and preserve in the Shanghai Library.[34] These included *myriad treasures* (apparently earlier editions in particular, since Gu Tinglong describes them as "books used by the common people in the Ming dynasty"). They also included a related genre, *minyong bianlan* 民用便覽 (brief guides for popular use).[35]

Guo Licheng 郭立誠 (fl. 1920), a graduate of the Beijing University History Department, also appreciated the link between the *myriad treasures* genre and folk culture. He began to study folklore (*minsu xue* 民俗學) formally in the early 1920s, when Gu Jiegang and others were doing the same.[36] In a chapter of his memoirs entitled "Embarking on This Path of Folklore Studies" (Zoushang minsuxue yanjiu de zhe tiaolu 走上民俗學研究的這條路), Guo describes his scholarly trajectory. It began with his exposure to *myriad treasures* and similar texts in his father's study.[37]

Guo's father, a scholar and expert on local customs, had a well-stocked library that included several fine editions of the classics, histories, and poetry—none of which Guo was allowed to touch as a child. The books he was able to freely flip through included the genre called *wanshi buqiuren* 萬事不求人 (myriad matters about which one will not need to ask), hybrid texts that combined the content and encyclopedic quality of *myriad treasures* with elements of earlier literacy primers.[38] From these and other texts Guo perused in his father's library—including a record of auspicious days, the *Yuxia ji* 玉匣記 (Record of the jade casket), the *Taishang ganying pian* 太上感應篇 (Treatise of Laozi on the response and return), and morality books (*shanshu* 善書)—he developed an understanding of old customs. His reading fueled a later passion for academic research.[39]

In addition to folklorists, various other Chinese scholars have acknowledged the value of *myriad treasures* as gateways to the rich world of vernacular culture. Some scholars have made reference to technical information found in such books. They include Chen Jingxi 陳景熙, a recent scholar of monetary currency in Chaoshan 潮汕, Guangdong. Chen quotes material on four kinds of counterfeit silver that circulated in the region from the first supplement to an expanded *myriad treasures* edition attributed to Tang Shaoyi 唐紹儀 (1862–1938), first premier of the Republic of China. Chen references Liang Size's 梁思澤 *Yinjing fami yaojue* 銀經發秘要訣 (Classic of revealing the secrets of silver [original preface dated 1826]) not by quoting Liang's text directly, but through its inclusion in the Tang Shaoyi *myriad treasures*.[40]

Xiao Yifei 肖伊緋 (b. 1975), an independent scholar in China and the author of some ten works on intellectual history and philosophy, is one of the few writers to highlight the neglect of vernacular texts even by scholars of popular literature (*su wenxue* 俗文學) and folklore. He notes that because *myriad treasures* are generally considered to be extremely crude (*dasu* 大俗) rather than greatly refined (*daya* 大雅), collectors ignore them in the same way that porcelain collectors covet pieces made in the official kilns (*guanyao* 官窯) and disdain works produced in popular kilns (*minyao* 民窯). Xiao describes his own firsthand experience of this disdain by recounting the reaction of fellow customers at a bookstall when he picked up a fragment of a *myriad treasure*. The crowd of book buyers immediately dispersed. Anxious to get the book off his hands, the owner offered Xiao an excellent price.[41]

The *Huajing* (Mirror of Flowers) in and beyond the *Myriad Treasures* Genre

The characterization of *myriad treasures* as "extremely crude" belies the nature of much of the content found in both the main *juan* of the compilations and their late Qing supplements. A prime example of this is the excerpts from Chen Haozi's late seventeenth-century botanical treatise, the *Mirror of Flowers,* which were included in the fourth supplement added to the Mao Huanwen lineage of compendia in 1894. The subject of Chen's text is ornamental plants (*guanshang zhiwu* 觀賞植物) and fruit trees. He recorded and classified more than three hundred kinds of flowers and fruit trees together with the growing expertise necessary to cultivate them.[42] The earliest Chinese record of growing and arranging potted plants, his text is distinguished from earlier agricultural works that were focused on cotton, hemp, silkworms, mulberry, and other foodstuffs.[43]

The *Mirror of Flowers* was repeatedly republished from the early Qing dynasty through the early twenty-first century, making it a valuable source to think with in considering the question of historical time and the shifting status of particular bodies of knowledge in modern China. Woodblock editions of the text were frequently reprinted in both China and Japan from the late seventeenth through the late nineteenth centuries, and various print forms of the text continued to be produced under various titles through the twenty-first century.[44] Two illustrated lithographed versions were published in China in 1914.[45] Typeset editions appeared in 1936 and 1937, a photocopied version in 1956, and an annotated version in 1962 (revised in 1980). Two editions with the same title, *Mizhuan Huajing* 秘傳花鏡 (Esoteric lore of the Mirror of flowers) appeared in 2001 and 2002.[46] Over the course of this history the *Huajing* was variously categorized as a work of empiricism, of science, or of useful vernacular knowledge.

THE *MIRROR OF FLOWERS* AND EMPIRICISM

Chen Haozi's passion for plants may have been an unintended consequence of his politics. At about age thirty when the Qing was established, he was unwilling to serve under the Manchus and returned to his native Hangzhou from Nanjing.[47] Writing in 1688 at the age of seventy-seven, Chen originally conceived of his treatise as a handbook on plants for the uninitiated. He claimed that his compatriots knew nothing about planting and producing. Instead, they led aimless lives in the world of commerce. If they weren't speculating on financial markets and pursuing profit, they were frantically pursuing official careers.[48] He specifically sought to overcome one aspect of their ignorance: the "superstitious" notion that planting had to be restricted to a specific growing season.[49]

In compiling the *Mirror,* Chen relied on both experience and research. He drew on both his own experience and that of his acquaintances who earned a living growing flowers or of his friends who had a particular interest in flowers.[50] In terms of research, he built upon and improved earlier treatises on flowers (*huapu* 花譜) by correcting errors and introducing original ideas. According to recent scholars, his work surpassed Wang Zhen's 王禎 (d. 1333) *Nongsang tongjue* 農桑通訣 (Secrets of mulberry farming) in its exploration of the physiological mechanism of grafting. It also went beyond Jia Sixie's 賈思勰 sixth-century *Qimin yaoshu* 齊民要術 (Essential techniques for the welfare of the people) and Guo Tuotuo's 郭橐駝 (Tang era) *Zhongshu shu* 種樹書 (Book on planting trees).[51]

THE *MIRROR OF FLOWERS* AND SCIENCE

By the mid- to late nineteenth century, scholars and observers assessed the *Mirror of Flowers* not only in relation to past Chinese agricultural works but in relation to the increasingly influential epistemology of science. Certain contemporary foreign experts, a group that was rarely generous in its characterization of indigenous forms of Chinese knowledge, commended the *Mirror*. They include the British Protestant missionary Alexander Wylie (1815–1887). In a column entitled "Repertoires of Science &c.," Wylie praised Chen's text as "one of the best works on flowers that has appeared in the present dynasty."[52]

The section of Chen's six-*juan*, 110,000-character text that was excerpted in the supplement to the *myriad treasures* included what commentators unanimously consider its "most brilliant" section, the second *juan*, entitled "Eighteen Methods for Growing Plants" (Kehua shiba fa 課花十八法).[53] This is also arguably the most scientific section. Chen's introduction to the *juan* explains that plants are a product of their environment: those in the north are able to endure extreme cold, while those in the south can tolerate intense heat.[54] The *juan* includes sections on "Methods for Expediting the Growth of Flowers" (Bianhua cuihua fa 變花催花法), "Determining When to Use Fertilizer" (Peiyong kefou fa 培雍可否法), "Growing New Plants from Cuttage" (Qiancha yisheng 扦插易生),[55] and "Arranging the Soil around Transplanted Falowers" (Yihua zhuanduo fa 移花轉垛法).[56] It also includes an influential section focused on below, "An Ingenious Method for Grafting Plants" (Jiehuan shenqi fa 接換神奇法).[57]

In contrast to his "superstitious" forebears, Chen believed the cultivation of plants should not be limited by the seasons. In a subsection on transplanting in *juan* 2, he claims that it is possible to "transplant and replant" (*yizai dingzhi* 移栽定植) at any time.[58] He further argues that the very nature of plants could be changed by the skilled cultivator. Red-colored ones can become purple, and small can become large. Those that are sour and bitter can become sweet, and those that are "malodorous can become fragrant." "Man can reverse nature" (*renli keyi huitian* 人力可以回天) through the "process of grafting" (*wei zai jiehuan de qi chuan* 惟在接換得其傳). He can also improve the quality of grafted species by crossing particular "rootstocks" (*zhenmu* 砧木) with particular "branches" (*jiesui* 結穗). Even plants that were not particularly similar such as peaches, plums, apricots, and kumquats could be grafted to one another.[59]

Editors of Republican daily-use materials who directly criticized the quality of the *myriad treasures* genre in their prefaces in an effort to assert the superiority and scientificness of their own compilations, nonetheless included Chen Haozi's

"Wondrous Methods for Grafting Plants" in their collections. In their texts, which include *Xinbian Riyong wanquan xinshu* 新編日用萬全新書 (Newly edited, completely thorough new book for daily use, 1921), *Treasure House of All Daily Things Necessary for Social Relations* (1929; introduced above), and *Jiating baike quanshu* 家庭百科全書 (Household encyclopedia, 1930), the editors failed to acknowledge either the *Huajing* itself or the *myriad treasures* as the source for the botanical expertise they shared.[60] They repurposed and repackaged this "old" knowledge in order to make it their own. While Chen had initially described six methods of grafting—using the body, the root, the bark, and the branches of a plant or tree—each of the subsequent texts added and subtracted from this material and featured only four or five of Chen's original methods. The *Treasure House of All Daily Things* also provided illustrations of the grafting process.[61]

Chen's work was also reprised in mainstream publications. These include the Commercial Press' encyclopedic *Zhiwuxue dacidian* 植物學大辭典 (Dictionary of botanical nomenclature, 1908–1917). The *Dictionary*, which adopted Carolus Linnaeus's (1707–1778) system of binomial classification, included the *Mirror of Flowers* as a source in select entries.[62]

The *Mirror of Flowers'* status as a work of science rose further at the turn of the twenty-first century. Contemporary mainland Chinese scholars have directly hailed Chen's late seventeenth-century treatise as "a work of science" (*yiben kexue zhuzuo* 一本科学著作) and as one of the bases for scientific research in the People's Republic of China.[63] Zhang Guotai's 張國泰 (fl. 1670) original preface to the work has also been included in a recent collection on early Chinese science and technology.[64]

This claim for the scientificness of the *Mirror of Flowers* is most consistently tied to Chen's material on agricultural selection in *juan* 2 of his text, which was reprinted both in editions of *myriad treasures* and in Republican daily-use texts. According to recent scholars, Chen's discussion of grafting reveals a sophisticated level of knowledge. He understood the stages of plant development, the need to select high-yield branches for grafting, and the potential for improving plant quality and creating new species through grafting.[65] Keenly aware of global hierarchies of scientific knowledge and the need to overcome notions of an epistemological lag in China, these authors fashion Chen Haozi as an expert on plant selection before his time. They claim that his assertions that artificial cultivation can modify botanic characteristics and that "man can conquer nature" (*renli keyi duo tiangong* 人力可以夺天工, *rending shengtian* 人定胜天) evince a knowledge of scientific agricultural selection that predates the work of the Russian botanist Ivan Vladimirovich Michurin (1855–1935), one of the alleged founding fathers of this field. Similar to Chen, Michurin developed methods for hybridizing geographically distant plants. He insisted that man cannot wait for favors from nature but must take them from nature.[66] Other scientific innovations recent scholars had credited Chen with include his discussion of insecticides, his method of classification, and his experimental data.[67]

Other PRC scholars have, however, taken a more minimalist view of Chen's scientific contributions—alerting us once again to the unstable epistemological status of particular bodies of knowledge over time. Yi Qinheng 伊钦恒, who was probably most familiar with Chen's treatise, having annotated it in 1962, states that in terms of science, the *Mirror of Flowers* was a product of its time. Chen had limited knowledge of astronomy and meteorology, traveled little, and lacked a full range of specimens. At the same time, he made many misclassifications, confusing certain vines with non-vines, for example.[68] For Yi, Chen was more horticulturalist than botanist. This view was shared by other Chinese scholars, who consider Chen's "secret methods" most relevant for cultivating household plants, and even by Joseph Needham, who, allegedly, called Chen China's "horticulturalist" (*yuanyi jia* 園藝家).[69] These scholars understood the *Mirror of Flowers* in emic rather than etic terms: from the perspectives of the cultural history of science and knowledge of early scientific achievements rather than from the perspective of Western or "universal" scientific standards.[70]

THE *MIRROR OF FLOWERS* AS VERNACULAR KNOWLEDGE

While various claims have been made over time for the scientific status of Chen Haozi's work, it was, ironically, a famous May 4th-era intellectual, Zhou Zuoren 周作人 (1885–1967), who most explicitly praised Chen's text as a repository of invaluable vernacular botanical knowledge.[71] In an essay that is a paean to the *Mirror,* Zhou was less concerned with evaluating its scientific merits than he was with extolling it as a lively alternative to the moribund practices of classical scholars. While Chen wrote from experience and brought plants to life through his own direct relationship with nature, classical scholars derived their knowledge of plants from textual research on the names of things (*mingwu kaozheng* 名物考證).[72]

Zhou celebrated the *Mirror of Flowers* as both an extremely ordinary text and an extraordinary one, "a book one often doesn't see," on a par with precious banned Ming editions.[73] He recounted first discovering the volume not in a library, bookstore, or rare book collection, but in a relative's home. Only twelve or thirteen years old at the time, he was so intrigued by the Chen's discussion of flowers that he convinced the relative to sell it to him for 200 *wen*. Although he later lost that edition, he purchased another one as an adult.[74]

Zhou compared the *Mirror* to earlier Chinese works on plants—Jia Sixie's *Essential Techniques for the Welfare of the People* and Li Shizhen's 李时珍 (1518–1593) *Bencao gangmu* 本草綱目 (Materia medica)—and noted that the focus on garden plots in Chen's text spoke most directly to farmers' practical concerns.[75] He ultimately categorized the work not as an agricultural treatise, however, but as a "small essay" (*xiao lunwen* 小論文) most akin to Li Yu's 李漁 (Hushang liweng 湖上笠翁, 1611–1679) *Xianqing yuji* 閒情偶寄 (Casual expressions of idle feeling). Published in 1671 (some seventeen years before the *Mirror of Flowers*), Li's *Casual Expressions of Idle Feeling* is a collection of inventive personal essays on eight highly eclectic topics including flowers and trees.[76] Zhou commended both Li's and Chen's works as welcome antidotes to the idiocy of essay writing (*yizhi zuowen zhi ben* 醫治作文之笨). He valued their ingenious observations of nature and human affairs, their original forms of expression, and their overall cleverness.[77]

At the same time, Zhou had high praise for the practical botanical knowledge in the treatise. Rather than teaching the reader about the unusual plants that one would place in a grand hallway or seek to cultivate in one's garden, it provides instruction on the kinds of plants one would be likely to encounter on daily walks in the countryside. These include bamboo leaves and Chinese violet (*zihua diding* 紫花地丁), blackberry lily/iris (*shegan ji hudiehua* 射干即蝴蝶花), rhododendron/Indian azalea (*Rhododendron simsii, shan zhizhu ji yingshan hong* 山躑躅即映山紅), saxifrage/heavenly lotus leaves (*huer cao ji tianhe ye* 虎耳草即天荷葉), and flatwood/always tiny (*pingdi mu ji laohuda* 平地木即老勿大).[78]

Zhou included an excerpt from his own diary in the essay in which he recounts picking handfuls of flatwood at Crow Rock tomb (Wushi musuo 烏石墓所) when he was fourteen. The entry, dated October 16, 1899, records the name of the plant, its size, and the nature of its leaves and seeds. Zhou further discusses how to care for the plant. He notes its preference for dry shade and explains how to pot it so that it will produce more buds the following year than if it was living in the wild. While this hardly counts as sophisticated botanical knowledge, it is a form of vernacular knowledge that Zhou prized. He claimed he could attribute his own unique understanding of botanical principles to his reading of the *Mirror of Flowers*.[79]

These various readings of the *Mirror of Flowers* and other late Qing and Republican vernacular texts underline the unstable epistemic status of particular bodies of knowledge over time. They further highlight the extent to which this status is determined by the physical textual form in which the information is packaged and the political contexts in which it is mobilized.

In terms of shifts over time, scholars working in East Asia, Europe, and North America have carefully studied late Ming block-printed editions of *myriad treasures*, while completely overlooking the countless editions of revitalized and expanded lithographed editions of these same texts at the turn of the twentieth century. The reason for this neglect is the influx of new, Western encyclopedic knowledge, which started to reach China from Japan at this time, trumping any innovations made to older genres. Even the editors of new-style Republican daily-use texts maligned contemporary editions of *myriad treasures* (from which they often drew material) in order to fashion themselves as purveyors of a new and newly imported brand of knowledge.

In terms of textual materiality, past and present scholars have overlooked excerpts from Chen Haozi's *Mirror of Flowers* when they appeared in the "crude and unscientific" *myriad treasures*, while esteeming it when it was used in entries of the *Dictionary of Botanical Nomenclature*, for example. Regarding the political inflection of epistemic value, Zhou Zuoren's seemingly apolitical celebration of the *Mirror* could be read as a critique of the arid intellectualism of certain of his peers, while Lu Xun's belittling of the *myriad treasures* was another plank in his indictment of "traditional" culture. Turn-of-the-twenty-first-century Chinese scholars' efforts to declare Chen Haozi's treatise scientific are engaged in an all too transparent move of national chauvinism.

While all knowledge is subject to the vagaries of time and politics, vernacular knowledge of the kind examined in this essay is particularly vulnerable to marginalization and denigration. More emic than etic, it can be dismissed as vestiges of cultural dead ends with little historical importance and no global resonance. Yet even these supposed dead ends can be politicized, as recent developments in the PRC attest.

The Xi Jinping 习近平 (b. 1953) regime has found the "Republican fever"—a renewed interest in and curiosity about Republican-era styles, ideas, and texts—which erupted in recent decades particularly dangerous. The "reprint fever" that has accompanied this nostalgia for things Republican has included pre-Republican texts such as the repeatedly republished *Mirror of Flowers*. It has also included texts with titles that echo earlier daily-use materials—for example, the *Wanshi buqiuren: Jiating shiyong xiaobaike* 万事不求人：家庭实用小百科 (Myriad matters about which you don't need to ask: Small practical encyclopedia for the household).[80]

This nostalgia for and curiosity about past modes of knowing has raised pointed questions that the regime would prefer to leave unaddressed: What was lost when the Republic collapsed? What has been sacrificed on the altar of political unity?[81] Threatened by such questions, the regime responded in 2013 with a condemnation of "historical nihilism" in Document 9. Exuding political paranoia, the document forbids scholars and citizens from favorably evaluating Republican culture.[82]

Sinology has taught us to fully contextualize our archival materials. The methods of New Sinology—informed by new fields of inquiry such as agnotology and the cultural history of knowledge—further underline the need to include in our studies extra-archival materials, such as those that have resurfaced in the Republican fever era. As the examples of *myriad treasures* and the *Mirror of Flowers* suggest, such texts are complex cultural palimpsests that were constantly overwritten with new meanings—from usefulness to uselessness to scientificness to historical nihilism—in different political moments. Tracing their often obfuscated ties to the formal archive and their shifting sedimented meanings over time provides invaluable insights into the knowledge culture and cultural politics of modern China.

Appendix: Editions of *Myriad Treasures*

Gailiang xin wanbao quanshu 改良新萬寶全書 (Revised new comprehensive compendium of collected treasures), 3 juan, 1 vol. (n.p.: Beiyang junfuqu, 1912, as indicated by the content of the text);

Huitu zengbu wanbao quanshu 繪圖增補萬寶全書 (Newest, illustrated, expanded, comprehensive compendium of myriad treasures) (n.p., n.d.; pre-1911, as indicated by the content of the text);

Jingdu wenjintang 京都文錦堂, *Zengbu wanbao quanshu* 增補萬寶全書 *(Expanded compendia of myriad treasures)*, 20 juan, 1 supplement, 6 vols. ([Beijing]: Jingdu wenjintang, 1901);

Longwen shuju 龍文書局, *Zengbu wanbao quanshu* 增補萬寶全書 *(Expanded compendia of myriad treasures)*, 20 juan, 6 supplements, 8 vols. (Shanghai: Longwen shuju, 1906);

Qixin shuju 啟新書局, *Zuixin huitu zengbu zhengxu wanbao quanshu* 最新繪圖增補正續萬全書 *(Newest, illustrated, expanded comprehensive compendium of myriad treasures)*, 8 vols. (Shanghai: Qixin shuju, ca. 1912);

Shanghai liuxian shuju 上海六先書局, *Zengbu wanbao quanshu* 增補萬寶全書 *(Expanded comprehensive compendium of myriad treasures)*, 6 vols. (Shanghai: Shanghai liuxian shuju, 1898);

Shanggu shanfang 尚古山房, *Huitu zengbu wanbao quanshu* 繪圖增補萬寶全書 *(Illustrated expanded compendia of myriad treasures)*, 8 vols. (Shanghai: Shanggu shanfang, 1912);

Tianbao shuju 天寶書局, *Huitu zengbu zhengxu wanbao quanshu* 繪圖增補正續萬寶全書 *(Illustrated, expanded, corrected, and continued comprehensive compendium of countless treasures)*, 8 vols. (Shanghai: Tianbao shuju, 1920);

Tianji shuju 天機書局, *Zengbu wanbao quanshu* 增補萬寶全書 *(Expanded comprehensive compendium of myriad treasures)*, 8 vols. (Shanghai: Tianji shuju, 1912).

Notes

1. For a sophisticated examination of vernacular knowledge, see a recent forum on "Vernacular Ways of Knowing" in *The American Historical Review,* in particular, Townsend, "Introduction," pp. 779–788. On emic and etic in this context, see p. 780.

2. On this view of "vernacularization," see Fissell, *Vernacular Bodies*, p. 6.

3. "The people" have been differently labeled over time: *yiban renmin* in early Republican texts, *pingmin* from the early 1920s, and *minzhong* in the later 1920s and 1930s under Guomindang rule. There has, of course, been overlap among these and a plethora of other terms.

4. On the Chinese common reader, see Judge, "In Search of the Chinese Common Reader," pp. 218–237.

5. Cynthia Brokaw similarly argues that the lack of research on what she calls "traditional books"—late imperial woodblock print editions—in studies of new media in the Republican period has limited our understanding of the early twentieth-century print world. Brokaw, "Commercial Woodblock Publishing in the Qing (1644–1911) and the Transition to Modern Print Technology," pp. 54–57. I extend Brokaw's argument to include lithographed books, and emphasize that these texts offer glimpses into the broader knowledge culture.

6. On agnotology, see Proctor and Schiebinger, eds., *Agnotology*. On New Sinology, see Barmé, "Towards a New Sinology," pp. 4–9, and the Introduction to this volume.

7. Wang, "Shenghuo, zhishi, yu wenhua shangpin," p. 6.

8. Printed in 4 vols. (Guiwentang, 1828; preface 1739).

9. For a more detailed discussion of the evolution of the content and material form of the genre, see Judge, "Science for the Chinese Common Reader?," pp. 362–365.

10. The scholar who has taken the most interest in the study of the genre up to the twentieth century is Sakai Tadao 酒井忠夫 (1912–2012), chief editor of the six-volume collection compris-

ing fourteen editions of *wanbao quanshu* between the Wanli 萬曆 (1572–1620) and Chongzhen 崇禎 (1627–1644) eras, *Chūgoku nichiyō ruisho shūsei*. Sakai has also produced pioneering scholarship on these materials. See Sakai, *Chūgoku nichiyō ruisho shi no kenkyū*. Niida Noboru 仁井田陞 (1904–1966) used the material on land contracts to examine Chinese legal history. Ogawa Yōichi 小川陽一 (b. 1934) has focused on the links between Chinese category books (*leishu* 類書) and fiction; see Ogawa, *Nichiyō ruisho ni yoru Min Shin shōsetsu no kenkyū*. Wang, "Shenghuo, zhishi, yu wenhua shangpin" (cited above), analyzes painting and calligraphy sections in Ming category books. For a general overview of the genre, see Wu, *Wanbao quanshu*, vol. 1, pp. 4–5.

11. Wu, *Wanbao quanshu*.

12. On the rise of the periodical press in this period, with a focus on the women's press, see Judge, Mittler, and Hockx, "Introduction," pp. 1–18. On the tension between *myriad treasures* and the Western-derived *baike quanshu* 百科全書 that were translated from Japanese, see Reynolds, "Japanese Encyclopaedias," pp. 137–189; Judge, "Myriad Treasures and One-Hundred Sciences," pp. 329–369. On compendia of Western knowledge, see Doleželová-Velingerová, and Wagner, "Chinese Encyclopaedias of New Global Knowledge (1870–1930)," pp. 1–27.

13. On this notion of supplement, see Derrida, *Of Grammatology*, pp. 269–316.

14. I have examined nine different editions of expanded *myriad treasures* in various libraries in East Asia, consulted four editions online and in reprinted collections, and have seen mention of an additional nine in advertisements and catalogs. For a list of those I have examined and made copies of, see the Appendix.

15. Xiao, "Wugong miji yu hun duanzi."

16. See, for example, Bao, ed., *Gaodeng xiaoxue shiyong nüzi shuhan wen,* an advertisement for which may be found in *Funü shibao* 婦女時報 19 (August 1916): front matter.

17. Haohao zi 皞皞子, "Xu" 敘 (Preface), *Guomin baoku quanshu*, cited in Yu, "Zhong-Xi zhishi jiaohui yu puji de yangben," p. 280. The *Liuqing ji* was compiled by Chen Mei 陳枚 (fl. 1742) in the early Qing dynasty. The text collected poetry and literature for practical use. Two copies appear on Brokaw's list of Sibao 四堡 imprints available online: http://publications.asiacenter.harvard.edu/publications/commerce-culture-sibao-book-trade-qing-and-republican; see Appendix G, p. 20.

18. Saoye shanfang 掃葉山房, "Liyan" 例言 (Introduction), in *Riyong wanshi baoku choushi bixu.*

19. Tianji shuju, Preface, in *Zengbu wanbao quanshu*. Between 1894, when the *myriad treasures* were first expanded, until 1912, the preface to the 1739 Mao Huanwen text was repeated verbatim in all expanded editions of this text.

20. For a fuller exploration of the relationship between Chinese and Japanese encyclopedic knowledge in this period, see Judge, "Myriad Treasures and One Hundred Sciences."

21. Edo intellectuals and publishers preserved original Chinese *myriad treasures*, reproduced them as *wakokuhon* 和刻本 (Japanese annotated versions of the [Chinese] texts), and integrated them into Japanese textual genres, most notably the *chōhōki* 重宝記 (treasury of knowledge). See also Lin, "The Transmission of Wanbao Quanshu 萬寶全書 in Edo Japan"; Lin, "The Transmission of *Wanbao quansh*u to Japan in the Early Edo Period," pp.1–29.

22. Reynolds, "Japanese Encyclopedias," pp. 160, 177.

23. *Chambers's Information* was translated as part of a massive project under the umbrella title of *Hyakka zensho* 百科全書 (Complete compendium of a hundred branches of knowledge) starting in 1873. Reynolds, "Japanese Encyclopedias," p. 163. The *Encyclopaedia Britannica* was translated as *Dai Ei hyakka zensho* 大英百科全書. On its circulation, see Yu, "Zhong Xi zhishi jiaohui yu puji de yangben," p. 281.

24. These Chinese translations include *Putong baike quanshu* 普通百科全書 (General encyclopedia), which had the alternate title *Bianyi putong jiaoyu baike quanshu* 編譯普通教育百科全書 (Compiled and translated encyclopedia for general education) and was published by the Shanghai Huiwenshe 會文社 in 1903. For information on this and other encyclopedias, see Wagner, "Encyclopaedia from China and Japan (19th and 20th Century)." For studies of *baike quanshu* see Yu, "Zhong Xi zhishi jiaohui yu puji de yangben"; Reynolds, "Japanese Encyclopedias."

25. For studies of *baike quanshu*, see Mittler, "Written for Him or for Her?," pp. 399–424; Yeh, "Civilizing Our People through the Everyday Application of New Knowledge," pp. 367–397.

26. *Myriad treasures* are rarely included in catalogs of either private or public collections. When they do appear, it is under the category of "Masters and Philosophers" (*zibu* 子部)—a miscellaneous mix that contained practical and technological knowledge together with, for example, Legalist treatises.

27. Lu, *Zhongguo xiaoshuo shi dalüe*, p. 319.

28. "Wanbao quanshu," pp. 116–117; Xiao, "Wugong miji yu hun duanzi."

29. In addition to Chinese fiction, Masuda's interests included science, geography, strange tales of the Opium War, and Japanese pirates in Qing China. On Masuda, see Fogel, "Introduction," pp. vii–ix.

30. Gu Tinglong had worked in the field of library science from 1933, and protected tens of thousands of books and documents in the midst of the second Sino-Japanese War. He later contributed these materials to the Shanghai tushuguan. Gu, *Gu Tinglong xueshu*, p. 114. He also saved what were labeled feudal daily-use materials from being destroyed at the time of the Cultural Revolution. Personal communication with an archivist at the Shanghai Library.

31. Gu, *Gu Tinglong xueshu*, p. 118.

32. Schneider, *Ku Chieh-Kang and China's New History*, pp. 166–169. At the same time, according to Schneider (p. 183), Gu considered the culture of the masses to be ignorant and ugly and in need of reform guided by the intelligentsia.

33. Gu, *Gouqiu Zhongguo tushu jihua shu*. I have been unable to see a copy of this text. It is held in a library in Germany but is too fragile to lend.

34. Gu, *Gu Tinglong xueshu*, p. 117.

35. Several works with similar titles were published in the Republic, including *Renren bixu riyong bianlan* and *Riyong bianlan*. Gu Jiegang's *Gouqiu Zhongguo tushu jihua shu* lists sixteen types of books, of which the twelfth, namely "old skills" (*jiu yishu* 舊藝術), overlaps with material found in *myriad treasures* because of the coverage of skills described in medical books (*yishu* 醫書), music books (*yuepu* 樂僕), chess manuals (*qipu* 棋譜), and painting manuals (*huapu* 畫譜). The thirteenth type, on educational texts, includes old-style children's primers (*duben* 讀本); see Gu, *Gu Tinglong xueshu*, p. 119.

36. The Beida Geyao xuehui 歌謠學會 (Peking University Folksong Study Society) was established then as well; Guo, *Guo Licheng de xueshu lunzhu*, p. 247. According to Schneider (*Ku Chieh-kang*, p. 136), the Folksong Study Society was called "Beida Geyao yanjiu hui," rather than "xuehui."

37. Guo, *Guo Licheng de xueshu lunzhu*, pp. 246–248.

38. On these texts, see Wu, "'Riyong' yu 'leishu' de jiehe," pp. 11–54.

39. Guo Licheng, *Guo Licheng de xueshu lunzhu*, pp. 246–248.

40. Chen cites Liang, via Tang Shaoyi 唐紹儀, ed., *Gailiang xin wanbao quanshu* 改良新萬寶全書 (also called *Zengbu wanbao quanshu, Xin zeng huitu wanbao quanshu xubian* 增補萬寶全書, 新增繪圖萬寶全書續編) (Minguo, lithographed, n.p., n.d). The title Chen gives for Liang's text is slightly different from the original or as it is recorded in most *myriad treasures*; Chen, "Chaoshan 'Qidui yin-Qidui piao' kao," p. 207.

41. Xiao, "Wugong miji yu hun duanzi."
42. Shu, "*Huajing* jianjie yu Qingdai chahua yishu," p. 4.
43. Yi Qinheng, "Jiaozhu *Huajing* yinyan" 校註花鏡引言 (Introduction to the annotated version of *Mirror of Flowers*), in his *Huajing jiaozhuben,* vol. 2; Shen, "Lun Chen Haozi de *Huajing,*" p. 51.
44. Alternative titles for the text include *Mizhuan Huajing* 秘傳花鏡 (Esoteric lore of the *Mirror of flowers*) and *Baihua zaipei mijue* 百花栽培秘訣 (Secret know-how for cultivating 100 flowers), which suggest the transmission of "secret techniques." Others are more descriptive, including *Yuanlin huajing* 園林花鏡 (The garden *Mirror of flowers*), and *Qunfang Huajing quanshu* 群芳花鏡全書 (Comprehensive volume on all flowers and the *Mirror of flowers*); Shen, "Lun Chen Haozi de *Huajing,*" p. 49. *Huitu yuanlin huajing* 繪圖園林花鏡 (Illustrated garden *Mirror of flowers*) highlights the illustrations in the text, which, according to different sources, ranged from 100 to 324. The lower estimate is given in Shu, "*Huajing* jianjie yu Qingdai chahua yishu," p. 4; the higher in Pan, "Chen Haozi de *Huajing* ji qi zai Riben de chuanbo," p. 315.
45. *Qunfang huajing* and *Huitu yuanlin huajing.*
46. The text was even more revered in Japan than in China. It was used as a textbook in Japan, and translated into Japanese, with editions dated 1688, 1719 (3 editions), 1735, 1773 (4), 1818, 1829 (9), and 1846. The text continued to be welcomed even in the Western-oriented Meiji period; Pan, "Chen Haozi de *Huajing* ji qi zai Riben de chuanbo," p. 315. New editions also appeared through the twentieth century, one in 1944, for example.
47. See Shen, "Lun Chen Haozi de *Huajing,*" p. 49; Feng, "*Huajing* zuozhe Chen Haozi kao," pp. 160–161; Wang, "'*Huajing* zuozhe Chen Haozi kao' bian," p. 195. We know little about Chen from official sources. His name does not appear in gazetteers of Hangzhou and Zhejiang, nor in the original *Qingshi gao* 清史稿 (Draft history of the Qing dynasty) (but it does in a later, expanded edition); Yi, "Jiaozhu *Huajing* yinyan," p. 1. Some insight can be gleaned from "Chen Fuyao xiansheng qishi shouxu" 陳扶搖先生七十壽序 (Chen Fuyao's preface on his seventieth birthday), cited in Shen, "Lun Chen Haozi de *Huajing,*" p. 49. According to some accounts, Chen was from a family of physicians, and while he was also competent in medicine, he earned his living by managing a publishing house/bookstore (*shufang* 書坊). Wang, "'*Huajing* zuozhe Chen Haozi kao' bian," p. 195.
48. Shen, "Lun Chen Haozi de *Huajing,*" p. 49.
49. Yi, "Jiaozhu *Huajing* yinyan," p. 5.
50. Yi, "Jiaozhu *Huajing* yinyan," p. 1.
51. Shen, "Lun Chen Haozi de *Huajing,*" p. 52; Yi, "Jiaozhu *Huajing* yinyan," p. 1.
52. Wylie, *Notes on Chinese Literature,* p. 120.
53. See for example, Yi, "Jiaozhu *Huajing* yinyan," p. 4.
54. Shanggu shanfang, *Huitu zengbu wanbao quanshu,* p. 52a; Shen, "Lun Chen Haozi de *Huajing,*" p. 50.
55. Shanggu shanfang, *Huitu zengbu wanbao quanshu,* p. 56a.
56. Shanggu shanfang, *Huitu zengbu wanbao quanshu,* p. 56b.
57. Shanggu shanfang, *Huitu zengbu wanbao quanshu,* p. 54a. In the upper register (what is generally considered to be the register with the less important material) above the section on plants, the supplement also includes an excerpt from the sixth *juan* of Chen's *Huajing,* namely "Qinshou linchong kao" 禽獸鱗蟲考 (Investigation of birds, animals, fish, insects). It describes the species, forms, habits, and ways of raising forty-five kinds of birds, animals, fish, and insects. *Huitu zengbu wanbao quanshu* titles this section "Yang shouniao fa" 養禽鳥法 (Methods for raising birds). The third to fifth *juan* further examine the names, form, habits and properties, growing place, use, and cultivation of flowers and trees. *Juan* 3 includes an important section on the classification of plants: "Huamu leikao" 花木類考 (Investigation of plant categories).

58. "Yihua zhuanduo fa," in Shanggu shanfang, *Huitu zengbu wanbao quanshu,* p. 57a; Shen, "Lun Chen Haozi de *Huajing,*" p. 50.

59. In Shanggu shanfang, *Huitu zengbu wanbao quanshu,* p. 54a; Shen, "Lun Chen Haozi de *Huajing,*" p. 50.

60. See, for example, *Xinbian Riyong wanquan xinshu, juan* 8, *ji* 16: "Nongye" 農業 (Agriculture); Saoye shanfang, *Riyong wanshi baoku choushi bixu,* vol. 14, *bian* 28: "Zhongzhi baoku" 種植寶庫 (Treasury of cultivating plants); *Jiating baike quanshu,* "Zhongzhi" 種植 (Cultivating plants).

61. See, for example, Saoye shanfang, *Riyong wanshi baoku choushi bixu,* vol. 14, *bian* 28: "Zhongzhi baoku."

62. On the global institutionalization of Linnaeus' system by the late nineteenth century, see Meng, *Shanghai and the Edges of Empire,* p. 55. The entry on "Yurui ji xipanlian" 玉蕊即西番蓮 (Jade stamen or passion flower) in *Zhiwuxue dacidian* references the *Huajing,* for example.

63. Wang, "'*Huajing* zuozhe Chen Haozi kao' bian,'" p. 191.

64. Ren, ed., *Zhongguo kexue jishu dianji tonghui.*

65. Shen, "Lun Chen Haozi de *Huajing,*" p. 50.

66. Shen, "Lun Chen Haozi de *Huajing,*" p. 50.

67. On insecticides, see Li Yuese (Joseph Needham), *Zhongguo kexue jishu shi,* pp. 401–402; cited in Shen, "Lun Chen Haozi de *Huajing,*" p. 51. I have not found anything corresponding to this quote in the original English text of Needham, where the *Huajing* is mentioned twice (pp. 596 and 617), but only in relation to the discussion of specific plants; see Daniels, Needham, and Menzies, *Science and Civilisation in China,* vol. 6: *Biology and Biological Technology,* part 3: *Agro-Industries and Forestry.*

68. Yi, "Jiaozhu *Huajing* yinyan," pp. 6–7.

69. Yi Qinheng, "Xiuding houji" 修訂後記 (Epilogue on the revised edition), in his *Huajing jiaozhuben,* p. 449; Pan, "Cheng Haozi de *Huajing* ji qi zai Riben de chuanbo," p. 315; Shen, "Lun Chen Haozi de *Huajing,*" p. 51, citing Needham. But the quotation does not seem to appear in the original version of this text.

70. Pan, "Cheng Haozi de *Huajing* ji qi zai Riben de chuanbo," p. 318.

71. Zhou, "Huajing," pp. 94–98.

72. On this tradition, see Yu Cuiling, "Bowu shuji: Zhong-Ri chuban jiaoliu yu zhishi wanghuan" 博物書籍：中日出版交流与知识往还 (Books on natural science: Sino-Japanese publication exchange and knowledge contacts), in his collection of essays, *Yinshua wenhua de chuanbao guiji,* pp. 149–153.

73. Zhou, "Huajing," p. 96.

74. Zhou, "Huajing," p. 97.

75. Zhou, "Huajing," p. 96.

76. The other seven topics are: composition of plays; production of plays; concubines' beauty and accomplishments; houses; furniture and objets d'art; food and drink; and health and pleasure. Hanan, *The Invention of Li Yu,* p. 28.

77. Zhou, "Huajing," p. 96.

78. Zhou, "Huajing," p. 97.

79. Zhou, "Huajing," p. 97.

80. Zhang, *Wanshi buqiuren.*

81. For a cogent discussion of these issues, see Chiang and Link, "Before the Revolution," pp. 49–51.

82. "Document 9: A ChinaFile Translation."

8 ◆ JANET Y. CHEN

In Search of a Standard National Language in Republican China

In the summer and autumn of 1926, visitors to the Sesquicentennial International Exposition in Philadelphia might have casually passed by an exhibit about Chinese education, set up in the Palace of Education and Social Economy. The pavilion was located in a lightly trafficked area, away from the more exciting amusements available elsewhere on the fairgrounds. Among the many entertainment options were boat rides to Treasure Island, a dance revue in a "Chinese Village," and replicas of the Taj Mahal and Mount Vernon.[1] Inside the Palace of Education, the American Eugenics Society's flamboyant booth dominated the scene, with flashing lights blaring warnings about the menace of "genetic mongrelization."[2] For visitors strolling past the stone lions flanking the display cases of the Chinese education exhibit, it would have been easy to overlook a bilingual time line, titled "DIAGRAM SHOWING THE EVOLUTION OF CHINESE FOR THE LAST FOUR MILLENIUMS" (sic) 國語四千年來變化潮流圖 (Guoyu siqian nian lai bianhua chaoliu tu). The poster delineated China's linguistic history, from the time of the legendary Yellow Emperor through the first part of the twentieth century.

The creator of the "diagram" was Li Jinxi 黎錦熙 (1890–1978), considered an authority on and a spokesperson for matters related to China's national language (guoyu 國語).[3] A dozen years earlier, as a young history instructor at Hunan First Normal School in Changsha, Li had encountered a student named Mao Zedong 毛澤東 (1893–1976). Much later in his career, Li would enjoy high stature as Chairman Mao's former teacher. In 1926, Li's reputation stemmed from the leading role he played in efforts to create and standardize the national language—as a member of the National Language Preparatory Committee, as an editor at Zhonghua Books in charge of the guoyu textbook division, and as a professor with academic appointments at several universities in Beijing. The historical chronology displayed in Philadelphia reflected Li's assessment of the project, as well as his vision for the future. For non-Chinese viewers, the poster emphasized the long history of Chinese civilization and its evolution. The message complemented the exposition's theme of progress and its commemoration of the 150th anniversary of the American Declaration of Independence. For a Chinese domestic audience, which Li addressed in two different published versions of the time line, he presented a forceful argument about the trajectory and meaning of linguistic change.[4] Concerning the latter, Li depicted an extended

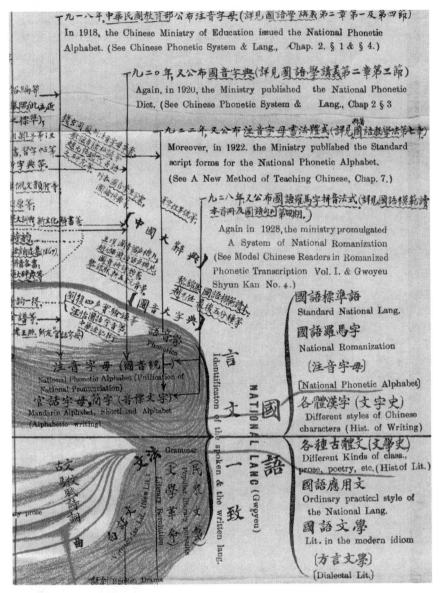

Figure 8.1. Li Jinxi, *Guoyu siqian nian lai bianhua chaoliu tu,* 1926.

process of historical development and the nation's linguistic heritage as converging upon one undated moment, circa 1924–1925 (Figure 8.1).

The progression registered moments of dramatic change, but largely without explanation—currents of "vernacular literature" culminating in a "literary revolution," and the emergence of a "national language" superseding the spoken medium of imperial officialdom (*guanhua* 官話, official language). A casual observer would not have intuited that between the lines of this apparently seamless chronology, there were enormous rifts in the project of "language unification." By reading between those lines, this chapter explores the tensions that were part and parcel of the process of linguistic change during the early decades of the twentieth century. I draw on techniques of New Sinology, with close attention to shifting linguistic, social, and material contexts, to reconsider the conventional wisdom about the history of China's national language. Whereas existing scholarship has emphasized script reform and the creation of the modern vernacular,[5] this study investigates the social effects and conflicts in the politics of speech standardization. Doing so reveals the instability of a national language in the infancy of formation.

The Currents of Change

For Li Jinxi and like-minded advocates for the national language, 1926 was a liminal moment. For more than a decade, the effort to create and standardize *guoyu* had alternately gained momentum and stalled. In 1913, the Education Ministry of the new Republican government had convened a Conference to Unify Pronunciation and invited eighty delegates to Beijing; the group's task was to determine a "national pronunciation" (*guoyin* 國音) and a phonetic notation system. Scholars (including Li Jinxi himself) have described the proceedings of the conference in detail: bickering that devolved into name calling and fistfights, and more than one hundred different phonetic notation systems put forward for consideration. Two successive chairmen—Wu Zhihui 吳稚暉 (1865–1953) and Wang Zhao 王照 (1859–1933)—quit in frustration before a third (Wang Pu 王璞, 1875–1929) finally corralled the unruly bunch and pushed through a compromise.[6] A public statement announced a new system of "national pronunciation," as reflected in approximately 6,500 characters and decided by majority voting. Northern speech patterns formed the basis for most of the sounds, but prominent elements of southern speech were included—for instance, three voiced initial consonants (万 / 兀 / 广) and a fifth tone (*rusheng* 入聲). A syllabary of thirty-nine signs made up the phonetic alphabet (*zhuyin zimu* 注音字母). The conference closed with the announcement of a seven-point implementation plan, which included: compilation of a dictionary of "national pronunciation"; a phonograph recording thereof; and teachers' compulsory use of *guoyu* as the medium of oral instruction.[7] By pushing through this compromise, however, the Conference to Unify Pronunciation sowed the seeds of contestation for years to come.

The debates became especially heated between 1919 and 1921, when primary schools and teacher training colleges were beginning to implement new curricular mandates, which shifted the battleground into the classroom. Among the contested issues: Which sounds and how many tones should constitute the "standard" for the "national pronunciation"? How should the phonetic alphabet be used pedagogically? Should *guoyu* be the exclusive medium of instruction in primary schools? How can students learn the national language if the teachers do not know how to speak it? Two main factions emerged—one for the "national pronunciation" (*guoyin* 國音) as it was determined by the 1913 conference, and the other for Beijinghua, or "Beijing/capital pronunciation" (北京話, also called *jingyin* 京音). The arguments were passionately fought, with heated exchanges in education journals and current affairs periodicals. Meanwhile, experts on either side proceeded to teach their version of spoken *guoyu* and to publish textbooks that professed a variety of views on its phonology. Adding to the muddle, two successive editions of a *Dictionary of National Pronunciation* appeared in 1919 and 1921 that featured inconsistent information.[8] Concurrently, two different phonograph recordings appeared for sale, both purporting to be models for pronunciation. One was made by Wang Pu in Shanghai (with Li Jinxi's help) in 1920, the other by Chao Yuen Ren 趙元任 (1892–1982) in New York City, a year later.[9] As Commercial Press founder Lufei Kui 陸費逵 (1886–1941) described it, the pages of school textbooks and journals revealed the linguistic chaos: "the vernacular writing has no fixed rules"; a hodgepodge of different varieties of *guanhua* intermingle with local speech (*tuhua* 土話). Citing the instructive experiences of Japan and Germany, Lufei opined that to "unify the national language is a colossal and monumentally difficult matter." Even with small populations, those two nations took many years to accomplish the goal, "much less China, with our 400 million people!" Progress would be slow, and in the interim, "it doesn't matter whether the pronunciation is entirely accurate or not"; likewise, mixing the classical with the vernacular and/or local dialects is fine—"it's a lot better than not knowing how to write at all."[10] As if to prove Lufei's point, to manage the competing phonologies, the *Guanhua zhuyin zimu bao* 官話注音字母報 (Phonetically annotated newspaper of the official language) adopted a dual notation system in December 1919. For six years the biweekly publication had spelled out the pronunciation of each character with *zhuyin zimu,* according to Beijing phonology, using interlinear phonetics to the right of the script. In the eighty-first issue, the paper switched to the "national pronunciation" (the hybrid standard created in 1913), an indication of its new allegiance to the *guoyin* camp. But in a conciliatory gesture, in cases where the two pronunciations differed, both were marked, on either side of the script.[11]

The uncertainty over the normative properties of the national language intensified when the Education Ministry announced a major policy change in 1920. Starting in the autumn term of that year, students in the first and second years of lower primary school would learn the written vernacular (*yutiwen* 語體文), replacing the literary language (*guowen* 國文). For the time being, students in grades three and above would continue to study the literary language. This mandate triggered another round of textbook revisions, as publishers in Shanghai rushed to produce new materials to conform to the revised curriculum.[12] Meanwhile, local education officials scrambled to find instructors capable of teaching both the spoken *guoyu* and the written vernacular. In Wuxi, the county magistrate instructed teachers to "temporarily follow the national pronunciation dictionary as the standard, so that in time unity may be achieved, and con-

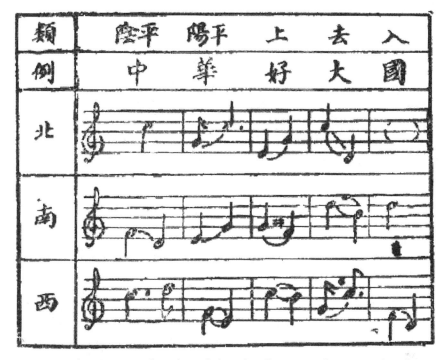

Figure 8.2. Chao Yuen Ren, "Wusheng de biaozhun," *Guoyu yuekan* 1, no. 8 (1922): 3.

fusion and fragmentation avoided."[13] Writing in *The Education Journal,* Shen Qi 沈圻 (dates unknown) observed that avid enthusiasm for studying the national language inspired hopes for the dawn of a new era.

> Yet what is the actual method for unifying the national language? There is blue-green *guanhua* [藍青官話], the language of the upper class of Beijing society, and what not. Which is actually to be the standard? There is Beijing pronunciation and national pronunciation, and what have you. Which is appropriate to use? Should the phonetic alphabet be revised, in part or in whole? When teaching the national language in primary schools, should the phonetic alphabet be learned first, later, or not at all? Should we learn or not learn the four tones? There are many questions but no consensus of opinion.[14]

The term "blue-green *guanhua,*" meaning neither entirely blue nor entirely green, referred to the hybrid quality of "official speech" mixed with local vernaculars, a situation that had long existed in the imperial era. Used by those who needed to communicate across dialect divides, its chief purpose was mutual intelligibility, with little concern for standardization. In contrast, as Shen declared, defining a clear standard was crucial to the national language unification project—a premise that his contemporaries largely agreed with, despite the lack of consensus about its specifications. "But since the standard has not yet been established, we can take, as a temporary standard, the language which is more common, or closer to the classical language."[15] Shen's improvisation here, inclined to opposite trajectories of the "common" and the "classical," could hardly solve the conundrum. In the long term, the temporary fixes generated further complications for the standardization effort.

How Many Tones?

Indeed, the inability of the experts and the educators to reach consensus about the pronunciation of the national language amplified the sense of disarray. For instance, in May of 1920, the National Language Unification Preparatory Committee voted to add a fortieth symbol (ㄜ) to the phonetic alphabet, an issue that had been under consideration for almost a year. At the same meeting, committee members also debated motions to revise or abandon the tones in the national pronunciation. In a proposal, Qian Xuantong 錢玄同 (1887–1939) asserted that tonal differentiation was "both completely impossible and completely unnecessary. . . . China should have a language that is much the same with minor differences, sufficient for mutual understanding." "Speech has its own natural tones," Qian added. "When speaking *guoyu,* Guangdong can use nine tones, eastern Zhejiang can use eight tones, Jiangsu can use seven, the southwest can use five, and the north can use four."

The Preparatory Committee did not go so far as to abolish the tones, but it did approve a motion that conceded: "In teaching the national pronunciation, it is not necessary to adhere rigidly to the tones."[16] In this decision, the committee concurred with Li Jinxi's flexible attitude toward tonal differentiation: "Let every person . . . mark the tones as he knows them, and he will not go wrong. . . . Moreover, the tones do not have significant bearing on the unification of pronunciation. When you speak, as long as the sound is correct in the pronunciation of the consonant, vowel, and medial, it is fine to use the tones of the local colloquial, or simply ignore them."[17] But rather than assuaging doubts, this accommodating approach fueled further disagreements. When Wu Zhihui visited Guangzhou in 1921 to deliver a series of lectures on the national language, one teacher publicly queried him on the issue, asking: the Ministry of Education identified five tones in 1918 (陰 / 平 / 陽 / 上 / 入) but "failed to specify which region's five tones should constitute the standard—why?" In response, Wu dismissed "the four tones" as an inconsequential artifact from the Six Dynasties period (220–589 CE), with "no great bearing on reality," certainly not worth the trouble to learn. Moreover, the notion of "the five tones" had been devised to placate the "old stubborns," who had threatened to "revolt" at the prospect of losing the fifth *rusheng* during previous deliberations on the phonology of *guoyu.* "The name [*rusheng*] was retained just to fool them. If you ask someone from the Ministry of Education to enunciate the fifth tone . . . even upon pain of death he could not do it."[18] In contrast to Wu Zhihui's scornful attitude, others rallied to the cause of tonal differentiation. For instance, Guo Houjue 郭後覺 (1895–1944), an editor at Zhonghua Books, offered an affirmative answer to the question: "Do tones actually have a function?"

Whereas Guo did not insist on any particular set of tones as normative, Chao Yuen Ren invoked the idea of a "standard five tones." At the same time, however, he accounted for the pitch variation of three major *guanhua* regions. Taking Beijing pronunciation as representative of the north, Nanjing for the south, and Chongqing for the west, he used musical notation to mark out the differences. Of the three, Chao considered Beijing pronunciation "the easiest to learn and the easiest to differentiate by ear."[19]

For his part, Yue Sibing 樂嗣炳 (1901–1984) differentiated between two types of *guoyu*. In the "crude" type, which Yue characterized as the ability to speak a few sentences of blue-green *guanhua* and write a few sentences of the vernacular *yutiwen*, there was "no need to be a stickler about the tones." For the "precise and exact" version of *guoyu*, tonal differentiation constituted an indispensable component of "the standard." Despite the doubts and suspicions many harbored, Yue averred that the "complex science" of establishing the standard, only in its "seedling" stage, awaited further research.[20] When some educators shared their research and analysis, however, a standard did not necessarily solidify. As veteran educator Fan Xiangshan 范祥善 (dates unknown) noted, "Opinions on the pronunciation of the five tones are not uniform." In his lectures on the phonetic alphabet (thirty-six lessons, published as a resource for middle-grade teachers), Fan explicated the five tones in detail. Yet he noted that some preferred to follow the old "four tones" (emphasizing the difference between the first and second); others adhered more closely to Beijing intonation (paying attention to the distribution of *rusheng* into the four other tones). Although Fan favored the latter method, "each approach has its own worthwhile aspects."[21]

In May of 1922, the Education Ministry approved and circulated a proposal from the Preparatory Committee to clarify "the method for marking the four tones of the phonetic alphabet." Despite the allusion to four, the system actually denoted five tones.[22] The directive also prompted more questions about the value or absurdity of tonal indicators for the phonetic alphabet, intertwining two sets of concerns, each with its own detractors. These issues came to the fore in a peculiar episode in the continuing tangle over pronunciation. The occasion was the forthcoming publication of *The Experimental Record of the Four Tones*, a study in speech phonetics by Liu Fu 劉復 (1891–1934),[23] a well-known scholar in the orbit of May 4th intellectual luminaries. Liu was then working toward his doctorate at the University of Paris. He conducted a series of phonetic experiments to measure pitch variations with an instrument of his own invention. The study featured twelve speakers from different dialect regions, recruited in Paris, to enunciate the eight tones of Guangzhou, the four (or five) tones of Chengdu, the four tones of Nanjing, and so on. In the introduction, Liu explained that the "four" in "four tones" did not imply a normative and should not be taken literally. In some places in China there are four tones, but in others five or eight—"for the sake of simplicity and convenience, I follow the old custom of loosely calling it four tones. This is not because I think that China has (or ought to have only) four tones."[24] After completing a draft of his book, he asked two prominent figures to contribute prefaces: Fu Sinian 傅斯年 (1896–1950),

then studying in London, and Wu Zhihui, who was directing the work-study program at the Sino-French Institute in Lyon.[25]

Fu Sinian largely obliged and sent a foreword with accolades.[26] Wu Zhihui, however, used the opportunity to launch a tirade, assailing the subject of the work as "useless rubbish" (*feiwu* 廢物) that belongs in a museum. Since Qian Xuantong ("a good friend of mine and Mr. Liu's") had already "declared war on the four tones . . . and pronounced a final death sentence," what was the point of this exercise? Although Liu's study had little to do with *zhuyin,* Wu vented: "The phonetic alphabet is just the phonetic alphabet. . . . Why have scholars dragged phonology and pronunciation techniques into it?" Embellished with accessories and ornaments, adding four tones here and five tones there, the phonetic alphabet ended up with "a bad case of indigestion." According to Wu, Liu Fu (an old friend) had asked him to write a "scholar's preface," not a laudatory puff piece, and to "interject differences of opinion freely." Wu certainly did not hold back; he penned a seventeen-page, handwritten diatribe, with glancing blows at the author. Liu Fu had "always been a believer in abolishing the four tones," Wu bristled—so why conduct research on something destined for the dustbin of history, with "no redeeming value whatsoever"? In short, "when the four tones are sent to the museum, Mr. Liu's *Experimental Record* can only accompany them as a narrative of their deeds."[27]

If Liu Fu felt offended by the disparaging substance or the tone of this rant, he did not say so. He chose to include Wu's preface in the publication and appended his own lengthy rejoinder. As a work of "research," Liu protested, his book did not advocate any particular position. Responding to Wu's caustic remarks about "adorning" the phonetic alphabet with tones, Liu maintained that the *zhuyin zimu* had nothing to do with the four tones. (On this issue, he said, we should simply shut our eyes and ignore those who are "kicking up a fuss.") As for the final verdict, "only the language itself has the prerogative to decide whether the four tones survive or not, it's not up to us." We may find many reasons to justify its demise, "but if it does not want to be eliminated, there is nothing we can do. Just like men's nipples. What function do they serve? Yet I have them, Xuantong has them, and Mr. Wu has them. The three of us actually cannot slice them off." Ultimately, even if the four tones are destined to become a gallery exhibit, "I will follow to study it in the museum."[28] As a coda to this exchange, Wu Zhihui added a final comment expressing his regret (sort of) for his taunting tone, "completely lacking a scholar's attitude." It was not much of an apology, however: "I can also imagine that my nonsense drivel of a preface will draw a lot of attention and discussion for Mr. Liu."[29]

In the Schools

This battle of words between old friends underscored the fractious debates over the basic features of the spoken national language. Yet despite the lack of consensus and the ambiguities, schools and local national language committees began implementation, even as the content of *what* to implement was still being debated. The process was predictably fraught, the results mixed. When Li Jinxi toured Jiangsu and Zhejiang in the winter of 1920–1921 to review the state of national language education, his companion Liu Ru 劉儒 (dates unknown) noted many inconsistencies. For example, some schools reported "no problems whatsoever" and some had *guoyu* classes conducted entirely in the local dialect. Some had tried to incorporate the *zhuyin zimu* but gave up in frustration; in others, the classical language continued to reign supreme. In short, positive news overlapped with disheartening evidence of inertia.[30] Two years later, the Jiangsu Provincial Education Association solicited feedback from its members, specifically requesting comments about "difficulties encountered" in school settings. The most common refrain in the responses converged on the opposition of families to the national language, with several permutations. In some cases, the resistance centered on the change from the classical curriculum to one based on the vernacular. In other instances, the new spoken *guoyu* provoked the ire of parents who viewed it as "strange and distant" from their own speech. Some evidently associated the national pronunciation with soldiers from the north, who were roaming the countryside during the intermittent civil wars of the time. In a form of guilt by association, the predatory behavior of these militia gangs prejudiced popular sentiment against *guoyu*. Influenced by such antagonistic attitudes, it was no wonder that "students have no interest in the national language." Indeed, parental disapproval could be acute, to the extent of withdrawing their children from school altogether. (One primary school reported an attrition rate of one-third after three years of trying to implement the national language.) As for the teachers, the lack of social support for the national language inevitably undermined their commitment. From the outset, they found *guoyu* "difficult to learn and difficult to teach." They had many questions but found few answers. Is it permissible to teach *guoyu* using dialect? What is the place of the phonetic alphabet in the curriculum? Since the government did not follow up or otherwise check on progress—and with clear evidence that "society does not believe in it"—most chose to abdicate responsibility for the national language.[31]

Other accounts from Jiangsu corroborated these developments, and also referred to geographical differences. In Wu County, for instance, schools in the metropolitan areas reportedly "tried their best" to implement the Education Ministry's directive in the fall of 1920. The Number Two Primary School in Xuguan encountered few obstacles and even "garnered the approval of many people." The results were not uniformly successful in urban areas, but it was not for lack of effort. In the rural districts, however, the teachers did nothing, purportedly out of fear or ignorance ("they sat on the city walls and watched the battle"). Some dared not challenge parents, out of consideration for keeping their "rice bowls." Others had no idea how to teach the national language, as they did not even know what it was. Finally, a cohort of teachers disapproved of the change to *guoyu* due to the enduring grip of "old ideology."[32]

And so the saga continued, with efforts to teach the new spoken *guoyu* entangling with misgivings about pedagogy and phonology, or intersecting with doubts about the national language project. Was *guoyu* to exist in tandem with—or in place of—the classical language in the school curriculum? For teachers and school administrators on the front lines of education, the question transcended intellectual debates to encompass practical issues—what to teach, and how? Moreover, the shaky fiscal basis for local education in a time of civil war meant that many schools struggled just to remain open, much less enact radical changes. Indeed, few could spare the resources needed to implement a national language curriculum, as Wu Zhihui observed. Advocates have "shouted until their lips are parched and their voices are hoarse"; the message has certainly spread to all in the education realm. In the absence of adequate funding and qualified teachers, however, at best there might be one instructor in a school for spoken *guoyu,* as an add-on to *guowen* classes—"treated as if it were a foreign language," disconnected from the other parts of the curriculum.[33] Perhaps the agenda had been overly ambitious, attempting too much all at once. Writing from Nanhui 南匯 County, one commentator claimed that in "hinterland" regions where local speech diverged significantly from *guoyu,* to demand primary school students learn the "national language" and the "national pronunciation" simultaneously verged on the impossible. "In my opinion," he stated, "we should not attach equal importance to both." Rather than insist on rigorous adherence to a national pronunciation, the priority should focus on achieving uniformity in the written language. In short, "when one speaks the national language, it is not necessary to use the national pronunciation."[34]

As these accounts indicate, the attempt to "unify the national language" introduced new fault lines of fragmentation. In 1923, the annual report of the Wuxi County Education Association delivered a blistering assessment. Enumerating "the reasons why the national language cannot be unified," Wu Meng 吳蒙 (dates unknown) observed that at all levels of education (normal, middle, and primary schools), few paid attention to *guoyu*. With teachers speaking in a blue-green *guanhua,* the students end up learning "a language that is neither donkey nor horse." The author pinned the blame for this woeful state of affairs on three groups. Among scholars, enmity between "the old school" and the "new literature" factions generated unequivocal opposition and mutual antipathy. In the publishing world, profiteers made cosmetic changes to existing products and repackaged them for sale as "national language textbooks." In government, the bureaucrats above espoused "empty words," while the local officials below evinced apathy. After seven years of promoting the national language, "there is virtually no achievement to speak of. This is truly a disgrace." To reverse the lack of faith in the national language, in schools and society at large, would require a colossal effort. But only by doing so might there be "some hope for a unified national language in ten years' time. Otherwise, forget about ten years, even after a hundred years it would be difficult to achieve progress!"[35] As Huang Zheng'an 黃正厂 (dates unknown) sarcastically observed, the warring factions, "having fought to the point of heads crushed and blood flowing," were taking a break out of exhaustion. But the cease-fire had not settled the question of what constituted the standard—the former antagonists are "only muddled together, not unifying."[36]

In 1925 the combatants in this round of the language wars called a truce—not because they had reconciled their differences, but because of an external enemy who emerged on the scene, in the person of a new minister of education. Zhang Shizhao 章士釗 (1881–1973) ordered the restoration of the Confucian classics to the school curriculum, in effect reversing changes that national language advocates had fought for and over.[37] Confronting this new foe, the former rivals put aside their differences, which now seemed trivial. Li Jinxi characterized the newly forged battle as a "defensive war." Writing in early 1926, Li averred that although Zhang Shizhao had set out to "destroy" the national language, he could not single-handedly reverse the tide. Despite many "casualties," Li believed that the national language would ultimately prevail.[38]

Four Thousand Years and Counting

When the Chinese Association for the Advancement of Education commissioned Li Jinxi to create a display for the Sesquicentennial International Exposition in 1926, these battle wounds were still fresh. Moreover, the upheaval created by a prolonged period of civil war meant that the political authority needed to implement educational reforms, and the financial resources to support them, were at best tenuous. Yet the genealogy Li produced made no explicit reference to any of the controversies discussed above, or to the instability of both the language and its nation. The upper half of the 4,000-year time line portrays the seamless evolution of *wenzi* 文字, rendered as "written characters and spoken language" in the corresponding English. The lower half addresses the development of *wenxue* 文學, or "literature and style of writing." As Li later explained, the series of red columns delineated periodization, progressing from the quasi-historical age of the sage-kings through the early 1920s. Using green ink, he charted the "currents and trends," so that one could discern the origins and development of the Chinese language "at a glance," with a particular emphasis on "the influence of outside trends" and "the power of popular literature."[39] As the two trajectories of *wenzi* and *wenxue* evolved over time, each splintered into multiple streams. For instance, sometime in the tenth century BCE, "the written and spoken idioms" began to diverge. In parallel, the "literature of the aristocracy" and the "literature of the people" separated as two branches. By the early twentieth century, the proliferation of new forms and styles, intersecting with foreign influences, emerged as waves of change, all flowing toward the unification of the written and the spoken language (see Figure 8.1, above). Li labeled the climax of this process "identification of the spoken and the written language" (*yanwen yizhi* 言文一致), which in the next step materialized as the "national language." At a glance, then, the pictorial representation of the Chinese language over four millennia suggests that despite the vicissitudes of time and the numerous divisive episodes, the nation's rich linguistic heritage ultimately merged into a singular moment of unity.

It is impossible to know definitively how much the 1926 display version differed from the edition published in Beijing the same year. By Li's later description, before publication he added the titles of major reference works and "important classics, authors, and works" for each period.⁴⁰ Rendered in vivid blue ink, these details populated the empty spaces on the poster, further amplifying the narrative of a bountiful heritage. Apart from these additions, whether Li made other changes to the published edition is unknown. More to the point, the impression of viewing the poster from afar, in an exhibition booth, would have differed significantly from purchasing a copy and studying it closely. Indeed, upon more careful scrutiny, the diagram inscribes somewhat ambiguous messages about the emergence of the national language in the twentieth century. For each of the three government directives—promulgating the *zhuyin zimu* phonetic alphabet (1918), publishing the national phonetic dictionary (1920), and standardizing the script forms for the *zhuyin zimu* (1922), respectively—Li instructs the reader to consult his published works, which he had in fact deployed as ammunition in the battles described above. A note appended to a chart in the uppermost right quadrant hints at a disjuncture between the "old" and the "standard" pronunciation, which had also been a hotly contested issue.⁴¹ The author appears to privilege Guoyu Luomazi 國語羅馬字 (Gwoyeu Romatzyh, known as GR) as the preferred system of phonetic notation, a provocative position asserted without explanation.⁴² Visually, as the torrents of linguistic change in the published time line swirl into riptides after the turn of the twentieth century, a nascent "national language" absorbs them. Two tiny rivulets emerge out of the crucible, with much left behind, relegated to the past.⁴³ Finally, after the decisive moment of unity, the national language immediately splinters into six major components, with two additional subparts:

- Standard National Language 國語標準語
- National Romanization 國語羅馬字
  (National Phonetic Alphabet) 注音字母
- Different styles of Chinese characters (history of writing) 各體漢字 (文字史)
- Different kinds of classics, prose, poetry, etc. (history of literature) 各種古體文 (文學史)
- Ordinary practical style of the National Language 國語應用文
- Literature in the modern idiom 國語文學
  (Dialectal literature) 方言文學

To an undiscerning passerby in Philadelphia or to a reader of the Beijing publication, it would not be immediately obvious that each of these components constituted a major battleground. But to those with even cursory knowledge of the radical changes being debated or the transformations occurring in the 1920s, it was rather disingenuous, if not downright misleading, to claim that the new literature of the vernacular, the status of the classics, the styles of Chinese characters, and a standardized national language were settled matters. Indeed, the legendary struggles over vernacular literature, now part of the iconic narrative of the birth of "modern Chinese literature," were being fought in the trenches of intellectual circles. Li was certainly aware of a recent book-burning incident, when a meeting of primary school educators (from three provinces, convening in Wuxi) culminated in a bonfire to destroy classical language textbooks.[44] No stranger to the disputes, Li had been embroiled in arguments over alphabetization and calls for a "script revolution" that provoked passionate polemics.[45] More generally, the project of creating a standardized national language had certainly proved to be more contentious than expected.

By the time the second edition of the "Diagram Showing the Evolution of Chinese" appeared, three years later in 1929, the national language project had the backing of a new central government. When Chiang Kai-shek unified China under Nationalist rule in 1927, the new regime provided a centralizing force for efforts to create a national language and make it a reality. Its future thus seemed secure, even if the phonological specifications of its spoken form were not definitively settled. Through the National Language Unification Preparatory Committee (reconvened in 1928 with Wu Zhihui as the chairman) and newly reconstituted agencies at the provincial and local levels, the KMT's Ministry of Education attempted to repair the damage from the previous decade of linguistic combat. The textbooks for national language instruction were a mess of conflicting approaches and contradictory information; the suspension of hostilities between the "national" and "Beijing pronunciation" factions had not definitively resolved the issue.[46] Given a new mandate by the KMT government, the Preparatory Committee set out to revise (again) the *Dictionary of National Pronunciation,* compile teaching materials, scrutinize the state of pedagogy in schools, and formulate strategies for "promoting the unification of the national language."[47] At the same time, although advocates of *guoyu* shared aspirations for achieving linguistic unity, they found themselves once again at odds over competing priorities: improving literacy, standardizing the spoken language, or attempting to pursue both goals simultaneously.

This was the context in which the second edition of Li Jinxi's time line appeared. It once again glossed over the disagreements, and instead proclaimed an unabashedly optimistic future for the national language agenda.[48] In a brief introductory note, Li explained that in using the term *guoyu,* he intended to invoke a "broad and general meaning . . . encompassing 4,000 years of changes in written characters and spoken language," as well as "the origin and development of literary schools." Beyond the details, Li stated, "However, my main point is the diagram's twentieth-century column, where with big waves of controversy there is a breakthrough from the world of the classical language . . . to converge in a large pool. Clearing the way and looking ahead, the six final components will build the future of the national language!" In presenting a linear narrative untroubled by disagreement, the revised time line erased two points of uncertainty: it expunged the allusion to an "old" pronunciation and explained the status of Guoyu Luomazi. Li's reference to the Education Ministry's designation of GR as "A System of National Romanization" did not, however, make clear its features or its relationship to the *zhuyin zimu* system. His pictorial representation, in fact, consigned *zhuyin* to a subordinate position—but according to the official directive, GR was to be the "secondary" system to *zhuyin.*

The most substantive modification in the revised time line filled in a formerly blank section with a chart reproducing the phonetic romanization system "by Matteo Ricci (an Occidental of the Ming Dynasty)."

Standardizing the Standard

Despite Li Jinxi's sanguine predictions of smooth sailing, the next decade proved to be turbulent for the fate of the national language. Since the phonology of Beijinghua constituted the basis for GR, the Education Ministry's endorsement thereof in effect affirmed northern speech as the standard pronunciation. This, however, did not match the original syllabary of the *zhuyin zimu*. Furthermore, despite Li's forecast of a peaceful coexistence of the two phonetic notation systems, detractors roundly criticized GR for its complexity, and especially for the insinuation that it could or would replace the Chinese script.[49] In practical terms, having two phonetic systems, both sanctioned for pedagogical and official use, stoked the anxieties of educators already unsure about the place of *zhuyin* in the curriculum, or vexed about the relationship of the phonetic to the script. In 1930, a government mandate addressed this issue by demoting the phonetic alphabet from *zimu* 字母 (alphabet) to *fuhao* 符號 (notation). By reinforcing its auxiliary status, the change signaled that phonetics were intended to function only as a guide to pronunciation, not to replace the script. "Calling it *zimu* has created misunderstanding and errors; therefore it should be changed to *fuhao,* so that the name will correspond to its true purpose."[50] Billed as "the cooperation of *zhuyin* and Hanzi," proponents hoped the change would facilitate mass education and improve literacy.[51]

Yet these efforts to set the national language on a firmer footing sowed more confusion—"the old pronunciation is no longer appropriate to use, but the new pronunciation has nothing to rely on."[52] For instance, which and how many *zhuyin* letters constituted the new standard pronunciation? Although the ascendance of Beijing phonology effectively rendered three of the forty phonemes irrelevant, the phonetic chart remained unchanged. Asterisks denoted the "dialect" status of 万, 兀, and 广 in some publications. In other instances, instructional manuals and dictionaries continued to characterize the system as consisting of forty letters, or described the fifth tone as an acceptable part of the national pronunciation.[53] In one particularly baffling iteration, a *zhuyin* handbook issued by the Ministry of Education enumerated forty symbols, but gave the following garbled explanation in lessons five and six:

> The number of annotation symbols is really quite small.
> In total there are only forty.
> We can divide them up to memorize.
> Not even seven or eight per day.
> In five days you will have memorized more than half.
> Then one more day and only three remain.
> Eliminate those three, but the rest you will memorize completely.

Have you got it down cold? Try to recite them.
How many times?
Once is not enough, do it twice.

The lesson concluded with a phonetic chart showing a syllabary of thirty-seven. A follow-up in lesson nine clarified that the new version of national pronunciation omitted three phonemes, but they could be used to "spell out the sounds of local vernaculars."[54]

During this period of transition, authoritative explanations were not consistently updated to correspond to changing linguistic standards. As Li Jinxi later commented, "the name remained but the reality had perished."[55] To begin the process of implementing the new standard, the Education Ministry issued an order in the spring of 1930, adding the spoken component to the existing menu of directives aimed at promoting the national language:

> The former instructions emphasized the written aspect and did not mention the language that the teacher should use as the medium of instruction. The pedagogy of the national language requires, on the one hand, the use of *yutiwen,* and on the other hand, the use of *guoyu* as the medium of instruction. In this way, what students read and hear will converge.... For this reason it is decreed that all middle and primary school teachers, within the scope of what is possible, should use "language that approximates standard *guoyu*" as the language of instruction.

To conclude, the ministry preemptively scolded teachers for both harboring erroneous assumptions and invoking them as excuses for inaction. Some paid only lip service to the national language and persisted in using local dialects to teach, claiming that the children cannot understand otherwise. Still others refused to speak *guoyu* for fear of embarrassment. This was the wrong attitude, the directive from Nanjing admonished, for "the so-called national language ... cannot avoid impurity"; it is inevitably a form of "southern tunes and northern tones." Although not ideal or satisfactory, "using impure *guoyu* as the language of instruction is still much better than using local dialects." Teachers must understand that the more practice they have in speaking, the more proficient they will become. "If you avoid speaking because of embarrassment, how will you improve in the future?"[56]

The Preparatory Committee also tried to reorganize the basis of the "national language" with the publication of a new pronunciation dictionary in 1932. The product of several years of revision and delays, the *Guoyin changyong zihui* 國音常用字彙 (Commonly used vocabulary of national pronunciation) reflected the shifting linguistic terrain.[57] In a long explanatory preface, the editors described the major changes incorporated into the new work: the inclusion of both *zhuyin* and GR for phonetic notation, and the shift to "Beiping pronunciation" as the standard phonology. The pocket-sized volume numbered merely seventy-six pages. To correct the contents of the 1921 edition to correspond to "Beiping pronunciation" was a vast undertaking, "not something that can be completed in a short time.... The present volume selects the most commonly used words, in order to meet the urgent need" for a new pronunciation dictionary.[58] In the prefatory remarks, the editors especially underscored the point that "the national pronunciation is not the same as taking the entirety of Beiping pronunciation." For example, the fifth *rusheng* tone "should be preserved" for both historical reasons and the needs of contemporaries. In regions where local speech depended on the fifth tone, making it difficult to "change over completely," the editors agreed that temporarily retaining "local tones" was acceptable. In addition, R-suffixation (the tongue-curling *er*-sound ubiquitous in northern phonology) was minimized and treated as an optional feature.[59]

Although *The Commonly Used Vocabulary of National Pronunciation* presented officially sanctioned parameters for spoken *guoyu*, previously published textbooks—based on the "old national pronunciation"—remained in circulation throughout the 1930s. Adding to the disarray, some savvy authors and publishers had anticipated the change and released "new national pronunciation" reference works, even before the authoritative guide appeared.[60] The contents thus varied and conflicted—with some obvious discrepancies, but others discernible only to those who painstakingly compared them, line by line. Indeed, one educator calculated that the difference between the "old" and the "new" constituted about 10 percent of the phonemic inventory. "Those who are studying the national pronunciation should make a comparative study of the new and old standard pronunciation, so that they can thoroughly understand the differences. Otherwise, when you see one book annotated in one way, and another book annotated in another way, you will be at a loss."[61] Although some faulted "unscrupulous marketers ... who only care about profits" for this situation, it was truly difficult to correlate the enormous output of published materials to the shifting standard. As a result, books featuring the "new" national pronunciation and those featuring the "old" were used in tandem.[62] In 1930, the education bureau in Kaifeng conducted an audit, instructing bookstores in the city to submit for inspection all *zhuyin* publications offered for sale. With the proliferation of such guides, "old and new are all mixed together." The auditors demanded verification as to whether they "correspond to the standard pronunciation and whether they contain errors."[63] Several years after the implementation of the new standard, complaints still abounded—of teachers directing their students to use obsolete editions of the dictionary, and of confusion about what constituted the features of standard pronunciation.[64]

Whither the National Language?

In the 1920s, the potent idea of a national language emerged as one of the pillars of modern Chinese nationalism. Although the experts could hardly agree on the specific content of *guoyu*, at a conceptual level those involved in the project's creation shared hopes that a unified language would strengthen China. In their aspiration, they often portrayed "Mandarin" as a coherent and preexisting entity, or as developing along a path leading to linguistic unity. Li Jinxi's time line visually narrated this teleology, mapping the development of the national language as moving inexorably toward a future of harmonious and unified purpose. Confident about the trajectory of the Chinese language, Li erased a recent past rife with conflicts. As he corralled the dissenting opinions into a single wave, his chronology rewrote the history of linguistic change as irreversible and untroubled by controversy. Li's intervention was not simply fantasy or prevarication, though there were elements of both. His "Diagram of Four Thousand Years" performed a didactic and epistemological function by naturalizing the history of the Chinese language, and by depicting *guoyu* as the inevitable outcome.[65]

Left unanswered, however, was the question of how long it would take to reach the promised land. Throughout the 1920s, those imagining a future of linguistic unity often hypothesized about the timetable for completing the quest. Such speculations, of course, depended on the goals imputed to the national language, varying definitions of standardization, as well as expectations about the relative strength or weakness of political authority. In 1925, for instance, speaking at the Conference of the National Language Movement, Lufei Kui had voiced the expectation that "the day of success will inevitably arrive . . . if we work hard, after a certain number of years there will surely be great achievements in national language unification." For the same occasion, Chao Yuen Ren (music) and Li Jinxi (lyrics) composed a commemorative song:[66]

> Today, after ten years, the national language movement can be considered a success
> Today the sun rises in the east
> Shining completely red over the national phonetic alphabet
> The blind can see, the deaf can hear
> Our national language has spread to the common people. . . .
> Movement, success!
> After ten years, the national language movement cannot yet be considered a success
> Today the sun rises slowly
> Shining faintly red over the national phonetic alphabet
> Quickly, strike the bell that heralds the dawn
> Awaken from the intoxicated dream
> When our national language has spread to the common people
> Only then will the movement be considered a success. . . .

With the first verse trumpeting the fruition of the movement, and the second characterizing it as an unfulfilled dream, the song underscored the incongruity embedded in assessments of the national language project. Had they accomplished all that they set out to do? Or has the journey only begun? From a longer-term view, would the ultimate realization of linguistic unification take a century, five hundred years, or a millennium? In some respects, Li Jinxi did not think that a specific time frame mattered. In 1930 he recalled that Wu Zhihui once forecast a timetable of a millennium for alphabetization, while Qian Xuantong had predicted it would take a century for China to jettison its script. "Taking the average,

I would say it will take five hundred years.... A hundred years would be fine, a little less is fine as well—it depends on our effort." But regardless of effort or intention, "everything in the world is apt to change, none more so than the language and writing system of a nation. Even if you do not want it to, it will change. This is a fundamental principle."[67] With a will of its own, the force of linguistic change would overcome every obstacle and surmount all challenges. As the dream of linguistic unification in China unfolded across a half century of war and revolution, these claims and assumptions would be tested in the years to come.[68]

Notes

1. *Philadelphia, the Birthplace of Liberty.*
2. Keels, *Sesqui!*, pp. 154–155, 167–169.
3. The twentieth-century incarnation of the term *guoyu* 國語 was a neologism from Japanese, meaning "national language." In the Qing dynasty, *guoyu* referred to Manchu as the language of the state.
4. Li, *Guoyu siqian nian lai bianhua chaoliu tu.* There are at least five extant copies of the 1926 edition in various libraries and seven copies of the 1929 version. The two editions are the same size, measuring 108 cm × 79 cm, folded and encased in fabric binders.
5. DeFrancis, *Nationalism and Language Reform in China;* Wang, *Shengru xintong;* Kaske, *The Politics of Language in Chinese Education, 1895–1919.* Kaske's study ends in 1919, while this essay focuses on developments in the 1920s and 1930s.
6. Li, *Guoyu yundong shigang, juan 2,* pp. 50–62; DeFrancis, *Nationalism and Language Reform,* pp. 55–59; Kaske, *The Politics of Language,* chapter 6. For a linguistic analysis, see VanNess Simmons, "Whence Came Mandarin?," pp. 63–88.
7. Kaske, *The Politics of Language,* p. 413; Li, *Guoyu yundong shigang,* p. 57.
8. Duyin tongyihui, comp., *Guoyin zidian;* Duyin tongyihui, comp., *Jiaogai guoyin zidian.*
9. There are no surviving copies of Wang Pu's phonograph recording, only the companion textbook: Dong, ed., *Zhongghua guoyin liusheng jipian keben.* A digitized version of Chao Yuen Ren's recording is in the Rulan Chao Pian Collection, Chinese University of Hong Kong, cataloged as *Jiu guoyu liushengpian* 舊國語留聲片. The companion textbook is *Guoyu liushengpian keben.*
10. Lufei, "Xiaoxuexiao guoyu jiaoshou wenti," pp. 1–7.
11. *Guanhua zhuyin zimu bao,* front matter. A year later, the publication jettisoned *guanhua* (official language) in its title to be renamed *Phonetically Annotated Newspaper for the National Language* (*Guoyu zhuyin zimu bao* 國語注音字母報).
12. Ministry of Education order, January 12, 1920, *Zhengfu gongbao* 政府公報, no. 1409 (January 15, 1920), *gongwen* 公文; Culp, "Teaching *Baihua,*" pp. 18–19.
13. *Shenbao* 申報, March 6, 1920, p. 7.
14. Shen, "Ruhe kewei xiaoxue guoyu jiaoshi," pp. 1–8.
15. Shen, "Ruhe kewei xiaoxue guoyu jiaoshi."
16. Qian Xuantong 錢玄同 explained this in detail in a long essay written in 1922. See Gao, *Gao Yuan guoyin xue,* pp. 6–7.
17. Li, *Guoyu xue jiangyi, shangpian* 5–6, pp. 13–14. Li initially published these lectures as a lengthy article in the journal *Minduo* 民鐸 (no. 6, May 1919, pp. 53–76), which Mao Zedong praised as "brilliant" (Mao, "Letter to Li Jinxi").
18. Wu, "Zhuyin zimu de taolun." This exchange appeared in the Guangzhou newspaper *Qunbao* 群報 in May 1921; *New Youth* magazine subsequently reprinted the letters. On the lin-

guistic history of the five tones in the Ming–Qing period, see VanNess Simmons, "Whence Came Mandarin?"

19. Guo, "Shengdiao jiujing you meiyou yongchu," pp. 5–6; Chao, "Wusheng de biaozhun," pp. 1–4. Chao's article was written in 1921 and was intended for publication elsewhere. By the time it appeared in the *National Language Monthly* journal a year later, Chao was in the United States. Thus, the editor emphasized that this was a piece of "old writing" and that the author had not been consulted about its publication.

20. Yue, "Zenyang yanjiu guoyu de shengdiao," pp. 1–5. Yue was the chief editor of the journal *National Language Monthly*.

21. Fan, *Zhuyin zimu jiangyi,* pp. 45–49.

22. *Jiaoyu gongbao* 教育公報 9, no. 5 (1922): *gongdu* 26. The first tone (陰平) is unmarked, with dots placed at the four corners for second, third, fourth, and fifth tone.

23. Liu, *Sisheng shiyan lu.* An article in 1922 provided a preview of the book; "Sisheng shiyan lu tiyao," pp. 1–4. Before going to Paris, Liu Fu (courtesy name Liu Bannong 劉半農) taught for a time at Beijing University and was credited with inventing the female pronoun 她.

24. Liu, *Sisheng shiyan lu,* p. 1.

25. Wu's tenure in Lyon (1921–1922) was difficult, punctuated by a riot in September 1921 that resulted in the deportation of more than a hundred Chinese students. The rabble-rousers included future leaders of the Chinese Communist Party such as Li Lisan 李立三 (1899–1967) and Cai Hesen 蔡和森 (1895–1931). See Levine, *The Found Generation,* pp. 121–130.

26. Fu, "Wei Liu Fu '*Sisheng shiyan lu*' zuoxu." Fu's preface is complimentary but a little odd. In the conclusion Fu writes that Liu had specifically asked him to discuss several points, but that he had forgotten them.

27. Wu, "Xu" 序 (Preface). For correspondence between Wu and Liu on this matter, see letters in Wu Zhihui Papers, KMT Party Archives (Taipei), files 08290, 02893, 02895.

28. Liu, "Xuzhui," pp. 19–25. Liu refers to a letter he wrote to Qian Xuantong, in which he had already expressed these sentiments about the vestigial utility of anatomical parts.

29. Wu, "Shu xuhou hou." Liu's book did not attract widespread attention, possibly due to the opaque and technical discussions of phonology. He did gain posthumous acclaim as a pioneer who "solved the four tones question," a topic in Chinese phonology that had eluded understanding for 1,500 years; see Bai, "Dao Liu Bannong xiansheng," pp. 13–15. Subsequent reprint editions of the book omitted the prefatory essays.

30. Liu, "Kaocha guoyu jiaoyu biji," pp. 1–5.

31. Yue, "Jiangsu sheng jiaoyuhui suo zhengji guoyu jinxing kunnan wenti de yijian."

32. Wang, "Xuguan dier xiao xuexiao 'guoyu jinxing' shang de dalüe baogao he di'er nian suo faxian de liangge kunnan wenti."

33. Wu, "Shanghai guoyu shifan xuexiao faqi xuanyan."

34. Wang, "Xiaoxue guoyu jiaoxue duiyu yanwen yizhi he duyin tongyi buneng binzhong." In 1924 the author considered Nanhui County part of "the hinterland" (*neidi* 內地); today it is in the Shanghai metropolitan area (Pudong).

35. Wu, "Guoyu buneng tongyi de yuanyin." An inspector's report in 1925 praised Wuxi County education authorities for their "earnest" efforts. When Liu Ru visited twenty-seven of the 206 schools in the county, he found that "a minority" still adhered to the classical language. The others had switched to "the national language," even if taught using local dialects or with inaccurate pronunciation (*Jiangsu jiaoyu gongbao* 江蘇教育公報 8, no. 2 [1925]: 27–35).

36. Zheng'an, "Biaozhunyu yu guoyu biaozhun." A teacher by training, Huang joined the national language textbook division of Zhonghua Books in 1923 and worked under Li Jinxi.

37. Compared to others, Zhang Shizhao's five-month tenure (July 28 to December 31, 1925) as minister of education was relatively long. In the revolving door of the Beiyang government, some officials lasted only a few weeks.

38. Li, "1925 nian guoyu jie 'fangyu zhan' jilüe." Li sent an impassioned letter to the minister of education in protest; see *Zhonghua jiaoyujie* 中華教育界 15, no. 7 (January 1926): appendix 1–5.

39. Li, *Guoyu siqian nian lai bianhua chaoliu tu* (1929 edition).

40. See explanatory note on the lower left-hand corner of the 1929 edition.

41. For the character 禾, the pronunciation is marked as ㄏㄨㄛ (*huo* in present-day *pinyin*), with the note: "the *guoyu* standard pronunciation should be ㄏㄜ; this chart follows the old pronunciation."

42. In a brief note in the lower left quadrant, Li used GR spelling to render the place of publication as "Beeijing," and to thank Jaw Yuanrenn (趙元任), Yiguu Shyuantorng (錢玄同, using Qian's newly adopted pseudonym 疑古), and Liou Bannnong (劉半農, or Liu Fu) for their consultation. The most unique feature of GR is "tonal spelling," which embedded the tone of each syllable within its spelling. For an early explanation, see Chao, "Guoyu Luomazi de yanjiu," pp. 87–117.

43. My thanks to Joachim Kurtz for pointing out how tiny these streams are.

44. Li, "Sansheng shixiao lianhehui fenmie chuxiao wenyan jiaokeshu zhi xuanyan." Li wrote about the incident, which occurred in December 1925, in "1925 nian guoyu jie 'fangyu zhan' jilu."

45. Li contributed a lengthy article to a special issue of the *National Language Monthly* journal (*Guoyu yuekan*, July 1922) devoted to discussions of the "Hanzi revolution" (漢字改革). A follow-up issue focused on the alphabetization question, for which Li wrote the preface (*Guoyu yuekan*, August 1924).

46. Between 1925 and 1926 several subcommittees of the Preparatory Committee passed resolutions to amend the standard pronunciation in favor of northern phonology. According to Li Jinxi's later account, "six committee members" (including himself) effectively pushed through the change, which was not officially promulgated until 1932 (see below).

47. "Guoyu tongyi choubei weiyuanhui guicheng" 國語統一籌備委員會規程 (Rules for the National Language Unification Preparatory Committee) (December 1928), in Li, *Guoyu yundong shigang*, pp. 191–192.

48. The advertised price for the 1929 edition was five *jiao*, comparable to other national language reference works.

49. The antipathy would intensify in the "new script" controversies of the late 1930s, with the emergence of Latinxua Xin Wenz as another competing system of alphabetization. See Wong, "The Chinese Latinization Movement, 1917–1958"; Zhong, *Chinese Grammatology*.

50. "Jiaoyubu xunling" 教育部訓令 (Instruction of the Education Ministry) (May 1930), in Li, *Xinzhu guoyu jiaoxue fa*, appendix 2.

51. Chen, "Zhuyin fuhao yu minzhong jiaoyu."

52. Ma, *Xinjiu guoyin bianyi*, preface.

53. Ma, *Guoyu zhuyin fuhao fayin zhinan*, pp. 7–8; Mu, *Guoyu fayin ji wenfa*, pp. 8–10, 32; Mu, "Zenyang xuexi guoyu?" p. 21.

54. Jiaoyubu, ed., *Zhuyin fuhao chuanxi xiaoce*, pp. 5, 45–47, 50.

55. Li, *Guoyu yundong shigang*, p. 90.

56. *Jiaoyubu gongbao* 教育部公報 2, no. 11 (March 16, 1930): 21–23. This directive was sent to all subsidiary provincial and municipal education agencies, and subsequently forwarded to schools for implementation (Chongqing Municipal Archive, 130/1/11, pp. 228–229; *Zhejiang jiaoyu xingzheng zhoukan* 浙江教育行政週刊 30 [March 24, 1930]: 6–7).

57. In 1927, Li Jinxi wrote to Wu Zhihui that the dictionary revision was nearly complete. Li, Qian Xuantong, and Chao Yuen Ren had divided up the tasks and met periodically for consultation. The National Language Unification Committee was effectively defunct—"existing in name only, without a single copper" of government funding to support any of the initiatives (Wu Zhihui Papers 02887).

58. Jiaoyubu guoyu tongyi choubei weiyuanhui, *Guoyin changyong zihui*, vol. 3.

59. Jiaoyubu guoyu tongyi choubei weiyuanhui, *Guoyin changyong zihui*, vols. 3–7, 11–12.

60. For example, Ma, *Xin guoyin gaiyao;* Lu and Ma, *Xin guoyin xuesheng zidian;* Qi, *Xin guoyin jiangxi keben;* Zhang et al., *Guoyin xin jiaoben jiaoshou shu.*

61. Cong, *Guoyin xue*, pp. 8–9.

62. *Shanghai xian jiaoyuju yuekan* 上海縣教育局月刊 22 (October 1929): 67; *Wuxi jiaoyu zhoukan* 無錫教育週刊 49 (1928): 26–32.

63. *Shijiu niandu Henan jiaoyu nianjian,* pp. 852–853. Of the more than one hundred books submitted, only five were rejected. The rest were approved as "appropriate for use" or "suitable for consultation."

64. Li, "Xiaoxue diji de shuohua jiaoxue wenti," p. 17; Li Bizhen, in *Dagong bao* 大公報 (Tianjin edition) (December 19, 1936), p. 14.

65. Time lines in early modern and modern Europe performed some of these functions as well. See Rosenberg and Grafton, *Cartographies of Time.*

66. "Zhonghua Minguo guoyu yanjiuhui shizhou nian jinian ge." The reference to the phonetic alphabet shining "red" alludes to plans for street signs in Beijing to be annotated (in red) with *zhuyin zimu*. The project was cancelled "due to continuing hostilities" in the ongoing civil war.

67. Li, "Yibai nian ye keyi," pp. 188–190.

68. David Moser provides a useful overview of language reform in the post-1949 period in *A Billion Voices*. My forthcoming book (*The Sounds of Mandarin*) investigates the divergent fate of *guoyu* in Taiwan and its socialist counterpart *putonghua* in the PRC.

9 ❖ MÅRTEN SÖDERBLOM SAARELA

A Guangxu Renaissance?
Manchu Language Studies in the Late Qing and Their Republican Afterlife

> Examined close up, our history looks rather vague and messy, like a morass only partially made safe for pedestrian traffic, though oddly enough in the end there does seem to be a path across it.
> —Robert Musil (1880–1942), trans. Sophie Wilkins,
> *The Man without Qualities* (1930–1933)

The Manchu Qing empire collapsed in 1911–1912. During the decades that followed, various regimes (warlords, imperialist Japan, authoritarian Nationalists) ruled parts of the old empire. Rapid intellectual change accompanied the political uncertainty. Scholars who lived through the transition often wore many hats, or so it appears in retrospect, as they are seen moving between educational, cultural, and political institutions, the publishing industry, and interacting with foreign colleagues. In the process, they gave shape to modern China's humanistic disciplines. Foreign traditions of Sinology that had achieved academic independence during the nineteenth century partially converged with this cluster of disciplines, as Chinese scholars traveled abroad and worked in the new universities within China. In this internationally informed context, they reconsidered the imperial as well as pre-imperial past from new points of view and with different purposes in mind.

The Manchu language had been a core part of the self-image of the Qing aristocracy and its banner troops. It remained an administrative language in parts of the imperial periphery and, in a few areas, a vernacular language.[1] At a time when forging a "national language" out of Chinese was an increasingly prominent political issue (see Chen's chapter in this volume), it was far from obvious that Manchu would have a place in the new century. In political time as well as in the periodization of Sinological university curricula (in Europe in particular), the late nineteenth and early twentieth centuries are treated as the modern period. In terms of written language, the means by which the period is inscribed in historical time, it is a moment characterized by a shift from literary to vernacular Chinese. I believe, however, that in addition to the attention that the Manchu language received from Sinologists abroad (as discussed by Perdue's chapter in this volume), Manchu still remained an object of study and a matter of interest within China as well.

This chapter will thus treat the study of Manchu language and Manchu documents as one part of the new Chinese humanities—that is, the disciplines that abroad were called Sinology—in this period of momentous scholarly developments, stretching from the 1890s to the 1930s. During the last decades of Qing rule, even though members of the imperial government and the provincial administration worked to overcome domestic unrest and foreign pressure through reforms that departed radically from earlier Manchu institutions and practice, the written Manchu language, one of the oldest emblems of the dynasty, remained a subject worthy of study. The generation of scholars who, either in their own scholarly work or through their expressed opinion, contributed to transforming Manchu studies into the academic discipline we know today grew up during these last decades of the empire. The chapter will use the example of publishing in the Jingzhou garrison, one of the most active sites of Manchu printing in this period, to illustrate late-Qing Manchu book culture as the point of departure for the new Manchu studies.

Suggesting a continuous engagement with the Manchu written language across the 1911 divide, I want to show that modern Manchu studies has a genealogy within China that I think is underappreciated. Manchu studies in fact had a place in some of the major historiographical and bibliographical undertakings of the Republican period. Whereas the Manchu language as late as 1911 was touted as a foundational institution of the empire, it was by the end of the same decade described as being in need of urgent philological attention, which some scholars indeed accorded it. Throughout the period, there was a continuous but changing engagement with Manchu.

Following the discussion of the Jingzhou garrison, I will review the discussion on the Manchu language in relation to *Qingshi gao* 清史稿 (Draft history of the Qing). I will then discuss how Manchu bibliography emerged in China in the 1930s and '40s. Finally, as a conclusion, I will briefly relate Republican Manchu studies to the reprinting and inventorying of Qing sources in the second half of the twentieth century.

A Guangxu Renaissance?

The renaissance invoked in the title of this chapter is not the only renaissance that scholars have identified in this crucial period in Chinese history. Notably, Hu Shi 胡適 (1891–1962) identified a "Chinese Renaissance" in the second and third decades of the twentieth century.[2] The word is here intended as a contrast not only to Hu, but also to Mary Wright's "T'ung-chi [Tongzhi] Restoration" (named after the reign-title of emperor Yi 毅, the Guangxu emperor's cousin). Wright's phrase referred to the revival of "a civilization" through the "extraordinary efforts of extraordinary men." The civilization revived was that of imperial China, not the Qing dynasty in particular. The men were government officials, both bannermen and civilians, who used new tools and organizations to restore Qing control domestically and strengthen it internationally. Intellectually the restoration was accompanied "by a revival of the traditional learning on which society was based,"[3] which was broadly speaking Confucian and not specifically Manchu. Hu's renaissance, likewise, had nothing to do with the Manchus or their language.

Some of the Confucian statesmen who realized Wright's restoration were included by Hu as forerunners to his Chinese renaissance. Hu distanced himself from his "conceited" use of the word "renaissance," but found it expedient nonetheless. Hu's renaissance was, unsurprisingly, even less Manchu than Wright's restoration. In Hu's account, Manchu was synonymous with the politically incompetent Qing court. Manchu language and cultural practices thus played no active role in the renaissance.[4] Hu knew that his Chinese renaissance referred to events—the polemical activities of himself and his friends—of a magnitude quite different from that of the European Renaissance to which it alluded.

Similarly, the renaissance of Manchu studies in the Guangxu period invoked here cannot match up to the Tongzhi restoration except by rhetorical sleight of hand. Yet juxtaposing the development of Manchu language studies with Hu's Chinese renaissance serves a purpose, as does contrasting the Tongzhi restoration and the Guangxu renaissance, if you will allow me this word. Whereas the turn away from classical literary forms that Hu advocated at the height of his renaissance distanced modern Chinese literary practice from what was historically a topic of choice for Sinologists—classical literature—the editorial and publishing projects of the Guangxu renaissance in the 1890s shored up Manchu learning and facilitated the later development of Manchu studies as a branch of the Chinese humanities, or of Sinology, in Republican China. Identifying a Guangxu renaissance and its twentieth-century aftermath, then, serves both to highlight the relevance of Manchu studies for Sinology in an age of cultural iconoclasm and to show that Sinology never was and indeed never can be focused only on canonical Chinese forms of expression.

Contrasting the Guangxu renaissance with Wright's Tongzhi restoration provides context. For it is precisely in light of the critical redirections of the institutional and political history of the empire, which Wright chronicled under the name of the restoration, that the increase in publication of Manchu-language books in the last thirty-five years of the dynasty appears so remarkable. The participation of bannermen notwithstanding, many of the new institutions, notably the provincial armies, that gave the dynasty a new lease on life were not banner institutions.[5] The chaos of the mid-nineteenth century and the subsequent institutional and legislative reforms had an important impact on the Manchu garrison communities. Late nineteenth-century bannermen were less able but also less constrained to rely on stipendiary soldiering.[6] Still, in some of the garrisons and in the commercial print shops of Beijing, Manchu books were published with greater frequency than in preceding decades. If the restoration was not a restoration of Manchu institutions, why did Manchu publishing rebound after order was restored in the early 1870s? Perhaps the renaissance apparent in Manchu-language publishing in the last thirty-five years of the Qing period to some extent reflected the galvanization of those bannermen who remained attached to their institutions and communities and sought a place for themselves in a future that was not yet decided.

Statistics show this increase in Manchu publishing. Evelyn Rawski aggregated titles in several catalogs of major Manchu library holdings and stated that 17.7 percent of 993 dated Manchu works, both chiro- and xylographs, are from the first half of the nineteenth century (1796–1851); 7.7 percent are from 1851–1875, showing an average yearly output that is similar to the preceding period (an average of about 0.3 titles per year); and 17.2 percent are from the remaining thirty-seven years of Qing rule (1875–1912), representing a final "surge" of publishing (an average of about 0.5 titles per year over the whole period, but, I conjecture, at a significantly higher rate before the turn of the century).[7]

Huang Runhua's 黄润华 studies of Manchu publishing exclude chirographs, which might not have circulated very widely, and give a more fine-grained time line, but include far fewer titles. The picture that emerges is similar, however. Huang lists twenty-two publications from private or commercial publishers (including reissues) for the first half of the nineteenth century (Jiaqing to Daoguang periods), then seven publications for the Xianfeng decade (1850–1861), a mere three for the Tongzhi reign, and a full twenty-six for the rest of the dynasty (including two from the abortive Xuantong reign [1908–1912]).[8]

Publishing that can in some measure be called official, including books that by all the evidence seem to have been written by individuals on their own initiative but printed by regional banner institutions, also exhibit this trend. The great projects that helped endow Manchu with the trappings of a learned language—including literature in various genres, largely the result of translation from Chinese and Mongolian, and linguistic reference works—ended already by the time of the Qianlong emperor's retirement in 1796. Accordingly, among the fifteen publications that Huang lists for the first half of the nineteenth century, the only voluminous works published by the court were collections of imperial pronouncements and tables and biographies having to do with the nobility in the Inner Asian dependencies. The court no longer sponsored publication of linguistic scholarship.[9]

Whereas Huang lists three official publications each for the Xianfeng and Tongzhi reigns, he lists fourteen for Guangxu, and even one for Xuantong. Huang's list is incomplete: an institution from the Tongzhi restoration, the Jiangsu Book Bureau (Jiangsu Shuju 江蘇書局), reprinted a work containing Manchu-script glosses in 1878.[10] Unlike earlier in the century, seven of the officially produced books that Huang lists for the Guangxu period are explicitly linguistic works. One of them (*Mongyol-un üsüg-ün quriyaysan bičig* | *Qinding Mengwen huishu* 欽定蒙文彙書 [Imperially authorized collection of Mongolian], 1892) was even a court publication.[11]

Despite an increase in the total output of books, the Guangxu period did not witness a return to the big editorial projects that characterized the Kangxi and Qianlong reigns. The aforementioned Mongolian-Chinese-Manchu dictionary that the court published was not the product of a group of scholars working for years on imperial command, as had been the case in the eighteenth century. Rather, it was published on the initiative of the imperial clansman Sungsen 松森 (fl. 1892), president of the Ministry of Dependencies, who obtained imperial permission to publish a work based on Sayišangy-a's 賽尚阿 (fl. mid-nineteenth century) privately produced manuscript dictionary, reworked with reference to eighteenth-century lexicons. Two department directors, one Mongol and one Chinese, completed this task in six months.[12]

Moreover, the publication of *Mongyol-un üsüg-ün quriyaysan bičig* reflected lexicographical work done by bannermen officials and clerks in the absence of direct orders from their superiors, and, at least at first, largely independently of any government support. This kind of grassroots scholarship had a long tradition, and it lay behind many of the other official Manchu studies publications of the Guangxu period.

The sine qua non for such interest in Manchu was, naturally, the continued relevance of the language for the bureaucracy. Statements about the decline of Manchu as an administrative language in the late Qing need qualification.[13] Evidently, some banner registries were still being kept exclusively in Manchu in Guangzhou in 1851 and Beijing in 1877 (Guangxu 3).[14] The reason that Chinese became used alongside Manchu in some contexts at court was that Cixi, who had not received the training of an emperor, knew very little Manchu. One authority has recently written that "even into the Guangxu era, Manchu officials appearing before the emperor were still expected to use Manchu."[15]

The "surge" in Manchu linguistic scholarship in the late Qing coincided with other efforts to reinforce cultural continuity. In 1889, a member of the Hanlin Academy memorialized the emperor with a request to produce a continuation of *Siku quanshu* 四庫全書 (Complete writings of the four repositories)—the Qianlong emperor's giant, late eighteenth-century manuscript transcription of books gathered from across the realm. The request was approved on the condition that the project be postponed, but the opportune moment never presented itself. In 1908 a second, independent proposal to continue *Siku quanshu* was made, this time in connection with a proposal to institute public libraries for the education of the citizenry.[16] More generally, with a weakened court and the Qing world visibly undergoing important changes, from at least the 1890s the culture of the imperial capital was increasingly documented in print, often by bannermen writers.[17] Chinese literature written by bannermen also received attention. In 1901, the Chinese bannerman Yang Zhongxi 楊鐘羲 (1865–1940) published *Baqi wenjing* 八旗文經 (Literary canon of the eight banners), a work that he had compiled together with his cousin Sheng-yu 盛昱 (1850–1900), an imperial clansman born to a Mongolian mother.[18]

Linguistic Scholarship in the Jingzhou Garrison

I will use the example of the Jingzhou garrison to illustrate some features of Guangxu-period Manchu linguistic scholarship, by which I mean books serving the study of language. In this period, bannerman scholars employed in the provincial garrisons continued to successfully obtain the local authorities' sponsorship for the publication of their work. The Chengdu garrison in 1878 published a bilingual edition of the *Four Books*[19]—useful reading for the translation examination that were many bannermen's path to a government career—followed by a flurry of publications from the Fanyi zongxue 翻譯總學 (Comprehensive translation school) at the Jingzhou garrison.[20]

The driving force behind the linguistic work in Jingzhou were the bannermen Zhi-kuan 志寬 (provincial graduate, presumably of the translation examination, 1867) and Pei-kuan 培寬 (provincial graduate, also presumably of the translation examination, 1873).[21] The pair's superiors, including garrison General-in-Chief Xiang-li-ting 祥立亭 (fl. 1890–97), underwrote the publication project.[22] Pei-kuan was senior instructor of Manchu (*Manzhou zong jiaoxi* 滿洲總教習) in the school that printed the books. In 1890, when the pair published a Manchu-Chinese transcription treatise, Zhi-kuan was platoon commander (rank 5a), but when they published a Manchu-Chinese vocabulary the following year, he had been promoted to expectant major commander of a Mongolian banner company (*Menggu houbu zuoling* 蒙古候補佐領; rank 4a).[23]

The culmination of Zhi-kuan's and Pei-kuan's linguistic scholarship in Jingzhou appears to have been *Qingwen zonghui* 清文總彙 (Comprehensive collection of Qing writing; 1897), the largest of their publications. The book was a combination of two of the most well-known privately compiled Manchu dictionaries of the eighteenth century. Zhi-kuan's and Pei-kuan's students combined the lemmata lists of the two works that had become worn from age and unclear in places.[24] After almost a year of carving, the blocks for the twelve volumes lay ready for printing late in the summer of 1897.[25] As a synthesis of earlier dictionaries, *Qingwen zonghui* was similar to *Mongγol-un üsüg-ün quriyaγsan bičig*, the court's contribution to lexicography in the 1890s.

Linguistic scholarship in the Jingzhou garrison was related to contemporary commercial publishing, as the activities of the Chinese bannerman Fungšan 鳳山 (1859–1911; provincial graduate of translation) show.[26] Fungšan had "always wanted to benefit future students by writing a book assembling the fixed rules of the Manchu language," but considered himself "of slight understanding and little knowledge" and did not dare to assume the task. Yet "one day," he wrote, he "mentioned [his unrealized plans] in a discussion with [his] colleague Mr. Wan[fu]." Fungšan was in for a surprise. Wanfu 萬福 (fl. 1867), a Mongolian bannerman,[27] pulled out a Manchu grammar that he had privately published a few years earlier, and now the two coworkers set out to revise it. Then, in the spring of 1893, the manager of the Assembled Treasures Hall (Juzhen Tang 聚珍堂) print shop wanted to (re)print (Ma. *foloro;* Ch. *chongzi* 重梓) the work. Juzhen Tang, operated by a Henan civilian, was known for its output of Chinese vernacular fiction. It was also one of Beijing's most visible publishers of Manchu books, with an expressed interest in locating unpublished manuscripts.[28] A year later, in 1894, Wanfu and Fungšan's book was published.[29]

A decade and a half later, in late June or July of 1911 (Xuantong 3/6) and thus a few months before the Wuchang uprising that toppled the Qing dynasty, Fungšan was again thinking about the future of Manchu studies. Now, close to two decades after he had worked on Manchu grammar with Wanfu in Beijing, Fungšan was several months into his tenure as general-in-chief (rank 1b) at Jingzhou. Two decades of military service had left him no time for scholarly work. Indeed, his official duties had included service in the leadership of the post-Boxer modernized banner units in Beijing, a task that led to a study trip to Japan in 1903.[30]

Together with Wanfu, Fungšan realized his ambition to write a Manchu grammar. Yet he had also been unable to pursue yet another long-standing plan. While preparing for the translation examination much earlier in his life, Fungšan had regretted having to flip so painstakingly through several Manchu lexicons in search of a word. There was no single, complete, and convenient Manchu dictionary. Fungšan had wanted to compile one, but never had the chance. When he arrived in Jingzhou early in that fateful *xinhai* year, he found *Qingwen zonghui* in his offices, compiled by the garrison instructors and printed by his predecessor Xiang-li-ting. "Reading it I was overcome with joy," Fungšan wrote. "It was as if someone here in this place had unexpectedly divined my wish of so many years ago, unrealized because of lack of time." Fungšan decided to reprint the work. And so, in the second printing of *Qingwen zonghui,* we see private, commercial, and government-sponsored publishing of Manchu language studies in the late Qing coalesce into a common effort to strengthen the study of the Manchu language.

When Fungšan reprinted Zhi-kuan and Pei-kuan's dictionary, he wrote a Chinese colophon (*ba* 跋) in which he framed continued investment in the Manchu language as an alternative to the "self strengthening" of unnamed constitutional reformers. Fungšan understood the Manchu language in terms of the new nationalism that was developing in China at this time under Japanese influence, presenting it as the "essence of the state" (*guocui* 國粹, from J. *kokusui,* often translated as "national essence"):[31]

> Some say that "Now our Sagacious Son of Heaven is repeatedly promulgating legal reforms and self-strengthening through enlightened edicts! Those of us gentlemen who welcome the new might even suggest abandoning the old order in its entirety. There does not seem to be any point in discussing matters of this art [of Manchu language studies]."
>
> "That is not so!" I respond. "Manchu [*Qing*] writing is the basis of our dynasty. It is, to use a simile, like someone's person. You can choose whatever is good from his outfit, language, and appearance and adopt it. One may act like some person, but not change one's reason for being [*shengming*]. Now is Manchu [*Qing*] writing not the Manchu [*Qing*] people's reason for being? For these reasons I will promote and praise it, so as to better preserve the essence of our state [*guocui*]!"[32]

What to make of this curious text? The "surge" of Manchu-language publishing in the Guangxu and Xuantong reigns, which I have spoken about as a renaissance, Huang Runhua calls "a dying flash" (*huiguang fanzhao* 迴光返照).[33] The expression is inappropriate, as it implies knowledge of the outcome. It is true that, with hindsight, it is difficult not to see the energy expended on Manchu language learning in this period as a sort of Qing version of the *Parallelaktion*, the celebration of the Austro-Hungarian Emperor Franz Joseph I's seventy-year reign in 1918 that the characters in Robert Musil's novel *The Man without Qualities* (*Der Mann ohne Eigenschaften*) are planning in 1913. Just as the reader of Musil's novel knows that both emperor and empire would be dead and gone by 1918, so the reader of Fungšan's colophon knows that the Manchu dynasty fell less than a year after the reprint of the twelve-volume dictionary. Yet ultimately Fungšan does not, unlike some of Musil's characters, seem out of touch with history; the Manchu language, as a mark of Manchu distinctiveness, was indeed an essential resource for the dynasty. With the fall of the empire, the language receded from prominence. Yet it did not do so all that quickly, as the remainder of this chapter will argue.

Little use was made of Fungšan's *Qingwen zonghui* reprint (I know of only one copy, which is held at Capital Library in Beijing). What happened just months after the printing blocks were carved explains why. On November 19, 1911, revolutionary forces began an attack on Jingzhou's outer defense cordon. After more than a month of fighting, the garrison was overrun and surrendered on December 23. After the defeat of the garrison, its schools were closed, producing a generation of ostracized banner descendants who, unlike their fathers, were illiterate or semi-illiterate.[34]

Fungšan played no part in these events. Earlier that fall, he was transferred to the garrison in Guangzhou. As he was about to enter the city proper on October 25, a group of revolutionaries set off bombs that killed Fungšan and a dozen members of the military escort.[35]

Fungšan published in genres of Manchu language studies that had existed for about two hundred years, but he also engaged with nationalist ideas characteristic of the early twentieth century and in the end was the victim of a political assassination. By his intellectual activities and his official life, Fungšan bridged two historical periods.

From Language of State to Historical Research Tool

As Fungšan so forcefully asserted, the Manchu language was inseparable from the Manchu empire. In the last years of the dynasty, steps were taken to "annul the differences between Manchus and the Chinese population by 1915."[36] The translation examination was abolished along with the civil service examination system in 1905, but the court opened a Higher School of Manchu and Mongolian languages in Beijing in 1908 to train administrators.[37] Furthermore, a network of new schools in Manchuria was instituted to train students in the relevant languages and prepare them for the Higher School.[38] After the fall of the Qing, however, Manchu was no longer a language of state. The keeping of government records had always accounted for the largest share of Manchu writing. It had been a major task of bannermen clerks (Ma. *bithesi*), an entry-level position and in many cases a step on a successful official career.[39] Just as literary

Chinese was maintained in large part through the civil service examinations, the regrowth of Manchu proficiency was ensured by the translation examination as a gateway to official service. After 1911, that institutional support was gone.

In the areas where Manchu was not a vehicle for everyday, spoken communication—that is, in the former garrisons of China proper and in Beijing, but not all parts of Manchuria and Xinjiang—little incentive remained to study the language. The primary reason that some people outside the communities that still spoke Manchu continued to value the language in the early twentieth century was its importance for understanding China's recent past and the empire's *Nachlass* of written and material culture. Manchu studies became a branch of Sinology as it developed in the Chinese Republic.

The crises that befell the imperial institutions in the last years of Qing rule enabled outsiders to access places that otherwise would have been closed to them. In 1905, Naitō Konan 內藤湖南 (1866–1934), exploiting his position as the advisor to a Japanese diplomat, was allowed to photograph a copy of an eighteenth-century edition of the earliest Manchu archive that he had previously discovered.[40] Soon thereafter, perhaps around 1916, a group of interested Qing officials began translating the same collection into Chinese. The translation was finished in 1918. Jin-liang 金粱 (1878/1881–1962/1965), a Manchu official and Qing loyalist, published this work in 1929 and in a revised edition in 1933.[41] It has not been seen as a very glorious beginning for Republican Manchu studies, because of both the poor scholarship and the political leanings of its editor.[42] However, the book represents new attention, from scholars in China, paid to the early, formative history of several Manchu institutions. One of those institutions, the Manchu written language itself, was ultimately neglected in a more impactful scholarly project, the *Draft History of the Qing*. Discussions surrounding the *Draft History*, however, indicate that its ultimate disregard of the Manchu language was not a foregone conclusion.

Manchu and the *Draft History of the Qing*

In 1914, Yuan Shikai's 袁世凱 (1859–1916) conservative government set up a commission headed by former Qing official and Chinese bannerman Zhao Erxun 趙爾巽 (1844–1927) to compile a history of the fallen dynasty. The project continued a tradition almost as old as the imperial era. Accordingly, its members were generally former Qing servants. In 1927, the undertaking prematurely came to an end when Zhao, old and dying, suddenly ordered the book printed.[43] Published as *Qingshi gao* in that year, the book was criticized for scholarly lapses as well as for a bias against the Qing dynasty's enemies, allegedly not acknowledging the legitimacy of the Xinhai Revolution. Meng Sen 孟森 (1868–1938)[44] called the book "anti-revolutionary" (*fan geming* 反革命), "anti-republican" (*fan Minguo* 反民國), and "opposed to the Chinese *ethnos*" (*fandui Hanzu* 反對漢族) for references made to the mid-nineteenth-century rebels using the traditional vocabulary of banditry.[45] We should keep in mind, however, that undertaking to write a history of the Qing dynasty implied an acknowledgment that the empire was, well, history. Tellingly, Luo Zhenyu 羅振玉 (1866–1940), whose strong Qing loyalties later took him to Pu-yi's 溥儀 (1906–1967) court in Manchukuo, immediately burned his letter of invitation to edit the history of the dynasty.[46]

Yet for a work that at least expressed nostalgia for the Manchu empire, the *Draft History* paid little attention to the Manchu language. The book was more a product of the Tongzhi restoration than the Guangxu renaissance, as it were. Critics said the compilers used mostly official Qing historiography and neglected to make any use of the archival documents now in the care of the Palace Museum,[47] many of which were in Manchu.

The initial plans for the project gave a somewhat different impression. As I will show, the words of the compilers show a commitment to Manchu, while also revealing a lack of familiarity with the Manchu record that might have contributed to the language's apparent absence from the final product.

Shortly after the project was launched, members of the commission contributed a list of points covering both the research to be conducted and the format of the book that would result from it. In the introduction to the list, six individuals headed by Yu Shimei 于式枚 (1859–1915),[48] a veteran of the Qing Guoshi Guan 國史館 (State Historiographer's Office)[49] who died shortly thereafter, began by praising the Great Qing (*Da Qing* 大清), which had "opened up the land and expanded the borders and made civilized teachings flourish" and deserved to be remembered in a history. Then, merely a few sentences into the statement, Yu et al. described the sources that the project should use. The chief source base should be the documents produced by the Qing central government, which the authors traced to the beginning of Manchu record-keeping in pre-conquest Manchuria, when "our dynasty in the eighth year of Tiancong [1634] ordered Preceptor Erdeni and others to create Manchu writing on the basis of Mongolian."[50] Some official eighteenth-century works had been vague or inaccurate on this point,[51] but as even scholars writing in a private capacity in the late Qing knew,[52] the received account, with a locus classicus in the Nurhaci *Veritable Records,* had it that the invention of Manchu had taken place in 1599 (Wanli 27), not 1634.[53] Yu et al. were not faithful to the historical record available to them, but their grandiose introduction remained within the Qing paradigm of Manchu as the language of the dynasty.

A similar acknowledgment of the importance of written Manchu among Qing institutions and concurrent ignorance of its history is seen in the compiler Jin Zhaofan's 金兆蕃 (1869–1951)[54] letter to the commission. Jin wanted to place Dahai's 達海 (posthumous title Wencheng 文成, d. 1632) biography first among the civil officials of the pre-conquest period, because Dahai "created the dynastic script." In reality, Dahai did not create the Manchu script. The authoritative sources, the archival record, and even Jin's colleagues attributed this achievement to Erdeni.[55] The mistaken dating suggests that the members of the historiography commission had not given the Manchu historical record that much thought. They had a good idea of how to do historical research, however.

The first point on their agenda was to "scan archival holdings" (*sou dangce* 搜檔冊), which they knew were not only in Chinese. They specified that "files in Manchu or Mongolian script must be entrusted to individuals competent in Manchu and Mongolian writing for indexing and abstracting."[56]

The format of the resulting book, it was noted, should follow that of the dynastic histories, specifically *Ming shi* 明史 (History of the Ming). Thus its chapters belonged to one of several established types. The six scholars provided a table of contents divided into these types. Among the traditional "treatises" (*zhi* 志), several had a focus that in a Qing context would demand a consideration of Manchu. The "bibliographical treatise" (*yiwen zhi* 藝文志), a kind of book inventory of which the canonical example was in *Han shu* 漢書 (Book of the Han), was one, as a voluminous literature in Manchu had been produced in the Qing period. Another treatise, which Yu et al. listed without further commentary, explicitly took Manchu as its focus: the "treatise on the dynastic language" (*guoyu zhi* 國語志).[57]

As the commission was discussing the methodology and format, individual scholars also submitted their views on how a history of the Qing should be written. Compilers working on the project, such as Jin Zhaofan or Wu Shijian 吳式鑑 (presented scholar in 1892),[58] who stressed the need to "inquire broadly among learned gentlemen of the Eight Banners" to unearth books on specifically Manchu topics (for example, shamanist state rituals),[59] counted among them. Scholars unaffiliated with the project also contributed opinions.

Zhang Zongxiang 張宗祥 (1881–1965),[60] an unaffiliated scholar, commented on the proposed "treatise on the dynastic language." The addition of such a treatise "cannot be avoided," Zhang wrote, citing the corresponding treatises in the histories of the Jurchen Jin (compiled in 1344–1345, under the Mongols) and the Mongol Yuan (compiled in 1370, under the Ming) as models.[61] Liang Qichao 梁啟超 (1873–1929), likewise not officially involved, submitted a proposal on the book's structure. He proposed changes (ultimately not heeded), but remained largely within the tradition of the dynastic histories.[62] Liang had urged the amalgamation of the Manchus and Chinese while the former were still in power,[63] but now that Qing power was history, he stressed the need to document Manchu specificity through a "treatise on the dynastic script" (*guoshu* 國書):

> The dynastic script was created for that one dynasty. Now, however, not even one in every ten thousand Manchus is able to understand it. Now that the cauldrons [i.e., the regime] have changed, we can all agree that [the Manchu language] will disappear completely. If it is not recorded in the Qing history, then how would it be transmitted in the future? It will thus be appended to the series of treaties.[64]

Furthermore, Liang wanted other languages of the Qing empire—Mongolian and Tibetan (*Tanggute* 唐古忒)—covered as well.

Kui-shan 奎善 (n.d.), a proofreader for the *Draft History*,[65] went beyond suggesting that a "treatise on the national language/script" should be included; he actually wrote a synopsis for one. In a note on the "Origin of Manchu Writing" (*Manwen yuanliu* 滿文源流), Kui-shan presented the received narrative that his superiors had failed to correctly reproduce in their list of editorial points. He added a commentary:

> Scripts are what replaced knotted cords [in prehistory, according to a widespread Chinese theory]. The scripts of all countries all contain remnants of the knotted-cord design in their tangles and bends, even though their system does not follow the same principle. Furthermore, scripts also differ according to the features of the land. Europe is rich in waterways, thus the scripts of England, France, and other countries there are written horizontally like the waves whipped up by the wind, like the ripples on the water's surface. The original home of the Manchus was rich in mountains and forests, therefore their script stands tall and upright like an ancient tree, like the lone peak. It is probably the case that when scripts are created, they are based in the minds of the people [*renxin*], and the soul [*ling*] of people's minds stem from the natural principles of Heaven and Earth. Things are not so by accident.[66]

As Fungšan before him, Kui-shan linked the Manchu language, or at least its script, to the essence of the Manchu people, here presented as their ancestral homeland. Kui-shan continued by praising the phonographic properties of the Manchu script, as had been common among scholars in the Qing period. The Manchu script allowed for many different combinations, and so it conformed to the nature of articulated sound (*yinlai* 音籟). Kui-shan did not shy from drawing a conclusion that I thought the anti-Manchu Republican revolution would have made impossible. He asserted Manchu's superiority over Chinese: "Manchu writing can even grasp points that Chinese writing is unable to grasp." Ultimately, however, Kui-shan's praise of Manchu has a hint of apology to it. Manchu writing was one of the great institutions of the Qing, but it did not represent Manchu repression of Chinese culture:

> It was, of course, an imperial creation. Propagated for several centuries, it did not wither. If we examine the matter further, we find that since entering the pass and establishing the cauldrons [in Beijing], there have been high officials who never learned Manchu, but the rulers were always accommodating and never forced it upon them. Until the Qianlong period [1736–1796], recently graduated Hanlin Bachelors were all ordered to enter the Academy for selection to study the dynastic language [*guowen* 國文]. Since the older candidates had a heavy accent, they were not very good at reading [Manchu] aloud. Before long, there were proposals to end the practice. "That was good, but also leaves you unsatisfied" [as it is said in the *Zuozhuan*].

> Yet now that we are compiling a history of the Qing dynasty, dare I suggest that we begin with the Manchu script. As the unique creation of the dynasty, it was the essence of the state [*guocui*], and it cannot easily be overlooked and unnoticed. I would suggest to first give a general account of its history, followed by the letters [*zimu* 字母], then various translations arranged by topic. Thereby future philologists [*zhengwen zhe* 徵文者] will have something to work from.[67]

Indeed, two versions of a thematic Manchu-Chinese vocabulary are found alongside Kui-shan's synopsis for a treatise on Manchu in the archive (in Taipei) of the Qing historiography commission.

The idea of a "treatise on the dynastic language" faced resistance, however. The card-carrying Republican revolutionary Yi Peiji 易培基 (1880–1937)[68]—in contrast to Yu Shimei et al., Zhang Zongxiang, and Liang Qichao—was vehemently opposed to it. In a journal article published in 1915, Yi argued against the inclusion of a treatise on Manchu on the grounds that it was contrary to the purpose of writing the history of fallen dynasties:

> The great import of historiography is in celebrating assimilation [*tonghua* 同化]. When the Manchus ruled over China, did they assimilate to China, or did China assimilate to them? The scholarship did not differ, the customs did not diverge, administrative procedure and ceremonies were clearly just as they had been before. This represents the Manchus' assimilation to China. Since they assimilated to China, a *History of the Qing* today is not the history of one house or one *ethnos*, but a great chronicle over the government and citizenry of our country, China, during 270 years.[69]

There was no place in such a history for a "Manchu dictionary."[70] The people of Yi's generation, growing up toward the end of Qing rule, did not speak Manchu. "The flourishing of the dynastic language," Yi ironized, had only been the "barbarian cackling" (*Huyu gaji*) of a few officials in the emperor's retinue.[71]

Meanwhile, as the history was being put together, the Qing archives suffered. In 1922–1924, Luo Zhenyu, who had refused to participate in the history project, helped save archival documents of the Qing imperial government from being recycled as scrap paper, including more than two thousand documents either wholly or partially written in Manchu.[72]

For whatever reason, the *Draft History* did not include a "treatise on the dynastic language" when it was published in 1927.[73] The Manchu language had indeed been omitted as both a topic of history writing and a subject of historical research. Despite mentions of the invention of Manchu in the list of points drawn up by Yu Shimei and his colleagues at the beginning of the project, the history of one of the Qing dynasty's most important institutions received little attention in the final product. In a lecture held in 1928, Ye Gongchuo 葉恭綽 (1881–1968),[74] a multitalented official, expressed his regret in this regard:

> The Manchu script, its creation and reform, has quite some history. It also has substantial connections with the culture of the Manchu Qing. In the past, all the important administrative documents were written in Manchu. And yet, the *Draft History of the Qing* does not give a detailed account of how it was created or reformed.[75]

However, the published book did include a "bibliographical treatise." The publishing business in Beijing had been markedly multilingual during Qing times, something that the treatise could not but reflect in its inclusion of imperially commissioned translations and lexicographical works.[76] The treatise was written by Zhu Shizhe 朱師轍 (1878–1969),[77] who was also the history project's chronicler.[78]

Fan Xizeng 范希曾 (1899–1930), who made notable contributions to Chinese bibliography before his premature death,[79] commented on Zhu's "bibliographical treatise." After remarking on genres and methods of bibliography, Fan noted that Qing print culture was characterized by the great number and diversity of books. "Now, books were not only written by Chinese individuals; there are books by Manchus, texts in Mongolian and Tibetan," as well as missionary compositions and translated works. Ignoring these books in the bibliographical treatise, as Fan thought Zhu had done, was to act in "ignorance of the particularities of the Qing period."[80]

Zhao Wanli 趙萬裏 (1905–1980),[81] writing for the press in 1928 under the pseudonym Lizhou 蠡舟,[82] made a similar point, but also stressed that books were not just written *by* Manchus; there were also books *in* Manchu:

> Giving a comprehensive reckoning of Qing documents presents certain difficulties, but two general points can be made that have thus far eluded the attention of contemporaries. One regards the writings by individuals of the eight banners, the other the books written in Manchu or translated into Manchu. A bibliographical treatise for a history of the Qing dynasty should thus be conscientiously compiled. There is no room for carelessness, and these two aspects must take priority.[83]

Through consultation of anthologies of literature by bannermen (Zhao mentioned Sheng-yu's collection), the first point could be addressed. "The second point is seemingly even more important," Zhao explained:

> The numbers of our countrymen who study Manchu and are able to successfully read it are dwindling, and Manchu-language books gradually disappear from circulation. If we do not increase our efforts to collect and edit them now, then not a trace will be left some centuries hence. . . . Alexeiev [V. M. Alekseev (d. 1951)?[84]] and other Russians engaged in this kind of work, and the Japanese have also made great efforts. Yet Mr. Zhu has not been capable of providing detailed records of the [Chinese] writings by bannermen. As for Manchu-language texts, they are found only in the philology section of the classics division [of the bibliography], which cursorily lists a dozen or so of the most common dictionaries and lexicons. This I single out as the [treatise's] greatest disappointment.[85]

It was perhaps not a coincidence that it was Zhao, a generation younger than most other writers commenting on the *Draft History* who are quoted in these pages, who was the one to compare the state of Manchu studies in China to the work done by foreign researchers. Unlike for scholars born in the 1870s and '80s, who had reached maturity in the Guangxu period, Manchu studies was for Zhao an international academic discipline among others. In Beijing, Zhao would have been able to witness firsthand how Manchu books were being bought up by foreign collectors and shipped overseas.[86]

In the 1920s, concern for the study of the Manchu language and the proper care of the Manchu written heritage were not limited to the discussions surrounding the *Draft History of the Qing*. Kung Ling-wei has shown that proposals were made to offer classes on Manchu language and literature at Peking University as early as 1922. Indeed, Chen Yinque 陳寅恪 (Yinke; 1890–1969), who had learned Manchu in Europe, taught Manchu and other Inner Asian languages in the capital's universities. He was, however, eventually compelled to shift the focus to Chinese-language sources, since by the early 1930s, the students were unreceptive to his "extremely specialized classes," according to one of Chen's colleagues at Tsinghua.[87]

Such setbacks notwithstanding, Zhao's and others' appeals to Chinese colleagues to join their foreign counterparts in compiling inventories of the Manchu *Nachlass* in both Chinese and Manchu was timely. In the decade following the publication of his review, bannermen scholars of the Guangxu generation did precisely that.

Manchu Bibliography in the 1930s

The unearthing and reprinting of historical sources was, alongside history writing, a prominent aspect of humanistic research in the late Qing and Republican periods. The book series *Sibu congkan* 四部叢刊 (Serial printings from the four divisions, 1920–1935) and *Sibu beiyao* 四部備要 (Ready essentials of the four divisions, 1924–1931) are well-known representatives of this publishing trend,[88] and there were new plans to reprint or complement the Qianlong emperor's *Siku quanshu*, or *Complete Writings of the Four Repositories*, which was seen as having been too selective. Its practice of censorship was one reason, as was the fact that it naturally only covered the first half of the Qing dynasty. To complement Qianlong's collection therefore in large part meant to engage in Qing bibliography, which, as Zhao pointed out, had an important Manchu aspect to it.

Manchu bibliography was in the 1930s practiced both in the context of updating *Siku quanshu* and otherwise. In 1932–1933, the Mongolian bannerman En-hua 恩華 (1879–1954) began compiling a record of books written by members of the eight banners in the Qing period, primarily but not only in Chinese, on the basis of investigations carried out in former garrison towns in Manchuria, China proper, and Xinjiang. He might have published an edition upon completing the draft in 1935, but we know for certain of a final version of *Baqi yiwen bianmu* 八旗藝文編目 (Edited catalog of eight-banner literature), including a list of errata, that appeared in 1941 as a privately published book. In 1943, Hellmut Wilhelm (1905–1990), one of the foreign bibliographers living in Beijing at the time, called En-hua "a well-known collector of books composed by bannermen."[89] En-hua's book went a long way toward fulfilling the first of Zhao Wanli's two bibliographical desiderata.

It looked as if Zhao's second desideratum, that of describing the Manchu-language texts produced by the banners, would also be satisfied in the 1930s and early 1940s. In 1933, Li Deqi 李德啟 (n.d.) published a catalog of some Manchu holdings in Beijing.[90] Without knowing Manchu, the young scholar Xie Guozhen 謝國楨 (1901–1982)[91] in the same year published a monograph that included an overview of early Qing sources.[92] Some of the Manchu sources in the old imperial palace that Xie described had been identified with the help of Chen Yinque.[93] But several of the scholars who worked on the newly discovered Manchu sources had been trained in Manchu in banner schools in the late Qing period. They included the Manchu bannerman Qi Zenggui 齊增桂; the Mongol Zhang Yuquan 張玉全, who had a merchant background; and Feng-kuan 奉寬 (1876–1943), a Manchu bannerman from the Mongolian Borjigin clan (of Chinggis Khan fame).[94]

Feng-kuan, who reached maturity in the Guangxu period, had a clerical career in the Ministry of War before 1911. He suffered a few years of unemployment after the Revolution, but was reinstated in 1916 with the Chinese name Bao Bian 鮑汴. When the Nationalists moved the central government to Nanjing in 1928, Feng-kuan resigned. Under his original name, he spent the rest of his professional life as a scholar and university teacher (of Manchu and Mongolian), with affiliations at Yenching and Peking Universities.[95] Perhaps it was during his time at the latter that he annotated *Mongγol-un üsüg-ün quriyaγsan bičig*, the court-sponsored dictionary from 1892, which entered the Peking University Library collection in 1930. In the second volume of this copy, a slip of paper has been inserted that says "I correct mistakes in the book as I go along (written by Feng-kuan)."[96] Thus the Manchu-language books extant in the capital's libraries themselves reflect Feng-kuan's importance for Manchu studies in the latter half of the Republican period.

Some years after helping Xie Guozhen identify the pre-conquest Manchu sources at the palace, Feng-kuan began a much greater project of Manchu bibliography as part of a Japanese-Chinese joint cultural undertaking.

The foreign powers that had received war reparations following the Boxer Rebellion at the turn of the century one after the other paid some of that money back to China by setting up joint cultural ventures. Japan in 1925 opened a joint humanistic research institute in China with indemnity funds, a project from its inception criticized in China as imperialist. The institute's first task was to compile a "Bibliographical Précis for a Continuation of the *Complete Writings of the Four Repositories*" (*Xuxiu "Siku quanshu" zongmu tiyao* 續修四庫全書總目提要), for which purpose a great number of books were gradually purchased. The project progressed through the outbreak of hostilities between the two countries, but finally came to a halt when the funding was withdrawn at the outbreak of Pacific War in 1941.[97]

By the time the project was interrupted, a voluminous collection of précis already existed in corrected manuscript copies. Thousands[98] of those pages, or 788 entries,[99] were written by Feng-kuan, who worked on the project from 1934. They covered a vast terrain. Officially, Feng-kuan's responsibilities were books relating to the *Shilu* 實錄 (Veritable records) and books on statecraft and administration (*zhengshu* 政書), but for whatever reason, he wrote numerous précis on Manchu and Mongolian texts as well as on Chinese works written by bannermen authors. Many of the works he covered fell under the "philology" (*xiaoxue* 小學) heading, which lay outside his formal charges.[100] Many of the items that he described were not books strictly speaking, but collections of administrative files and other documents that we would consider archival material. Much of it dates from the late Qing, including many undated "transmitted manuscript copies" (*chuan chaoben* 傳鈔本). Consciously or not, Feng-kuan's précis presented the reader with an inventory of the literary world available to a Guangxu-period metropolitan bannerman, which was indeed what Feng-kuan had been for the first half of his life. Important historical events and the lived experiences of Manchus across the *xinhai* divide shine through Feng-kuan's summaries of these manuscripts. One described work treated the Boxer Rebellion and the occupation of Beijing by the Eight Nation army. Another, by the Manchu bannerwoman Wen-zhong 文仲, detailed (in Chinese) a trip to the neighboring hills and their temples in the summer of 1923. Wen-zhong was a teacher in a school for girls at Fragrant Hill (Xiangshan 香山) in the Beijing suburbs, where she died from overwork at the age of only twenty-one *sui*.[101] Like her predecessors in the Guangxu period, she documented the capital region's cultural heritage. Feng-kuan's précis were themselves arguably part of the same effort of documentation.

At times, Feng-kuan expresses regret over the lost Qing world. Describing a block-printed charter for a charitable school from 1898, Feng-kuan noted that "in the four sectors of the fallen dynasty's capital, privately established charitable schools numbered no less than forty, not counting public schools." Supplying the students with room, board, and free tuition, these schools made morally upright individuals out of the gifted poor, so different from "today's schools, whose fees prevent households of sub-middle-class standing from attending."[102]

Finally, Feng-kuan used the précis to comment on the *Draft History of the Qing*. Yi-geng's 奕賡 (fl. first decades of the nineteenth century)[103] *Qingyu renming yi Han* 清語人名譯漢 (Manchu names translated into Chinese) provided the occasion.[104] Feng-kuan noted that this book followed the format of the expressions of Jurchen terms seen in the *History of the Jin*, as well as of the Qianlong version of that work, reprinted in 1878 and using the Manchu script for Jurchen and other Inner Asian–language terms. Zhang Zongxiang had in the early years of the Qing history project singled out precisely this section of the *History of the Jin* as a model for the prospected "treatise on the dynastic language." Now Feng-kuan noted that "the *Draft History of the Qing*, compiled in the Republic, does not contain such a section, for which scholars faulted it." Yi-geng's book, then, "can remedy this deficiency of the *Draft History* and, I think, serve as a bridge leading to research into the dynastic language."[105]

Feng-kuan's descriptions are a valuable source on Manchu bibliography. Some of the collections he used, including that of the South Manchuria Railway Company in Dalian (one of the most interesting in China), have only recently been cataloged in print, generally with less detail than that given by Feng-kuan.[106] Writing in the 1930s, Feng-kuan invites comparison with the foreign

Manchu bibliographers in Beijing to whom Zhao Wanli referred. Yet whereas the bibliographies of Manchu sources written by Walter Fuchs (1902–1979), who was one of these expatriate scholars, have been routinely cited since their publication in the 1930s,[107] Feng-kuan's work remained in manuscript in the library of what is now the Chinese Academy of Sciences, whose predecessor institution inherited the project after Japan's withdrawal.

It was only in 1971 that Feng-kuan's précis of Manchu books were published.[108] The publication, issued in Taipei, was based on a prewar Japanese lithograph covering parts of the original manuscript. On the mainland, work on the précis began in earnest only in the 1980s,[109] leading eventually to the publication of an edited portion of the original manuscripts in 1993. Feng-kuan's précis of Manchu books were, "due to editorial and typographical difficulties," not included in this publication, Luo Lin 羅琳 of the library of the Chinese Academy of Sciences explained, but were saved for "a separate volume that will conclude the project."[110] The planned volume never appeared, but Feng-kuan's précis were instead printed together with the rest of the manuscripts in facsimile in 1996. Around the same time, plans were made to print a continuation of the *Siku quanshu* itself—that is, print facsimiles of original works, not bibliographical précis. The project, still bearing the title *Continuation of the "Complete Writings of the Four Repositories,"* concluded in 2002 after 1,800 volumes had been published. None of them, however, contained any books in which Manchu was used as anything more than an auxiliary script.[111]

In the 1910s and '20s, writers and interested readers alike wanted an official history of the Qing to contain a treatise on the Manchu language and a list of Manchu books, but in the end they got neither. Then, in the 1930s, it looked as if one of the greatest bibliographic undertakings of the period would lead to an inventory of the Manchu literary heritage and, perhaps, eventually to its publication in reprint. War, turmoil, and a changing intellectual landscape prevented that from happening. Feng-kuan's manuscript, after a long wait, appeared in facsimile and En-hua's bibliography finally appeared in an accessible edition in 2006. Kui-shan's treatise on Manchu, however, still lies unpublished among the files of the Qing historiography commission in Taipei.

By bringing several instances of Manchu research up for discussion, I wanted to show that already in the early years of the Republic, Manchu studies were developing from a means to maintain a language of state, studied with renewed intensity in the last decades of imperial rule, into a historical academic discipline in China. Many of the scholars who either worked directly on Manchu topics, or stressed their urgency in learned journals or in the press, had grown up during the last thirty-five years of Qing rule that I have called, half in jest, the Guangxu renaissance. The 1911 Revolution was certainly disruptive for the study of Manchu; Fungšan, an active promoter of Manchu linguistic literature in the late Qing period, was even killed by it, and the printing of Zhi-kuan and Pei-kuan's dictionary that he sponsored in Jingzhou is almost unknown today. Yet with half their lives in the Manchu empire and half in the Republic, scholars such as En-hua and Feng-kuan survived, persisted, and bridged the study of Manchu as a dynastic language to its study as a language of primarily historical documents and books.

The Qing tradition of Manchu studies was even to some extent carried on even further. The career of Feng-kuan's third son, Bao Yuwan 鮑育萬 (1897–1960), shows the survival of Qing Manchu studies into the People's Republic. Bao, who unlike his father used the family's Chinese name, graduated from Manchu school in 1912 after three years of study. He worked on several officially sponsored scholarly projects in the early Republic, being attached to the Qing historiography commission in 1927. Shadowing his father, he worked as a proofreader on the *Xuxiu siku quanshu* project. After the revolution of 1949, Bao worked at the archives in the old Imperial Palace, where he sorted through Manchu memorials in the mornings and cataloged Manchu books in the afternoon. He spent his last professionally active years translating Manchu documents at the archive. The work of Bao Yuwan and his colleagues laid the groundwork for the opening of the Qing archives to researchers years later. Without access to these archives, much of the historical research on the Qing period during the past several decades, especially on its Manchu aspects, would hardly have been possible.

Much time passed between the editorial activities of Zhi-kuan and Pei-kuan in Jingzhou and Bao Yuwen's archival work in the 1950s. The times also changed. The institution of the banners, the language of written bureaucratic Manchu, and the technology of xylographic printing all disappeared. Yet bannermen and the Manchu language remained part of post-imperial China. Conversely, changes to the banner establishment, but also efforts to recover and document the literary heritage of the Qing dynasty, began decades before the fall of the Manchu dynasty. Thus, 1911 does not represent a clean divide except for a general level at most.

The Manchu language remained relevant, in certain places and for certain people, into the late Qing and beyond. The presence of this third language alongside different forms of Chinese means that changes within the realm of written language in the early twentieth century cannot be construed simply as literary Chinese versus a new national language. Language shifts played a part in Hu Shi's "Chinese Renaissance," and the study of—mostly pre-Hu Shi—Chinese texts characterizes Sinology. Yet Chinese texts were extremely varied before Hu Shi's renaissance, and they never existed in isolation from other languages and written traditions, including that of Manchu.

However, drawing attention to the continued presence of Manchu in the Chinese linguistic landscape around the turn of the twentieth century does not mean that Manchu is an absolute necessity for Sinological research on the late Qing. I do not agree with Erich Hauer (1878–1936) that the "Sinologue *should* study Manchu" (my emphasis). The Sinolog(ist) should study whatever is important for the period and topic under scrutiny, which might or might not involve Manchu. Yet Hauer was indeed right to point out that Sinology has to be more than the study of canonical texts in literary Chinese.

Notes

This chapter is a second take on a topic that I briefly discussed in a blog post some years ago: Saarela, "The Cost of a Manchu Dictionary in the Guangxu Period." I thank David Porter, Yangyang Su, and Qiu Yuanyuan for their help and advice when writing this new version; Grace Fong and Sarah Schneewind for their comments when I presented it in Tel Aviv on May 15, 2017; Ori Sela for his comments on the penultimate written version; Joshua Fogel for correcting mistakes; and Jonathan Hill for providing a reference.

1. See Saarela, "Manchu Language."
2. I owe the realization that Hu Shi was important for this discussion to Blitstein, "Multiple Renaissances."
3. Wright, *The Last Stand of Chinese Conservatism*, pp. ix, 50. The first quotation is from the author's summary of her original thesis, written for the second edition.
4. Hu, "The Renaissance in China," pp. 15–25.
5. Wright, *The Last Stand of Chinese Conservatism*, chapter 9.
6. Crossley, *Orphan Warriors*, chapters 5–7, esp. pp. 147–150, 164–176, 178–179; Rhoads, *Manchus and Han*, chapters 2–3.
7. Rawski, "Qing Publishing in Non-Han Languages," table 8.2 and p. 311. Also Rawski, "Qing Book Culture and Inner Asia," p. 198. The remaining books date from before the nineteenth century, with most books dating from the Qianlong reign (30.6 percent).
8. Huang, "Manwen fangke tushu shulun," pp. 220–237.
9. According to some sources, a set of glossaries with Manchu and Chinese transcriptions of Inner Asian terms in the Liao, Jin, and Yuan dynastic histories, which had been included in manuscript in *Siku quanshu* 四庫全書 (Complete writings of the four repositories), is a possible exception, as some sources say it was only printed in 1824. Qing-gui, *Guochao gongshi xubian*, pp. 903–904; Huang, "Manwen guanke tushu shulun," pp. 178–201. Other research dates the printing of this work to 1787, however. Zhang, "Wuying Dian ben," pp. 107–108.
10. Listed, with prices, in *Jiangsu Shuju chongding heshi jiamu, shi bu*, p. 3b.
11. On the copy I consulted (Sungsen, ed., *Qinding Mengwen huishu* 欽定蒙文彙書 | *Mongyolun üsüg-ün quriyaysan bičig*), the Mongolian title (which does not say "imperially authorized") figures only on slips pasted onto the outside cover of the volumes. The printed running title is in Chinese. Both titles are pictured in Gugong bowuyuan, ed., *Tongwen zhi sheng*, pp. 141–143.
12. Chunhua, *Qingdai Man-Mengwen cidian yanjiu*, pp. 340–344 (item 216); Brunnert and Hagelstrom, *Present Day Political Organization of China*, pp. 98, 101 (item 290).
13. For example, Rhoads, *Manchus and Han*, p. 53.
14. "Manwen pu"; *Xuxiu "Siku quanshu" zongmu tiyao (gaoben)*, facsimiles of mss. by multiple authors: 5:151 and 6:223 are by Feng-kuan 奉寬 (Jinan: Qi-Lu shushe, 1996), written during 1931–1942, 5:177–178 (for Beijing).
15. Murata, "The Late Qing 'National Language' Issue and Monolingual Systems," p. 115; Murata, "Rasuto-enperazu wa nani go de hanashite ita ka?," p. 13.
16. Liu, "Guangxu chao 'xuxiu *Siku quanshu*' shuping," pp. 93–95.
17. Naquin, *Peking*, pp. 696–697.
18. Momose, "Shêng-yü."
19. Huang, "Manwen guanke tushu shulun," p. 199.
20. The flyleaf of Zhi-kuan and Pei-kuan, *Duiyin jizi*, 2 vols., copy held at Capital Library, Beijing, reads *Fanyi zongxue* 翻譯總學; the preface (pp. 2a and 4a) reads *Baqi zongxue* 八旗總學.
21. Zhi-kuan and Pei-kuan, *Duiyin jizi, xu*, pp. 3b–4a.
22. Zhi-kuan and Pei-kuan, *Qingwen zonghui*, vol. 12, *ba*, p. 1b.

23. Zhi-kuan and Pei-kuan, *Duiyin jizi, xu*, p. 4a; Zhi-kuan and Pei-kuan, *Dan Qingyu*, vol. 8, p. 34a. The two were from different banners (Bordered White and Bordered Yellow). The translation of their titles follows Brunnert and Hagelstrom, *Present Day Political Organization of China*, pp. 335–336 (item 746) and pp. 510–511 (items 970–971), but Pei-kuan's title has no perfect equivalent in that book.

24. Zhi-kuan and Pei-kuan, *Qingwen zonghui*, 1st ed., vol. 1, *xu*, p. 1b.

25. Zhi-kuan and Pei-kuan, *Qingwen zonghui*, vol. 12, *ba*, pp. 2a–b.

26. We have these dates from Zhang and Qin, "Feng-shan jiangjun beici an xintan," p. 85.

27. *Xuxiu "Siku quanshu" zongmu tiyao (gaoben)*, vol. 6, p. 160.

28. Rawski, "Qing Publishing in Non-Han Languages," p. 307; Widmer, "*Honglou Meng Ying* and Its Publisher, Juzhen Tang of Beijing." Widmer notes that the print shop's name implies movable-type printing, which it also used for its monolingual Chinese titles.

29. Wanfu, *Chongke Qingwen xuzi zhinan bian*, Fungšan's preface, *xu*, pp. 1b–2a: *bi, kemuni manju gisun-i toktoho kooli be isamjafi bithe arame, amaga taci[r]e urse de tusa araki seme gûnihade, beye ulhihengge cinggiya sahangge komso babe tulbime, gelhun akû cihai salihakû, tere inenggi emu yamun-i gucu wan agu-i emgi ere turgun be leoleme sisiname ofi, siyan šeng emu bithe be tucibufi minde tuwabuha de* | 余嘗思將清文成法集而為書以益後進，而自問淺識寡見，未敢自專，一日與同寅萬公語及其故，先生出一卷示余. The book was reissued just two years before the fall of the dynasty: Wanfu, *Chongke Qingwen xuzi zhinan bian* (1909).

30. Rhoads, *Manchus and Han*, p. 83.

31. For a discussion of the term, see Hon, "Revolution as Representation." To my knowledge, the claim to a "Manchu" *guocui* by bannermen has not yet received scholarly attention.

32. Zhi-kuan and Pei-kuan, *Qingwen zonghui*, vol. 12, *ba*, 2a–b: 閱之喜不自勝。蓋余曩年欲爲而未暇者，不意此地竟有人先得我心者也。或曰：「方今聖天子屢頒明詔變法自強！一般喜新之士方議廢棄舊制之無遺。似一藝之事未足重輕。」余曰：「不然！清文爲我國之根本，譬如人之一身，衣裳，冠履，言語，形容無一不可擇善而從，依人作態，而其生命不能改也. 彼清文者，其清人之生命乎？余故表而彰之，亦保存國粹之一助也！」。

33. Huang, "Manwen fangke tushu shulun," p. 224.

34. Pan, "Xinhai geming yu Jingzhou zhufang baqi," pp. 24–25.

35. *Qingshi gao*, p. 12785 (chapter 469); Zhang and Qin, "Feng-shan jiangjun beici an xintan."

36. Brunnert and Hagelstrom, *Present Day Political Organization of China*, p. 68.

37. Brunnert and Hagelstrom, *Present Day Political Organization of China*, pp. 264–265 (item 627) and p. 271; Li, "Mouxin yu duanben."

38. Liu, "Qingdai 'guoyu qishe' zhengce yanjiu," pp. 104–107.

39. Elliott, *The Manchu Way*, pp. 151–152; Rhoads, *Manchus and Han*, pp. 44, 46; Brunnert and Hagelstrom, *Present Day Political Organization of China*, p. 102 (item 293).

40. Fogel, *Politics and Sinology*, pp. 112–113.

41. *Neige cang "Manwen laodang,"* vol. 1, preface, p. 6; Nakami, "The Manchu Bannerman Jinliang's Search for Manchu-Qing Historical Sources," p. 175.

42. Chen, "Jin-liang *Manzhou bidang* pingjia"; cf. Crossley, *Orphan Warriors*, pp. 210–211.

43. Zou, Han, and Lu, "*Qingshi gao* zuanxiu shimo yanjiu." Also on the history of the project, see Qingshi zuanxiu weiyuan hui, "*Qingshi gao* zuanxiu zhi jingguo."

44. Xu, Cai, Ji, and Cu, eds., *Minguo renwu da cidian*, vol. 1, p. 954.

45. Fu, "*Qingshi gao* pinglun shang," vol. 2, pp. 550, 560; Fu, "*Qingshi gao* pinglun xia," vol. 2, p. 603; also see Zhu, *Qingshi shuwen*, pp. 229, 237, 271, 315–318; Meng, "*Qingshi gao* yingfou jingu zhi shangque," vol. 2, pp. 712–714. For context, see Dong, "How to Remember the Qing Dynasty."

46. Yang and Whitfield, "Chronology of Luo Zhenyu (1866–1940)," p. 253.

47. Fu, "*Qingshi gao* pinglun shang," pp. 556–557; also in Zhu, *Qingshi shuwen*, pp. 234–235.

48. Xu, Cai, Ji, and Cu, eds., *Minguo renwu da cidian*, vol. 1, p. 27.

49. Brunnert and Hagelstrom, *Present Day Political Organization of China*, p. 74 (item 205).
50. Yu, Miao, Wu, Yang, and Tao, "Kaiguan banfa jiu tiao," p. 82: 拓土開疆，文教昌明.... 我朝天聰八年命額爾德尼巴克什等由蒙古文創立滿文。
51. For example, Hûng Jeo, Maci, and Ortai, eds., *Han-i araha jakûn gûsai tung j'i bithe*, p. 236, 1b-2a; *Baqi tongzhi, chu ji*, p. 236, 1a-b.
52. Fu-ge, *Ting yu congtan*, p. 216 (chapter 11).
53. *Da Qing Manzhou shilu, Da Qing Taizu Gao huangdi shilu*, pp. 108-110.
54. Xu, Cai, Ji, and Cu, eds., *Minguo renwu da cidian*, vol. 1, p. 873.
55. Jin, "Shang Qingshi Guan zhang di yi shu," p. 134: 達文成創制國書，故以為第三冊之首。
56. Yu, Miao, Wu, Yang, and Tao, "Kaiguan banfa jiu tiao," pp. 82–83: 滿蒙字檔須延認滿文，蒙文者編號並摘由。
57. Yu, Miao, Wu, Yang, and Tao, "Kaiguan banfa jiu tiao," p. 89.
58. Zou, Han, and Lu, "*Qingshi gao* zuanxiu shimo yanjiu," p. 87.
59. Wu, "Chen zuanxiu tili," pp. 143–144: 遍訪八旗博雅君子。
60. Xu, Cai, Ji, and Cu, eds., *Minguo renwu da cidian*, vol. 2, p. 1820.
61. Zhang, "Chen zuanxiu Qingshi banfa," p. 187: "國語志"不得不添，此《金》，《元史》所當取法者也。
62. Zou, Han, and Lu, "*Qingshi gao* zuanxiu shimo yanjiu," p. 90.
63. Rhoads, *Manchus and Han*, pp. 3–5.
64. Liang, "Qingshi shangli chugao," p. 23: 國書為一代製作，今則滿人中解者不及萬一矣，鼎革以往，淪漸蓋所共睹，清史不紀，後何述焉？故以殿臺志之末; also in Zhu, *Qingshi shuwen*, p. 101.
65. Song, "*Qingshi gao* guan neiben, guan waiben shiguan zhiming biao," p. 221.
66. Kui-shan, "Guoyu zhi," vol. 2 (no pagination): 文字所以代結繩，無論何國文字，其糾結屈曲無不含有結繩遺意，然體制不一則。又以地勢而殊。歐洲多水故英法諸國文字橫行，如風浪，如水紋。滿洲故里多山林，故文字矗立高聳，如古樹，如孤峯。蓋製造文字本乎人心，人心之靈實根於天地自然之理。非偶然也。Kui-shan's text is also quoted and discussed in Ye, *Qing qianqi de wenhua zhengce*, pp. 56–57.
67. Kui-shan, "Guoyu zhi," vol. 2 (no pagination): 即漢文所不能到之處，滿文亦能曲傳而代達之宜乎皇王製作，行之數百年，而流傳未艾也。又考自入關定鼎以來，執政臣工，或有未曉者，歷朝俱優容之，未嘗施以強迫。至乾隆朝所有新科庶常，均令入館學習國文之舉。因年長舌強，誦讀稍差。行之未久，而議遂寢。亦美猶有憾者！爾茲編纂清史，伊始竊以書法，爲一朝創製國粹，未便闕而不錄。謹首述源流大畧，次述字母，次分類繙譯庶使，後世徵文者有所考焉。Cf. the different translation of the cited *Zuozhuan* passage in Couvreur, trans., *Tch'ouen ts'iou et Tso tchouan*, vol. 2, pp. 534–535.
68. Xu, Cai, Ji, and Cu, eds., *Minguo renwu da cidian*, vol. 1, p. 861.
69. Yi, "Qingshi limu zhengwu," p. 32: 史之大義，崇尚同化。滿洲之主中國，同化於中國乎？中國同化於滿洲乎？學術不異，風俗未殊，典章禮教，彰然猶昔。此滿洲同化於中國也。同化於中國，則今之『清史』，非一家一族之史，乃我中國二百七十年政府與國民之大事紀也。
70. Yi, "Qingshi limu zhengwu," p. 32: 滿洲之文書。
71. Yi, "Qingshi limu zhengwu," p. 33: 清語者，吾儕小民固不攷習。繆君曾為有清文學侍從之臣，亦知彼胡語嘎咭者，果何謂耶？是國語之盛。
72. Yang, "Deciphering Antiquity into Modernity," pp. 179–181; Brown, "Archives at the Margins," pp. 252–256.
73. Zou, Han, and Lu, "*Qingshi gao* zuanxiu shimo yanjiu," p. 91.
74. Xu, Cai, Ji, and Cu, eds., *Minguo renwu da cidian*, vol. 2, pp. 1939–1940.
75. Ye, "Qingshi ying ruhe zuanxiu," vol. 2, 541–542: 滿洲的文字，他的創造和改革，很有一番歷史。就是對於滿清文化的關係，也不少。從前一切重要的典章文件，都是用滿文寫的。但是關於怎樣的創造，怎樣改革，清史稿沒有詳細記載。
76. *Qingshi gao*, vol. 15, chapter 145, pp. 4248, 4252, 4263; chapter 146, p. 4267. Zhu also listed books for which both Manchu and Chinese versions existed, but as he named only the

Chinese titles, I assume that he was not referring to the Manchu versions (was he aware of them?).

77. Ding, "Zhu Shizhe shengping zhushu jiqi san dai cangshu," pp. 61–68.
78. See Zhu, *Qingshi shuwen*.
79. Xu, Cai, Ji, and Cu, eds., *Minguo renwu da cidian*, vol. 1, pp. 844–845.
80. Fan, "Ping *Qingshi gao* yiwenzhi," pp. 1137–1138: 且清代書籍,有異夫前代者,尤不得不博考,蓋非特漢人著述也,有滿族之書,有蒙藏之文 … 有西洋教士之書,有翻譯書 … 多所闕略,此則不知清代有特色者. Also in Zhu, *Qingshi shuwen*, p. 279.
81. Xu, Cai, Ji, and Cu, eds., *Minguo renwu da cidian*, vol. 2, pp. 2289.
82. Chen, *Wang Guowei yu jindai Dong-Xifang xueren*, pp. 389–390.
83. Zhao, "Ping Zhu Shizhe *Qingshi gao* yiwen zhi," pp. 1153–1154: 清代文獻較難統計,而世人尚未充分注意者,約有二事,一為八旗人之著述,二為滿文書及其譯書,故清史藝文志,須加意纂集,而不容草率者,亦必以此二事為先. Also in Zhu, *Qingshi shuwen*, p. 292.
84. Walravens, "V. M. Alekseev—Leben und Werk." The problem is that I see no indication in Alekseev's list of publications that he was engaged in bibliographical research.
85. Zhao, "Ping Zhu Shizhe *Qingshi gao* yiwen zhi," p. 1154: 關乎後者,似尤為重大,國人之習滿文,能通其讀者,日見少,而滿文書籍流行日見稀,設此時不加搜輯,則數千百載後,必無徵 … 此事俄人Alexeiev 等,均嘗從事,日人亦嘗致力於此用力,乃朱君於八旗人之著述,已未能詳加著錄,而於清人,亦僅於經部小學類,略見十數最普通之字典字書,此吾人所引為絕大之遺憾者也.
86. One example: Heijdra, "The East Asia Library and the Gest Collection at Princeton University," pp. 120–135.
87. Kung, "Chen Yinke yu Dongfang yuwen xue," pp. 57, 64.
88. Li, "*Sibu congkan* he *Sibu beiyao*"; Culp, "New Literati and the Reproduction of Antiquity," pp. 103–104.
89. Wilhelm, "Second List of Sinological Books Published in China since 1938," p. 340; cf. the editor's preface in En-hua, *Baqi yiwen bianmu*.
90. Li, ed., *Guoli Beiping tushuguan, Gugong bowuyuan tushuguan Manwen shuji lianhe mulu*.
91. Xu, Cai, Ji, and Cu, eds., *Minguo renwu da cidian*, vol. 2, p. 2722. Xie did not have a bannerman background.
92. Xie, "Qing kaiguo shiliao kaoxu lunding bubian."
93. Guanglu and Li, "Qing Taizu chao *Lao Manwen yuandang* yu *Manwen laodang* zhi bijiao yanjiu," pp. 4–5.
94. Shan, "Zhengli Manwen laodang ji," p. 324.
95. Dai, "Zaoqi gu wenzi xuezhe—Bao shi fuzi"; Xu, "*Xuxiu 'Siku quanshu' zongmu tiyao* xiaoxue lei Manwen tushu tiyao tanxi."
96. Sungsen, *Qinding Mengwen huishu*; note slip in vol. 2 reads: 書中錯誤隨手改正（奉寬記）.
97. Guo, "*Xuxiu Siku tiyao* zuanxiu kaolüe."; Peng, "*Xuxiu siku quanshu zongmu tiyao* kaolüe"; Luo, "*Xuxiu Siku quanshu zongmu tiyao* bianzuan shi jiyao"; Luo, "*Xuxiu Siku quanshu zongmu tiyao gaoben* zuanxiu shimo"; Li, "*Shiko zensho no zokushū o meguru rekishiteki tenkai ni kansuru ichi kōsatsu*"; Yamane, *Tōhō bunka jigyō no rekishi: Shōwa zenki ni okeru Nit-Chū bunka kōryū*, chapters 1–2.
98. A total of 872 printed pages, each containing four manuscript pages, thus 3,488 pages.
99. Guo, "*Xuxiu Siku quanshu zongmu tiyao* de zhengli fangfa yu pingjia," p. 25. I do not know how much money Feng-kuan made from this, but Luo Zhenyu was paid thirty dollars (*yinyuan* 銀元) per entry: Guo, "*Xuxiu Siku tiyao* zuanxiu kaolüe," p. 20.
100. Wang, ed., *Xuxiu Siku quanshu tiyao*, vol. 1, pp. 8–9, and the table of contents, pp. 128–130.
101. *Xuxiu "Siku quanshu" zongmu tiyao (gaoben)*, vol. 5, pp. 233, 235.

102. *Xuxiu "Siku quanshu" zongmu tiyao (gaoben)*, vol. 5, p. 192: 遜朝京師四城, 除官學外, 私立義學不下四十餘處, 皆供給學生食宿, 津貼膏火, 免費讀書... 今學校收費, 中戶以下不能問津之不同.
103. Fang, "Yin-lu," p. 926.
104. Yi-geng, "Qingyu renming yi Han." I do not know what the manuscript looked like; this printed version, at least, does not contain Manchu script but is arranged in the order of the Manchu syllabary.
105. *Xuxiu "Siku quanshu" zongmu tiyao (gaoben)*, vol. 6, pp. 206–207: 民國纂修『清史稿』適無此門, 學者病之... 可補『清史稿』之缺, 謂爲研治國語之津梁.
106. Yang and Zhang, *Dalian Tushuguan cang shaoshu minzu guji tushu zonglu*; Beijing shi minzu guji zhengli chuban guihua xiaozu, *Beijing diqu Manwen tushu zongmu*.
107. Fuchs, "Neues Material zur mandjurischen Literatur aus Pekinger Bibliotheken"; Fuchs, *Beiträge zur Mandjurischen Bibliographie und Literatur*, and other publications.
108. Wang, *Xuxiu Siku quanshu tiyao*.
109. Li, "*Shiko zensho* no zokushū o meguru rekishiteki tenkai ni kansuru ichi kōsatsu," pp. 161–162.
110. Luo, "Zhengli shuoming," vol. 1, p. 4: 因存在整理和排版的困難, 計畫集中附在全書最後部分出版.
111. Li, "Senkyūhyakukyūjū nendai ni okeru *Shiko zensho* kanren sōsho no kankō oyobi sono bunkateki imi," pp. 8–9. A few linguistic titles contained Manchu script used as phonetic notation, but these books were not included *qua* Manchu books but as books on Chinese phonology.

The Textual Time Machine
Truth, Facts, and the *Shuowen*, 1770–1932

Modern histories of the Qing dynasty often divide it into two periods: "High Qing" and "Late Qing." The first—a period of sociopolitical success, splendor, territorial expansion, and a general *Pax Manchurica* maintained by the three great emperors (Kangxi, Yongzheng, and Qianlong); the second—a period of social unrest, rebellions, Western intrusions, successive failures, and deterioration of social, economic, and political institutions. It is no coincidence that the authoritative *Cambridge History of China* series divided Qing history into two, with the year 1800 serving as a dividing line. Links between the two periods have been analyzed mostly in terms of how the final decades of the first embedded the second one's roots of decline—usually described as manifesting in corruption, fiscal and institutional malfunction, lack of reform, wrongheaded negotiations with Western powers, or the peaceful era's unmanageable population growth. Any threads of substantial continuity between High Qing and Late Qing are understood as succumbing to a break between former splendor and later failure, and they stayed severed.

In intellectual history, we must pay attention also to a certain development during the mid-Qing (seen as the years that spanned the two periods, that is, roughly 1750–1850). I refer, namely, to a style of scholarship and analysis that was called evidential learning, which subsequently suffered attacks from the early nineteenth century onward. A major debate between so-called Han scholars (i.e., "philologists") versus Song scholars (i.e., "philosophers") formed the context in which evidential learning was cast aside and statecraft learning embraced. Finally, with the radical breaks that occurred at the turn of the twentieth century, as "modernity" kicked in, Western learning (science and philosophy in particular) superseded the "old learning," which remained only as a symbol of something perceived as China's intellectual degeneration. With this narrative in mind, we see more breaks than continuities. In particular, as many of the leading writers became focused on the practical world, especially during the second half of the nineteenth century, the promise of the eighteenth-century "philological turn" seems not to have endured into the Late Qing. Any perceived links between Qianlong-era and Republican-era scholarship would seem even more far-fetched, at best.

However, in order to hold onto such complex links and be able to see and discuss certain connecting threads, we should consider the *Shuowen* as a case study. The changes and continuities related to its study shed important light, I believe, on both Qing eras and the Republican era as well. The case of the *Shuowen*—which I use heuristically as a "time machine"—allows us to penetrate the close interaction between time, language, and power: a linguistic text that transformed over time on the one hand (in uses and form), but that cuts through conventional periodizations on the other—a text that both sustained identities and facilitated their crystallization, thereby becoming a formidable tool in the hands of so-called conservatives, reformers, and nationalists alike. This general genealogy is also an important part of the longer history of the formation of New Sinology, from the Chinese angle.

The *Shuowen jiezi* 說文解字 (Analysis of simple graphs as an explanation of complex characters) is a Han dynasty philological text that deals mostly with the etymology of characters found in classical texts. While the work had been in circulation and use for many centuries prior to the Qing, and required no "rediscovery" of sorts, during the mid-Qing the ways in which it was used—its status and importance (concrete and symbolic)—changed dramatically. From the 1770s, the *Shuowen* became one of the central textual objects of inquiry in China, a centrality that persisted all the way to the late 1920s and early 1930s with the monumental collection of *Shuowen* editions and studies by Ding Fubao 丁福保 (1874–1952).[1] The continued engagement with the *Shuowen*—not simply as a storehouse of "facts" or truisms for those interested in something else (the Classics, early China, linguistics, etc.), but as a subject of research in its own right—elicits the question: Why?

Such a long, continual commitment to *Shuowen* studies, across some of the most turbulent moments in China's history, also suggests that there is more than one answer to "why"; in fact, the reasons pertaining in the prosperous late eighteenth century were not necessarily similar to those in the wake of the Opium Wars and Taiping Rebellion of the mid-nineteenth century or to those in the twentieth century. The *Shuowen*, in short, served very different purposes, and was part of different intellectual-social-political climates and agendas.

In this chapter I analyze the transformation and persistence of *Shuowen* studies. The consequent argument runs as follows: during the last decades of the eighteenth century a tsunami of *Shuowen* studies dramatically transformed the status and usage of the text; the vaunted status of both the *Shuowen* and its traditional commentaries and studies continued throughout the nineteenth century, spanning the Opium Wars and Taiping Rebellion, and received attention from some who were called "reformers," "statecraft-thinkers," and "self-strengthening" protagonists. At the turn of the twentieth century, after the Sino-Japanese War, and as new notions of nation, history, and classicism arose, the Han-era work retained its status, yet the reasons for its study and for its praise changed from those that preceded.

I use the notion of a "time machine" to convey the idea that, put simplistically, during the eighteenth and nineteenth centuries, the *Shuowen* was part of a desire to get closer to antiquity. It allowed scholars to come as close as possible (with some exceptions) to the language of the classical texts, and hence to be able to recover their meanings, and thence to recover and put into motion the ancient (true) Way (道). With antiquity, the ancients, and the Way as the loci of truth, facts, and modes of behavior, scholars found the *Shuowen* to be a useful means for reaching those goals: this was all part of the "philological turn" of the eighteenth century. The *Shuowen* (along with other philological texts) symbolized the philological turn, the correct methodology, and the way to get the Way right. The upheavals of the mid-nineteenth century, while generating various movements to make the country—its army and administration—stronger and more effective, did not cause overall doubt in the Way. Therefore, the continued interest in the *Shuowen* was still related to the idea that it could conduct historical actors during the Qing to the right, ancient, Way.

At this time, especially at the turn of the twentieth century, antiquity was beginning to be understood as a problem rather than the solution to sociopolitical and cultural anxieties. As a time machine, it was becoming obsolete. Nonetheless, intellectuals wanted a new time machine (metaphorically, of course, although we do have time travel fiction of the period too)—one that could transport them into the future (i.e., "modernize"). A significant part of this future orientation of intellectuals meant the molding of a new, national identity—alongside a new understanding of the term "civilization," with its demands and potential gains. With this agenda in mind, the past was critical for the future: it provided an important segment of and for the new Chinese identity as well as an explanatory model that was filled with national pride: it showed why China was, and perhaps is/will be, a glorious civilization. The *Shuowen* could thus serve several purposes to achieve the main goals of state-building, modernization, and the creation of shared national identity with a proud place among other nations, including:

1. a splendid relic of ancient Chinese civilization, providing access to ancient wisdom;
2. a reminder to Chinese and others of how the Chinese language (mainly script) flourished for so long a time, without rupture (a somewhat problematic argument for philologists);
3. a tool in helping to build linguistic genealogies and language reforms;
4. proof that important new terminologies so prominent throughout Chinese society were in fact rooted in indigenous, ancient Chinese (while, at times, finding linguistic unity within the many regional variations);
5. demonstration of the uniqueness of the Chinese character-based script, related to a unique national identity and perhaps mind; and
6. for those pursuing "scientific history," it was a tool for understanding antiquity "scientifically," or for doubting it when the need arose (but not in order to revive antiquity–*au contraire,* to put it behind museum glass or research/textbook covers as an object that belongs in a past, a past that serves the modern present from afar).

Another aspect of the history of *Shuowen* studies concerns the change in what constituted truth and facts, from the eighteenth to the twentieth centuries. If the sort of textual antiquity that the *Shuowen* represented stood for timeless truth and facts for the earlier scholars, then for the later ones, at the turn of the twentieth century, truth and facts meant something very different. Textual studies could unravel ancient meanings in ancient texts; indeed, if used "scientifically," such studies had importance (depending on for whom and for what end). But ancient texts and their meanings eventually no longer corresponded to contemporary truths and facts, which then had to be sought elsewhere (with new categories, like science and philosophy, taking hold).

With so many different uses, it should not come as a surprise that the *Shuowen* in the early decades of the twentieth century could draw to it such diverse scholars with different, even contradictory, agendas and inclinations. Be it National Essence, National Learning, Doubting Antiquity, Modernism, Traditionalism, Buddhism, Anarchism, and so on—each scholar could find what he wanted in the text. And while many criticized earlier philologists for their "uselessness" (among other flaws), these twentieth-century scholars nonetheless followed the eighteenth- and nineteenth-century philological footsteps, even if most of them had very different aims from those of the earlier group of philologists. Therefore, while the Qian-Jia period (marking the reign periods of emperors Qianlong 乾隆, 1736–1796, and Jiaqing 嘉慶, 1796–1820) produced a wave of *Shuowen* enthusiasm that emanated from anxieties about Ru 儒 (that is, the "true," or "real") identity, about meandering too far from the main path of ancient knowledge, and about a wish to draw closer to antiquity, it was in the early twentieth century, with enormous anxieties about China's national identity and its future, that made the *Shuowen* highly relevant, while concurrently the figure of Kongzi 孔子 (Confucius), the classics assigned to him, and his Ru followers were all being more or less rejected.

The Qian-Jia Period (1736–1820) and Ancient Learning

During the final decades of the eighteenth century, the status of the *Shuowen* rose dramatically. With modest beginnings that were often assigned to Hui Dong 惠棟 (1697–1758), interest in the work increased, especially from the 1770s. This surge in interest can be seen, for example, in Wang Mingsheng's 王鳴盛 (1722–1798) assertion that "the *Shuowen* is the world's paramount type of book; one who reads all the books in the world but not the *Shuowen* is as one who has not read [at all]. However, one who is capable of understanding the *Shuowen* even without having read the rest of the books, must be regarded as a comprehensive Ru" (說文為天下第一種書，讀徧天下書，不讀說文，猶不讀也；但能通說文，餘書皆未讀，不可謂非通儒也).[2] The issue was not one of "rediscovery"—the *Shuowen* had been in use and circulation long before the 1700s—but the scope of its use and its significance were unheard of prior to the 1770s.

The main reason for such a change was that the *Shuowen* allowed scholarly learning to "come close to antiquity" (進乎古). Wang Mingsheng, in his preface to Sun Xingyan's 孫星衍 (1753–1818) *Wenzi tang ji* 問字堂集 (Collected writings from the Hall of Lexical Inquiries), expressed this notion clearly, along with the notion of connecting the present (今) with antiquity (古): "[consider] those who love antiquity like Sun [Xingyan]. Their learning comes close to antiquity, and can also connect with the present" (好古如孫君, 其學進乎古, 而又能通于今).³ Qian-Jia era scholars understood the long history of Ru scholarship and conduct as a manifestation of a rupture between antiquity and their own present, a rupture that was linked to the Qin burning of books (213 BCE), to the problematic nature of Wei-Jin period (220–420 CE) scholarship, and, more recently, to the deplorable practices of Song (960–1279) and Ming (1368–1644) scholars.

Qian-Jia scholars aimed to restore the integrity of antiquity, not simply because they "loved antiquity" (that too), but because they saw antiquity as the source of true knowledge (and truth in general), as the source of their identity as Ru, and as the fountainhead of practical knowledge concerning how to build and maintain self, society, and state (in short—All under Heaven, and also the entire cosmic order). The rupture with antiquity, for them, could not be bridged by contemplation, meditation, introspection, or various "idle chatter" (清談), which they regarded as "to chisel into air" (鑿空).⁴ Since the truth of antiquity was only to be found in ancient texts, and since the rupture was predominantly textual, the bridge between antiquity and the present had to be built with textual building blocks. The *Shuowen* (along with many other philologically oriented texts) thus supplied the building blocks for the bridge to antiquity and ultimately the Way.

We should also remember, however, that as an ancient writing the *Shuowen* suffered from textual problems along the way on its long course from the Han to the Qing. Furthermore, it was not the words of the ancient (often mythical) sages, but a scholarly composition by a real person. Therefore, as Qian-Jia scholars began using the *Shuowen* so frequently, they actually aimed to correct it, to make sure the textual building blocks were the correct ones. In light of this, numerous publications and research projects (by individuals or teams) appeared. The *Shuowen* was both a means for getting to antiquity and an object of inquiry in its own right: the philologists did not want to set the time-machine dial on "Kongzi" only to find that they were taken to Han times.

Weng Fanggang 翁方綱 (1733–1818), a prominent northern official, epigrapher, and Cheng-Zhu (Song learning) defender, wrote in 1812:

> The study of textual research has as its main priority getting to the core of meanings and principles, not the delight in extensiveness or in pettiness, nor the delight in deviations [from orthodoxy], nor self-praise. Not praising oneself, not delighting in deviation, not delighting in extensiveness and in pettiness, but nonetheless exerting oneself in textual research, this can be said to be [true] textual research.... Textual research is simply the opposite of the study of empty chattering over meanings and principles. In general, what is considered textual research is the desire to support the search for actual truths [found in] meanings and principles.... The process of comprehending the Classics and learning about antiquity must be preceded by textual research.⁵
> 考訂之學, 以衷於義理為主, 其嗜博, 嗜瑣者非也, 其嗜異者非也, 其矜己者非也. 不矜己, 不嗜異, 不嗜博, 嗜瑣, 而專力於考訂, 斯可以言考訂矣.... 考訂者, 對空

談義理之學而言之也,凡所為考訂者,欲以資義理之求是也....通經學古之事,必於考訂先之.

If one wanted to make a valid argument—for instance, supporting or objecting to the Cheng-Zhu or any other tradition—one would have to anchor one's words in textual research—that is, in philology—and the *Shuowen* was the most important anchor. Thus, throughout the nineteenth century, treatises and books focusing on philology continued to be published in vast numbers. Proponents of exact and rigorous textual-philological studies were gradually, from the early nineteenth century, becoming known as "Han learning" scholars, precisely because of their stress on Han-era scholarship. The chief means for accomplishing that was, of course, the *Shuowen*.

Before and between Wars: The *Shuowen* Undercurrent Continues in the Nineteenth Century

The philological zeitgeist based on this flourishing of "evidential scholarship" and textual research, especially concerning the *Shuowen* and other ancient works, continued to reign supreme during the nineteenth century. Even scholars such as Wei Yuan 魏源 (1794–1856), who objected to the so-called Han learning scholars—claiming they "confined the wise and bright under heaven and led [them] to follow a useless path" (錮天下聰明知慧,使盡出于無用之一途)— still accepted the priority of meticulous textual research in making various arguments.[6] Indeed, Wei himself engaged in philological research, and his work on the history of the Yuan dynasty was indebted to Qian-Jia philologically oriented scholarship, such as Qian Daxin's 錢大昕 (1728–1804) *Yuanshi shizu biao* (元史氏族表, Table of clan names for Yuan history), and *Yuanshi yiwenzhi* (元史藝文志, Bibliographical treatise for Yuan history).[7]

Moreover, the *Huangchao jingshi wenbian* 皇朝經世文編 (Collected essays on statecraft of the glorious [Qing] dynasty), of which Wei Yuan was the chief compiler, included philological research and abundant references to philological studies. Philology was central to, and was understood as part and parcel of, statecraft. And despite the enormous difficulties the Qing faced during the 1840s and 1850s, in the form of the Opium Wars and the Taiping Rebellion, philology was still understood at the very least as a key to the survival of the *dao* in many people's eyes.

And survival was not taken for granted. Yu Yue's 俞樾 (1821–1907) case demonstrates that he was worried about nothing less than the "abandonment of the Way" (舍道). Yu linked his anxieties about Ru identity to a longing for the Qianlong era, which produced so many gifted scholars, especially Dai Zhen 戴震 (1724–1777). That era represented a legacy that Yu Yue had received from his mentors, who were Dai's students. Later, Yu's appreciation for Dai was transferred to Yu's student Zhang Binglin 章炳麟 (Taiyan 太炎, 1868–1936), who promoted the study of Dai Zhen, yet Dai Zhen's—and others'—ascendance and appreciation in the early twentieth century were related to new factors, which will be discussed in the following section.[8]

In order to promote the continuity of the Way, Yu, like many of his peers, leaned heavily upon the *Shuowen*. In 1862, he wrote that,

> Since Qin and Han [times] onward, the classical texts in Seal Script continually changed, while of the profundity of characters created by the ancient sages only a tiny percent of the very many survived; the only solid base was the one book by Xu Shen 許慎 of the Han dynasty—the *Shuowen jiezi*. A scholar who is born today and desires to follow from the texts and observe the Way has no origin point other than this [book]. Yet later generations of scholars have discarded solid facts and competed in empty talk. *Shuowen* studies were [thus] abandoned without [further] discussions.
> 自秦漢以來, 篆籀遞變, 而古聖人剙造文字之精微, 其存十一於千百者, 實賴有漢許叔重氏《說文解字》一書。士生今日, 而欲因文見道, 外是無由矣。乃後世學者, 舍實事而競空言。說文之學廢而不講。[9]

Yu bemoaned pre–Qian-Jia scholarship for discarding the *Shuowen* and with it concrete studies, while delving into empty talk. He regarded Qian-Jia scholars as marking a fundamental change is this regard: "The classical skills in my dynasty[, however,] flourished and thrived, and scholars knew [they needed to] follow paleography in order to comprehend etymology; to follow etymology in order to comprehend meanings and principles" (我朝經術昌明, 士知由文字而通訓詁, 由訓詁而通義理). Yu was well aware (like Qian-Jia scholars before him) that the *Shuowen* was a later compilation, not a sage-time work, and hence the need to research it and to "choose what is right [in it] while separating what is wrong" (擇其是而違其非). Nonetheless, all in all, Yu expressed his "trust and love of it [the *Shuowen*]" (信而好之), thereby reminding the reader of Kongzi's use of these words, except that Kongzi's object of trust and love was antiquity and/or the ancients. The literary allusion would thus directly link *Shuowen* to antiquity.

Similarly, Zhang Zhidong 張之洞 (1837–1909), in 1871, expressed clear-cut opinions regarding the *Shuowen:* "[If] one seeks to comprehend meanings and principles, one must begin with phonology and etymology; [if] one desires to comprehend phonology and etymology, one must begin with the *Shuowen*" (求通義理, 必自音訓始, 欲通音訓, 必自說文始). Zhang thought that anyone who "reads books is doing none else but valuing the opinions of the ancients" (讀書貴得古人意而已),[10] and certainly the *Shuowen* would have been the ultimate source.

After the mid-nineteenth century, *Shuowen* appreciation was not only relevant to those elite scholars who were considered to be "traditionalists." Feng Guifen 馮桂芬 (1809–1874), a mastermind, perhaps, of the self-strengthening movement, likewise shared such appreciation. He stressed that "one cannot neglect to read the *Shuowen*" (不可不讀説文),[11] and not just any *Shuowen*—Duan Yucai's 段玉裁 (1735–1815) *Shuowen* research came first. Feng wrote; "one cannot neglect to read Duan's commentary [on the *Shuowen*]" (不可不讀段注). He, too, regarded the great rise of classical and philological learning during his dynasty with admiration, after many dynasties in which such studies had been declining. Feng saw Hui Dong as the one who began this new classicism (after a few initial steps by Gu Yanwu 顧炎武 [1613–1682]), and then Zhu Yun 朱筠

(1729–1781), Duan Yucai, Qian Daxin, Dai Zhen, and others. The Qian-Jia era was, for Feng, the apogee of *Shuowen* and philological learning, the backbone of classical studies. Feng even composed his own *Shuowen* research, in which he corrected some of Duan Yucai's findings.

Feng Guifen's senior colleague, Zeng Guofan 曾國藩 (1811–1872), often credited with subduing the Taiping Rebellion and presiding over the self-strengthening movement, came to appreciate philological research and engage in it, especially as concerns the study of ritual. Similarly, Li Hongzao 李鴻藻 (1820–1897), a prominent minister and grand councilor involved in the self-strengthening movement and a participant in negotiations with Western nations and in Western learning, also pursued philology well into the 1880s. Likewise, Li Hongzhang 李鴻章 (1823–1901) expressed great respect for Duan Yucai's *Shuowen* studies. In around 1888, he was invited to write a preface to a certain just-discovered Jiaqing-era book that shed light on Duan's *Shuowen* scholarship. Li stated that the fortunate turning point of *Shuowen* studies began in the Qianlong era. The remark reveals that Li Hongzhang had an acute understanding of the *Shuowen*'s transmission, including Feng Guifen's role in it.[12]

It is important to note that while there arose this intense interest in philology and its role in approaching historical facts, there was at the same time a significant change among scholars in their use of science in order to approach natural facts. During the Qian-Jia period, and in many ways all the way to the 1850s, science in general terms was understood by elite scholars as part and parcel of their culture, including specific Western scientific ideas that had been arriving already for over a century. The *Shuowen*, and philology in general, therefore, was understood as vital for scientific endeavors.

Yet, by the 1850s, an important shift took place. Science (and technology) began to be understood as something apart from scholarly culture as expressed through the ancient texts and their commentaries. The reasons for European successes in science and technology, along with their military prowess (proved in the Opium Wars and Taiping Rebellion), as opposed to Qing losses and technological disadvantages, began to be interpreted as fundamental and not merely due to random transmission problems. It began to dawn on Qing scholars that scientific and technological success may not, by default or at all, be related to antiquity, and as they wished to integrate technological improvements with the survival of the realm, they had to accept European supremacy, without assuming it all came down from the classics. At the same time, the classics and their Way were still the backbones of their cultural and political identity and authority, and were not something to get rid of altogether. The way to do it was to separate technological means (new, Western) from civilizational essence (Chinese, classical). In a nutshell, the scientific-technological quantum leap Qing scholars (and officials) encountered—in the form of steam gunships, for example—could no longer be explained away as simply a modification of their own ancient ways. Mid-nineteenth-century European science and technology were new and different; they demanded a different categorical reasoning, and they therefore broke away from the classical hold. The older association of the *Shuowen* with science was broken; but as far as running the state, society, and self, the *Shuowen*, its philology, and its impact on notions of antiquity, its stance in present affairs, and the acceptance of the paramount supremacy of the ancient Way remained intact and were highly esteemed. This esteem was not only part of *Shuowen* prefaces and postscripts (a natural habitat for inflated praise), but can be seen through the vast engagement with the *Shuowen* in a host of publications (and reprints) throughout the nineteenth century, many of which were descendants of Qian-Jia research on philology, and Duan Yucai's work in particular (see Appendix A and B).

Turning a Page in the *Shuowen:* From the Sino-Japanese War to the Republic

While the great rebellions and wars of the mid-nineteenth century did not induce scholars to doubt the ancient Way itself, the Sino-Japanese War of 1894–1895, along with events in its aftermath, certainly did. An increasing number of intellectuals began to feel and pronounce such doubts. The Way of the ancients seemed less and less relevant to the cause of "making the state wealthy and its army strong" (富國強軍); even the great accomplishments in *Shuowen* studies may not have provided the key for future success. And as new categories and fields of knowledge and practice—new philosophy (including new ideas about state, nation, society, and their relationships) and science in particular—began to hold sway over the minds and hearts of Chinese intellectuals, antiquity and the ancient Classics, for which the *Shuowen* was the key, ran the risk of being either irrelevant or an outright problem (as possible accomplice in causing China's deterioration).

Indeed, growing numbers of intellectuals expressed such notions about antiquity and its textual delegates, as they fixed their eyes on the future rather than on the past. Debates about antiquity raged, and even the *Shuowen* was at times questioned. One of the most famous of such debates was the one precipitated by Gu Jiegang 顧頡剛 (1893–1980) as part of the *Gushibian* 古史辨 (Ancient history debates) publications, especially during the 1920s. In that debate, which extended well beyond *Shuowen* issues per se, Gu—a proponent of the "we doubt antiquity" (疑古) position—presented the *Shuowen* as a problematic tool for understanding the past. Liu Yizheng 柳詒徵 (1880–1956), on the other hand, defended the *Shuowen* and presented it as a powerful scientific tool for historical research, thus doubting Gu's position.[13] Although the 1920s were times in which those deemed more traditionalist did not often gain the upper hand, eventually, the *Shuowen* dodged the bullet and continued to serve as a key for aiding a nation under construction. How so?

One intellectual who explicitly stated the importance of the past for any present or future goals of the old-new Chinese nation was Zhang Binglin, mentioned above. And among the things of the past that he regarded as essential for the Chinese, the *Shuowen* was of great importance, a view that came no doubt from his scholarly lineage, as we saw. But they were also tied to his notions of language in general, and, as well, to his notions of the role of antiquity within the new national zeal. In short, the *Shuowen* supplied for Zhang the origins of linguistic form and meaning: a long history that united the nation, and, importantly, a sign of the greatness of Chinese civilization. Given the linguistic reforms being discussed by many intellectuals of the time, the *Shuowen* provided a tool for use by the reformers. It accorded with ancient precepts and represented progress with, perhaps, Chinese characteristics. Zhang also made it clear that philological interests were closely related to nationalism and patriotism.[14] Indeed, even when he was in Japan during the 1900s, he found it essential to teach the *Shuowen* to younger fellow revolutionaries, such as Qian Xuantong 錢玄同 (1887–1939) and Lu Xun 魯迅 (1881–1936).[15]

Similarly, National Essence enthusiasts saw the *Shuowen* as a gateway to the new China, and Liu Shipei's engagement with the *Shuowen* speaks to that effect. And for modern school curricula, the *Shuowen* was likewise encouraged during the 1910s and well into the May 4th era (that is, well into the 1920s).

Of course, studying the *Shuowen* did not necessarily mean endorsing antiquity and its treasured textual tradition: Wu Zhihui 吳稚暉 (1865–1953), for example, argued that the Chinese "national treasures . . . should be thrown into the toilet."[16] Lu Xun advised in 1918 that "the Chinese national essence . . . amounts to a fart" (中國國粹 . . . 等於放屁).[17] And Qian Xuantong thought that "the destruction of Confucian learning and Daoist religion is the fundamental solution if China is not to perish and if the Chinese people are to become a civilized people of the twentieth century."[18]

Nonetheless, even those who denounced the Classics in such harsh words kept the *Shuowen*. Lu Xun, who famously associated classical learning with cannibalism, kept several editions of the *Shuowen* in his library, added his handwritten notes to them, and perhaps used the lexical definitions in *Shuowen* for his writings and translations. Qian Xuantong, highly involved in linguistic reforms, taught phonetics, and at times praised the *Shuowen* (although at other times he dismissed it), as did Wu Zhihui, who had been the one to suggest throwing such national treasures into the toilet. Furthermore, as linguistic reforms were discussed time and again, the *Shuowen* was used to build strategies, and as dictionaries (themselves, in several ways, a major tool and product of nationalism) were produced, once again the *Shuowen* had a purpose. Use (or misuse) of the *Shuowen* could also grant ancient legitimacy to ideological and political stands of the day, be they for questions of race and nation, or for the Chinese understanding of the status of women.

Those early twentieth-century days were also a time of importance in collecting and curating national treasures. In some cases, material treasures were placed and displayed in museums, images were collected and published in books, and some textual treasures per se were collected into thematic projects. One of those was the greatest *Shuowen* project of the time: the *Shuowen jiezi gulin* (說文解字詁林) (Forest of explanations on the analysis of characters and explanation of writing). The chief collector, perhaps better termed curator, was Ding Fubao (introduced earlier).

Ding was a celebrity of sorts by the 1920s, a well-known and connected collector, translator (from Japanese), and publisher, who already had many volumes of collected materials published in the fields of mathematics, medicine, and Buddhism. He is also credited with a major Buddhist dictionary (well before the *Shuowen gulin* was published), and his son—Zhou Yunqing 周雲青 (credited with the republication of the *Zhonghua da zidian*, just a few years after the *Gulin* project)—compiled collations of ancient texts, including a text series dealing with astronomy.

According to Ding, he began collecting *Shuowen* editions in 1895, and, as an avid bibliophile, had managed to gather a substantial number of them by the early 1920s. In his various prefaces to the project, Ding struck a traditional manner: he narrated the origins of the Chinese writing system in the Yellow Emperor, then to Confucius and the establishment of the Classics, finally arriving at the history and importance of the *Shuowen*. Ding's traditional introduction notwithstanding, other contributors of prefaces and postscripts described the project using different, modern, tones.

Thus when, in 1926, Meng Sen 孟森 (1868–1938) wrote the first preface to Ding Fubao's project (apart from Ding's own preface), he emphasized several aspects: the *Shuowen* in general (and the writing system it stood for, the six ways of character formation in particular, or *liushu* 六書) was a marker of Chinese civilization; it demonstrated, according to Meng, the "uniqueness of the Chinese nation" (*wuguosuo duyou* 吾國所獨有) and its "fabulously long" (*qianwan nian* 千萬年) and continual history; it allowed, by understanding the formation of the written characters, an understanding of "social history" (*shehui lishi* 社會歷史); it was scientific, and the *Shuowen gulin* would ensure a "scientific application in the future" (*jianglai kexue zhi yong* 將來科學之用). Meng saw it as imperative that anyone who wanted to reform the written language should first thoroughly research and know its origins, namely antiquity, in order to "search for the new" (*qiuxin* 求新). He also acknowledged that *Shuowen* studies had been the greatest and most important achievement of the Qing period (Duan Yucai in particular), and he listed a line of scholarly descent from the mid-Qing to his own day.

Wu Zhihui likewise wrote prefaces to the *Shuowen gulin*. In a 1932 preface he, like Meng Sen, stressed the connection and continuation of the Chinese writing system for "four or five thousand years" (*siwuqian nian* 四五千年). All of those writing prefaces and postscripts to the *Shuowen gulin* used classical Chinese to convey their messages, not any type of vernacular or *baihua*, perhaps attesting to the linguistic continuity they endorsed. Indeed, the style of the prefaces and postscripts seems often to resonate with mid-Qing assertions about the *Shuowen*. It should also be noted that both Wu and Meng wrote favorable prefaces to Ding's publication of Buddhist texts a few years earlier.

The point here is not that everyone loved and appreciated the *Shuowen*; some did, some did not, some asserted one thing in one context and the opposite in another. The point is that the *Shuowen* became an important national tool. For those genuinely interested in the classical tradition it could be used for new ideas about the past; for those with resentment toward the classics it could serve for building and enhancing national pride.

In a way, the rationale behind all of the importance attached to the *Shuowen* in early twentieth-century China was not so different from the rationale in India for attaching importance to Paninian grammar. Pāṇini's analysis of the Sanskrit language, dating to the middle of the first millennium BCE, had been the cornerstone of Sanskrit linguistic (with philosophical underpinnings) thought in premodern India. In the nineteenth century, as Western scholars became aware of these texts, Pāṇini was hailed by them as a paramount linguist, and his work as the first scientific and critical endeavor that predated the modern discipline. Thus, in the late nineteenth and early twentieth centuries, Indian (Hindu) nationalists used Pāṇini—the person and his texts—as part of their efforts at the "nationalization of Sanskrit," which was "a major topic of socio-political interest throughout India."[19] In both cases, an ancient linguistic text became a beacon for nationalist feelings, and in both cases, from a living part of past tradition, such a text became a ground on which to construct a future nation. We should also consider the new (even if with limited impact) genre of *"gulin"* and the format of that project: if, for about a century and a half, the *Shuowen* was in constant flux from analysis, editing, commentary, and discovery, then with the *gulin* edition the many different *Shuowen*s (plural) were all collected into a magnificent centerpiece. Magnificent but less alive; the *gulin* was more relevant as a centerpiece, showcasing the past, less so as a dynamic part of a living culture—present- and future-oriented. Furthermore, as truth became less a matter of texts, especially ancient texts, and more linked to new scientific and philosophical evidence, those seeking truth engaged less with the concrete, ancient, textual facts and more with what was understood as scientific. To research the *Shuowen*, therefore, could mean a scientific understanding of the *past,* but not an unearthing of *present-day* facts.

Nonetheless, scholars in modern China continued to explore the *Shuowen*, research it, and gain new insights into its subtleties. Still, *Shuowen* research and use in the modern era, for the most part, did not aim to make the Way of antiquity alive again, but rather to cast it in modern, scientific ways. If unearthing the language of the classics before the twentieth century meant, potentially, a powerful time machine with which users could get to antiquity, that ancient language ceased to play such a role later on; yet mastering it, through the *Shuowen,* still provided power of authority and precedence, and identity anchors, to its modern users.

Appendix A: The Japan (Mis-)Connection

Scholars have identified many parallels in the scholarship of the Qing and Tokugawa periods, specifically in the development in Japan of "ancient learning" (*kogaku* 古學) and evidential-learning methodology (*kōshōgaku* 考證學).

I believe exploring the *Shuowen*'s history in Japan during the eighteenth and nineteenth centuries highlights the conclusions of this chapter. In particular, it emphasizes how the use of the *Shuowen* in China had so much to do with questions of identity, certainly at the turn of the twentieth century, as that identity was tied to the nation. To expect, then, a parallel rise in *Shuowen* studies in Tokugawa or Meiji Japan might bring disappointment. Japanese scholars engaged with the *Shuowen* in ways similar to early and pre-Qing scholars, that is, as a text that could assist in solving specific textual riddles, but not as a major object of inquiry in its own right; the late eighteenth century and early nineteenth century did not mark any remarkable change in Japanese *Shuowen* studies despite the many resemblances between Qing and Tokugawa philological turns. It was only after Duan Yucai's *Shuowen jiezi zhu* arrived in Japan—in the 1820s, in all likelihood through the Nagasaki trading port—that Japanese scholars began to concentrate some effort on the *Shuowen*. But in any event there were relatively few scholars who worked on it.

The 1826 publication of a *Shuowen* edition in Japan, based on Mao Jin's 毛晉 (1599–1659) and Mao Yi's 毛扆 (b. 1640) rendition of Xu Xuan's 徐鉉 (916–991) *Shuowen*—the *Jigu ge Shuowen* 汲古閣説文 (The *Shuowen* from the Pavilion for Absorbing Antiquity)—steered some discussions on the subject. This edition, often called *Setsumon shinpon* 説文真本 (The authentic *Shuowen*), had already been corrected by Duan Yucai in his *Jigu ge Shuowen ding* 汲古閣説文訂 (Corrected *Shuowen* from the Pavilion for Absorbing Antiquity) three decades earlier, but this was the first time it was published in Japan. One of the first Japanese to deal with the *Shuowen* in this manner was Matsuzaki Kōdō 松崎慊堂 (1771–1844), who, in 1827, also delved into Duan's *Shuowen jiezi zhu*, discussed it with other Japanese scholars, and organized a small "*Shuowen* gathering" (*Setsumon* kai 説文会) wherein *Shuowen*-related matters were deliberated. Interestingly, according to his diary, Kōdō borrowed the *Shuowen jiezi zhu* from his superior at the prestigious academy Shōheikō 昌平黌 in Edo. This was Hayashi Jussai 林述齋 (1768–1841), known to be a follower of Zhu Xi 朱熹 (1130–1200). Kōdō began examining more thoroughly the *Shuowen* (and the *Erya* too) with his friends, who shared his scholarly taste: Ichino Meian 市野迷庵 (1765–1826), Kariya Ekisai 狩谷掖齋 (1775–1835), and Yamanashi Tōsen 山梨稲川 (1771–1826) all were ardent textualists. In turn, the next generation of scholars, especially Kojima Seisai 小島成齋 (1796–1862), Okamoto Kyōsai 岡本況齋 (1797–1878), and Shibue Chūsai 澀江抽齋 (1805–1858), continued to focus on philological issues, yet, as the final decades of the Tokugawa era saw a change in taste (such as nativist *kokugaku* 國學 trends, for which *Shuowen* may have been seen as a foreign object, and later Western learning), such isolated focus did not turn into a wave of Japanese scholarship. Although great scholars, like Naitō Konan, regarded highly the earlier scholars who worked on the *Shuowen*, Chinese and Japanese alike, the fate of the *Shuowen* in Japan was never similar to that in China; the *Shuowen* in Japan was not tied to national identity (perhaps was even contrary to it), and could not serve as a "time machine"—neither for early *kokugaku* scholars nor for later nationalists.[20]

Appendix B: Major *Shuowen* and *Erya* Studies of the Nineteenth Century (esp. between the Opium War and the Sino-Japanese War, 1839–1894)

Table 10.1. List of Nineteenth-Century Shuowen/Erya Studies

No.	Author	Title	Notes
1.	Di Kui 苗夔	說文繫傳校勘記	1839 postscript by Cheng Peiyuan
2.	Feng Guifen 馮桂芬 (1809–1874)	說文段注考	Written during the Tongzhi reign period (1862–1874), was not printed
3.	Gong Zizhen 龔自珍 (1792–1841)	說文段注札記	
4.	He Shaoji 何紹基 (1799–1873)	說文段注駁正	
5.	Hu Zhuo 胡焯 (1804–1852)	校補說文解字繫傳	
6.	Huang Yizhou 黃以周 (1828–1899)	唐本說文真偽辨	
7.	Li Hongzao 李鴻藻 (1820–1897)	爾雅不二字	1883 and 1885 printed editions
8.	Lin Changyi 林昌彝 (1803–1876)	段氏說文注刊訛	
9.	Lin Changyi	說文二徐本辨訛	
10.	Ma Shouling 馬壽齡 (fl. 1868)	說文段注撰要	1868 preface by Qiao Songnian 喬松年 (1815–1875)
11.	Pan Yantong 潘衍桐 (1841–1899)	爾雅正郭	1891 printed edition
12.	Qian Guisen 錢桂森 (1827–1902)	說文段注鈔案	
13.	Shen Tao 沈濤 (1792–1861)	說文古本考	
14.	Tan Xian 譚獻 (1832–1901)	說文解字注疏	
15.	Wang Rensi 王仁俊 (1866–1913)	說文解字考異訂	
16.	Wang Shaolan 王紹蘭 (1760–1835)	說文段注訂補	1888 preface by Li Hongzhang
17.	Wang Yun 王筠 (1784–1854)	說文解字繫傳考正	
18.	Wang Yun	校祁刻本說文繫傳	
19.	Wang Yun	說文繫傳校錄	Wang worked on this book alternately in the 1830s and 1840s; it was published in 1857
20.	Xu Han 許瀚 (1797–1866)	某先生校桂注說文條辨	1843 postscript
21.	Xu Hao 徐灝 (1810–1879)	說文解字注箋	
22.	Xu Hao	說文段注箋	
23.	Ye Huixin 葉蕙心 (b. 1815)	爾雅古注斟	
24.	Zhu Junsheng 朱駿聲 (1788–1858)	說文段注拈誤	
25.	Zhu Junsheng	經韻樓說文注商	
26.	Zhu Junsheng	小字本說文簡端記	
27.	Zhu Xuedan 朱學聃 (b. 1814)	爾雅諍郭	1890 printed edition

(continued)

Table 10.1. List of Nineteenth-Century Shuowen/Erya Studies (*Continued*)

No.	Author	Title	Notes
28.	Cheng Peiyuan 承培元	說文繫傳校勘記	1835
29.	Wang Yun	說文句讀	1850. Wang began working on this book in 1841. It also has a preface by Zhang Mu dated 1844.
30.	Lu Shiyi 呂世宜 (1784–1855)	古今文字通釋	1853. 1879 printed edition by Lu's student, Long Xilin 龍溪林
31.	Zhu Shiduan 朱士端 (1786–1872)	說文校定本	1854; 1863 preface
32.	Mo Youzhi 莫友芝 (1811–1871)	唐寫本說文木部箋異	1863
33.	Yu Yue 俞樾 (1821–1907)	爾雅平議	1864
34.	Yan Zhangfu 嚴章福	說文校議	1865. Yan (who was Yan Kejun's relative) worked on the book alternately from 1844 to 1861
35.	Chen Changzhi 陳昌治	說文校字記	1873
36.	Xie Zhangting 謝章鋌 (1820–1903)	說文大小徐本錄異	1885
37.	Wang Shunan 王樹楠 (1851–1936)	爾雅郭注佚存補訂	1892
38.	Tian Wuzhao 田吳炤 (1870–1926)	說文二徐箋異	1896

The list above includes only studies that deal directly with the *Shuowen* and/or *Erya* as their principal subject matter in book form (the list is not inclusive of all genres).[21] Many short essays on specific problems related to *Shuowen*/*Erya* studies were composed during this time, which the table does not include. The data come from the following sources: Lin, *Qingdai Xuxue kao*; Ding, comp. and ed., *Shuowen jiezi gulin*, esp. vol. 1; Zhu Zuyan 朱祖延, comp. and ed., *Erya gulin*, and its *Xulu*; Zhao, ed., *Qingdai xueshu cidian*.

Notes

This research was supported by Israeli Science Foundation grant 134/18.

1. I do not suggest that after the 1930s the text lost its appeal; I end my discussion with Ding Fubao since his collection became central for almost any *Shuowen* study thereafter.

2. Wang, "*Shuowen jiezi zhengyi* xu," vol. 1, p. 328. The *Shuowen jiezi zhengyi*, for which Wang Mingsheng wrote the preface, was a work by Chen Zhan 陳鱣 (1753–1817).

3. Wang Mingsheng, "Xu" 序 (Preface), in Sun, *Wenzi tang ji*, p. 4; see also p. 3 for the *Shuowen* as a major means of getting antiquity right.

4. For example, Qian, *Shijiazhai yangxin lu*, vol. 7, *juan* 18, p. 502; Wang, "Wang Rongfu *Shuxue* xu," appendix, pp. 60–61; Cheng, "*Shuowen yinjing kao* xu."

5. See Shen, *Weng Fanggang nianpu*, p. 514; Chen and Zhu, *Qian-Jia xueshu biannian*.

6. See Wei, *Guwei tang ji*, *juan* 4, pp. 148–150; Elman, *Classicism, Politics, and Kinship*, p. 120.

7. See Jiang, "Wei Yuan jingshi zhiyong de bianji sixiang"; Liu, "*Yuanshi xinbian* de lishi bianzhuan chengjiu"; Zhu and Wang, "Qian Daxin zai Yuan shixue shang de gangxian ji yingxiang"; Chen, "Qian Daxin yu Yuan shixue"; Leonard, *Wei Yuan and China's Rediscovery of the Maritime World,* pp. 16–17.

8. For more on Yu Yue, see Qiu, *Dai Zhen xue de xingcheng,* pp. 11–75; see Yang, "Lun wan Qing xuejie zongshi Yu Yue de xueshu chengjiu ji yingxiang." Elman noted Yu Yue's "overall attack on Chinese medicine . . . which may have been prompted by the deaths of his wife and children due to illness"; Elman, *On Their Own Terms,* pp. 274, 406; see also Liu, "Yu Yue feizhi Zhongyi sixiang genyuan tansuo"; Luo, "Lun Yu Yue zai wan Qing xueshu shi shang de diwei," p. 115, and esp. p. 101. That Yu criticized some aspects of ancient Chinese knowledge while upholding others, used new terminology but held the traditional structure, attests to the *problématique* of strict categorization among today's scholars.

9. See Ding, comp., *Shuowen jiezi gulin zhengxu hebian,* vol. 1, p. 285.

10. See Ding, comp., *Shuowen jiezi gulin zhengxu hebian,* vol. 1, pp. 225–226.

11. See Ding, comp., *Shuowen jiezi gulin zhengxu hebian,* vol. 1, pp. 214–215.

12. See Li, "*Shuowen Duan zhu dingbu* xu," vol. 1, p. 217. For Zhang Zhidong's praise of the *Shuowen* and of the dynasty's scholars' achievements in the field, see his preface to the *Shuowen jiezi yizheng* 說文解字義證 (Proofs of the meanings in the *Shuowen jiezi*), in Ding, comp., *Shuowen jiezi gulin zhengxu hebian,* vol. 1, pp. 225–226.

13. For this episode see, for example, Hon, "Ethnic and Cultural Pluralism."

14. See Kaske, *The Politics of Language in Chinese Education, 1895–1919,* esp. pp. 349–365.

15. See Zhang, "Cong Zhang Taiyan Shuowen shouke biji kan Zhang Taiyan dui Yu Yue, Sun Yirang ershi de xueshu jicheng."

16. See Shih, *Lure of the Modern,* p. 55.

17. See Lu, *Lu Xun shuxin ji,* p. 17.

18. Zarrow, *China in War and Revolution, 1895–1949,* p. 137.

19. Smith, "'Ambiguity at Its Best!.'" See also Ramaswamy, "Sanskrit for the Nation"; Prakash, "The Modern Nation's Return in the Archaic."

20. For more on this topic see, for example, Fujiyama, "Edo kōki no kōshōgakusha to Dan Gyokusai no *Setsumon chō.*"

21. For a similar table concerning the Qianlong-Jiaqing era (1736–1820), see my *China's Philological Turn,* pp. 199–204.

11 ◈ KANG XIAOFEI 康笑菲

A Time to Heal or a Time to Kill
Confessions in the Anti-Shaman Campaign at Communist Yan'an, 1944–1945

On April 16, 1944, a crowd of more than 2,000 peasants and government workers gathered to witness a public trial in the city plaza of Yan'an 延安, the capital of the communist Shaan-Gan-Ning Border Region (Shaan Gan Ning bianqu 陝甘寧邊區) during the second Sino-Japanese War. The culprit being tried was Yang Hanzhu 楊漢珠, a shaman from Baijiaping 白家坪 village in the suburbs of Yan'an.[1] Yang was accused of having murdered the twenty-six-year-old daughter-in-law of the Chang 常 family. She had passed out after having a miscarriage. Yang denounced the modern medicine practiced by a doctor from the government-run hospital. He claimed that the woman was afflicted by a ghost (*guibing* 鬼病). In light of that, he performed a series of exorcist rituals, during which he allegedly whipped, burned, and pierced iron nails into her body until she breathed her last breath. The rituals cost the Chang family over one million *yuan*,[2] which subsequently drove the family into bankruptcy.

The trial was held by the Yan'an city judicial court in conjunction with several other agencies of the city government. The court also found Yang guilty of having previously caused the deaths of many other women in similar healing rituals. Yang made a public confession, acknowledging that he indeed had committed the crimes, that the gods and ghosts he had invoked were fake, and that his malpractice was nothing but "superstition" used to extort money. Yang's confession stirred up widespread anger among the people in attendance, who demanded that Yang be shot to death right away. The court delivered the following verdict: Yang's crimes indeed deserved a death sentence. However, he cheated mainly for money and did not murder deliberately. Thus, he should be punished with leniency—with a five-year term of imprisonment. The trial, nevertheless, according to a stern journalist's account, taught the masses to smash superstitions and believe in modern medicine. People began to condemn shamans and warned each other that "if anyone still holds superstitious beliefs in ghosts and spirits, his family will be destroyed just like the Changs."[3]

On April 29, 1944, the above story, alongside a major editorial entitled "Carry Out the Anti-Shaman Fight" (Zhankai fandui wushen de douzheng 展開反對巫神的鬥爭), appeared on the front page of *Liberation Daily* (*Jiefang ribao* 解放日報), the official newspaper of the Chinese Communist Party (CCP). The two pieces ushered in an intense Anti-Shaman Campaign in Yan'an. From April to

October 1944, *Liberation Daily* published forty-eight reports of anti-superstition measures. In 1945, it continued to cover the campaign, with thirty-four news articles. These propagandistic reports attacked shamanistic healing practices, promoted the power of modern medicine, and proclaimed a resolution to transform village shamans from parasitic layabouts (*erliuzi* 二流子) into productive laborers in rural society.

The Anti-Shaman Campaign of 1944–1945 was the first mass campaign against traditional religion in the history of the Communist Party. The campaign propaganda offers an excellent entry point to study the CCP's language of state building in relation to the twentieth-century, modernist, reconstruction of Chinese religions. The latter had much to do with May 4th enlightenment values of science and evolutionism and with Marxist-Leninist atheism. The CCP regarded religion and revolution as two incompatible temporalities in the evolution of humankind. Religion was a product of China's "feudal" past and a tool of class exploitation. The inevitable future of the revolution would bring the socio-economic development of human society to the highest level, and class and religion would eventually disappear.[4]

How did the CCP-run Yan'an government carry out this ideology in wartime social conditions? What kind of power politics did the language of these two temporalities create between the CCP and the rural populace? In what ways did CCP propaganda reveal interconnections rather than mere disjunctions between religion and revolution? This essay takes a New Sinology approach to address these questions. It focuses on the Party newspaper's extensive coverage of the campaign's confessional meetings, for which Party workers summoned shamans from the Yan'an region and urged them to confess that in their healing practices they had killed people and destroyed families. These meetings marked an important step for the CCP to extend the freshly developed mechanism of intraparty thought reform into a rural populace. Through a close reading of the propaganda materials, the essay uncovers key vocabularies, categorization schemes, and narrative designs with which the Party attempted to implement a new knowledge structure among the rural populace. It reveals that beneath the Party's outright attacks on "feudal superstition," Party propaganda selectively used traditional language and ritual culture to build its political power. In recasting the shamanistic practices from "a time to heal" to "a time to kill," the Party agents became new ritual masters who presided over confessional meetings and public trials. They embodied scientific miracles, legal justice, and political righteousness all at once. The Anti-Shaman Campaign's propaganda offers important insights into the Communist Revolution's tenacious connection with China's "feudal" past.

Religion, Superstition, and the CCP's Modernizing Programs in Yan'an

Religion as a separate and private sphere of human experience within the broad society is a modern Western invention. The concept of separation of church and state was rooted in the European Enlightenment values of science, reason, and progress. It shaped the foundation of the modern nation-state around the world from the eighteenth century on.[5] Chinese reformers and revolutionaries of the first half of the twentieth century adopted the Western concepts of "religion" (*zongjiao* 宗教) and "superstition" (*mixin* 迷信) that had been discussed in Japan in the late nineteenth century.[6] In upholding the principle of religious freedom, the Chinese reformers, joined by lay and monastic elites, recognized the legal status and spiritual leadership of five organized religions—Protestantism, Roman Catholicism, Islam, Buddhism, and Daoism. What emerged was a long process of reinventing traditional Chinese religions on a "Christian normative model."[7] Buddhism and Daoism were uprooted from their traditional connections with temple cults and community life. They reemerged as acceptable religions only if they met three basic criteria: provide ethical and spiritual principles, build a well-organized church-like structure under a national association, and make a commitment to the nation-state and social welfare.[8] The reform leaders denounced as superstition (thus the antithesis of Chinese modernization) all traditional religious practices that revolved around family, lineage, and community and that ranged from ancestor worship and ghost pacification to temple cults and festivals. Communal shrines and temples were destroyed or converted into schools and other public facilities.[9] Ritual specialists such as shamans, geomancers, and fortune-tellers were condemned as parasites and perpetuators of "superstition."[10]

Early communist leaders were initially prominent champions of Western Enlightenment values. They acknowledged the positive role of religious teachings in sustaining the moral and spiritual development of humankind and supported religious freedom. In the meantime, taking a Marxist stand of historical materialism and class struggle, they maintained that religion only existed in the lower stages of human evolution, when humankind was unable to understand the scientific principles that lay behind all natural phenomena in the universe. According to their ideals, after the triumph of science, reason, and democracy that would attend the future development of a classless society, religion would meet its demise. In this regard, religion was reduced to mere "beliefs in gods and spirits," which they deemed to be illusions and backward thinking. Therefore, unlike the reformers' overhaul of religions, the communists condemned all religions as superstition, and all religious institutions as tools of class exploitation.[11]

The CCP's ideological rhetoric of religion had to face harsh realities in its revolutionary base in rural China, where multiple forms of traditional religions, or "superstitions," had a strong hold on peasant life. The Jiangxi Soviet (1931–1934) had issued radical laws to confiscate religious properties, ban ritual activities, and deprive all religious professionals of their political and economic rights, but there is little evidence that the short-lived CCP government there was able to actually carry out these laws. During the subsequent Long March (1934–1935), the CCP found that it was impossible to eradicate "superstitions." Moreover, in order for the Red Army to draw on local resources for its survival, it was necessary to show respect for the religions of the many ethnic groups who were willing to supply help.[12] In order to establish a broad "united front" against the Japanese invasion, the Yan'an government also formed alliances with the Elder Brother Society and adopted tolerant policies toward religions, especially those of ethnic and foreign minorities.[13]

The Anti-Shaman Campaign captures a historical moment in which the CCP had to strike a balance between its ideological claims and the much-needed pragmatic policies for the rural societies of the Yan'an-centered Border Region. The Border Region's official statistics in 1944 show that of a total population of 1,500,000, over 1,000,000 were illiterate, more than 2,000 were shamans, and the infant mortality rate was as high as 60 percent. In contrast, "good and bad all together," it had only 1,000 doctors of Chinese medicine among the rural population, and 200 doctors of Western medicine who served in the government and the military. In addressing this reality, the Party called for a "New Culture Movement" against "feudal superstition, illiteracy, unhygienic habits, and other old customs."[14]

These were by no means new problems for the CCP, but it was not until 1944 that the Party was politically and economically ready to take up these cultural issues. In 1944, the Sino-Japanese War was drawing to an end, and it had become politically necessary for the CCP to pose itself as a modernizing force in order to compete for legitimacy in the postwar government. In a number of speeches Mao delivered to the Party during this time, he called for a shift of CCP focus from military to economic and cultural construction. Most notably, he developed and advocated his 1940 formulation of the New Democracy as the foundation of postwar state building.[15] In his landmark essay, "On New Democracy," Mao famously made Marxism Chinese by inserting the Communist Revolution as an inevitable stage of human evolution that would move the Chinese nation from a "semifeudal/semicolonial" past to a socialist future. It was the CCP's historical mission to lead the revolutionary efforts in order to transform the old culture of the Chinese peasants and build a "national, scientific, and mass culture."[16] In 1945, Mao declared that his New Democracy was "much more progressive and comprehensive than Sun Yat-sen's doctrine," thus asserting the CCP's advantage over its Nationalist rival in taking up national leadership.[17]

The Border Region's "New Culture Movement" was the Party's timely response to Mao's political agenda. By 1944, an intraparty Rectification Movement in Yan'an had firmly established Mao's absolute power within the Party and remolded the Party into a "single discourse community" that some scholars describe as the "Yan'an mafia."[18] Following Mao's famous "Talks on Literature and Arts at the Yan'an Forum" in 1942, Communist cultural workers were now required to submit to the Party line, immerse themselves in the language and culture of peasants and soldiers, and become the "cultural army operating in concert with the CCP's military and political forces."[19]

The economic situation in 1944 provided cultural workers with fitting conditions to carry out Mao's political agenda. The severe economic crisis from 1941 to 1943 prevented the CCP government from investing in any significant social and cultural reforms beyond the need for survival. By 1944, the Border Region's economic situation had significantly improved. Even though the CCP-run opium trade and taxation policies probably played a much more critical role, Party propaganda understandably credited the economic success to the Great Production Movement (*dashengchan yundong* 大生產運動), which peaked in 1943 and 1944.[20] This success allowed the CCP to provide its limited resources to the rural populace and to support various social reform programs, but wartime political and economic exigencies also required the Party to follow the lines of the United Front and scale back from the radical stand of class struggle.

Under such conditions, the CCP's rhetoric that encouraged the destruction of the old focused on shamanistic healers as the easiest target of "superstition" and ignored all other rural religious establishments. The campaign would drive the shamans into the under-filled labor force needed for the Great Production Movement. The ritual expenses that had always been condemned as excessive waste since imperial and Republican times would be redirected to the Border Region's coffers to support productivity and the war effort. Most of all, in rendering the shamanistic healing as dregs of the "feudal past" and shamans as killers, the CCP would establish its claim of leadership in rural China's march into the modern age.[21]

Exposing the Evil of the Old: Classifications and Personal Confessions

On June 18, 1944, the Party newspaper published a long editorial exposing the whole range of the "shamans' arts of cheating." It appeared on the same page with an equally long report entitled "Shaman Bai Conghai's Confession." Despite the obvious bias in the former and the repentant tone in the latter, these two pieces are still the most informative ethnographies of shamanic practices in Shaanbei. The editorial and the individual confession authenticate each other: the former takes an "etic" point of view to survey and classify the whole range of popular religious practices in Shaanbei that the Party newspaper deems to be superstitious and fraudulent, while the latter confirms the shaman's quackery from an "emic" perspective. These two pieces were later collected in a chapter in the Anti-Shaman Campaign booklet published by the Border Region government. The title of the chapter summarizes well the Party's definition of shamanistic practices: "The many evil crimes of shamans" (Wushen de zui'e zhongzhong 巫神的罪惡種種).

Any classification scheme, according to Foucault, is in itself the working of power. This is because it shatters older, familiar thought, establishes a new conceptual framework of cultural categories, and produces a mechanism of disciplines, regulations, and social control.[22] Confession in modern society has also become the "most highly valued technique for producing truth." It effectively subjects the confessor to the authority of those who demand, hear, and judge the confession.[23] In the case of Yan'an's Anti-Shaman Campaign propaganda, as we will see below, the Party made a special effort to classify local ritual specialists and encourage, or more likely coerce, shamans to make confessions. By imposing a secular lens on the "evil crimes" of the shamanistic ritual practices, the Party assumed moral as well as temporal authority in its vehement attacks on the old knowledge structure of Shaanbei's rural populace.

The editorial begins by listing seven categories: *shenguan* 神官 (spirit official), *shiwu* 師婆 (or *nüwu* 女巫, shamaness), *wushen* 巫神 (also, shaman), *fashi* 法師 (ritual master), *mengxian* 夢仙 (dream diviner), *qiansong* 遷送 (soul deliverer), and *majiao* 馬腳 (horse servant). The editorial indicates that *wushen*, that is, shaman, was the most popular word used in the Border Region, and it is also used as a general term touching on all the categories. The specific category of *wushen* was further divided into two types: those who "pretended to be gods and demons themselves" (*zhuangshen zhuanggui* 裝神裝鬼), and those who specialized in "the dirty business of sending off gods or catching, exorcising, and beating demons" (*songshen zhuogui qugui dagui de goudang* 送神捉鬼驅鬼打鬼的勾當). The editorial states that the second type was particularly "barbaric and cruel" and had ended many lives, because it invoked all kinds of violence upon the bodies of patients, including poking steel needles (*ding gangzhen* 釘鋼針), ironing the flesh (*lao pifu* 烙皮膚), lying down on the blades of long knives (*shui zhadao* 睡鍘刀), and burning pubic hair (*shao yinmao* 燒陰毛).[24] The editorial describes many such practices in great detail, then denounces them as circus tricks and magic designed to fool the patients into spending their money.

The editorial sees its task as exposing traditional rituals and divination practices as illogical and irrational. Number one on the list of the "arts of cheating" was called *shen bagua* 神八卦 (spirit hexagrams) and *gui bagua* 鬼八卦 (ghost hexagrams). Drawing on popularized *Yijing* styles of divination techniques, shamans diagnosed symptoms based on cosmological correlations between time periods and one's state of health. Each day was presided over by a particular spirit, and one fell sick as a result of offensive remarks made to that spirit: *shen bagua* was used to diagnose male patients, and *gui bagua* was used for female patients. The editorial calls the use of hexagrams absurd, because every diagnosis came in the form of the glib pronouncements that easily fitted into preexisting formulas: "The shaman's mouth is like a bottomless bucket."

The editorial breaks the subject matter down even further. It discusses two major healing rituals found in Shaanbei. The first was *saohun* 掃魂 (sweeping souls, also known as *zhaohun* 招魂 or summoning souls), both the word and actions harking back in some respects to ancient funerary rites. It consisted of four steps: setting up the altar (*qitan* 起壇), making a divination inquiry (*zhangua* 占卦), expelling the illness (*rangbing* 禳病), and protecting one's body (*hushen* 護身). Once a shaman had raised the altar and reached a divination diagnosis, he would use a needle (*zhen* 針, a play on the word *zhen* 真, meaning true, pure) to sew a piece of red cloth into a green cloth. The red represented the lost soul of the patient and the green the horse on which the soul rode. He then pinned the horse on the patient's shoulder—the higher it was, the better the chance of recovery. Then he would find a person born in the year of either the horse or the rooster; he would dress that person up in red (upper) and green (lower) and let him hold a basket in one hand and a broom in the other. As he swept the floor and called up loudly for the return of the soul, this person would walk around until the shaman finally located the lost soul and collected it into the basket. The two would return to the altar in the patient's home, and the shaman would circle the altar three times each, clockwise and counterclockwise, tapping the patient with the basket. The process purportedly returned the soul to the body of the patient. After giving a warning such as "Stay indoors for three days!" the shaman would depart regardless of the result. Sometimes the shaman searched for the soul all by himself, either walking or riding a horse, and as such he would receive a chicken as extra compensation.

A certain rite called *xiayin* 下陰 (descent to the underworld) was much less used because it was more dangerous and, as the editorial states, more "ridiculous." It was performed when an ailing patient's family was wealthy enough to afford its particularly high cost. The shaman would claim that the patient had violated the rules of either the "celestial jail" or the "underworld jail." The remedy was for the shaman to dig a two- to three-foot-deep pit and use it in a soul-searching journey to other worlds. The shaman would crawl into the pit after sunset and be totally buried in it, having only a tiny hole through which a rope connected him to a bell hanging on a pole in a courtyard. Incense sticks would be burned outside, and someone would stay up and periodically report to the buried shaman what was going on outside: "The cocks have crowed!" "It is nearly dawn!" "Somebody just passed by." Monetary rewards for this were attractive, but in fact shamans who dared to undertake such a semi-suicidal mission gained much respect and even reverence among fellow villagers; and some indeed died of suffocation during the process. The editorial, however, discredits any sincerity and honesty in the ritual. It emphasizes the shamans' cowardice and shrewdness by explaining that they would keep three objects in the pit: a lamp to calm him, water in a basin to help absorb his body heat, and a live chicken to indicate whether there was enough oxygen left in the pit. As soon as the chicken started to choke, the shaman would ring the bell, and his assistant waiting outside would quickly dig him out.[25]

The editorial quotes shaman Bai Conghai's "confession" to corroborate its accusations: "I was very frightened staying in that pit all alone. I could not get myself either to lie down or sit down. All I could do was stare at that little hole. If I felt good, I could stay there for one more incense-stick burn, and if I did not feel good, I would ring the bell and kick the pole for people to dig me out when it was time for another." Bai also confessed: "The fraudulent practice of *xiayin* is really dangerous. I only dared to do it several times a year when I was young and don't dare to do it now that I am getting old.... The famous shaman Liu Wanyi of Ansai County and shaman Tian Yingsan of Xiaolaoran both died of suffocation. Where were their patron spirits then?"[26]

As once again carried in the editorial, we learn of Bai's confession that most times shamans appeared to have gone into the pit with their hands tied in order to show that their strength was solely derived from their patron deities, but in fact this had nothing to do with supernatural protection: the shamans were actually tied with slipknots so that they could untie themselves while in the pit and retie the knots just before they came out. In order to avoid risking their lives, some "shrewd" shamans would send a rooster to the underworld on their behalf. The patient's family provided the rooster. The shaman would stick a chopstick into the rooster's mouth, insert a pin through the rooster's eye, and nail it to a wall. He then covered the rooster with a piece of red cloth, thus sending it on its journey to the other world. Two hours later, he took away the red cloth and let the rooster go. If the rooster ate grain that was spread on the ground, the soul had returned and the patient would recover; and if the rooster failed to notice the grain, then the patient was left on his or her own. The editorial comments that the rooster always ate the grain, since the shaman never really pierced its eyes, which would be as if the brain were pierced, but only its nostrils; he acted so swiftly that nobody could see clearly what he did. In this way the shaman could in the end claim both the rooster and the piece of cloth as his compensation.[27]

The high mortality rate and poor sanitary conditions made ritual blessings attractive as active protection for newborn babies and young children in rural Shaanbei. People routinely hired shamans to make "life-extension strings" (*xuming sheng* 續命繩), a cotton collar that strung several copper coins together for children to wear around their necks. They also relied on shamans to draw a charm to destroy the "Curse of Nine Daughters" (*jiunüsha* 九女煞). The charm would liberate the cursed family from the fate of having only daughters and further their prospects of getting a male heir. Furthermore, it was a widespread belief in Shaanbei that children got sick because their souls were taken away and delivered to the underworld by "fast runners" (*jijiaozi* 急腳子), these being female soul stealers.[28] Only a shaman would have the power to summon all the gods and spirits in a local temple, knock down an empty rice bowl in front of the horse god, and thereby catch the "fast runner" and force her to release the children's souls. In the Party propaganda, the "life-extension string" was nothing but a device with which the shaman blackmailed people for money. The mythical characters that the shaman drew on the charm were merely the result of some material (chemical) reactions and thus an illusionary trick. And as for the "fast runner," "the masses thought the shaman's method was efficacious," but, the editorial explains, this was only the shaman's "bluff" (*chuiniu* 吹牛).[29]

From Healing to Killing

The rich ethnographic details in the editorial draw on shamans' oral confessions and journalists' interviews at the village level. How did the Party's propaganda then use these materials to convince the rural populace that "a time to heal" was actually "a time to kill"? First, Mao's mass-line politics was at work here. The targeted audience of the *Liberation Daily* was grassroots cadres with moderate or no education and the largely illiterate rural population. The Party's campaign messages in newspaper editorials would be routinely circulated into the rural populace through the newly implemented propaganda mechanism of village newspaper study sessions and public meetings.[30] Local people surely experienced various of the procedures offered by shamans in their everyday lives, but there is little evidence that they thought about the same sort of classifications as those listed in the editorial. And rarely would they have been exposed to such a complete gamut of shamanic rituals and in such an organized, didactic manner all at once.

Second, the editorial uproots shamanistic healing rituals from the traditional cosmological worldview and places them in a secular framework imposed from an authoritative political level. Traditional Chinese medicine and healing hinged on beliefs in *qi* as the fundamental element of all life forms and the systematic correspondences of yin-yang and five phases in a holistic universe shared by both humans and spirits. It also depended on ritual specialists for the exorcising of demons and the resultant well-being of individuals and communities.[31] The editorial's rendering of the familiar ritual details would in and of itself have sparked interest in the magical, the dramatic, and the supernatural among local cadres and villagers. However, the Party's propaganda was not about experiencing rituals for healing and exorcism, but about listening to new categories, and discussing and criticizing them in newspaper study sessions and at mass campaign meetings. The editorial presents the rituals as isolated occurrences without any rational context; as such, they must have appeared irrational, false, and ridiculous. The ethnographic details only served to establish the authenticity of the editorial's accusations of the shamanistic "art of cheating."

Third, the editorial's educational effect was built on the rhetorical art of selective representation. It excludes certain practices that had been originally inseparable from the shamanic ritual practices listed above. Impelled by the mass-line principle and the pronounced commitment to new forms of national culture, the Party earnestly deployed native and traditional resources. The dearth of medical resources, however, forced it to prioritize public health, demographic growth, and labor supply over the eradication of superstitions. As a result, it had to carefully separate "superstition" from "tradition." Ritual exorcism was singled out as the campaign target. In contrast, herbs, needles, and moxibustion, which had been an integral part of shamanic healing practices in Shaanbei, were now disassociated from "shamans" and repackaged as the "science" of traditional Chinese medicine.[32] In the same vein, the editorial does not mention the popular profession of blind storytellers, even though as a social category these men were heavily involved in fortune-telling, ritual healing, and other "superstitious" services in Shaanbei.[33] These blind men had little prospect of employment in the labor force; moreover, their expertise and popularity in narrative singing afforded them great potential to become the Party's popular cultural workers as long as they followed Party directions to cleanse all "superstitious" elements from their practices.[34] In this context, the editorial defines shamans not as a generic category in Shaanbei's rural life; rather, it is a label exclusively reserved for ritual healers per se. It focuses on exposing the evil of ritual exorcism and transforming shamans from parasitic healers or wanton killers into productive laborers.

No doubt both editorials and shamans' confessions in *Liberation Daily* were well-designed campaign strategies to deliver the Party's anti-shaman messages. Nevertheless, the propaganda's mechanism of discrimination and manipulation inadvertently reveals telling differences between these two kinds of narrative. First, while newspaper reports overwhelmingly featured female patients as victims, the shamans' confessions mentioned, often matter-of-factly, patients of all kinds: men, women, and children. This diversity confirms that shamanic services were routine in Shaanbei, where the illiteracy rate was high and traditional doctors few. Second, the shamans unequivocally denounced the very existence of gods and spirits; they also confessed that they cheated people for money and that their healing techniques were their own clever designs rather than divine intervention. But other than the above-mentioned feature story about Yang Hanzhu and the editorial condemning the "arts of cheating," few shamans acknowledged in their confessions having taken any life or having physically mistreated anyone. In fact, several shamans were quoted as saying that although they reprimanded Yang for his crimes, they insisted on the validity of their own healing practices because those were utterly different from Yang's.[35]

Note also the narrative differences between the editorial and Bai Conghai's confession. As mentioned above, the two appeared side by side in *Liberation Daily,* and the editorial drew heavily on the latter, which became widely publicized. Bai's confession started with the statement that "I have been a shaman for fifteen years. Big or small, I don't know how many people's illnesses I have treated, nor how many lives I have wasted."[36] Even with that required self-abasement, one still detects a hint of suppressed pride. Many would have thought that Bai could not have sustained a business based on sheer cheating and causing deaths for as long as fifteen years. Bai went on to acknowledge that he was a layabout and chose to become a shaman because he could "win [people's] respect" after he had swindled money out of them. If he cured people, they would credit it to the efficacy of his patron gods and praise his extraordinary skills, and if he failed, he would not be blamed because it was common understanding that "the gods only cure illnesses but don't extend lives."[37] He, of course, intended to follow the campaign rhetoric to show the uselessness of his healing rituals and the treachery of his magic, but he inadvertently revealed, in minute detail, the complex ritual procedures and techniques he had mastered, and how high a price the local people were willing to pay for his services. In fact, Bai's confession inadvertently reveals that being a shaman in rural Shaanbei was a respectable and even desirable vocation.

Mass Meetings and the Political Rituals of Confession

The Rectification Movement set up a useful model for all CCP campaigns in the years to come. It consisted of several stages, including the Cadre Examination Campaign (*shen'gan* 審幹), the Anti-Espionage Campaign (*fanjian* 反奸 or *sufan* 肅反), and the Rescue Campaign (*qiangjiu* 搶救). These consecutive inner-party campaigns involved carefully planned procedures of both reeducation and coercion. Everybody was subjected to Party review and scrutiny. The campaign usually started with public lectures delivered by Mao and other top Party leaders or the reading of key documents authored by them. Further discussions and digestion of the lectures/documents would then be conducted in small group study sessions. During and in between these sessions, Party members and rank-and-file cadres had to reexamine their inner thoughts. Above all, they had to write confessions about their personal history, their family history, and any wrongs they had done in the past. They were also encouraged to submit secret allegations against others and to make public denunciations. They would have to go through repeated rounds of criticism and self-criticism in small sessions and mass meetings before they were rehabilitated. Some participated voluntarily, but most did so under tremendous collective pressure. All strove to make confessions in order to become a new Party member loyal to the Maoist line. Those who voiced different opinions, or were slow to comply with the Party line, were struggled against in mass meetings and often were subjected to brutal persecution.[38]

The Anti-Shaman Campaign adopted the new ideology and operational principles that had been invented and developed during the Rectification Movement. It targeted, however, a different social group—not Party cadres and intellectuals but rural masses with little or no education. The campaign methodologies were adjusted accordingly. Mass meetings constituted one of the most common campaign features. Participants did not need literary skills. The goal was to efficiently assert the Party's absolute power over the evils of shamans and to mobilize rural audiences with mass-line tactics, public spectacles, and voluntary identifications with the Party's cause.

Contemporary newspaper articles record two kinds of mass meetings held during the campaign. The Party used Yang Hanzhu's trial cited above to launch the campaign. The public trial established the model for the campaign to condemn the evil of shamans.[39] It started with a narrative recounting a shaman's malpractices and the harms he had caused. It then turned to the public anger that demanded harsh punishment of the shaman, which broke into violent acts. This kind of spontaneous violence justified mass support of the Party agenda. Yet eventually the party-state would have to tame this energy and turn it into more "rational," but no less dramatic, party-directed and regulated campaign mechanisms. In the end, the agents of the party-state intervened, acknowledging the rightfulness of the public anger, but curtailing it by exercising justice with prudence and public consent, as we saw above in the leniency shown to Yang. The campaign goal was thus accomplished: both the masses and the shamans were educated to become new citizens who denounced ghosts and spirits, believed in the Party and science, and raised awareness of hygienic standards for themselves and their families.

The second type of mass meeting aimed at the rehabilitation of individual shamans. Such meetings were called upon at county and district levels.[40] After making confessions in such meetings, the shamans were supposed to have shaken off their old professions and to have become new productive laborers. In July 1944, the Yan'an County government called an anti-shaman meeting that lasted for more than three days, and preparation required several steps. First, shortly before the scheduled meeting, the government workers conducted a preliminary investigation of the shamans in a manner similar to those used in the Cadre Examination campaign. They went into villages and identified, interviewed, and collected background information about individual shamans. They then singled out the most "obedient and honest" (*laoshi tanbai* 老實坦白) shamans as their first targets of education. Next, under the influence (or pressure) of the initial educational efforts, these "obedient and honest" shamans became the first ones to make confessions. They acknowledged that their gods and spirits were all fraudulent and that they took up the profession for no other reason than to make money. They were not literate enough to write reports to examine themselves or others, but the rationale of criticism and self-criticism remained the same. The government held up these shamans as models of rehabilitation thereafter, and led them on a tour for the purpose of educating other shamans and villagers. The Party newspaper states that "the shamans are encouraged to not only make confessions about themselves, but also expose other shamans"—a commonplace strategy of the Rectification Movement.[41]

Only after they had secured a number of rehabilitated shamans did the Party workers launch the three-day meeting. On July 14, they summoned a total of fifty-nine shamans in Yan'an County to attend. The meeting opened and ended with province-level and local CCP officials' public speeches. The officials exhorted shamans to denounce all gods and spirits, abandon their old selves, and become new productive citizens. The speeches were followed by a new round of reeducation, during which the Party workers first conducted one-on-one educational sessions with each shaman, then grouped them into small study sessions, and finally brought all of them together into several mass meetings of criticism and self-criticism. "Shamans know shamans the best," so the participating shamans not only confessed their own crimes but also "competed" in informing against others. In the end, the most "progressive" shaman, named Zhao Shixian 趙世賢, led eight shamans from his own district to make a pledge:

> We will participate in productive labor. We will not be shamans anymore. We will catch any [practicing] shaman as soon as we see one. Should any of us resume the practice again, he will pay a fine of three pigs and five years' labor service.
> 我們參加生產, 不當巫神。見巫神就抓, 誰要再犯, 願罰三口豬, 五年勞役。[42]

Other shamans followed suit and offered names of more than eighty who had not come to the meeting. The meeting concluded with an anti-shaman pact and a public letter signed by all fifty-nine of the attending shamans. The anti-shaman pact read:

> We make this compact: we will never practice the profession of shaman.
> 我們約定, 再不務神。
> Invoking and sending off spirits; hacking and slashing demons: with these we deceive people.
> 遣送斬剁, 都是騙人。
> We will devote ourselves to hygienic practices and do away with superstitions.

講求衛生，破除迷信。
We must rectify ourselves from all the bad habits and addictions.
各種嗜好，都要改正。
We will participate in productive labor, and take good care of our households.
參加生產，鬧好家務。
We will supervise each other and educate others.
互相監督，教育別人。
If we violate this compact, we will be subject ourselves to punishments.[43]
違犯此約，甘受處分。

Political rituals of confession and group self-criticism were important mechanisms of ideological control. Unlike the Soviet Bolsheviks, who tended to keep this kind of ritual inside their own party (aimed notoriously at the political elite), the CCP extended it from the Party leadership to all cadres during the Rectification Movement and began to utilize it in village organizations thereafter. These practices would finally penetrate into the basic levels of Chinese society after 1949, when the CCP changed from winning popular support to consolidating control over the entire society. In this light, the political rituals of shamans' confessions, as well as the public trials and mass meetings, marked the beginning of this "mass-line" process. The propaganda created significant psychological fear and peer pressure on the shamans and forced them to question the profession, give up their moral sense of self, and conform to officially promoted values.[44]

Beneath the surface of the new campaign methodology, however, we can still detect the power of tradition, which might have helped the Party perpetuate its messages more efficiently in rural society. The whole process of listening to lectures, investigating self and others, as well as making a compact, can be found in the village rituals of community compact since the Song dynasty (960–1279). The first community compact was created in Lantian, Shaanxi, by the Neo-Confucian scholar-official Lü Dajun 呂大鈞 (1029–1080). The system became widespread in China during the Ming and Qing, and it was still well in place in the Yan'an region under the communist Border Region government.[45] The purpose of the community compact was to disseminate Confucian moral precepts into village communities, to use collective pressure to transform "evil customs," and to maintain "the rule of ritual" under the leadership of local gentry elites.[46] The compact was set up through a common agreement by community or lineage leaders. It was sanctioned through a sophisticated ritual procedure of kowtowing before the tablet honoring the moral teachings of the emperor, then reciting them and listening to sermons about them. After this, all participants would review their behavior. Good behavior would be "declared, praised, and recorded in a Good Deed Register," and bad behavior would be "revealed, criticized, and recorded in a separate register."[47]

It is an important yet much overlooked fact that confession and self-criticism were also familiar elements in Chinese religious traditions. The Yan'an study groups and self-criticism sessions much resembled the self-examination routine undertaken between masters and disciples in Confucian academies since the late Ming. The oath taken by all participating shamans pledged to "give up evil and return to good" (*gaixie guizheng* 改邪歸正), a stock phrase echoing Confucian moral rehabilitation and transformation.[48] Furthermore, confessions of sins were used in Daoist ritual healing and Buddhist monastic disciplines. In repenting their sins and subjugating themselves to divine entities and to their communities, the confessors took oaths to rectify their deviant behavior and regained a new self, physically, spiritually, or morally.[49] When the intraparty thought reform mechanism was brought into the rural populace, Party propaganda workers may have found it easier to draw on the traditional penitential language to allow shamans and fellow villagers to make sense of the new situation.

Making confessions and expressing oaths and contractual agreements were also part and parcel of traditional legal culture. A distinct feature of the late imperial judicial system was that a magistrate could only close a case after he had successfully extracted confessions from the accused. The confession was far more important than the evidence in this traditional judicial process. It served to "establish an objective truth," and indicated that the accused had acknowledged and repented his or her crime and therefore had the potential to be rehabilitated.[50] In his seminal study on religion and Chinese judicial rituals, Paul Katz has documented the various forms and long history of the Chinese oath-making tradition. People took oaths to pledge allegiance, settle conflicts, express their determination and commitment, or prove their innocence. Gods and spirits were routinely invoked as witnesses and supervising authorities, often facilitated by spirit mediums and other ritual specialists. Some oath-taking rituals involved trials of flesh similar to those we have seen in the shamanistic exorcistic rituals mentioned above, such as "pulling objects out of pots of boiling oil" (*laoyoutang* 撈油湯) and "holding or walking on red-hot iron objects" (*retie shenpan* 熱鐵神判). It is especially worth noting that these oath-taking rites were never part of the official legal procedure in either imperial or modern times, but they did remain widely practiced throughout mainland China and Taiwan.[51]

The same can also be said about the penalties the reformed shamans vowed for in their pledge. Under Soviet influence, the Border Region's High Court adopted a general policy to enforce criminal punishment through labor service and to preclude fines paid in cash or in kind.[52] Even if the shamans might not have been fully aware of the High Court's penal code, they must have become very familiar with the five-year sentence that Yang Hanzhu had received, through repeated study sessions and lectures. Yet nowhere in the Border Region's official penal code would one find a clause that required payment of fines in cash, let alone in kind.[53] The fine of three pigs in the shamans' pledge seems to be more in tune either with the kind of payment shamans usually received for their healing services or what was stipulated in contracts and agreements that had been used outside of the official legal system in the long history of rural societies.[54]

It is also telling that a military officer who successfully cracked down on a severe case of ghost-haunting staged by a shaman was hailed as "Zhang Qingtian" 張青天, meaning "Judge Zhang" or "Blue-Sky Zhang." This title alludes to the

Song dynasty official Bao Zheng 包拯 (999–1062), who had become a legendary figure emblematic of justice against worldly corruption and demonic aggressions in popular religion and folklore.[55] The success of Officer Zhang invoked both actual military support (soldiers and guns) and the symbolic power of the imperial as well as celestial bureaucracy. In renouncing the shamans' ritual power, the Party agents asserted new rituals and judicial authorities. Using confessions and public trials, they educated the rural populace and granted the shamans opportunities to relieve themselves, either voluntarily or not, of feelings of guilt as parasitic healers and to reinvent themselves as "new men." It subordinated grassroots revolutionary energy to the party-state's hegemony and promoted what Whyte describes as "a rewarding sense of solidarity and mutual concern" in fighting for a higher common cause.[56]

Yan'an's Anti-Shaman Campaign in 1944–1945 demonstrates the CCP's attempt to deploy state-building power against its Nationalist rivals in the context of a broad, contemporary urge to modernize China's rural society. It is important to place the campaign in historical perspective. Shamans were frequent targets of official suppression and elite criticism in imperial times, but they were attacked with a different rationale then. Late-imperial Confucian elites conceived of themselves as living in the same moral universe as the shamans, and the two relied on different methods and forms to compete over access to the magic of the same unseen world. The Confucian elite considered shamanistic access undesirable and might describe shamanistic claims of spiritual connection as fraudulent. Nevertheless, few if any Confucian scholars ever questioned the very existence of the spiritual world.[57] By contrast, anti-shaman rhetoric in the twentieth century, including that of the Chinese Communists and the various campaigns undertaken by the Nationalists before them, was built on secular ground. Twentieth-century socialist-inspired rhetoric worldwide promoted a linear, progressive, and future-oriented worldview. It left no room for gods, spirits, or any other "supernatural" forces in the social, economic, and political lives of modern citizens. But in China the departure of modernists from the Confucian tradition was not so very abrupt and clean-cut. Both Nationalist and CCP campaigns echoed the views of old Confucian critics in condemning shamanistic rituals for being a drain on local financial and human resources. Moreover, communist cultural workers (in another context) inherited a Confucian bias against shamans concerning sexual corruption.[58]

In the case of the Yan'an campaign, the communists deployed both old and new resources for their political agenda. The latter differed significantly from that used by urban-based Nationalist predecessors in the 1920s and '30s. As Rebecca Nedostup has shown, the Nationalist campaign in the Jiangnan region focused more on the economy of superstitious practices, such as imposing taxes, restricting the publication of "superstitious" materials, and finding new employment for "superstitious" persons by advocating the principle of "self-reliance."[59] The CCP, in contrast, expanded the mass-line principles and Rectification Movement methods of inner-party cadre training and thought reform into the cultural transformation of the rural population in northwestern Base Areas at large. In the meantime, the CCP was also sensitive to rural conditions and peasant culture in Shaanbei. It resorted to self-criticism and self-examination of the superstitious persons in conjunction with traditional practices of confession, oath-taking, and ritual repentance. Furthermore, instead of focusing on the principle of "self-reliance," the CCP's rituals of public trials and confessions aimed at subordinating shamanistic ritual power to the combined authority of the Party and science. It thus upheld the party-state's claim to be a superior force of Chinese modernization.

The public trials and confessions indicate the ambiguous status of shamans in Communist state-building programs during this particular time period. While the campaign rhetoric condemned the healing practices as businesses that killed people, neither the rituals of confession nor the public trials were designed to punish the shamans as murderers. In fact, as the court's sentence at Yang Hanzhu's trial shows, the purpose of the campaign was to eradicate shamanistic practices and rehabilitate shamans. The latter were granted the prospect of "giving up evil and returning to good." As long as they gave up their old selves, the party-state would offer them a new life and make them members of the "people."

The Anti-Shaman Campaign set useful precedents for the CCP's thought-reform programs for the "dangerous classes" in the post-1949 PRC state.[60] The campaign was short-lived, and the rhetoric of class struggle took over CCP propaganda in the forthcoming Civil War that played out before 1949. The propaganda soon reframed the two opposing sides of the cultural war as between the "people" under the leadership of the CCP and the old social order of the ruling class—rural landlords, urban capitalists, and the Nationalist government. Individual shamans might still be cast as victims of the old social order. As such, through confessional rituals and other means of education and coercion, it was considered possible to redeem them from the influence of these evils. As a political category, however, shamans and other ritual specialists would be increasingly associated with the evil power of the ruling class during the immediate land reform and in subsequent political campaigns.[61] Mass meetings, public trials, and rituals of confession became national exercises on an everyday basis, while practices associated with religion and superstition were subjected to total eradication without further discernment. Although it was short-lived and geographically limited, Yan'an's Anti-Shaman Campaign foreshadowed how Party propaganda would deploy resources from the "Old China" to support the forthcoming "New China." It supplies a deeper insight into the power mechanism of propaganda as the current Chinese regime has called upon both traditional culture and Maoist legacies for the "great rejuvenation of the Chinese nation."

Notes

1. Mircea Eliade (1907–1986) distinguishes shamans from spirit mediums: the former specialize in ecstasy and magical flight, and their ritual is mainly concerned with "life, health, the

world of light, against death, diseases, sterility, disasters, and the world of darkness." They are most often male, and they control animal spirits. The latter are usually women and of low status; unlike shamans, they are prone to spirit possessions. Eliade, *Shamanism*, p. 590; Winkelman, "Shamanism in Cross-Cultural Perspective." There is no clear evidence that the Shaanbei people distinguished shamans and spirit mediums in the same way that Eliade did. I use the term shaman more freely to include both categories, and I introduce indigenous categorizations whenever the sources are available. On questioning Eliade's definitions with Chinese examples, see also Sutton, "From Credulity to Scorn," pp. 2–3, fn. 7; Yang, "Shamanism and Spirit Possession in Chinese Modernity," pp. 52–53, fn. 1.

2. The currency was likely the *bianbi* 邊幣 that had been issued by the Border Region government since 1941 to replace the Nationalist government's *fabi* 法幣. According to Gunther Stein (1900–1961), a foreign journalist who visited Yan'an, the Border Region bank stipulated the official exchange rate of 1 U.S. dollar for 1,350 *yuan bianbi*, and the currency was worth even more on the black market; Stein, *The Challenge of Red China*, pp. 197–199. The Chinese journalist Zhao Chaogou 趙超構 (1910–1992) also visited Yan'an in 1944 and recorded that several cheap clay dolls cost him over ten thousand *yuan* in *bianbi*; Zhao, *Yan'an yiyue*, p. 74.

3. Mu, "Benshi Baijiaping wushen Yang Hanzhu shanghai renming panchu tuxing."

4. Yang, "Introduction," in *Chinese Religiosities*, pp. 19–25; Yang, *Religion in China*, pp. 3–64. See also Dubois and Chi, "Opiate of the Masses with Chinese Characteristics," pp. 1–20.

5. Asad, "Religion, Nation-State, Secularism."

6. The earliest uses of *zongjiao* for "religion" and *mixin* for "superstition" appeared in Japan in 1869 and 1889, respectively. On the Japanese origins of these terms and how they were adopted in China, see Josephson, *The Invention of Religion in Japan*, esp. pp. 192–253; Suzuki, "Religion (*shūkyō*) and Freedom (*jiyū*)"; Chen, "'Zongjiao'"; Huang, "Mixin guannian de qiyuan yu yanbian"; Yang, "Introduction," pp. 11–19; Nedostup, *Superstitious Regimes*, pp. 7–11; Goossaert and Palmer, *The Religious Question in Modern China*, pp. 43–89; Katz, *Religion in China and Its Modern Fate*, pp. 9–12.

7. Goossaert and Palmer, *The Religious Question in Modern China*, pp. 73–79.

8. Goossaert and Palmer, *The Religious Question in Modern China*, p. 58.

9. On the early twentieth-century anti-superstition and temple destruction campaigns, see, among others, Duara, *Culture, Power, and the State*, pp. 118–157; Goossaert, "1898: The Beginning of the End for Chinese Religion?"; Nedostup, *Superstitious Regimes*; Poon, *Negotiating Religion in Modern China*; Goossaert and Palmer, *The Religious Question in Modern China*, pp. 50–55; Kang Bao (Paul Katz), "Jindai Zhongguo zhi simiao pohuai yundong"; Qi, "Qingji Wenzhou diqu de miaochan banxue."

10. Nedostup, *Superstitious Regimes*, pp. 191–226; Poon, *Negotiating Religion in Modern China*, pp. 67–92.

11. Chen, *Zhongguo Gongchandang yu Zhongguo de zongjiao wenti*, pp. 11–20, 76–79; Goossaert and Palmer, *The Religious Question in Modern China*, pp. 140–141; Yang, "Introduction"; Yang, *Religion in China*, pp. 57–63.

12. Yang, "Introduction"; Goossaert and Palmer, *The Religious Question in Modern China*, pp. 139–143.

13. Chen, *Zhongguo Gongchandang yu Zhongguo de zongjiao wenti*, pp. 28–76.

14. Mao, "Wenhua gongzuo zhong de tongyi zhanxian"; Li, "Guanyu wenjiao gongzuo de fangxiang." Li was vice president of the Border Region government, and this was the speech he delivered at the second meeting of the Shaan-Gan-Ning Border Region Congress on December 6, 1944. See also Keating, *Two Revolutions*, pp. 233–240. Adam Chau speculates, with good reason, that the actual number of shamans may have been much higher. See Chau, "Popular Religion in Shaanbei, North-Central China," p. 41.

15. Mao, "Guanyu Shaan-Gan-Ning Bianqu de wenhua jiaoyu wenti"; Mao, "Zai Zhongguo Gongchandang diqici quanguo daibiao dahuishang de koutou zhengzhi baogao."

16. The publication of Mao's essay was later considered the birth of "Mao Zedong Thought." See Dirlik, "The Discourse of 'Chinese Marxism'"; Holm, *Art and Ideology in Revolutionary China*, pp. 74–81 (quotation on p. 74).

17. Dirlik, "Discourse of 'Chinese Marxism,'" p. 325.

18. Apter and Saich, *Revolutionary Discourse in Mao's Republic*, p. 26. For critical views of this movement, see also Chen, *Yan'an de yinying*; Gao, *Hong taiyang shi zenyang shengqi de*. For a more sympathetic evaluation of the Rectification Movement, see Selden, *China in Revolution*.

19. Holm, *Art and Ideology in Revolutionary China*, pp. 91–94; Judd, "Prelude to the 'Yan'an Talks.'" On the Yan'an talks, see also McDougall, *Mao Zedong's "Talks at the Yan'an Conference on Literature and Art."*

20. Selden, *China in Revolution*, pp. 169–196; Keating, *Two Revolutions*; Chen, "The Blooming Poppy under the Red Sun."

21. On the Nationalist anti-superstition campaign as an important underside of the public health reform, see Nedostup, *Superstitious Regime*, pp. 191–226, esp. pp. 215–224.

22. Foucault, *The Order of Things*; Rabinow, "Introduction," in *The Foucault Reader*, pp. 3–29.

23. Foucault, *The History of Sexuality*, pp. 58–59.

24. "Wushen de pianshu" 巫神的騙術 (Shamans' arts of cheating), in *Zhankai fandui wushen de douzheng*, pp. 5–6.

25. "Wushen de pianshu," pp. 7–10.

26. "Wushen de pianshu," pp. 9–10; "Wushen Bai Conghai de tanbai" 巫神白從海的坦白 (Shaman Bai Chonghai's confession), in *Zhankai fandui wushen de douzheng*, pp. 38–39.

27. "Wushen de pianshu," p. 10.

28. Adam Chau finds that there are mainly two kinds of demonic beings in contemporary Shaanbei: the "paralysis monsters" (*tanjiezi* 癱羯子, or castrated male goats) that "supposedly kidnap children's souls and cause them to go into paralytic fits," and the mischievous "hairy ghost gods" (*maoguishi* 毛鬼神), who "employ different techniques to harm people and their property, making people fall ill or causing valuables to disappear; Chau, "Popular Religion in Shaanbei, North-Central China," p. 49. The former is similar to the *jijiaozi* and the latter bears typical characteristics of fox spirits. On the latter, see Kang, *The Cult of the Fox*.

29. "Wushen de pianshu," pp. 11–14.

30. Stranahan, *Molding the Medium*.

31. Unschuld, *Medicine in China*, pp. 4–9.

32. On the remaking of traditional knowledge about the Chinese body and medicine into "science" during PRC times, see, among others, Palmer, *Qigong Fever*, pp. 102–135; Croizier, *Traditional Medicine in Modern China*, pp. 151–209; Taylor, *Chinese Medicine in Early Communist China, 1945–1963*; Scheid, *Chinese Medicine in Contemporary China*.

33. On the blind storytellers, or bards, as ritual specialists in Shaanbei, see Jones, *Ritual and Music in North China*, vol. 2: *Shaanbei*, pp. 30–41.

34. On the reformation of traditional storytellers into Party cultural workers, see Hung, "Reeducating a Blind Storyteller"; Jones, *Ritual and Music in North China*, esp. pp. 43–54 on the Yan'an period; Wu, *Reinventing Chinese Tradition*, pp. 88–121.

35. "Bai Lang yisheng quanshuo wushen zhuanbian" 白浪醫生勸說巫神轉變 (Dr. Bai Lang persuades a shaman to reform himself) and "Fan wushen yingxiong Shi Yuexiang" 反巫神英雄史月祥 (Anti-shaman hero Shi Yuexiang), in *Zhankai fandui wushen de douzheng*, pp. 67–72.

36. "Wushen Bai Conghai de tanbai," p. 33.

37. "Wushen Bai Conghai de tanbai," p. 45.

38. Chen, *Yan'an de yinying*; Gao, *Hong taiyang shi zenyang shengqi de*. Selden holds a more sympathetic view of the Rectification Movement but still discusses the "immense psychological power groups can wield over their members" so that individuals would be compelled to conform to group norms and values; Selden, *China in Revolution*, pp. 156–157. See also Smith, *Thought Reform and China's Dangerous Classes*, pp. 105–108.

39. On an example to follow this model, see Feng, "Nao 'gui,' zhuo 'gui.'" The confession meetings discussed below often followed much the same procedure as this public trial.

40. One such confession meeting was held in Fuxian 鄜縣 (today's Fuxian 富縣, about eighty kilometers south of Yan'an city); see "Qunzhong juxing fan wushen dahui." Another "mass meeting of shamans' confessions" was held in a township of Yanchuan xian 延川縣 (about eighty km northeast of Yan'an city); see "Yanchuan Yongyuan qu sanxiang qunzhong tongguo fandui wushen banfa."

41. "Yan'an xian zhaokai fan wushen dahui."

42. "Yan'an xian zhaokai fan wushen dahui."

43. "Fan wushen gongyue"; "Yan'an xian de fan wushen dahui," in *Zhankai fandui wushen de douzheng*, pp. 55–57.

44. On the origin and the impact of the communist mass-line politics in thought reform, see Whyte, *Small Groups and Political Rituals in China*, pp. 10–17, 25–33; Smith, *Thought Reform and China's Dangerous Classes*, pp. 93–138.

45. Übelhör, "The Community Compact (Hsiang-yüe) of the Sung and Its Educational Significance"; Zhang and Guo, "Yan'an shiqi jiceng zhengquan jianshe yanjiu."

46. Liu, *Confucian Rituals and Chinese Villagers*, pp. 167–179.

47. McDermott, "Emperor, Élite, and Commoners"; Liu, *Confucian Rituals and Chinese Villagers*, pp. 170–171, fn. 17.

48. Legal scholars of China have pointed out that modern Chinese concepts of punishment and rehabilitation were influenced as much by Western penal theories as "Confucian beliefs in teaching proper moral behavior and its positive effect on social stability." See Mühlhahn, *Criminal Justice in China*, pp. 75–76. Jan Kiely shows that Confucian moral transformation remained critical in Chinese penal reforms in the late nineteenth and twentieth centuries, although to a lesser degree in early PRC thought reforms; see Kiely, *The Compelling Ideal*.

49. Wu, "Self-Examination and Confession of Sins in Traditional China."

50. Mühlhahn, *Criminal Justice in China*, p. 49.

51. Katz, *Divine Justice*, pp. 61–81.

52. Ai Shaorun, "Shaan-Gan-Ning Bianqu xingfa de tedian" 陝甘寧邊區刑罰的特點 (Special features of Shaan-Gan-Ning Border Region criminal penalties), in *Shaan-Gan-Ning Bianqu falü fagui huibian*, compiled by Ai and Gao, pp. 98–100. On Soviet influence, see Mühlhahn, *Criminal Justice in China*, pp. 148–153.

53. "Xingfa zong fenze caoan" 刑法總分則草案 (Draft of the general and specific provisions of the penal code), in *Shaan-Gan-Ning bianqu falü fagui huibian*, compiled by Ai and Gao, pp. 103–126.

54. On the traditional use of contracts, see Hansen, *Negotiating Daily Life in Traditional China*. For an excellent case study of the contrast between imperial law and customary law in village life, see Hase, *Custom, Land and Livelihood in Rural South China*. I thank Valerie Hansen for alerting me of the use of contractual terms and penalty clauses in customary practices and for providing me with several references.

55. The story was first reported in *Jiefang ribao*, August 15, 1944. On Judge Bao in English, see Idema, *Judge Bao and the Rule of Law*; Blader, *Tales of Magistrate Bao and His Valiant Lieutenants*.

56. Whyte, *Small Groups and Political Rituals in China,* p. 16.

57. Sutton, "From Credulity to Scorn," p. 33; Kendall, "The Cultural Politics of 'Superstition' in the Korean Shaman World."

58. This feature of the communist anti-shaman rhetoric is discussed in Kang, "Women's Liberation and Anti-Superstition in Wartime Communist Propaganda, 1943–50," pp. 64–96.

59. Nedostup, *Superstitious Regime,* pp. 191–226.

60. Smith, *Thought Reform and China's Dangerous Classes.*

61. On the general connection between the ruling class and religion (or superstition) in CCP propaganda, see Hinton, *Fanshen,* pp. 165–185; Smith, *Thought Reform and China's Dangerous Classes,* pp. 97–98; Goossaert and Palmer, *The Religious Question in Modern China,* pp. 146–150. On the sustaining power of "superstitions" and sectarian religions in Maoist times, see Smith, "Talking Toads and Chinless Ghosts"; Dubois, *The Sacred Village,* pp. 141–151, 166–172.

BIBLIOGRAPHY

Afinogenov, Gregory. *Spies and Scholars: Chinese Secrets and Imperial Russia's Quest for World Power.* Cambridge, MA: Belknap Press of Harvard University Press, 2020.

Ai Shaorun 艾绍润 and Gao Haishen 高海深, comp. *Shaan-Gan-Ning Bianqu falü fagui huibian* 陕甘宁边区法律法规汇编 (Collection of Shaan-Gan-Ning Border Region laws and regulations). Xi'an: Shaanxi renmin chubanshe, 2007.

Aleni, Giulio (Ai Rulüe 艾儒略). *Shengmeng ge* 聖夢歌 (A song of sacred dreams). In *Yesuhui Luomadang'anguan Ming-Qing Tianzhujiao wenxian* 耶穌會羅馬檔案館明清天主教文獻 (Chinese Christian texts from the Roman archives of the Society of Jesus), edited by Nicolas Standaert 鐘鳴旦 and Adrian Dudink 杜鼎克, vol. 4. Taipei: Ricci Institute, 2002.

———. *Tianzhu jiangsheng yinyi* 天主降生引義 (An explanation of Our Lord's incarnation). Wulin: Tianzhu chaoxingtang, n.d.

Allan, Sarah. *Buried Ideas: Legends of Abdication and Ideal Government in Early Chinese Bamboo-Slip Manuscripts.* Albany: State University of New York Press, 2015.

Allard, James. "Idealism in Britain and the United States." In *The Cambridge History of Philosophy 1870–1945,* edited by Thomas Baldwin. pp. 43–59. Cambridge: Cambridge University Press, 2003.

Apter, David E., and Tony Saich. *Revolutionary Discourse in Mao's Republic.* Cambridge, MA: Harvard University Press, 1998.

Asad, Talal. "Religion, Nation-State, Secularism." In *Nation and Religion: Perspectives on Europe and Asia,* edited by Peter van Der Veer and Hartmut Lehmann, pp. 178–196. Princeton, NJ: Princeton University Press, 1999.

Bai Dizhou 白滌洲. "Dao Liu Bannong xiansheng" 悼劉半農先生 (Mourning Mr. Liu Bannong). *Duli pinglun* 獨立評論 110 (1934): 13–15.

Bao Tianxiao 包天笑, ed. *Gaodeng xiaoxue shiyong nüzi shuhan wen* 高等小學適用女文 (Girls' letter-writing manual, upper-level elementary school). Shanghai: Youzheng shuju, n.d.

Baqi tongzhi, chu ji 八旗通志, 初集 (Comprehensive treatises of the Eight Banners, first installment). Beijing: Wuying dian, 1739. Xylograph, held at Harvard-Yenching Library, call number: t 4718 2008.

Barmé, Geremie R. "Towards a New Sinology." *Chinese Studies Association of Australia Newsletter* 31 (May 2005): 4–9.

Barthes, Roland. *S/Z.* Translated by Richard Miller. New York: Hill and Wang, 1974.

Beijing shi Minzu guji zhengli chuban guihua xiaozu 北京市民族古籍整理出版规划小组. *Beijing diqu Manwen tushu zongmu* 北京地区满文图书总目 (General catalog of Manchu sources in the Beijing area). Shenyang: Liaoning minzu chubanshe, 2008.

Bell, John. *A Journey from St. Petersburg to Peking, 1719–1722.* Edited by J. L. Stevenson. Edinburgh: Edinburgh University Press, 1965.

Ben-Dor Benite, Zvi. *The Ten Lost Tribes: A World History.* New York: Oxford University Press, 2009.

"Ben Kong" 本空 (pseud.). "Riben yinmou Da Qing diguo" 日本陰謀大清帝國 (Japan's great conspiracy to reinstate the Qing Diguo). *Jiaoguo zhoubao* 教國週報 21 (1932): 2–3.

Berlin, Isaiah. *Four Essays on Liberty.* Oxford: Oxford University Press, 1969.

Bernal, Martin. "Liu Shih-p'ei and National Essence." In *The Limits of Change,* edited by Charlotte Furth, pp. 90–112. Cambridge, MA: Harvard University Press, 1976.

Bernstein, Gail Lee. *Japanese Marxist: A Portrait of Kawakami Hajime, 1879–1946.* Cambridge, MA: Harvard University Press, 1976.

Blader, Susan. *Tales of Magistrate Bao and His Valiant Lieutenants.* Hong Kong: Chinese University of Hong Kong, 1998.

Blitstein, Pablo. "Multiple Renaissances: The Chinese Roots of a Widespread Idea in the Euro-American World." Paper presented at Tel Aviv University, May 14, 2017.

Brokaw, Cynthia. "Commercial Woodblock Publishing in the Qing (1644–1911) and the Transition to Modern Print Technology." In *From Woodblocks to the Internet: Chinese Publishing and Print Culture in Transition, circa 1800–2008,* edited by Cynthia Brokaw and Christopher A. Reed, pp. 39–58. Leiden: Brill, 2010.

Brook, Timothy. *Great State: China and the World.* London: Profile Books, 2021.

Brook, Timothy, Hans van Walt van Praag, and Miek Boltjes. *Sacred Mandates: Asian International Relations since Chinggis Khan.* Chicago: University of Chicago Press, 2018.

Brooks, Linda M. *The Menace of the Sublime to the Individual Self: Kant, Schiller, Coleridge, and the Disintegration of Romantic Identity.* Lewiston, NY: Edwin Mellen Press, 1995.

Brown, Shana J. "Archives at the Margins: Luo Zhenyu's Qing Documents and Nationalism in Republican China." In *The Politics of Historical Production in Late Qing and Republican China,* edited by Tze-ki Hon and Robert J. Culp, pp. 247–270. Leiden: Brill, 2007.

Brunnert, H. S., and V. V. Hagelstrom. *Present Day Political Organization of China.* Translated by A. Beltchenko and E. E. Moran, edited by N. T. Kolessoff. Shanghai: Kelly and Walsh, 1912.

Buckley, Chris. "Xi Jinping Thought Explained: A New Ideology for a New Era." *New York Times,* February 26, 2018. https://www.nytimes.com/2018/02/26/world/asia/xi-jinping-thought-explained-a-new-ideology-for-a-new-era.html.

Cai Jianguo 蔡建国. *Cai Yuanpei yu jindai Zhongguo* 蔡元培与近代中国 (Cai Yuanpei and modern China). Shanghai: Shanghai shehui kexue chubanshe, 1997.

Cai Yuanpei 蔡元培. *Cai Yuanpei wenji* 蔡元培文集 (Collected works of Cai Yuanpei). Edited by Gao Pingshu 高平叔. Taipei: Jinxiu chuban, 1995.

———. *Cai Yuanpei xiansheng yiwen leichao* 蔡元培先生遺文類鈔 (Classified surviving writings of Mr. Cai Yuanpei). Edited by Sun Dezhong 孫德中. Taipei: Fuxing shuju, 1966.

———. "Replacing Religion with Aesthetic Education." Translated by Julia F. Andrews. In *Modern Chinese Literary Thought: Writings on Literature, 1893–1945,* edited by Kirk A. Denton, pp. 182–189. Stanford, CA: Stanford University Press, 1996.

———. *Zhongxue xiushen jiaokeshu* 中學修身教科書 (Middle school self-cultivation textbook). Shanghai: Shangwu, 1907–1908.

Carrai, Maria Adele, Jean-Christophe Defraigne, and Jan Wouters. *The Belt and Road Initiative and Global Governance.* Cheltenham, UK: Edward Elgar Publishing 2020.

Carroll, John. "Beauty contra God: Has Aesthetics Replaced Religion in Modernity?" *Journal of Sociology* 48, no. 2 (June 2012): 206–223.

Chan, Marjorie. "In Memoriam: Edwin G. Pulleyblank 蒲立本 (1922–2013)." *Journal of Chinese Linguistics* 42, no. 1 (2014): 252–266.

Chang, Hao (Zhang Hao). *Liang Ch'i-ch'ao and Intellectual Transition in China, 1890–1907.* Cambridge, MA: Harvard University Press, 1970.

Chao Yuen Ren (Zhao Yuanren) 趙元任. "Guoyu Luomazi de yanjiu" 國語羅馬字的研究 (Studies in the romanization of the national language). *Guoyu yuekan* 國語月刊 1, no. 7 (1922): 87–117.

———. "Wusheng de biaozhun" 五聲的標準 (The standard for the five tones). *Guoyu yuekan* 國語月刊 1, no. 8 (1922): 1–4.

Chau, Adam. "Popular Religion in Shaanbei, North-Central China." *Journal of Chinese Religions* 31, no. 1 (2003): 39–79.

Chen Di 忱迪. "Zhuyin fuhao yu minzhong jiaoyu" 注音符號與民眾教育 (Phonetic notation and mass education). *Guoyu zhoukan* 國語週刊 20, no. 2 (September 12, 1931): 2.

Chen Guoqiu 陈国球. *Wenxue shi shuxie xingtai yu wenhua zhengzhi* 文学史书写形态与文化政治 (Modes of writing and the cultural politics of literary history). Beijing: Beijing daxue chubanshe, 2004.

Chen Hongxiang 陈鸿祥. *Wang Guowei yu jindai Dong-Xifang xueren* 王国维与近代东西方学人 (Wang Guowei and Asian and Western intellectuals). Tianjin: Tianjin guji chubanshe, 1990.

Chen Hsi-yuan 陳熙遠. "'Zongjiao': Yige Zhongguo jindai wenhua shi shang de guanjianci" 「宗教」：一個中國近代文化史上的關鍵詞 ("Zongjiao" [Religion]: A keyword in the cultural history of modern China). *Xin shixue* 新史學 13, no. 4 (2002): 37–66.

Chen, I-Hsin. "From God's Chinese Names to a Cross-Cultural Universal God: James Legge's Intertextual Theology in His Translation of Tian, Di, and Shangdi." *Translation Studies* 9, no. 3 (2016): 268–281.

Chen Jiexian 陳捷先 (Ch'en Chieh-hsien). "Jin-liang *Manzhou bidang* pingjia" 金梁「滿洲祕檔」評價 (A review of Jin-liang's *Secret Manchu archives*). In *Qingshi zabi* 清史雜筆, vol. 2, pp. 55–68. Taipei: Xuehai chubanshe, 1977.

Chen Jingxi 陈景熙. "Chaoshan 'Qidui yin-Qidui piao' kao: Qingmo Minchu difang xuwei bizhi yanjiu" 潮汕「七兌銀'七兌票」考：清末民初地方虛位幣制研究 (Investigation of Chaoshan "seven silver cash, seven cash in banknotes": Research on the local counterfeit currency system in the late Qing and early Republic). *Chaoxue yanjiu* 潮学研究 10 (2002): 205–210.

Chen Jinlong 陳金龍. *Zhongguo Gongchandang yu Zhongguo de zongjiao wenti: Guanyu dangde zongjiao zhengce de lishi kaocha* 中國共產黨與中國的宗教問題：關於黨的宗教政策的歷史考察 (The Chinese Communist Party and China's religion question: A historical investigation of the Party's policy on religion). Guangzhou: Guangdong renmin chubanshe, 2006.

Chen, Pingyuan *Touches of History: An Enquiry into "May Fourth" China*. Translated by Michel Hockx et al. Leiden: Brill, 2011.

Chen Qitai 陈其泰. "Qian Daxin yu Yuan shixue" 钱大昕与元史学 (Qian Daxin and Yuan historiography). *Zhejiang xuekan* 浙江学刊 4, no. 111 (1998): 118–122.

Chen Yan 陳衍. "He xin yu shi xu" 何心與詩叔 (Talking of the mind and poetry). In *Chen Yan shilun heji* 陳衍詩論合集 (Comprehensive collection of Chen Yan's commentaries on poetry), edited by Chen Zhonglian 錢仲聯, pp. 1056–1057. Fuzhou: Fujian renmin chubanshe, 1999.

Chen Yung-fa 陳永發. "The Blooming Poppy under the Red Sun: The Yan'an Way and the Opium Trade." In *New Perspectives on the Chinese Communist Revolution,* edited by Tony Saich and Hans J. van de Ven, pp. 263–298. Armonk, NY: M. E. Sharpe, 1995.

———. *Yan'an de yinying* 延安的陰影 (Yan'an's shadow). Taipei: Zhongyang yanjiuyuan jindaishi yanjiusuo, 1990.

Chen Zuwu 陈祖武 and Zhu Tongchuang 朱彤窗. *Qian-Jia xueshu biannian* 乾嘉学术编年 (Scholarship of the Qianlong-Jiaqing [reign periods] on a yearly basis). Shijiazhuang: Hebei renmin chubanshe, 2005.

Cheng Yaotian 程瑤田. "*Shuowen yinjing kao* xu" 說文引經考序 (Preface to Examination of *Shuowen* quotations of the Classics). In Cheng Jisheng 程際盛, *Shuowen yinjing kao* 說文引經考 (Examination of Shuowen quotations of the Classics). Rare Books Collection, Fudan University Library, Shanghai, Ms. #374889 (3107).

Chiang, Louisa, and Perry Link. "Before the Revolution." *New York Review of Books* 45, no. 10 (June 7, 2018): 49–51.
Chow, Kai-wing, Ng On-cho, and John B. Henderson, eds. *Imagining Boundaries: Changing Confucian Doctrines, Texts, and Hermeneutics*. Albany: State University of New York Press, 1999.
Chunhua 春花. *Qingdai Man-Mengwen cidian yanjiu* 清代满蒙文词典研究 (Research on Manchu- and Mongol-language dictionaries of the Qing period). Shenyang: Liaoning minzu chubanshe, 2008.
Cohen, Alvin. "Brief Note: The Origin of the Yellow Emperor Era Chronology." *Asia Major* 25, no. 2 (2012): 1–13.
Cohen, Paul. *Between Tradition and Modernity: Wang T'ao and Reform in Late Ch'ing China*. Cambridge, MA: Council on East Asian Studies, Harvard University, 1988.
———. *Discovering History in China: American Historical Writing on the Recent Chinese Past*. New York: Columbia University Press, 1984.
Cong Jiesheng 叢介生. *Guoyin xue* 國音學 (Study of national pronunciation). Shanghai: Shijie shuju, 1933.
Couvreur, Séraphin, trans. *Tch'ouen ts'iou et Tso tchouan: La chronique de la principauté de Lòu*. 3 vols. Paris: Les Belles Lettres, 1951 [1914].
Croizier, Ralph C. *Traditional Medicine in Modern China: Science, Nationalism, and the Tensions of Cultural Change*. Cambridge, MA: Harvard University Press, 1968.
Crossley, Pamela Kyle. *Orphan Warriors: Three Manchu Generations and the End of the Qing World*. Princeton, NJ: Princeton University Press, 1990.
———. *A Translucent Mirror: History and Identity in Qing Imperial Ideology*. Berkeley: University of California Press, 1999.
Csikszentmihalyi, Mark, ed. *Readings in Han Chinese Thought*. Indianapolis: Hackett Publishing, 2006.
Culp, Robert. "New Literati and the Reproduction of Antiquity: Contextualizing Luo Zhenyu and Wang Guowei." In *Lost Generation: Luo Zhenyu, Qing Loyalists and the Formation of Modern Chinese Culture,* edited by Yang Chia-ling and Roderick Whitfield, pp. 99–121. London: Saffron, 2012.
———. "Teaching *Baihua*: Textbook Publishing and the Production of Vernacular Language and a New Literary Canon in Early Twentieth-Century China." *Twentieth-Century China* 34, no. 1 (November 2008): 4–41.
Da Qing diguo quantu 大清帝國全圖 (Complete map of the great Qing state). Shanghai: Shangwu, 1905.
Da Qing diguo xinbian fadian 大清帝國新編法典 (New legal code of the great Qing state). Shanghai: Dongya Shushe, 1906.
Da Qing Manzhou shilu, Da Qing Taizu Gao huangdi shilu 大清滿洲實錄, 大清太祖高皇帝實錄 (Manchurian veritable records of the Great Qing; Veritable records of the Lofty Emperor of the Great Qing) (1636–1739). Facsimile of ms. Taipei: Huawen Shuju, 1969.
Dai Xinying 戴鑫英 (Batu 巴图). "Zaoqi gu wenzi xuezhe—Bao shi fuzi" 早期古文字学者—鲍氏父子 (Pioneering scholars of historical scripts: The Baos, father and son). *Manzu yanjiu* 满族研究 4 (2003): 86–87.
Daniels, Christian, Joseph Needham, and Nicholas K. Menzies. *Science and Civilisation in China,* vol. 6: *Biology and Biological Technology,* part 3: *Agro-Industries and Forestry*. Cambridge: Cambridge University Press, 1996.
Davis, Natalie Zemon. *Trickster Travels: A Sixteenth-Century Muslim between Worlds*. New York: Hill and Wang, 2006.

de Crespigny, Rafe. *A Biographical Dictionary of Later Han to the Three Kingdoms: (23–220 AD)*. Leiden: Brill, 2007.
DeFrancis, John. *Nationalism and Language Reform in China*. Princeton, NJ: Princeton University Press, 1950.
Derrida, Jacques. *Of Grammatology*. Translated by Gayatri Chakravorty Spivak. Baltimore: Johns Hopkins University Press, 1976.
Diaz, Emmanuel, Jr. *Jingjiao liuxing Zhongguo beisong zhengquan* 景教流行中國碑頌正詮 (The text and ode of the stele on the spread of Jingjiao in China: An orthodox interpretation). Bibliotèque national de France 1190.
Di Cosmo, Nicola. "Nurhaci's Gambit: Sovereignty as Concept and Praxis in the Rise of the Manchus." In *The Scaffolding of Sovereignty: Global and Aesthetic Perspectives on the History of a Concept*, edited by Zvi Ben-Dor Benite, Stefanos Geroulanos, and Nicole Jerr, pp. 102–123. New York: Columbia University Press, 2017.
Ding Fubao 丁福保, comp. and ed. *Shuowen jiezi gulin* 說文解字詁林 (Forest of explanations on the analysis of characters and an explanation of writing). 12 vols. Taipei: Taiwan shangwu yinshuguan, 1966.
——, comp. *Shuowen jiezi gulin zhengxu hebian* 說文解字詁林正續合編 (Joint compilation of the *Corrected and continued forest of explanations* of the *Analysis of characters and explanation of writing*). Taipei: Dingwen shuju, 1977.
Ding Hong 丁红. "Zhu Shizhe shengping zhushu jiqi san dai cangshu" 朱师辙生平著迹及其三代藏书 (The life and work of Zhu Shizhe and his collection of writings from the preimperial period). *Zhongguo dianji yu wenhua* 中国典籍与文化 4 (2000): 61–68.
Dirlik, Arif. "The Discourse of 'Chinese Marxism.'" In *Modern Chinese Religion: 1850–2015*, edited by Vincent Goossaert, Jan Kiely, John Lagerwey, et al., pp. 305–327. Leiden: Brill, 2016.
Dobson, W. A. C. H., trans. *Mencius*. Toronto: University of Toronto Press, 1969.
"Document 9: A ChinaFile Translation." *ChinaFile*, November 8, 2013. http://www.chinafile.com/document-9-chinafile-translation.
Doleželová-Velingerová, Milena, and Rudolf G. Wagner. "Chinese Encyclopaedias of New Global Knowledge (1870–1930): Changing Ways of Thought." In *Chinese Encyclopaedias of New Global Knowledge*, edited by Milena Doleželová-Velingerová and Rudolf G. Wagner, pp. 1–27. Berlin: Springer-Verlag, 2014.
Dong, Madeleine Yue. "How to Remember the Qing Dynasty: The Case of Meng Sen." In *The Politics of Historical Production in Late Qing and Republican China*, edited by Tze-ki Hon and Robert J. Culp, pp. 271–294. Leiden: Brill, 2007.
Dong Wen 董文, ed. *Zhonghua guoyin liusheng jipian keben* 中華國音留聲機片課本 (Zhonghua national pronunciation phonograph record textbook). Shanghai: Zhonghua, 1920.
Downing, Charles Toogood. *The Fan-Qui in China, in 1836–7*. London: H. Colburn, 1838.
Du Songbo 杜松柏, ed. *Qing chu shihua fanyi chubian* 清初詩話訪佚初編 (First collection of found early Qing poetry colloquies), vol. 7. Taipei: Xin wenfeng chuban gongsi, 1987.
Duara, Prasenjit. *Culture, Power, and the State: Rural North China, 1900–1942*. Stanford, CA: Stanford University Press, 1988.
Dubois, Thomas. *The Sacred Village: Social Change and Religious Life in Rural North China*. Honolulu: University of Hawai'i Press, 2005.
Dubois, Thomas, and Chi Zhen 池桢. "Opiate of the Masses with Chinese Characteristics: Recent Chinese Scholarship on the Meaning and Future of Religion." In *Marxism and Religion*, edited by Lü Daji 呂大吉 and Gong Xuezeng 龔学增, pp. 1–20. Leiden: Brill, 2014.
Duiker, William J. "The Aesthetics Philosophy of Ts'ai Yuan-p'ei." *Philosophy East and West* 22, no. 4 (October 1972): 385–401.

———. *Ts'ai Yüan-p'ei: Educator of Modern China*. University Park: Penn State University Press, 2003.
Dunn, Ross E. *The Adventures of Ibn Battuta, a Muslim Traveller of the Fourteenth Century*. Berkeley: University of California Press, 1986.
Duyin tongyihui 讀音統一會. *Guoyin zidian* 國音字典 (Dictionary of national pronunciation). Shanghai: Shangwu, 1919 (1920).
———. *Jiaogai guoyin zidian* 校改國音字典 (Revised dictionary of national pronunciation). Shanghai: Shangwu, 1921.
Eliade, Mircea. *Shamanism: Archaic Techniques of Ecstasy*. Translated by Willard R. Trask. Princeton, NJ: Princeton University Press, 1964.
Elliott, Mark C. *The Manchu Way: The Eight Banners and Ethnic Identity in Late Imperial China*. Stanford, CA: Stanford University Press, 2001.
Elman, Benjamin A. *Classicism, Politics, and Kinship: The Ch'ang-chou School of New Text Confucianism in Late Imperial China*. Berkeley: University of California Press, 1990.
———. *On Their Own Terms: Science in China, 1550–1900*. Cambridge, MA.: Harvard University Press, 2005.
———. "'Where Is King Ch'eng?': Civil Examinations and Confucian Ideology during the Early Ming, 1368–1415." *T'oung Pao* 79, nos. 1–3 (1993): 23–68.
Elman, Benjamin A., and Martin Kern, eds. *Statecraft and Classical Learning: The Rituals of Zhou in East Asian History*. Leiden: E. J. Brill, 2010.
En-hua 恩华. *Baqi yiwen bianmu* 八旗艺文编目 (Edited catalog of eight-banner literature). Edited by Guan Jixin 关纪新. 1941 typeset edition. Shenyang: Liaoning minzu chubanshe, 2006.
"Fan wushen gongyue" 反巫神公約 (The anti-shaman pact). *Jiefang ribao* 解放日報, July 21, 1944.
Fan Xiangshan 范祥善. *Zhuyin zimu jiangyi* 注音字母講義 (Lectures on the phonetic alphabet). Shanghai: Shangwu, 1922.
Fan Xizeng 范希曾. "Ping Qingshi gao yiwenzhi" 評清史稿藝文志 (Review of the bibliographical treatise in the *Draft history of the Qing*). In *Youguan "Qingshi gao" bianyin jingguo ji ge fang yijian huibian* 有關清史稿編印經過及各方意見彙編 (Collection of material relating to the process of compiling and publishing *Draft history of the Qing* as well the as opinions of various parties), edited by Xu Shishen 許師慎, vol. 2, pp. 1135–1151. Taipei: Zhonghua Minguo shiliao yanjiu zhongxin, 1979.
Fang, Chao-ying. "Tulišen." In *Eminent Chinese of the Ch'ing Period (1644–1912)*, edited by Arthur W. Hummel, pp. 784–787. Washington, DC: United States Government Printing Office, 1943.
———. "Yin-lu." In *Eminent Chinese of the Ch'ing Period (1644–1912)*, edited by Arthur W. Hummel, pp. 925–926. Washington, DC: United States Government Printing Office, 1943.
Fang Dongshu 方東樹. "*Dongming wenji* xu" 東溟文集序 (Preface to Writings from the Eastern Sea). In *Dongming wenji* (1820), in *Zhongfu tang wenji* 中復堂文集 (Complete works from the Restoration Hall), vol. 1, *Taibei xian Yonghe zhen* (As it then was), 1b. Wenhai chubanshe, 1974.
———. *Zhaomei zhanyan* 昭昧詹言 (Tidbits on Discerning Right from Wrong). Beijing: Renmin wenxue chubanshe, 2006 [1961].
Fang Xiaoyue 方孝岳. "Wode gailiang wenxue guan" 我之改良文學觀 (My views on literary reform). *Xin qingnian* 新青年 3, no. 2 (April 1, 1917).
Feng Lihua 馮利華. "*Huajing* zuozhe Chen Haozi kao" 花鏡作者陳淏子考 (An investigation of the author of the *Mirror of flowers*, Chen Haozi). *Wenxian* 文獻 2 (April 2002): 159–162.

Feng Senling 馮森令, "Nao 'gui,' zhuo 'gui': 'Chumu gui,' 'Xiexing gui,' 'Hongxie nüyaojing' dou zhuading le" 鬧'鬼,' 捉'鬼': '出墓鬼,' '血腥鬼,' '紅鞋女妖精'都抓定了 ("Ghosts" haunted, "Ghosts" captured: The "Revenant Ghost from the Grave," the "Blood Stench Ghost," and the "Female Demon in Red Shoes" all securely caught). *Jiefang ribao* 解放日報, August 12, 1944.

Feng Ziyou 馮自由, "Xingzhonghui shiqi zhi geming tongzhi" 興中會時期之革命同志 (Comrades from the period of the Revive China Society). In *Geming yishi* 革命逸史 (Anecdotes from the revolution), vol. 3, p. 33. Shanghai: Shangwu yinshuguan, 1945.

Fissell, Mary E. *Vernacular Bodies: The Politics of Reproduction in Early Modern England.* Oxford: Oxford University Press, 2004.

Fitzgerald, John *Awakening China: Politics, Culture and Class in the Nationalist Revolution.* Stanford, CA: Stanford University Press, 1998.

Fogel, Joshua A. "Introduction: Masuda Wataru and the Study of Modern China." In Masuda Wataru, *Japan and China: Mutual Representations in the Modern Era,* pp. vii–ix. Richmond, UK: Curzon Press, 2000.

———. *Maiden Voyage: The Senzaimaru and the Creation of Modern Sino-Japanese Relations.* Berkeley: University of California Press, 2014.

———. *Politics and Sinology: The Case of Naitō Konan (1866–1934).* Cambridge, MA: Council on East Asian Studies, Harvard University, 1984.

Foucault, Michel. *The History of Sexuality: An Introduction.* Translated by Robert Hurley. New York: Vintage, 1978.

———. *The Order of Things: An Archeology of the Human Sciences.* New York: Vintage, 1994.

Fu Sinian 傅斯年. "Wei Liu Fu '*Sisheng shiyan lu*' zuoxu" 為劉復 '四聲實驗錄' 作序" (Preface to Liu Fu's *Sisheng shiyan lu*) (2nd preface, January 1923). In Liu Fu, *Sisheng shiyan lu* 四聲實驗錄 (Experimental record of the four tones). Shanghai: Qunyi shushe, 1924.

Fu Zhenlun 傅振倫. "*Qingshi gao* pinglun shang" 清史稿評論上 (Review of *Draft history of the Qing* 1). In *Youguan "Qingshi gao" bianyin jingguo ji ge fang yijian huibian* 有關清史稿編印經過及各方意見彙編 (Collection of material relating to the process of compiling and publishing *Draft history of the Qing* as well the as opinions of various parties), edited by Xu Shishen 許師慎, vol. 2, pp. 544–578. Taipei: Zhonghua Minguo shiliao yanjiu zhongxin, 1979.

———. "*Qingshi gao* pinglun xia" 清史稿評論下 (Review of *Draft history of the Qing* 2). In *Youguan "Qingshi gao" bianyin jingguo ji ge fang yijian huibian* 有關清史稿編印經過及各方意見彙編 (Collection of material relating to the process of compiling and publishing *Draft history of the Qing* as well the as opinions of various parties), edited by Xu Shishen 許師慎, vol. 2, pp. 579–610. Taipei: Zhonghua Minguo shiliao yanjiu zhongxin, 1979.

Fuchs, Walter. *Beiträge zur Mandjurischen Bibliographie und Literatur.* Tokyo: Deutsche Gesellschaft für Natur- und Volkerkunde Ostasiens, 1936.

———. "Neues Material zur mandjurischen Literatur aus Pekinger Bibliotheken." *Asia Major* 7 (1932): 469–482.

Fu-ge 福格. *Ting yu congtan* 聽雨叢談 (Conversations gathered while listening to the rain). (Written after 1850; Lidai shiliao biji congkan; Qingdai shiliao biji typeset edition). Edited by Wang Beiping 汪北平. Beijing: Zhonghua shuju, 1984.

Fujiyama Kazuko 藤山和子. "Edo kōki no kōshōgakusha to Dan Gyokusai no *Setsumon chō*" 江戶後期の考証学者と段玉裁の『説文解字注』 (Late Edo period evidential learning scholars and Duan Yucai's *Shuowen jiezi zhu*). *Otsuma Journal of Comparative Culture* 4 (2002): 98–115.

Gailiang xin wanbao quanshu 改良新萬寶全書 (Revised new comprehensive compendium of collected treasures). 3 *juan*, 1 vol. N.p.: Beiyang junfuqu, 1912.

Gao Hua 高華. *Hong taiyang shi zenyang shengqi de: Yan'an Zhengfeng yundong de lailong qumai* 紅太陽是怎樣升起的：延安整風運動的來龍去脈 (How the red sun rose: The origin and development of the Yan'an rectification campaign). Hong Kong: Chinese University Press, 2011.

Gao Yuan 高元. *Gao Yuan guoyin xue* 高元國音學 (Gao Yuan's studies of national pronunciation). Shanghai: Shangwu, 1922.

Gilbert, Martin. *Letters to Auntie Fori: Five Thousand Years of Jewish History*. New York: Schocken Books, 2002.

Gildow, Douglas M. "Cai Yuanpei (1868–1940), Religion, and His Plan to Save China through Buddhism." *Asia Major* 31, no. 2 (2018): 107–148.

Goodman, Howard L. *Ts'ao P'i Transcendent: The Political Culture of Dynasty-Founding in China at the End of the Han*. Seattle: Scripta Serica, 1998.

Goossaert, Vincent. "1898: The Beginning of the End for Chinese Religion?" *Journal of Asian Studies* 65, no. 2 (2006): 307–336.

Goossaert, Vincent, and David Palmer. *The Religious Question in Modern China*. Chicago: University of Chicago Press, 2011.

Grant, Asahel. *The Nestorians; or, The Lost Tribes*. London: John Murray, 1841.

Gregory, Alan. "Philosophy and Religion." In *Romanticism: An Oxford Guide*, edited by Nicholas Roe, pp. 102–114. Oxford: Oxford University Press, 2005.

Gu Jiegang 顧頡剛. *Gouqiu Zhongguo tushu jihua shu* 購求中國圖書計畫書 (Program for seeking out and purchasing Chinese books). Guangzhou: Guoli Zhongshan daxue tushuguan yanjiuhui, 1927.

———. *Gushi bian zixu* 古史辨自序 (Introduction to the debates on ancient history). Beijing: Shangwu yinshuguan, 2011.

Gu, Ming Dong and Xian Zhou. "Sinology, Sinologism, and New Sinology." *Contemporary Chinese Thought* 49, no. 1 (2018): 1–6.

Gu Tinglong 顾廷龙. *Gu Tinglong xueshu* 顾廷龙学术 (Gu Tinglong's scholarly studies). Edited by Liu Xiaoming 刘小明. Hangzhou: Zhejiang renmin chubanshe, 2000.

Guanglu 廣祿 and Li Xuezhi 李學智. "Qing Taizu chao *Lao Manwen yuandang* yu *Manwen laodang* zhi bijiao yanjiu" 清太祖朝「老滿文原檔」與「滿文老檔」之比較研究 (Comparative research on the *Old original Manchu archives* and the *Old Manchu archives*). *Zhongguo Dongya xueshu yanjiu jihua weiyuan hui nianbao* 中国典籍与文化 4 (1965): 1–165.

Guanhua zhuyin zimu bao 官話注音字母報 (Phonetically annotated newspaper for the official language). Beijing: Zhuyin zimu chuanxisuo, 1919.

Gugong bowuyuan 故宫博物院, ed. *Tongwen zhi sheng: Qinggong cang minzu yuwen cidian* 同文之盛：清宫藏民族语文辞典 (Standardizing the written language: Dictionaries of different ethnic languages from the Qing palace). Beijing: Zijincheng chubanshe, 2009.

Guo Houjue 郭後覺. "Shengdiao jiujing you meiyou yongchu" 聲調究竟有沒有用處 (Do the tones actually have any use?). *Guoyu yuekan* 國語月刊 1, no. 8 (1922): 5–6.

Guo Licheng 郭立誠. *Guo Licheng de xueshu lunzhu* 郭立誠的學術論著 (Guo Licheng's academic writings). Taipei: Wenshizhe chubanshe, 1993.

Guo Shaoyu 郭紹虞 and Wang Wensheng 王文生, eds. *Zhongguo lidai wenlun xuan* 中国历代文论选 (Chinese essays on literature through the ages). Shanghai: Shanghai guji chubanshe, 1980.

Guo Yongfang 郭永芳. "Xuxiu Siku quanshu zongmu tiyao de zhengli fangfa yu pingjia" 《续修四库全书总目提要》的整理方法与评价 (Evaluation and method for managing bibliographical précis to the continuation of the *Complete writings of the Four Repositories*). *Tushu qingbao gongzuo* 图书情报工作 4 (1988): 21–25, 16.

———. "*Xuxiu Siku tiyao* zuanxiu kaolüe: *Xuxiu Siku tiyao* zhuanti yanjiu zhi yi" 《续修四库提要》纂修考略—《续修四库提要》专题研究之一 (Cursory examination of the compilation of the *Bibliographical précis to the continuation of the [complete books of the] four reposito-

ries: A first study on the topic of the *Bibliographical précis to the continuation of the [complete books of the] four repositories*). *Tushu qingbao gongzuo* 图书情报工作 5 (1982): 15–20.

Guomin baoku quanshu 國民寶庫全書 (Complete treasury for citizens). Shanghai: Zhonghua shuju, 1919.

Guoyu liushengpian keben 國語留聲片課本 (National language phonograph record textbook). Shanghai: Shangwu, 1922.

Hanan, Patrick. *The Invention of Li Yu.* Cambridge, MA: Harvard University Press, 1988.

Hansen, Valerie. *Negotiating Daily Life in Traditional China: How Ordinary People Used Contracts, 600–1400.* New Haven, CT: Yale University Press, 1995.

Hanyu da cidian 漢語大詞典 (Great dictionary of Chinese). 10 vols. Shanghai: Hanyu da cidian chubanshe, 1994.

Hartog, François. *Regimes of Historicity: Presentism and Experiences of Time.* New York: Columbia University Press, 2017.

Hase, Patrick H. *Custom, Land and Livelihood in Rural South China: The Traditional Land Law of Hong Kong's New Territories, 1750–1950.* Hong Kong: Hong Kong University Press, 2013.

Hauer, Erich. "Why the Sinologue Should Study Manchu." *Journal of the North China Branch of the Royal Asiatic Society* 61 (1930): 156–164.

Heijdra, Martin J. "The East Asia Library and the Gest Collection at Princeton University." In *Collecting Asia: East Asian Libraries in North America, 1868–2008,* edited by Peter X. Zhou, pp. 120–135. Ann Arbor, MI: Association for Asian Studies, 2010.

Hevia, James L. *English Lessons: The Pedagogy of Imperialism in Nineteenth-Century China.* Durham, NC: Duke University Press, 2003.

Hinton, William *Fanshen: A Documentary of Revolution in a Chinese Village.* New York: Vintage, 1966.

Holm, David. *Art and Ideology in Revolutionary China.* New York: Clarendon Press, 1991.

Hon, Tze-Ki. "Ethnic and Cultural Pluralism: Gu Jiegang's Vision of a New China in His Studies of Ancient History." *Modern China* 22, no. 3 (1996): 315–339.

———. "Revolution as Representation: Meanings of 'National Essence' and 'National Learning' in *Guocui xuebao*." In *The Challenge of Linear Time: Nationhood and the Politics of History in East Asia,* edited by Viren Murthy and Axel Schneider, pp. 257–276. Leiden: Brill, 2014.

———. *The Yijing and Chinese Politics: Classical Commentary and Literati Activism in the Northern Song Period, 960–1127.* Albany: State University of New York Press, 2012.

Hou Han shu 後漢書 (History of the Later Han). Beijing: Zhonghua shuju, 1965.

Hsuan, Hua, trans. *The Vajra Prajna Paramita Sutra.* Burlingame, CA: Dharma Realm Buddhist University, 2002.

Hu, Shih. "The Renaissance in China" (address given November 9, 1926). In *English Writings of Hu Shih: Chinese Philosophy and Intellectual History,* edited by Chih-p'ing Chou, vol. 2, pp. 15–25. Heidelberg: Springer, 2013.

——— 胡適. *Wushi nian lai Zhongguo wenxue* 五十年來中國文學 (Chinese literature in the last fifty years). In *Hu Shi shuo wenxue bianqian* 胡适说文学变迁 (Hu Shi on literary transformation). Shanghai: Shanghai guji chubanshe, 1999.

Huang Kewu 黃克武. "Mixin guannian de qiyuan yu yanbian: Wusi kexueguan de zai fanxing" 迷信觀念的起源與演變：五四科學觀的再反省 (Origin and evolution of the concept of mixin/superstition: A review of May Fourth scientific views). *Dongya guannian shi jikan* 東亞觀念史集刊 9 (2015): 153–226.

Huang Lin 黃霖. *Jindai wenxue piping shi* 近代文学批评史 (History of modern literary criticism). Shanghai: Shanghai guji chubanshe, 1993.

Huang Runhua 黄润华. "Manwen fangke tushu shulun" 满文坊刻图书述论 (Account of commercial publishing in Manchu). *Wenxian* 文献 2 (1999): 220–237.

———. "Manwen guanke tushu shulun" 满文官刻图书述论 (Account of state publishing in Manchu). *Wenxian* 文献 4 (1996): 178–201.

Hucker, Charles O. *A Dictionary of Official Titles in Imperial China*. Stanford, CA: Stanford University Press, 1985.

Huitu yuanlin huajing 繪圖園林花鏡 (Illustrated garden *Mirror of flowers*). Shanghai: Jinzhang shuju, 1914.

Huitu zengbu wanbao quanshu 繪圖增補萬寶全書 (Newest, illustrated, expanded, comprehensive compendium of countless treasures). N.p., n.d. (pre-1911).

Hummel, Arthur W., ed. *Eminent Chinese of the Ch'ing Period (1644–1912)*. Washington, DC: United States Government Printing Office, 1943.

———. "What Chinese Historians Are Doing in Their Own History" (paper read before the meeting of the American Historical Association at Indianapolis, December 31, 1928). *American Historical Review* 34, no. 4 (1929): 715–724.

Hung, Chang-tai. "Reeducating a Blind Storyteller: Han Qixiang and the Chinese Communist Storytelling Campaign." *Modern China* 19, no. 4 (1993): 395–426.

Hûng Jeo, Maci, and Ortai, eds. *Han-i araha jakûn gûsai tung j'i bithe* (Comprehensive treatises of the Eight Banners). Beijing: Wuying dian, 1739.

Huters, Theodore. *Bringing the World Home: Appropriating the West in Late Qing and Early Republican China*. Honolulu: University of Hawai'i Press, 2005.

———. "From Writing to Literature: The Development of Late Qing Theories of Prose." *Harvard Journal of Asiatic Studies* 47, no. 1 (June 1987): 51–96.

———. *Qian Zhongshu*. Boston: Twayne Publishers, 1982.

Idema, Wilt L. *Judge Bao and the Rule of Law: Eight Ballad Stories from the Period 1250–1450*. Singapore: World Scientific Publishing, 2010.

Imanishi Shunjū 今西春秋. *Kōchū Iikiroku* 校注異域錄; *Tulišen's I-Yü-Lu*. Tenri: Tenri daigaku Oyasato kenkyūjo, 1964.

———. *Manshū jitsuroku, Man-Wa Mō-Wa taiyaku* 満洲実録: 満和蒙和対訳 (Manchu veritable records: Manchu-Japanese [and] Mongolian-Japanese side-by-side translations). Tokyo: Tōsui shobō, 1992.

Jenco, Leigh. "Histories of Thought and Comparative Political Theory: The Curious Thesis of 'Chinese Origins for Western Knowledge,' 1860–1895." *Political Theory* 42, no. 6 (December 2014): 658–681.

Jian Bozan 翦伯贊 et al., eds. *Zhongwai lishi nianbiao: Gongyuan qian 4500 nian—gongyuan 1918 nian* 中外历史年表: 公元前 4500 年—公元 1918 年 (A Sino-foreign history timeline: 4500 BCE–1918 CE). Beijing: Zhonghua shuju, 1918.

Jiang Xianhan 蒋先寒. "Wei Yuan jingshi zhiyong de bianji sixiang" 魏源经世致用的编辑思想 (On Wei Yuan's editorial thinking in statecraft and practicality). *Shaoyang xueyuan xuebao* 邵阳学院学报 6, no. 5 (October 2007): 1–4.

Jiangsu Shuju chongding heshi jiamu 江蘇書局重訂核實價目 (List of assessed and rectified prices at the Jiangsu Book Bureau). Suzhou: Jiangsu shuju, 1893.

Jiaoyubu 教育部, ed. *Zhuyin fuhao chuanxi xiaoce* 注音符號傳習小冊 (Handbook for learning phonetic notation), 13th ed. Shanghai: Zhonghua shuju, 1935 [1930].

Jiaoyubu guoyu tongyi choubei weiyuanhui 教育部國語統一籌備委員會. *Guoyin changyong zihui* 國音常用字彙 (Commonly used vocabulary of national pronunciation). Shanghai: Shangwu, 1932.

Jiating baike quanshu 家庭百科全書 (Household encyclopedia). Shanghai: Xinhua shuju, 1930.

Jin Guantao 金觀濤 and Liu Qingfeng 劉青峰. *Guannian shi yanjiu* 觀念史研究 (Studies in conceptual history). Beijing: Falü chubanshe, 2009.

Jin Zhaofan 金兆蕃. "Shang Qingshi Guan zhang di yi shu" 上清史馆长第一书 (First letter submitted to the head of the Qing History Commission). In Zhu Shizhe 朱师辙, *Qingshi shuwen* 清史述闻 (Record of things heard regarding Qing history), pp. 134–135. Shanghai: Shanghai shudian chubanshe, 2009 [1957].

Jingdu wenjintang 京都文錦堂. *Zengbu wanbao quanshu* 增補萬寶全書 (Expanded compendia of countless treasures). 20 *juan*, 1 supplement, 6 vols. Beijing: Jingdu wenjintang, 1901.

Jones, Stephen. *Ritual and Music in North China*, vol. 2: *Shaanbei*. Burlington, VT: Ashgate, 2007.

Josephson, Jason Ānanda. *The Invention of Religion in Japan*. Chicago: University of Chicago Press, 2012.

Judd, Ellen R. "Prelude to the 'Yan'an Talks': Problems in Transforming a Literary Intelligentsia." *Modern China* 11, no. 3 (1985): 377–408.

Judge, Joan. "In Search of the Chinese Common Reader: Vernacular Knowledge in the Age of New Media." In *The Edinburgh History of Reading*, vol. 2: *Common Readers*, edited by Jonathan Rose, pp. 218–237. Edinburgh: Edinburgh University Press, 2020.

———. "Myriad Treasures and One-Hundred Sciences: Vernacular Chinese and Encyclopedic Japanese Knowledge at the Turn of the Twentieth Century." In *Reconsidering the Sinosphere: Cultural Transmissions and Transformations*, edited by Qian Nanxiu, Richard Smith, and Zhang Bowei, pp. 329–369. Amherst, NY: Cambria Press, 2020.

———. "Science for the Chinese Common Reader? Myriad Treasures and New Knowledge at the Turn of the Twentieth Century." *Science in Context* 30, no. 4 (Winter 2017): 359–383.

Judge, Joan, Barbara Mittler, and Michel Hockx. "Introduction: Women's Journals as Multigeneric Artifacts." In *Women and the Periodical Press in China's Long Twentieth Century: A Space of Their Own?*, edited by Michel Hockx, Joan Judge, and Barbara Mittler, pp. 1–18. Cambridge: Cambridge University Press, 2018.

Kang Bao 康豹 (Paul Katz). "Jindai Zhongguo zhi simiao pohuai yundong: Yi Jiang Zhe diqu wei taolun zhongxin" 近代中國之寺廟破壞運動：以江浙地區為討論中心 (Temple destruction campaigns in modern China, the Jiangsu and Zhejiang region). In *Gaibian Zhongguo zongjiao de wushi nian* 改變中國宗教的五十年, 1898–1948 (Fifty years of reforming Chinese religion, 1898–1948), edited by Kang Bao and Gao Wansang 高萬桑 (Vincent Goossaert), pp. 1–38. Taipei: Institute of Modern History, Academia Sinica, 2015.

Kang, Xiaofei 康笑菲. *The Cult of the Fox: Power, Gender and Popular Religion in Late Imperial and Modern China*. New York: Columbia University Press, 2006.

———. "Women's Liberation and Anti-Superstition in Wartime Communist Propaganda, 1943–50." *Nan Nü: Men, Women and Gender in China* 19, no. 1 (2017): 64–96.

Karl, Rebecca. *Staging the World: Chinese Nationalism at the Turn of the Twentieth Century*. Durham, NC: Duke University Press, 2002.

Kaske, Elisabeth. *The Politics of Language in Chinese Education, 1895–1919*. Leiden: Brill, 2008.

Katz, Paul. *Divine Justice: Religion and the Development of Chinese Legal Culture*. New York: Routledge, 2009.

———. *Religion in China and Its Modern Fate*. Waltham, MA: Brandeis University Press, 2014.

Kaufman, Alison. "China's Discourse of 'Civilization': Visions of Past, Present, and Future." *ASAN Forum*, February 19, 2018. http://www.theasanforum.org/chinas-discourse-of-civilization-visions-of-past-present-and-future/.

———. "Xi Jinping as Historian: Marxist, Chinese, Nationalist, Global." *ASAN Forum*, October 15, 2015. http://www.theasanforum.org/xi-jinping-as-historian-marxist-chinese-nationalist-global/.

Keating, Pauline B. *Two Revolutions, Village Reconstruction and the Cooperative Movement in Northern Shaanxi, 1934–1945.* Stanford, CA: Stanford University Press, 1997.
Keels, Thomas. *Sesqui!* Philadelphia: Temple University Press, 2017.
Keevak, Michael. *The Story of a Stele: China's Nestorian Monument and Its Reception in the West, 1625–1916.* Hong Kong: Hong Kong University Press, 2008.
Kendall, Laurel. "The Cultural Politics of 'Superstition' in the Korean Shaman World: Modernity Constructs Its Order." In *Healing Powers and Modernity,* edited by Linda H. Connor and Geoffrey Samuel, pp. 25–41. Westport, CT: Bergin & Garvey, 2001.
Kern, Martin. "The 'Harangues' (*Shi* 誓) in the *Shangshu*." In *Origins of Chinese Political Philosophy: Studies in the Composition and Thought of the Shangshu (Classic of Documents),* edited by Martin Kern and Dirk Meyer, pp. 281–319. Leiden: Brill, 2017.
Kiely, Jan. *The Compelling Ideal: Thought Reform and the Prison in China, 1901–1956.* New Haven, CT: Yale University Press, 2014.
Kiyama Hideo 木山英雄. "'Wenxue fugu' yu 'wenxue geming'" '文學復古'與'文學革命' ("Literary archaism" and "literary revolution"). In *Wenxue fugu yu wenxue geming* 文学復古與与文學革命 (Literary archaism and literary revolution), edited and translated by Zhao Jinghua 趙京華, pp. 209–210. Beijing: Beijing daxue chubanshe, 2004.
Koselleck, Reinhart. *Futures Past: On the Semantics of Historical Time.* New York: Columbia University Press, 2018.
——. *Sediments of Time: On Possible Histories.* Stanford, CA: Stanford University Press, 2020.
Krimmer, Elisabeth, and Patricia Anne Simpson, eds. *Religion, Reason, and Culture in the Age of Goethe.* Rochester, NY: Camden House, 2013.
Kuhn, Philip A. *Rebellion and Its Enemies in Late Imperial China: Militarization and Social Structure, 1796–1864.* Cambridge, MA: Harvard University Press, 1970.
Kui-shan 奎善. "Guoyu zhi" 國語志 (Treatise on the dynastic language). Ms. originating in the Qing Historiography Bureau (Guoshi Guan 國史館). Held at National Palace Museum Library, Taipei; call number: 219000001.
Kung Ling-wei 孔令偉. "Chen Yinke yu Dongfang yuwen xue: Jianlun Neiya shi ji yuwen xue de weilai zhanwang" 陳寅恪與東方語文學—兼論內亞史及語文學的未來展望 (Chen Yinke and Oriental philology: A reflection on the future of Inner Asian history and philology). *Xin shixue* 新史學 31, no. 1 (2020): 53–102.
Lau, D. C., trans. *Confucius: "The Analects."* Hong Kong: Chinese University Press, 2000.
Legge, James, trans. *The Chinese Classics: With a Translation, Critical and Exegetical Notes, Prolegomena, and Copious Indexes.* Oxford: Clarendon Press, 1893.
——, trans. *The Chinese Classics,* vol. 2: *The Yi King.* Hong Kong: Hong Kong University Press, 1970.
——, trans. *Confucian Analects.* In *The Chinese Classics.* Taipei: Wenxing shudian, 1966.
——, trans. *The Four Books.* Taipei: Culture Book Co., 1981.
Leibold, James. "Competing Narratives of Racial Unity in Republican China: From the Yellow Emperor to Peking Man." *Modern China* 32, no. 2 (2006): 181–220.
——. *Reconfiguring Chinese Nationalism.* New York: Palgrave Macmillan, 2007.
Leonard, Jane Kate. *Wei Yuan and China's Rediscovery of the Maritime World.* Cambridge, MA: Harvard University Press, 1984.
Leontiev, Aleksei. *Puteshestvie kitaiskogo poslannika k kalmytskomy Ayuke-Khany, c opisaniem zemel' obychaev rossiiskikh.* St. Petersburg: Akademii Nauk, 1762.
Levenson, Joseph. *Confucian China and Its Modern Fate: A Trilogy.* Berkeley: University of California Press, 1968.

Levine, Marilyn. *The Found Generation: Chinese Communists in Europe during the Twenties*. Seattle: University of Washington Press, 1993.

Lewis, Mark. *The Early Chinese Empires: Qin and Han*. Cambridge, MA: Belknap Press of Harvard University Press, 2007.

Li Bizhen 李壁貞. "Xiaoxue diji de shuohua jiaoxue wenti" 小學低級的說話教學問題 (Problems of teaching the spoken language in the lower primary grades). *Jiangxi difang jiaoyu* 江西地方教育 38 (1936): 17.

Li Changqing 李常慶 (Ri Chanchin). "Senkyūhyakukyūjū nendai ni okeru *Shiko zensho* kanren sōsho no kankō oyobi sono bunkateki imi 1990" 年代における四庫全書関連叢書の刊行およびその文化的意味 (The publication of book series related to the *Complete writings of the Four Repositories* in the 1990s and its cultural significance). *Nihon toshokan jōhō gakkaishi* 日本図書館情報学会誌 52, no. 1 (2006): 1–15.

———. "*Shiko zensho* no zokushū o meguru rekishiteki tenkai ni kansuru ichi kōsatsu" 『四庫全書』の続修をめぐる歴史的展開に関する一考察 (An investigation concerning the historical developments surrounding the continuation of the *Complete writings of the Four Repositories*). *Nihon toshokan jōhō gakkaishi* 日本図書館情報学会誌 51, no. 4 (2005): 153–165.

Li Deqi 李德啓, ed. *Guoli Beiping tushuguan, Gugong bowuyuan tushuguan Manwen shuji lianhe mulu* 國立北平圖書館、故宮博物院圖書館滿文書籍聯合目錄 (Union catalog of Manchu books in National Beiping Library and the National Palace Museum Library). Beijing: Guoli Beiping tushuguan ji Gugong bowuyuan tushuguan, 1933.

Li Dingming 李鼎铭. "Guanyu wenjiao gongzuo de fangxiang" 关于文教工作的方向 (On the direction of cultural and educational work). In *Shaan-Gan-Ning Bianqu zhengfu wenjian xuanbian* 陕甘宁边区政府文件选编 (Selected collections of Shaan-Gan-Ning Border Region government documents), vol. 8, p. 458. Xi'an: Shaanxi sheng dang'an guan and Shaanxi sheng shehui kexueyuan, 1988.

Li Dingxia 李鼎霞. "Sibu congkan he Sibu beiyao" 《四部丛刊》和《四部备要》 (Serial printings from the Four Divisions and ready essentials of the Four Divisions). *Wenshi zhishi* 文史知识 3 (1982): 33–37.

Li Hongzhang 李鴻章. "*Shuowen Duan zhu dingbu* xu" 說文段注訂補 (Preface to the *Shuowen Duan zhu dingbu*). In *Shuowen jiezi gulin zhengxu hebian* 說文解字詁林正續合編 (Joint compilation of the *Corrected and continued forest of explanations* of the *Analysis of characters and explanation of writing*), compiled by Ding Fubao 丁福保. Taipei: Dingwen shuju, 1977.

Li Jinxi 黎錦熙. "1925 nian guoyu jie 'fangyu zhan' jilüe" 年國語界防禦戰紀略 (Chronicle of the "defensive war" of 1925 in the national language world). *Jingbao fukan* 京報副刊 406 (February 5, 1926): 1–5.

———. *Guoyu siqian nian lai bianhua chaoliu tu* 國語四千年來變化潮流圖 (Diagram showing the evolution of the national language over the last four millennia). Beiping: Wenhua xueshe, 1929.

———. *Guoyu xue jiangyi* 國語學講義 (Lectures on national language). Shanghai: Shangwu, 1919.

———. *Guoyu yundong shigang* 國語運動史綱 (Outline history of the national language movement). Shanghai: Shangwu, 1934.

———. "Sansheng shixiao lianhehui fenmie chuxiao wenyan jiaokeshu zhi xuanyan" 三省師小聯合會焚滅初小文言教科書之宣言 (Proclamation on destroying primary classical textbooks from the Federation of Normal Primary Schools in three provinces). *Zhonghua jiaoyu jie* 中華教育界 15, no. 8 (February 1926): 8–9.

———. *Xinzhu guoyu jiaoxue fa* 新著國語教學法 (New method for teaching the national language). Shanghai: Shangwu, 1930.

———. "Yibai nian ye keyi" 一百年也可以 (One hundred years would also be okay). *Guoyu luomazi zhoukan* 國語羅馬字週刊 (1930). Reprinted in his *Guoyu yundong shigang* 國語運動史綱 (Outline history of the national language), pp. 188–190. Shanghai: Shangwu, 1934.

Li Lin 李林. "Mouxin yu duanben: Qingmo Man-Mengwen gaodeng xuetang kaolun" 谋新与端本: 清末满蒙文高等学堂考论 (Seek the new and keep to the origins: An examination of the Higher School of Manchu and Mongolian Languages). *Minzu jiaoyu yanjiu* 民族教育研究 6 (2015): 59–67.

Li Xiaoqian 李孝迁. *Yuwai Hanxue yu Zhongguo xiandai shixue* 域外汉学与中国现代史学 = (Sinology and modern historiography in China). Shanghai: Guji chubanshe, 2014.

Li Yuese 李约瑟 (Joseph Needham). *Zhongguo kexue jishu shi: Diliu juan* 中国科学技术史：第六卷 (The history of science and technology in China, vol. 6). Beijing: Kexue chubanshe, 2006.

Li Zhizao 李之藻. "Du Jingjiaobei shuhou" 讀景教碑書後 (Written after reading the stele on the spread of Jingjiao in China). In *Jingjiao liuxing Zhongguo beisong bing xu* 景教流行中國碑頌並序 (Preface to the text and ode of the stele on the spread of Jingjiao in China). Bibliotèque national de France 1188.

Li Zongze 李宗澤. "Cai Yuanpei sixiang zhong de Deguo ziyuan" 蔡元培思想中的德國資源 (The German sources of Cai Yuanpei's thought). In *Jindai Dong-Xi sixiang jiaoliu zhong de chuanbozhe* 近代東西思想交流中的傳播者 (Modern intellectual interactions, east-west: The disseminators), edited by Yang Zhende 楊貞德, pp. 199–229. Taipei: Zhongyang yanjiuyuan, Zhongguo wenzhe yanjiusuo, 2017.

Liang Qichao 梁啟超. *Intellectual Trends in the Qing Period.* Translated by Immanuel C. Y. Hsü. Cambridge, MA: Harvard University Press, 1959.

———. *Qingdai xueshu gailun* 清代學術概論 (Intellectual trends in the Qing period). Edited by Zhu Weizheng 朱维铮. Shanghai: Shanghai guji chubanshe, 1998.

———. "Qingshi shangli chugao" 清史商例初稿 (First draft of suggested principles for a history of the Qing). *Zhongguo yizhou* 中國一周 559 (January 9, 1961): 21–24.

———. *Shixue lunzhu sizhong* 史學論著四種 (Four essays in historiography). Changsha: Yuelu shushe, 1998.

———. *The So-Called People's Will: A Comment on the Secret Telegrams of the Yuan Government.* Shanghai: n.p., 1916.

Lin, Kuei-ju. "The Transmission of Wanbao Quanshu 萬寶全書 in Edo Japan." Paper presented for the panel Encyclopedic Audiences: Readership of Late Ming and Late Qing Compendia for Everyday Life, Association of Asian Studies in Asia, Taipei, June 2015.

———. "The Transmission of *Wanbao quanshu* to Japan in the Early Edo Period: Their Role in the Compilation of Educational Texts." *Lingua Franca: The History of the Book in Translation* 6 (2020): 1–29.

Lin Mingbo 林明波. *Qingdai Xuxue kao* 清代許學考 (Examination of Xu [Shen] studies of the Qing period). Taipei: Jiaxin shuini gongsi wenhua jijinhui (yanjiu lunwen 28), 1964.

Lin Wushu 林悟殊. *Tangdai Jingjiao zaiyanjiu* 唐代景教再研究 (Reexamination of Chinese Nestorianism). Beijing: Zhongguo shehui kexue chubanshe, 2003.

Link, Perry. "On Translation." In *Texts and Transformations: Essays in Honor of the 75th Birthday of Victor H. Mair,* edited by Haun Saussy, pp. 17–30. Amherst, NY: Cambria Press, 2018.

Liu Chengyu 劉成禺. "'Hongxian Huangdi' de yirang" 洪憲的揖讓 (Voluntary yieldings of the Hongxian emperor). In *Shizaitang zayi* 世載堂雜憶 (Various opinions from the Shizai Pavilion). Taipei: Wenhai, 1966.

———. "Hongxian jishi shi" 洪憲紀事詩 (Poetic account of the Hongxian dynasty). *Wuwu zazhi* 戊午雜誌 1, no. 1 (1918): 209–215.

———. *Hongxian jishi shi benshi buzhu 4 juan* 洪憲紀事詩本事簿注 4卷 (Register of sources for poems commemorating the Hongxian dynasty, four fascicles). Chongqing: Jinghua yinshuguan, 1945.

———. *Yuan Shikai dangguo: Hongxian jishi shi benshi buzhu* 袁世凱當國: 洪憲紀事詩本事簿注 (Yuan Shikai's party-state: Register of sources for poems commemorating the Hongxian dynasty). Taipei: Xinrui wenchuang chuban, 2018.

Liu Dapeng 刘大鹏. *Tuixiangzhai riji* 推想斋日记 (Diary from the Chamber to Which One Retires to Ponder). Taiyuan: Shanxi renmin chubanshe, 1990.

Liu Fu 劉復. *Sisheng shiyan lu* 四聲實驗錄 (Experimental record of the four tones). Shanghai: Qunyi shushe, 1924.

———. "Xuzhui" 序贅 (Redundant preface). In *Sisheng shiyan lu* 四聲實驗錄 (Experimental record of the four tones), pp. 19–25. Shanghai: Qunyi shushe, 1924.

Liu Jialin. "Inception, Inheritance and Innovation: Sima Qian, Liang Qichao and the Modernization of Chinese Biography." In *Different Lives: Global Perspectives on Biography in Public Cultures and Societies,* edited by Hans Renders and David Veltman, pp. 217–229. Leiden: Brill, 2020.

Liu Lanxiao 刘兰肖. "*Yuanshi xinbian* de lishi bianzhuan chengjiu" 《元史新編》的历史編撰成就 (History, composition, and accomplishment of the *New compilation of the Yuan history*). *Shandong ligong daxue xuebao* 山东理工大学学报 26, no. 1 (January 2010): 93–97.

Liu Ru 劉儒. "Kaocha guoyu jiaoyu biji" 考察國語教育筆記 (Notes on investigation of national language education). *Jiaoyu zazhi* 教育雜誌 13, no. 6 (June 1921): 1–5.

Liu Shipei 劉師培. "Junzheng fugu lun," 君政復古論 (On the virtuous ruler and the restoration if antiquity). In *Liu Shenshu xiangsheng yishu* 劉申叔先生遺書 (The writings of Liu Shenshu [Shipei]), vol. 55 shang-zhong (facsimile, vol. 3, pp. 1955–1957). Taipei: Daxin shuju, 1965 [1935].

———. "Lun Tang-Yu shanrang yu Minguo zhidu butong" 論唐虞禪讓與民國制度不同 (On the difference between the abdication of Tang-Yu and the republican system). *Shuntian shibao* 順天時報, December 7, 1915.

———. *Lun wen zaji* 論文雜記 (Notes on writing). Beijing: Renmin wenxue chubanshe, 1984.

———. *Zhongguo zhonggu wenxue shi Han Wei Liuchao zhuan jiawen yanjiu* 中国中古文学史汉魏六朝专家文研究 (History of medieval Chinese literature: Studies of the Han, Wei, and Six Dynasties prose). Beijing: Zhongguo huabao chubanshe, 2010 [1933].

Liu Xiangyuan 刘祥元. "Guangxu chao 'xuxiu *Siku quanshu*' shuping" 光绪朝"续修《四库全书》"述评 (An evaluation of the "Continuations of the *Complete Writings of the Four Repositories*" of the Guangxu period). *Yixue tushuguan lilun yu shijian* 医学图书馆理论与实践 4 (2010): 93–95.

Liu Yanchen 刘彦臣. "Qingdai 'guoyu qishe' zhengce yanjiu" 清代"国语骑射"政策研究 (The "dynastic language, horsemanship, and archery" policies of the Qing period). PhD dissertation, Dongbei shifan daxue, 2010.

Liu Yazi 柳亚子. *Nanshe congke* 南社从刻 (Collected block printings of the Southern Society). Yangzhou: Jiangsu guangling guji keyinshe, 1996.

Liu, Yonghua. *Confucian Rituals and Chinese Villagers: Ritual Change and Social Transformation in a Southeastern Chinese Community, 1368–1949.* Leiden: Brill, 2013.

Liu Zesheng 刘泽生. "Yu Yue feizhi Zhongyi sixiang genyuan tansuo" 俞樾废止中医思想根源探索 (Research on the origin of Yu Yue's ideas concerning abolishing Chinese medicine). *Zhonghua yishi zazhi* 中华医史杂志 31, no. 1 (July 2001): 171–174.

Longwen shuju 龍文書局. *Zengbu wanbao quanshu* 增補萬寶全書 (Expanded compendia of countless treasures). 20 *juan*, 6 supplements, 8 vols. Shanghai: Longwen shuju, 1906.

Lönnroth, Harry. *Philology Matters! Essays on the Art of Reading Slowly.* Leiden: Brill, 2017.

Lu Shanqing 卢善庆. *Zhongguo jindai meixue sixiang shi* 中国近代美学思想史 (Intellectual history of modern Chinese aesthetics). Shanghai: Huadong shifan daxue chubanshe, 1991.

Lu Xun 鲁迅. "A Layman's Remarks on Writing" (1934). In *Lu Xun: Selected Works,* translated by Yang Xianyi and Gladys Yang, pp. 102–125. Beijing: Foreign Languages Press, 1980.

———. *Lu Xun quanji* 鲁迅全集 (Collected works of Lu Xun). Beijing: Renmin wenxue chubanshe, 2005.

———. *Lu Xun shuxin ji* 鲁迅书信集 (Collected letters of Lu Xun). Beijing: Renmin wenxue chubanshe, 1976.

———. *Zhongguo xiaoshuo shi dalue* 中国小说史大略 (Outline of the history of Chinese fiction). Shanghai: Shanghai kexue jishu wenxian chubanshe, 2015.

Lu Yiyan 陸衣言 and Ma Guoying 馬國英. *Xin guoyin xuesheng zidian* 新國音學生字典 (New national pronunciation dictionary for students). Shanghai: Shangwu, 1929.

Lufei Kui 陸費逵. "Xiaoxuexiao guoyu jiaoshou wenti" 小學校國語教授問題 (National language pedagogy problems in primary school). *Zhonghua jiaoyu jie* 中華教育界 8, no. 1 (1919): 1–7.

Luo Jialun 羅家倫, ed. *Guomin ribao huipian* 國民日報彙編 (*Guomin ribao* compilation). Taipei: Zhongyang wenwu gongyingshe, 1983.

Luo Lin 罗琳 (羅琳). "*Xuxiu Siku quanshu zongmu tiyao gaoben* zuanxiu shimo" 《續修四庫全書總目提要稿本》纂修始末 (The compilation of the draft version of the bibliographical précis to the continuation of the *Complete writings of the Four Repositories*). *Shumu jikan* 书目季刊 13, no. 3 (1996): 3–11.

———. "*Xuxiu Siku quanshu zongmu tiyao* bianzuan shi jiyao" 《续修四库全书总目提要》编纂史纪要 (Outline of the compilation history of bibliographical précis to the continuation of the *Complete writings of the Four Repositories*). *Tushu qingbao gongzuo* 图书情报工作 1 (1994): 45–50.

———. "Zhengli shuoming" 整理說明 (Notes on the editing process). In *Xuxiu Siku quanshu zongmu tiyao: Jing bu* 續修四庫全書總目提要：經部 (Bibliographical précis for a continuation of the *Complete Writings of the Four Repositories: Classics Division*), compiled by Zhongguo kexue yuan tushuguan 中國科學院圖書館, vol. 1, pp. 1–5. Beijing: Zhonghua Shuju, 1993.

Luo Xiongfei 罗雄飞, "Lun Yu Yue zai wan Qing xueshu shi shang de diwei" 论俞樾在晚清学术史上的地位 (On Yu Yue's position in the history of late Qing scholarship). *Suzhou daxue xuebao* 蘇州大學學報 1 (January 2007): 99–103.

Ma Guoying 馬國英. *Guoyu zhuyin fuhao fayin zhinan* 國語注音符號發音指南 (Pronunciation guide to the national phonetic notation). Shanghai: Shangwu, 1931.

———. *Xin guoyin gaiyao* 新國音概要 (Essentials of the new national pronunciation). Shanghai: Dongfang bianyi suo, 1929.

———. *Xinjiu guoyin bianyi* 新舊國音變異 (Differences between new and old national pronunciation). Shanghai: Dongfang bianyishe, 1928.

Ma Xinmin 馬辛民 and Li Xueqin 李學勤, eds. *Shisanjing zhushu (biao dian ben): Shangshu zhengyi* 十三経注疏 (標點本)：尚書正義 (Commentaries and subcommentaries to the thirteen classics, punctuated: True meaning of the *Book of history*). Beijing: Beijing daxue chubanshe, 1999.

Ma Yong. "From Constitutional Monarchy to Republic: The Trajectory of Yuan Shikai." *Journal of Modern Chinese History* 6, no. 1 (2012): 15–32.

Ma Zhendong 馬震東. *Yuan Shikai dangguo shi* 袁世凱黨國史 (History of the party-state of Yuan Shikai). Beijing: Tuanjie chubanshe, 2008.

"Manwen pu" 滿文譜 (Manchu-language record). Ms., 1851, held at Sun Yat-sen Library, Guangzhou; call number: 32104.

Mao Huanwen 毛煥文. *Zengbu wanbao quanshu* 增補萬寶全書 (Expanded complete compendia of countless treasures). 4 vols. N.p.: Guiwentang, 1828.

Mao Zedong 毛澤東(毛泽东). "Guanyu Shaan-Gan-Ning Bianqu de wenhua jiaoyu wenti" 關於陝甘寧邊區的文化教育問題 (On issues concerning cultural education in the Shaan-Gan-Ning Border Region) (March 22, 1944). In *Mao Zedong wenji* 毛泽东文集 (Writings of Mao Zedong), vol. 3, pp. 106–122. Beijing: Zhongyang wenxian yanjiushi, 1993.

———. "Letter to Li Jinxi," September 5, 1919. In *Mao's Road to Power: Revolutionary Writings, 1912–1949*, edited by Stuart R. Schram, vol. 1, pp. 414–415. Armonk, NY: M. E. Sharpe, 1992.

———. "Wenhua gongzuo zhong de tongyi zhanxian" 文化工作中的统一战线 (The United Front in cultural work). In *Mao Zedong xuanji* 毛泽东选集 (Selected works of Mao Zedong), vol. 3, pp. 1011–1013. Beijing: Renmin chubanshe, 1991. http://marx.xmu.edu.cn.

———. "Zai Zhongguo Gongchandang diqici quanguo daibiao dahuishang de koutou zhengzhi baogao" 在中国共产党第七次全国代表大会上的口头政治报告 (Oral political report at the Seventh National Congress of the Chinese Communist Party) (April 24, 1945). In *Mao Zedong wenji* 毛泽东文集 (Writings of Mao Zedong), vol. 3, pp. 303–355. Beijing: Zhongyang wenxian yanjiushi, 1993.

Martin, François. "Des faux qui ne trompent personne: Les textes d'abdication sous les Six Dynasties." *Extrême-Orient Extrême-Occident* (2010): 13–39.

McDermott, Joseph P. "Emperor, Élite, and Commoners: The Community Pact Ritual of the Late Ming." In *State and Court Ritual in China,* edited by Joseph P. McDermott, pp. 299–351. New York: Cambridge University Press, 1999.

McDougall, Bonnie S. *Mao Zedong's "Talks at the Yan'an Conference on Literature and Art": A Translation of the 1943 Text with Commentary.* Ann Arbor: University of Michigan Press, 1980.

Mei Zengliang 梅曾亮. *Baijian shanfang wenji* 柏梘山房詩文集 (Collected poetry and prose of Mei Zengliang). Edited by Peng Guozhong 彭國忠 and Hu Xiaoming 胡曉明. Shanghai: Shanghai guji chubanshe, 2005.

Meng Sen 孟森. "*Qingshi gao* yingfou jingu zhi shangque" 《清史稿》應否禁錮之商榷 (A discussion on whether the *Draft history of the Qing* should be banned). In *Ming-Qing shi lunzhu jikan* 明清史论著集刊 (Collected papers on Ming and Qing history), vol. 2, pp. 690–716. Beijing: Zhonghua shuju, 2006 [1929].

Meng Yue. *Shanghai and the Edges of Empire.* Minneapolis: University of Minnesota Press, 2006.

Mitamura Taisuke 三田村泰助. *Naitō Konan* 内藤湖南. Tokyo: Chūō kōron, 1972.

Mittler, Barbara. "Written for Him or for Her? China's New Encyclopaedias and Their Readers." In *Chinese Encyclopaedias of New Global Knowledge,* edited by Milena Doleželová-Velingerová and Rudolf G. Wagner, pp. 399–424. Berlin: Springer-Verlag, 2014.

Miyajima Tatsuo 宮島達夫. "*Kyōsantō sengen* no yakugo" 「共産党宣言」の訳語 (Translated terminology in the *Communist Manifesto*). In *Gengo no kenkyū* 言語の研究 (Studies in language), edited by Gengogaku kenkyūkai 言語学研究会 (Linguistics research group), pp. 425–517. Tokyo: Mugi shobō, 1979.

Moser, David. *A Billion Voices: China's Search for a Common Language.* Scoresby, Australia: Penguin Books, 2016.

Momose, Hiromu. "Shêng-yü." In *Eminent Chinese of the Ch'ing Period (1644–1912),* edited by Arthur W. Hummel, pp. 648–650. Washington, DC: United States Government Printing Office, 1943.

Mu Qing 穆青. "Benshi Baijiaping wushen Yang Hanzhu shanghai renming panchu tuxing" 本市白家坪巫神楊漢珠傷害人命判處徒刑 (Shaman Yang Hanzhu of Baijiaping village of Yan'an city harms lives and is sentenced to prison time). *Jiefang ribao* 解放日報, April 29, 1944.

Mu Xiude 穆修德. *Guoyu fayin ji wenfa* 國語發音及文法 (National language pronunciation and grammar). Beiping: Wenhua, 1932.

———. "Zenyang xuexi guoyu?" 怎樣學習國語 (How does one learn the national language?) *Shenbao* 申報 (supplement) (January 28, 1934): 21.

Mühlhahn, Klaus. *Criminal Justice in China: A History*. Cambridge, MA: Harvard University Press, 2009.

Muller, A. Charles, comp. and trans. *The Sutra of Perfect Enlightenment: Korean Buddhism's Guide to Meditation*. Albany: State University of New York Press, 1999.

Murata Yūjirō 村田雄二郎. "The Late Qing 'National Language' Issue and Monolingual Systems: Focusing on Political Diplomacy." Translated by Margaret Mengxi Li. *Chinese Studies in History* 49, no. 3 (2016): 108–125.

———. "Rasuto-enperazu wa nani go de hanashite ita ka? Shinmatsu no 'kokugo' mondai to tan'itsu gengosei" ラスト・エンペラーズは何語で話していたか？清末の「國語」問題と単一言語制 (What language did the last emperors speak? The problem of the "national language" in the late Qing period and the monolingual system). *Kotoba to shakai* 言葉と社会 3 (2000): 6–31.

Musil, Robert. *The Man without Qualities*. Translated by Sophie Wilkins. New York: Vintage International, 1996.

Naitō Konan 內藤湖南. "Shakaishugi o tore" 社會主義を取れ (Adopt socialism!). *Ajia* 亞細亞 54 (August 29, 1892). In *Naitō Konan zenshū* 內藤湖南全集 (Collected works of Naitō Konan) (hereafter NKZ), edited by Naitō Kenkichi 內藤乾吉 and Kanda Kiichirō 神田喜一郎, vol. 1, pp. 624–632. Tokyo: Chikuma shobō, 1972.

———. "Shina ni kaere" 支那に還れ (Go back to China!). *Ōsaka mainichi shinbun* 大阪毎日新聞 (May 25–30, 1926). In NKZ, vol. 8, pp. 171–181.

———. "Shina no chūkokusha" 支那の忠告者 (Chinese advisers). *Ōsaka mainichi shinbun* (January 1, 1921). In NKZ, vol. 5, pp. 143–145.

———. *Shina ron* 支那論 (On China). Tokyo: Bunkaidō shoten, 1914. In NKZ, vol. 5, pp. 291–408.

———. "Shinkoku no rikken seiji" 清國の立憲政治 (Constitutional government in China). *Ōsaka mainichi shinbun* 大阪毎日新聞 (June 25, 1912). In NKZ, vol. 5, pp. 411–431.

———. *Shin Shina ron* 新支那論 (On the new China). Tokyo: Hakubundō, 1924. In NKZ, vol. 5, pp. 483–543.

———. *Tōyō bunka shi kenkyū* 東洋文化史研究 (Studies in the cultural history of East Asia). Tokyo: Kōbundō, 1936.

Nakami Tatsuo. "The Manchu Bannerman Jinliang's Search for Manchu-Qing Historical Sources." In *Tumen jalafun jecen akū: Manchu Studies in Honour of Giovanni Stary*, edited by Alessandra Pozzi, Juha Antero Janhunen, and Michael Weiers, pp. 171–186. Wiesbaden: Harrassowitz, 2006.

Naquin, Susan. *Peking: Temples and City Life, 1400–1900*. Berkeley: University of California Press, 2000.

Nedostup, Rebecca. *Superstitious Regimes: Religion and the Politics of Chinese Modernity*. Cambridge, MA: Harvard University Asia Center, 2009.

Neige cang "Manwen laodang" 內阁藏本满文老档 (The *Old Manchu archives* held at the Grand Secretariat) (1774). 20 vols. Facsimile of ms. Shenyang: Liaoning minzu chubanshe, 2009.

Nihon kokugo dai jiten 日本国語大辞典 (Great dictionary of the Japanese language), 2nd ed. 14 vols. Tokyo: Shōgakukan, 2006.

Nora, Pierre. "Between Memory and History: *Les Lieux de Mémoire.*" *Representations* 26 (1989): 7–24.
Norman, Jerry, Keith Dede, and David Prager Branner. *A Comprehensive Manchu-English Dictionary.* Cambridge, MA: Harvard University Press, 2013.
Nylan, Michael. *The Five "Confucian" Classics.* New Haven, CT: Yale University Press, 2001.
———. "Mapping Time in the Shiji and Hanshu Tables 表." *East Asian Science, Technology, and Medicine* 43 (2016): 61–122.
———. "Sima Qian: A True Historian?" *Early China* 23/24 (1998–1999): 203–246.
Ogawa Yōichi 小川陽一. *Nichiyō ruisho ni yoru Min Shin shōsetsu no kenkyū* 日用類書による明清小説の研究 (Studies of Ming-Qing fiction based on daily-use encyclopedias). Tokyo: Kenbun shuppan, 1995.
Okada Hidehiro 岡田英弘. *Kōkitei no tegami* 康熙帝の手紙 (The letters of the Kangxi Emperor). Tokyo: Chūō kōronsha, 1979.
Okamoto, Takashi 岡本隆司. *En Seigai: gendai Chūgoku no shuppatsu* 袁世凱: 現代中国の出発 (Yuan Shikai, a starting point for modern China). Tokyo: Iwanami shoten, 2015.
Ōmura Izumi 大村泉. "Kōtoku Shūsui Sakai Toshihiko yaku *Kyōsantō sengen* no seiritsu denshō to Chūgokugo yaku e no eikyō" 幸徳秋水・堺利彦訳「共産党宣言」の成立・伝承と中国語訳への影響 (The formation and transmission of the translation of the *Communist Manifesto* by Kōtoku Shūsui and Sakai Toshihiko and its influence on the Chinese translation). *Ōhara shakai mondai kenkyū zasshi* 大原社会問題研究雑誌 603 (January 2009): 1–13.
Ono Kazuko. *Chinese Women in a Century of Revolution.* Translation edited by Joshua A. Fogel. Stanford, CA: Stanford University Press, 1989.
Palmer, David *Qigong Fever: Body, Science and Utopia in China.* New York: Columbia University Press, 2007.
Pan Honggang 潘洪钢. "Xinhai geming yu Jingzhou zhufang baqi" 辛亥革命与荆州驻防八旗 (The eight banners of the Jingzhou garrison and the Xinhai revolution). *Manzu yanjiu* 满族研究 2 (1992): 21–28.
Pan Jixing 潘吉星. "Chen Haozi de *Huajing* ji qi zai Riben de chuanbo" 陈涅子的《花镜》及其在日本的传播 (The dissemination of Chen Haozi's *Mirror of flowers* in Japan). *Qingbao xuekan* 情报学刊 4 (1992): 315–316, 318.
Pankenier, David W. "The Cosmo-Political Background of Heaven's Mandate." *Early China* 20 (1995): 121–176.
Peng Mingzhe 彭明哲. "*Xuxiu siku quanshu zongmu tiyao* kaolüe" 《續修四庫全書總目提要》考略 (Cursory examination of the bibliographical précis to the continuation of the *Complete writings of the Four Repositories*). *Xiangtan Daxue xuebao (shehui kexue ban)* 湘潭大學学报(社會科學版) 2 (1994): 80–83.
Perdue, Peter C. *China Marches West: The Qing Conquest of Central Eurasia.* Cambridge, MA: Harvard University Press, 2005.
———. "Tulišen." In *Oxford Companion to World Exploration,* edited by David Buisseret, pp. 2, 314–315. Oxford: Oxford University Press, 2007.
———. "Where Do Correct Political Ideas Come From? Writing the History of the Qing Empire and the Chinese Nation." In *The Teleology of the Modern Nation-State: Japan and China,* edited by Joshua A. Fogel, pp. 174–199. Philadelphia: University of Pennsylvania Press, 2005.
Perkins, Justin. *A Residence of Eight Years in Persia.* Andover, MA: Allen, Morrill & Wardwell, 1843.
Philadelphia, the Birthplace of Liberty: Official Souvenir View Book. Circa 1926 pamphlet in the Special Collections Research Center, Henry Madden Library, California State

University, Fresno. http://www.worldsfairs.amdigital.co.uk/Documents/Details/HMLSC_cpam_BX10_EXP926b-16boxed (accessed July 25, 2017).

Pines, Yuri. "Disputers of Abdication: Zhanguo Egalitarianism and the Sovereign's Power." *T'oung Pao* 91, nos. 4–5 (2005): 243–300.

———. *Envisioning Eternal Empire: Chinese Political Thought of the Warring States Era*. Honolulu: University of Hawai'i Press, 2009.

———. *The Everlasting Empire: The Political Culture of Ancient China and Its Imperial Legacy*. Princeton, NJ: Princeton University Press, 2012.

Pollock, Sheldon I. "Future Philology? The Fate of a Soft Science in a Hard World." *Critical Inquiry* 35, no. 4 (2009): 931–961.

Pollock, Sheldon I., Benjamin A. Elman, and Ku-ming Kevin Chang. *World Philology*. Cambridge, MA: Harvard University Press, 2015.

Poon, Shuk-wah. *Negotiating Religion in Modern China: State and Common People in Guangzhou, 1900–1937*. Hong Kong: Chinese University of Hong Kong, 2011.

Prakash, Gyan. "The Modern Nation's Return in the Archaic." *Critical Inquiry* 23, no. 3 (Spring 1997): 536–556.

Proctor, Robert N., and Londa Schiebinger, eds. *Agnotology: The Making and Unmaking of Ignorance*. Stanford, CA: Stanford University Press, 2008.

Pulleyblank, Edwin. *Chinese History and World History: An Inaugural Lecture*. Cambridge: Cambridge University Press, 1955.

Putong baike quanshu 普通百科全書 (General encyclopedia) or *Bianyi putong jiaoyu baike quanshu* 編譯普通教育百科全書 (Compiled and translated encyclopedia for general education). Shanghai: Huiwenshe, 1903.

Qi Gang 祁剛. "Qingji Wenzhou diqu de miaochan banxue" 清季溫州地區的廟產辦學 (Building schools with temple property in late-Qing Wenzhou). In *Gaibian Zhongguo zongjiao de wushi nian* 改變中國宗教的五十年, 1898–1948 (Fifty years of reforming Chinese religion, 1898–1948), edited by Kang Bao and Gao Wansang 高萬桑 (Vincent Goossaert), pp. 39–74. Taipei: Institute of Modern History, Academia Sinica, 2015.

Qi Tiehen 齊鐵恨. *Xin guoyin jiangxi keben* 新國音講習課本 (Textbook of new national pronunciation lectures). Shanghai: Zhonghua, 1929.

Qian Daxin 錢大昕. *Shijiazhai yangxin lu* 十駕齋養新錄 (Records of the cultivation of the new from the study of the ten yokes). In *Jiading Qian Daxin quanji* 嘉定錢大昕全集 (The entire collected writings of Qian Daxin of Jiading), edited by Chen Wenhe 陳文和. Nanjing: Jiangsu guji chubanshe, 1997.

Qing-gui 慶桂. *Guochao gongshi xubian* 國朝宮史續編 (Compilation on the palace history of our dynasty, sequel). Edited by Zuo Buqing 左步清. 2 vols. Beijing: Beijing guji chubanshe, 1994 [1807].

Qingshi gao 清史稿 (Draft history of the Qing). Edited by Zhao Erxun 趙爾巽. Beijing: Zhonghua shuju, 1977 [1927].

Qingshi gao. In *Qingshigao xiaozhu* 清史稿校注 (Annotated draft history of the Qing), edited by Guoshiguan 國史館. Taipei: Taiwan shangwu, 1999.

Qingshi zuanxiu weiyuan hui 清史纂修委員會. "*Qingshi gao* zuanxiu zhi jingguo" 清史稿纂修之經過 (The process of compiling the *Draft history of the Qing*). *Zhongguo yizhou* 中國一周 557 (December 26, 1960): 8–20.

Qiu Juli 邱居里. "Jia Kui yu shixue" 贾逵与史学 (Jia Kui and historiography). *Shixue yanjiu* 史学研究 4, no. 124 (2006): 70–72.

Qiu Weijun 丘為君. *Dai Zhen xue de xingcheng* 戴震學的形成 (Formation of Dai Zhen studies). Taipei: Lianjing chubanshe, 2004.

Qixin shuju 啟新書局. *Zuixin huitu zengbu zhengxu wanbao quanshu* 最新繪圖增補正續萬全書 (Newest, illustrated, expanded comprehensive compendium of countless treasures). 8 vols. Shanghai: Qixin shuju, ca. 1912.

Qu Qiubai 瞿秋白. "Diguozhuyi de yongpu yu Zhongguo pingmin" 帝國主義的傭僕與中國平民 (Servants of imperialism and the common Chinese people). In *Qu Qiubai wenji* 瞿秋白文集 (Writings of Qu Qiubai). http://50.22.193.73/thread-233164-1-1.html (accessed March 2017).

"Qunzhong juxing fan wushen dahui" 群眾舉行反巫神大會 (The masses held an anti-shaman meeting). *Jiefang ribao* 解放日報, June 3, 1944.

Rabinow, Paul, ed. *The Foucault Reader*. New York: Pantheon Books, 1984.

Ramaswamy, Sumathi. "Sanskrit for the Nation." *Modern Asian Studies* 33, no. 2 (1999): 339–381.

Rawski, Evelyn S. "Qing Book Culture and Inner Asia." In *Books in Numbers: Seventy-Fifth Anniversary of the Harvard-Yenching Library,* edited by Wilt L. Idema, pp. 197–235. Cambridge, MA: Harvard-Yenching Library, Harvard University, 2007.

———. "Qing Publishing in Non-Han Languages." In *Printing and Book Culture in Late Imperial China,* edited by Cynthia Joanne Brokaw and Kai-wing Chow, pp. 304–331. Berkeley: University of California Press, 2005.

Red Pine [Bill Porter]. *The Diamond Sutra*. Berkeley: Counterpoint, 2001.

Reed, Christopher A. *Gutenberg in Shanghai: Chinese Print Capitalism, 1876–1937*. Vancouver: University of British Columbia Press, 2004.

Reilly, Thomas. *The Taiping Heavenly Kingdom: Rebellion and the Blasphemy of Empire*. Seattle: University of Washington Press, 2014.

Ren Jiyu 任继愈, ed. *Zhongguo kexue jishu dianji tonghui: Nongxue juan* 中国科学技术典籍通汇, 农学卷 (Collection of ancient Chinese books on science and technology: Volume on agricultural science). Zhengzhou: Henan jiaoyu chubanshe, 1994.

Renren bixu riyong bianlan 人人必須日用便覽 (A brief guide for daily use that everyone needs). Shanghai: Yongzheng shuju, 1916.

"A Report of Nestorians 景教記事." In *Liuhe congtan* 六合叢談 (Universal forum), vol. 6, pp. 11b–13b. Shanghai: Mohai shukuan and the London Missionary Society Press, 1857.

Reynolds, Douglas R. "Japanese Encyclopaedias: Their Background and Hidden Impact on Late-Qing Chinese Encyclopaedias." In *Chinese Encyclopaedias of New Global Knowledge (1870–1930): Changing Ways of Thought,* edited by Milena Doleželová-Velingerová and Rudolf G. Wagner, pp. 137–189. Berlin: Springer-Verlag, 2014.

Rhoads, Edward J. M. *Manchus and Han: Ethnic Relations and Political Power in Late Qing and Early Republican China, 1861–1928*. Seattle: University of Washington Press, 2000.

Richard, Timothy. *Forty-Five Years in China*. New York: Frederick A. Stokes, 1916.

Riyong bianlan 日用便覽 (Information for daily use at a glance). Shanghai: Yongzheng shuju, 1916.

Rosenberg, Daniel, and Anthony Grafton. *Cartographies of Time: A History of the Timeline*. Princeton, NJ: Princeton Architectural Press, 2010.

Rossokhin, Ilarion. *Opisanie puteshestviia koim ezdili Kitayskie poslanniki v Rossiiu, byvshie v 1714 godu y Kalmytskago Khana Aiuki na Volge*. St. Petersburg: n.p., 1764.

Saarela, Mårten Söderblom. "The Cost of a Manchu Dictionary in the Guangxu Period." Manchu Studies Group, blog post, March 4, 2013. http://www.manchustudiesgroup.org/2013/03/04/715/ (accessed January 11, 2017).

———. "Manchu Language." *Oxford Research Encyclopedia of Asian History*. https://doi.org/10.1093/acrefore/9780190277727.013.447.

Sakai Tadao 酒井忠夫. *Chūgoku nichiyō ruisho shi no kenkyū* 中国日用類書史の研究 (Research on Chinese daily-use category books). Tokyo: Kokusho kankōkai, 2011.

———, ed. *Chūgoku nichiyō ruisho shūsei* 中國日用類書集成 (Complete collectanea of Chinese daily-use category books). 14 vols. Tokyo: Kyūko shoin, 1999–2004.

Saoye shanfang 掃葉山房. *Riyong wanshi baoku choushi bixu* 日用萬事寶庫酬世必需 (Treasure house of all daily things necessary for social relations). Shanghai: Saoye shanfang, 1929.

Saunier, Pierre-Yves. *Transnational History*. New York: Palgrave Macmillan, 2013.

Saussy, Haun, ed. *Texts and Transformations: Essays in Honor of the 75th Birthday of Victor H. Mair*. Amherst, NY: Cambria Press, 2018.

Scheid, Volker. *Chinese Medicine in Contemporary China: Plurality and Synthesis*. Durham, NC: Duke University Press, 2002.

Schlesinger, Jonathan. *A World Trimmed with Fur: Wild Things, Pristine Places, and the Natural Fringes of Qing Rule*. Stanford, CA: Stanford University Press, 2017.

Schneider, Julia. *Nation and Ethnicity: Chinese Discourses on History, Historiography, and Nationalism (1900s–1920s)*. Leiden: Brill, 2017.

Schneider, Laurence A. "From Textual Criticism to Social Criticism: The Historiography of Ku Chieh-kang." *Journal of Asian Studies* 28, no. 4 (1969): 771–788.

———. *Ku Chieh-Kang and China's New History: Nationalism and the Quest for Alternative Traditions*. Berkeley: University of California Press, 1971.

Sela, Ori. *China's Philological Turn*. New York: Columbia University Press, 2018.

———. "From Writing to Literature: The Development of Late Qing Theories of Prose." *Harvard Journal of Asiatic Studies* 47, no. 1 (June 1987): 51–96.

Selden, Mark. *China in Revolution: Yenan Way Revisited*. New York: Routledge, 1995.

The Sesquicentennial International Exposition, Philadelphia, June First to December First, 1926. Pamphlet in the Special Collections Research Center, Henry Madden Library, California State University, Fresno. http://www.worldsfairs.amdigital.co.uk/Documents/Details/HMLSC_upam_BX18_AMD653 (accessed July 25, 2017).

Shan, Patrick Fuliang. *Yuan Shikai: A Reappraisal*. Vancouver: University of British Columbia Press, 2018.

Shan Shiyuan 单士元. "Zhengli Manwen laodang ji" 整理满文老档记 (Notes on sorting through the old Manchu archive) (written in 1931, updated in 1991). In *Wo zai Gugong qishi nian* 我在故宫七十年 (My seventy years at the National Palace), pp. 321–326. Beijing: Beijing shifan daxue chubanshe, 1997.

Shanggu shanfang 尚古山房. *Huitu zengbu wanbao quanshu* 繪圖增補萬寶全書 (Illustrated expanded compendia of countless treasures). 8 vols. Shanghai: Shanggu shanfang, 1912.

Shanghai liuxian shuju 上海六先書局. *Zengbu wanbao quanshu* 增補萬寶全書 (Expanded comprehensive compendium of countless treasures). 6 vols. Shanghai: Shanghai liuxian shuju, 1898.

Shen Jin 沈津. *Weng Fanggang nianpu* 翁方綱年譜 (Biography of Weng Fanggang). Taipei: Zhongyang yanjiuyuan Zhongguo wenzhe yanjiusuo, 2002.

Shen Qi 沈圻. "Ruhe kewei xiaoxue guoyu jiaoshi" 如何可為小學國語教師 (How to become a primary school national language teacher). *Jiaoyu zazhi* 教育雜誌 13, no. 6 (June 1921): 1–8.

Shen Yuwu 沈雨梧. "Lun Chen Haozi de *Huajing*" 论陈淏子的花镜 (On Chen Haozi's *Mirror of flowers*). *Zhejiang shifan daxue xuebao (shehui kexue ban)* 浙江师范大学学报（社会科学版）4, no. 35 (2010): 49–53.

Shih, Shu-mei. *Lure of the Modern: Writing Modernism in Semicolonial China, 1917–1937*. Berkeley: University of California Press, 2001.

Shijiu niandu Henan jiaoyu nianjian 十九年度河南教育年鑑 (Henan education yearbook for 1930). Kaifeng: n.p., 1931.

Shu Yinglan 舒迎瀾. "*Huajing* jianjie yu Qingdai chahua yishu" 花鏡简介与清代插花艺术 (A brief introduction to *Mirror of flowers* and the art of flower arranging in the Qing dynasty). *Yuanlin* 園林 2 (2002): 4–5.

Sima Qian 司馬遷. *Records of the Grand Historian of China*. Translated by Burton Watson. New York: Columbia University Press, 1991.

"Sisheng shiyan lu tiyao" 四聲實驗錄提要 (Summary of *Sisheng shiyan lu*). *Chenbao fukan* 晨報副刊 (April 1922): 1–4.

Smith, Aminda M. *Thought Reform and China's Dangerous Classes: Reeducation, Resistance and the People*. Lanham, MD: Rowman & Littlefield, 2012.

Smith, Eric D. "'Ambiguity at Its Best!': Historicizing G. V. Desani's *All about H. Hatterr*." *Ariel* 40, nos. 2–3 (2009): 111–134.

Smith, Richard. *The I Ching: A Biography*. Princeton, NJ: Princeton University Press, 2013.

Smith, Steve (S. A.). "Talking Toads and Chinless Ghosts: The Politics of 'Superstitious' Rumors in the People's Republic of China, 1961–1965." *American Historical Review* 111, no. 2 (2006): 405–427.

Song Xi 宋晞. "*Qingshi gao* guan neiben, guan waiben shiguan zhiming biao" 清史稿關內本關外本史館職名表 (Tables of individuals of the historiography commission and their tasks in the *extra muros* and *intra muros* editions of *Draft history of the Qing*). In *Youguan "Qingshi gao" bianyin jingguo ji ge fang yijian huibian* 有關清史稿編印經過及各方意見彙編 (Collection of material relating to the process of compiling and publishing *Draft history of the Qing* as well the as opinions of various parties), edited by Xu Shishen 許師慎, vol. 1, pp. 219–222. Taipei: Zhonghua Minguo shiliao yanjiu zhongxin, 1979.

Souciet, Étienne, and Antoine Gaubil. *Observations Mathématiques, Astronomiques, Geographiques, Chronologiques, et Physiques, Tirées des Anciens Livres Chinois; Ou Faites Nouvellement aux Indes et à la Chine*. 3 vols. Paris: Chez Rollin, 1729.

Spira, Ivo. *A Conceptual History of Chinese -Isms: The Modernization of Ideological Discourse, 1895–1925*. Leiden: Brill, 2015.

Standaert, Nicolas. *Handbook of Christianity in China*, vol. 1: *635–1800*. Leiden: Brill, 2001.

Stary, Giovanni. *Manchu Studies: An International Bibliography*. Wiesbaden: O. Harrassowitz, 2003.

Staunton, George. *Narrative of the Chinese Embassy to the Khan of the Tourgouth Tartars in the Years 1712, 13, 14, and 15; by the Chinese Ambassador, and Published, by the Emperor's Authority, at Pekin*. London: John Murray, 1821.

Stein, Gunther. *The Challenge of Red China*. London: McGraw-Hill, 1945.

Stranahan, Patricia. *Molding the Medium: The Chinese Communist Party and the Liberation Daily*. Armonk, NY: M. E. Sharpe, 1990.

Strassberg, Richard E., trans. *Inscribed Landscapes: Travel Writing from Imperial China*. Berkeley: University of California Press, 1994.

Sun Jiang. "Continuity and Discontinuity: Narratives of the Yellow Emperor in Early Twentieth-Century History Textbooks." *Frontiers of History in China* 8 (2013): 176–201.

Sun Xingyan 孫星衍. *Wenzi tang ji* 問字堂集 (Collected writings from the Hall of Lexical Inquiries). Beijing: Zhonghua shuju, 1996.

Sun Yat-sen. *San Min Chu I: The Three Principles of the People*. Translated by Frank W. Price. Edited by L. T. Chen. Shanghai: Commercial Press, 1929.

Sungsen 松森, ed. *Qinding Mengwen huishu* 欽定蒙文彙書 | *Mongγol-un üsüg-ün quriyaγsan bičig* (Imperially authorized collection of Mongolian writing). 17 vols. Xylograph, 1892. Held at Peking University Library; call number: SB 419.2 3097.

Sutton, Donald S. "From Credulity to Scorn: Confucians Confront the Spirit Mediums in Late Imperial China." *Late Imperial China* 21, no. 2 (2000): 1–39.

Suzuki, Shūji 鈴木修次. "Religion (*shūkyō*) and Freedom (*jiyū*)." In *The Emergence of the Modern Sino-Japanese Lexicon: Seven Studies,* translated and edited by Joshua A. Fogel, pp. 81–112. Leiden: Brill, 2015.

Swartz, Wendy, Robert Ford Campany, Yang Lu, and Jessey J. C. Choo, eds. *Early Medieval China: A Sourcebook.* New York: Columbia University Press, 2014.

Tamaoka Atsushi 玉岡敦. "*Kyōsantō sengen* hōyaku shi" 「共産党宣言」邦訳史 (The Japanese translation history of the *Communist Manifesto*). https://jshet.net/docs/conference/75th/tamaoka.pdf (accessed July 2017).

———. "*Kyōsantō sengen* hōyaku shi ni okeru Kōtoku Shūsui Sakai Toshihiko yaku (1904, 1906 nen) no ichi" 「共産党宣言」邦訳史における幸徳秋水・堺利彦訳（1904, 1906年）の位置 (The place of the translation by Kōtoku Shūsui and Sakai Toshihiko, 1904 and 1906, in the Japanese translation history of the *Communist Manifesto*). *Ōhara shakai mondai kenkyū zasshi* 大原社会問題研究雑誌 603 (January 2009): 14–26.

Taylor, Kim. *Chinese Medicine in Early Communist China, 1945–1963.* New York: Routledge, 2011.

Teng, Emma J. *Taiwan's Imagined Geography: Chinese Colonial Travel Writing and Pictures, 1683–1895.* Cambridge, MA: Harvard University Asia Center, 2004.

Tianbao shuju 天寶書局. *Huitu zengbu zhengxu wanbao quanshu* 繪圖增補正續萬寶全書 (Illustrated, expanded, corrected, and continued comprehensive compendium of countless treasures). 8 vols. Shanghai: Tianbao shuju, 1920.

Tianji shuju 天機書局. *Zengbu wanbao quanshu* 增補萬寶全書 (Expanded comprehensive compendium of countless treasures). 8 vols. Shanghai: Tianji shuju, 1912.

Townsend, Camilla. "Introduction: Breaking the Law of the Preservation of Energy of Historians." *American Historical Review* 123, no. 3 (June 2018): 779–788.

Trüper, Henning. *Orientalism, Philology, and the Illegibility of the Modern World.* London: Bloomsbury Publishing, 2020.

Tse, Wicky. *The Collapse of China's Later Han Dynasty, 25–220 CE: The Northwest Borderlands and the Edge of Empire.* London: Routledge, 2018.

"Tuizheng wu shanrang ziyang" 退政無禪讓字樣 (A surrender to power is not *shanrang*). *Shuntian shibao* 順天時報, October 7, 1911.

Turner, James. *Philology: The Forgotten Origins of the Modern Humanities.* Princeton, NJ: Princeton University Press, 2015.

Übelhör, Monika. "The Community Compact (Hsiang-yüe) of the Sung and Its Educational Significance." In *Neo-Confucian Education: The Formative Stage,* edited by William Theodore de Bary and John Chaffee, pp. 371–388. Berkeley: University of California Press, 1989.

Unschuld, Paul U. *Medicine in China: A History of Ideas.* Berkeley: University of California Press, 1985.

VanNess Simmons, Richard. "Whence Came Mandarin? Qīng Guānhuà, the Běijīng Dialect, and the National Language Standard in Early Republican China." *Journal of the American Oriental Society* 137, no. 1 (2017): 63–88.

Wagner, Rudolf G. "Encyclopaedia from China and Japan (19th and 20th Century)." http://www.asia-europe.uni-heidelberg.de/en/research/d-historicities-heritage/d11/bibliographic-descriptions/encyclopaedia-china-japan.html (accessed October 2020).

Waley, Arthur, trans. *The Analects of Confucius.* New York: Vintage Books, 1938.

Waley-Cohen, Joanna. *Exile in Mid-Qing China: Banishment to Xinjiang, 1758–1820.* New Haven, CT: Yale University Press, 1991.

———. "The New Qing History." *Radical History Review* 88 (2004): 193–206.

Walravens, Hartmut. "V. M. Alekseev—Leben und Werk. Eine Bibliographie: Aus sowjetische Quellen zusammengestellt und übersetzt." *Oriens Extremus* 21, no. 1 (1974): 67–95.
"Wanbao quanshu" 萬寶全書 (Complete compendia of myriad treasures). *Ziluolan* 紫羅蘭 1 (1943): 116–117.
Wanfu 萬福. *Chongke Qingwen xuzi zhinan bian* 重刻清文虛字指南編 | *Nonggime dasame foloho manju gisun-i untuhun hergen-i temgetu jorin bithe* (Guide to the empty characters of the Manchu language, printed with additions and corrections). Edited by Fungšan 鳳山. 2 vols. Xylograph. Beijing: Juzhen tang, 1894.
———. *Chongke Qingwen xuzi zhinan bian* 重刻清文虛字指南編 | *nonggime dasame foloho manju gisun-i untuhun hergen-i temgetu jorin bithe* (Guide to the empty characters of the Manchu language, printed with additions and corrections), vol. 8: *Ural alt'ai inmun ch'ongsŏ 1*. Edited by Fungšan 鳳山. Beijing: Jinggutang, 1909.
Wang, Chaohua. "Cai Yuanpei and the Origins of the May Fourth Movement: Modern Chinese Intellectual Transformations, 1890–1920." PhD dissertation, University of California, Los Angeles, 2008.
Wang Cheng-hua (Wang Zhenghua) 王正華. "Shenghuo, zhishi, yu wenhua shangpin: Wan Ming Fujian ban 'Riyong leishu' yu qi shuhua men" 生活知識與文化商品：晚明福建版「日用類書」與其書畫門 (Daily life, commercialized knowledge, and cultural consumption: Late-Ming Fujian household encyclopedias on calligraphy and painting). *Zhongyang yanjiuyuan jindaishi yanjiusuo jikan* 中央研究院近代史研究所集刊 41 (September 2003): 1–85.
Wang Dongjie 王东杰. *Shengru xintong: Guoyu yundong yu xiandai Zhongguo* 声入心通：国语运动与现代中国 (The sound of the heart: The national language movement and modern China). Beijing: Beijing shifan daxue chubanshe, 2019.
Wang Fansen 王汎森. *Fu Ssu-nien: An Intellectual Biography*. New York: Cambridge University Press, 2000.
——— et al. *Zhongguo jindai sixiang shi de zhuanxing shidai: Zhang Hao yuanshi qizhi zhushou lunwenji* 中國近代思想史的轉型時代：張灝院士七秩祝壽論文集 (The transitional period in the history of modern Chinese thought: Essays in honor of academician Zhang Hao's seventieth birthday). Taipei: Lianjing Press, 2007.
Wang Guowei 王国维. "Wenxue xiaoyan" 文学小言 (Desultory remarks on literature). In *Zhongguo lidai wenlun xuan* 中國歷代文論選 (Chinese essays on literature through the ages), edited by Guo Shaoyu 郭紹虞 and Wang Wensheng 王文生, vol. 4, p. 378. Shanghai: Shanghai guji chubanshe, 1980.
Wang Hui 汪晖. *China from Empire to Nation-State*. Translated by Michael Gibbs Hill. Cambridge, MA: Harvard University Press, 2014.
Wang Jia'ao 王家鰲. "Xuguan dier xiao xuexiao 'guoyu jinxing' shang de dalüe baogao he di'er nian suo faxian de liangge kunnan wenti" 滸關第二小學校「國語進行」上的大略報告和第二年所發現的兩個困難問題 (General report on national language implementation at Xuguan Number Two Primary School and two difficult problems discovered in the second year). *Guoyu yuekan* 國語月刊 1, no. 5 (1922): 1–2.
Wang Jian 王建. "'*Huajing* zuozhe Chen Haozi kao' bian" 「花鏡作者陳淏子考」辨 (Debate on "Study of the author of *Mirror of flowers*, Chen Haozi"). *Wenxian* 文獻 2 (April 2003): 191–195.
Wang Mingsheng 王鳴盛. "*Shuowen jiezi zhengyi* xu" 說文解字正義敘 (Preface to *The correct meaning of the Shuowen Jiezi*). In *Shuowen jiezi gulin zhengxu hebian* 說文解字詁林正續合編 (Joint compilation of the *Corrected and continued forest of explanations* of the *Analysis of characters and explanation of writing*), compiled by Ding Fubao 丁福保. Taipei: Dingwen shuju, 1977.

Wang Niansun 王念孫. "Wang Rongfu Shuxue xu" 汪容甫述學敘 (Preface to Wang Rongfu's [Zhong] Discourses on learning). In Wang Zhong 汪中, Xinbian Wang Zhong ji 新编汪中集 (New edition of Wang Zhong's writings). Yangzhou: Guangling shushe, 2005.

Wang Xianqian 王先謙. "Houxu" 後序 (Postscript). In Yang Rongzhi, Jingjiao beiwen jishi kaozheng 景教碑文紀事考正 (Investigations and rectifications on the Records regarding the Nestorian stele). New Taipei City: Ganlan, 2015.

———. "Xu" 序 (Preface). In Yang Rongzhi, Jingjiao beiwen jishi kaozheng. 景教碑文紀事考正 (Investigations and rectifications on the Records regarding the Nestorian stele). New Taipei City: Ganlan, 2015.

Wang Yueyin 王曰因. "Xiaoxue guoyu jiaoxue duiyu yanwen yizhi he duyin tongyi buneng bingzhong" 小學國語教學對於言文一致和讀音統一不能並重 (In primary school national language education unity of speech-writing and the unification of pronunciation cannot be regarded as equally important). Nanhui xian lichen nannü xiaoyouhui zazhi 南匯縣立城南女校校友會雜誌 4 (1924): 149–150.

Wang Yunwu 王雲五, ed. Xuxiu Siku quanshu tiyao 續修四庫全書提要 (Bibliographical précis to the continuation of the Complete writings of the Four Repositories). 13 vols. Taipei: Taiwan shangwu yinshu guan, 1971.

Wang, Zheng. Never Forget National Humiliation: Historical Memory in Chinese Politics and Foreign Relations. New York: Columbia University Press, 2014.

Wasaki Kōtarō 和崎光太郎. "Taishō jiyū kyōiku to 'sekka shisō': Kawai kundō jiken to sono shūhen" 大正自由教育と「赤化思想」：川井訓導事件とその周辺 (Liberal education in the Taishō era and "Communist thought": The Kawai training incident and its surrounding circumstances). Shinano 信濃 59, no. 10 (October 2007): 753–770.

Wechsler, Howard. Offerings of Jade and Silk: Ritual and Symbol in the Legitimation of the T'ang Dynasty. New Haven, CT: Yale University Press, 1985.

Wei Yuan 魏源. Guwei tang ji 古微堂集 (Collected works of the Hall of Ancient Subtleties). Shanghai: Guoxue fulunshe, 1909.

———. Haiguo tuzhi 海國圖志 (Illustrated gazetteer of the maritime nations). Zhengzhou: Zhongzhou guji chubanshe, 1991.

———. Wei Yuan ji 魏源集 (The writings of Wei Yuan). Beijing: Zhonghua shuju, 1976.

Weinberger, Eliot, and Octavio Paz. Nineteen Ways of Looking at Wang Wei (with More Ways). New York: New Directions Books, 2016.

Whyte, Martin K. Small Groups and Political Rituals in China. Berkeley: University of California Press, 1974.

Widmer, Ellen. "Honglou Meng Ying and Its Publisher, Juzhen Tang of Beijing." Late Imperial China 23, no. 2 (2002): 33–52.

Wilhelm, Hellmut. "Second List of Sinological Books Published in China since 1938." Monumenta Serica 8 (1943): 336–393.

Wilhelm, Hellmut, and Cary F. Baynes. The I Ching; Or, Book of Changes: The Richard Wilhelm Translation. Princeton, NJ: Princeton University Press, 1972.

Williams, Raymond. Keywords: A Vocabulary of Culture and Society, new ed. Oxford: Oxford University Press, 1983.

———. The Politics of Modernism: Against the New Conformists. London: Verso, 1989.

Winkelman, Michael. "Shamanism in Cross-Cultural Perspective." International Journal of Transpersonal Studies 31, no. 2 (2012): 47–62.

Wong, Chi Man. "The Chinese Latinization Movement, 1917–1958: Language, History, and Politics." PhD dissertation, New York University, 2013.

Wright, Mary C. The Last Stand of Chinese Conservatism: The T'ung-chih Restoration, 1862–1874, 2nd ed. Stanford, CA: Stanford University Press, 1962 [1957].

Wu Chang-shing 吳昶興, ed. *Da Qin Jingjiao liuxing Zhongguo bei: Da-Qin Jingjiao wenxian shiyi* 大秦景教流行中國碑：大秦景教文獻釋義 (Da Qin stele commemorating the spread of *Jingjiao* in China: Explications of the documents of *Jingjiao* from Da Qin). New Taipei City: Ganlan, 2015.

Wu Huifang 吳蕙芳. "'Riyong' yu 'leishu' de jiehe, cong *Shilin guangji* dao *wanshi buqiuren*"「日用」與「類書」的結合, 從《事林廣記》到《萬事不求人》 (The link between "daily use" and "category books," from the *Comprehensive records of all matters* to *Myriad matters about which one will not need to ask*). In *Ming-Qing yilai minjian shenghuo zhishi de jiangou yu chuandi* 明清以來民間生活知識的建構與傳遞 (The construction and transmission of popular daily knowledge from the Ming and Qing dynasties), pp. 11–54. Taipei: Taiwan xuesheng shuju, 2007.

———. *Wanbao quanshu: Ming-Qing shiqi de minjian shenghuo shilu* 萬寶全書：明清時期的民間生活實錄 (Comprehensive compendia of countless treasures: A veritable record of popular life in the Ming and Qing periods). Taipei: Hua Mulan wenhua gongzuo fang, 2005.

Wu Jingheng 吳敬恆 (Wu Zhihui 吳稚暉). "Shu xuhou hou" 書序後後 (Afterword to the redundant book preface). In Liu Fu, *Sisheng shiyan lu* 四聲實驗錄 (Experimental record of the four tones). Shanghai: Qunyi shushe, 1924.

———. "Xu" 序 (Preface). In Liu Fu, *Sisheng shiyan lu* 四聲實驗錄 (Experimental record of the four tones). Shanghai: Qunyi shushe, 1924.

Wu, Ka-Ming. *Reinventing Chinese Tradition: The Cultural Politics of Late Socialism*. Urbana: University of Illinois Press, 2015.

Wu Meng 吳蒙. "Guoyu buneng tongyi de yuanyin" 國語不能統一的原因 (Reasons why the national language cannot be unified). *Wuxi xian jiaoyuyhui niankan* 無錫縣教育會年刊 4 (October 1923): *yanjiu* 1–4.

Wu, Pei-yi. "Self-Examination and Confession of Sins in Traditional China." *Harvard Journal of Asiatic Studies* 39, no. 11 (1979): 5–38.

Wu Rulun 吳汝綸. "*Tianyan lun* xu"《天演論》序 (Preface to *Evolution and ethics*). In *Yan Fu ji* 嚴復集 (The Yan Fu collection), edited by Wang Shi 王栻, vol. 5, p. 1318. Beijing: Zhonghua shuju, 1986.

———. "Yu Yao Zhongshi" 與姚仲實 (To Yao Zhongshi). In *Zhongguo jindai wenlun xuan* 中國近代文論選 (Selected modern essays on literature), edited by Luo Genze 羅根澤 and Guo Shaoyu 郭紹虞, p. 307. Beijing: Renmin wenxue chubanshe, 1962.

Wu, Shengqing. *Modern Archaics: Continuity and Innovation in the Chinese Lyric Tradition*. Cambridge, MA: Harvard University Asia Center, 2013.

Wu Shijian 吳士鑒. "Chen zuanxiu tili" 陳纂修體例 (Presented compilation principles). In Zhu Shizhe 朱師轍, *Qingshi shuwen* 清史述聞 (Record of things heard regarding Qing history), pp. 140–154. Shanghai: Shanghai shudian chubanshe, 2009 [1957].

Wu Zhihui 吳稚暉. "Shanghai guoyu shifan xuexiao faqi xuanyan" 上海國語師範學校發起宣言 (Manifesto at the launching of the Shanghai National Language School). Circa February 1924, housed in Wu Zhihui Papers, KMT Party Archives (Taipei), file 03077.

———. "Zhuyin zimu de taolun" 注音字母的討論 (Discussing the phonetic alphabet). *Xin qingnian* 新青年 9, no. 2 (1921): 1–14.

Wylie, Alexander. *Notes on Chinese Literature: With Introductory Remarks on the Progressive Advancement of the Art; and a List of Translations from the Chinese into Various European Languages*. Shanghai: American Presbyterian Mission Press, 1867.

"Xi Gives Trump a Chinese History Lesson." *Straits Times*, November 9, 2017. https://www.straitstimes.com/asia/east-asia/xi-gives-trump-a-chinese-history-lesson.

Xiao Yifei 尚伊緋. "Wugong miji yu hun duanzi: Tanxun *Wanbao quanshu* zhong de "mengliao" 武功秘笈與荤段子：探尋《萬寶全書》中的「猛料」(Secret books on martial arts and obscene storytelling, searching for "hot items" in *Wanbao quanshu*). http://club.history.sina.com.cn/viewthread.php?action=printable&tid=4704566 (accessed April 14, 2017).

Xie Guozhen 謝國楨. "Qing kaiguo shiliao kaoxu lunding bubian" 清開國史料考敘論訂補編 (Critical examination of the sources for early Qing history, emended version). In *Ming-Qing shiliao congshu ba zhong* 明清史料叢書八種 (Eight collections of sources from the Ming and Qing periods), vol. 6: *Qingchu shiliao si zhong* 清初史料四種 (Four sources from the early Qing period), pp. 163–206. Beijing: Tushuguan chubanshe, 2005 [1933].

Xinbian Riyong wanquan xinshu 新編日用萬全新書 (Newly edited completely thorough new book for daily use). Shanghai: Guangyi shuju, 1921.

Xu Guangqi 徐光啟. "Jingjiaotang beiji" 景教堂碑記 (Stele inscription on the Nestorian temple). In *Xu Guangqi ji* 徐光啟集 (Writings of Xu Guangqi), vol. 2, pp. 531–533. Beijing: Zhonghua shuju, 1963.

Xu Li 徐莉. "*Xuxiu 'Siku quanshu' zongmu tiyao* xiaoxue lei Manwen tushu tiyao tanxi" 《续修四库全书总目提要》小学类满文图书提要探析 (Forays in the Manchu works in the philology section of *Bibliographical summaries for the "Sequel to the 'Complete writings of the Four Repositories'"*). *Manyu yanjiu* 满语研究 52, no. 1 (2011): 104–117.

Xu Shishen 許師慎, ed. *Youguan "Qingshi gao" bianyin jingguo ji ge fang yijian huibian* 有關清史稿編印經過及各方意見彙編 (Collection of material relating to the process of compiling and publishing *Draft history of the Qing* as well the as opinions of various parties). 2 vols. Taipei: Zhonghua Minguo shiliao yanjiu zhongxin, 1979.

Xu Youchun 徐友春, Cai Hongyuan 蔡鴻源, Ji Peng 季鵬, and Xu Jianchuan 徐建傳, eds. *Minguo renwu da cidian* 民國人物大辭典 (Unabridged biographic lexicon of the Chinese Republic), rev. ed. 2 vols. Shijiazhuang: Hebei renmin chubanshe, 2007.

Xuxiu "Siku quanshu" zongmu tiyao (gaoben) 續修四庫全書總目提要(稿本) (Bibliographical précis for the *Sequel to the "Complete writings of the Four Repositories"* [draft edition]). Edited by Zhongguo Kexueyuan tushuguan 中國科學院圖書館. 38 vols. Facsimiles of manuscripts written in 1931–1942. Jinan: Qi-Lu shushe, 1996.

Yamane Yukio 山根幸夫. *Tōhō bunka jigyō no rekishi: Shōwa zenki ni okeru Nitchū bunka kōryū* 東方文化事業の歴史：昭和前期における日中文化交流 (A history of East Asian cultural enterprises: Sino-Japanese cultural exchange in the early Shōwa period). Tokyo: Kyūko shoin, 2005.

Yanabu, Akira. "The Tennō System as the Symbol of the Culture of Translation." *Japan Review* 7 (1996): 147–157.

"Yan'an xian zhaokai fan wushen dahui" 延安縣召開反巫神大會 (The Yan'an County government convened an anti-shaman mass rally). *Jiefang ribao* 解放日報, July 21, 1944.

"Yanchuan Yongyuan qu sanxiang qunzhong tongguo fandui wushen banfa" 延川永遠區三鄉群眾大會通過反對巫神辦法 (The mass meeting at the Third Township of Yongyuan district of Yanchuan County passed the anti-shaman methods). *Jiefang ribao* 解放日報, June 28, 1944.

Yang Chia-ling. "Deciphering Antiquity into Modernity: The Cultural Identity of Luo Zhenyu and the Qing Loyalists in Manzhouguo." In *Lost Generation,* edited by Yang Chia-ling and Roderick Whitfield, pp. 173–209. London: Saffron, 2012.

Yang Chia-ling and Roderick Whitfield. "Chronology of Luo Zhenyu (1866 1940)." In *Lost Generation,* edited by Yang Chia-ling and Roderick Whitfield, pp. 239–281. London: Saffron, 2012.

Yang Chia-ling and Roderick Whitfield, eds. *Lost Generation: Luo Zhenyu, Qing Loyalists and the Formation of Modern Chinese Culture.* London: Saffron, 2012.

Yang, Fenggang. *Religion in China, Survival and Revival under Communist Rule.* New York: Oxford University Press, 2012.

Yang Fengmou 楊豐陌 and Zhang Benyi 張本義. *Dalian Tushuguan cang shaoshu minzu guji tushu zonglu* 大連圖書館藏少數民族古籍圖書總錄 (General catalog of books by ethnic minorities in the holdings of Dalian Library). Shenyang: Liaoning minzu chubanshe, 2004.

Yang, Mayfair, ed. *Chinese Religiosities: Afflictions of Modernity and State Formations*. Berkeley: University of California Press, 2008.

———. "Shamanism and Spirit Possession in Chinese Modernity: Some Preliminary Reflections on a Gendered Religiosity of the Body." *Review of Religion and Chinese Society* 2 (2015): 51–86.

Yang Rongzhi 楊榮鋕. *Jingjiao beiwen jishi kaozheng* 景教碑文紀事考正 (Investigations and rectifications on the records regarding the Nestorian Stele). In *Da-Qin Jingjiao liuxing Zhongguo bei: Da-Qin Jingjiao wenxian shiyi* 大秦景教流行中國碑：大秦景教文獻釋義 (Da Qin stele commemorating the spread of *Jingjiao* in China: Explications of the documents of *Jingjiao* from Da Qin), edited by Wu Chang-shing 吳昶興, pp. 335–564. New Taipei City: Ganlan, 2015.

Yang Ximei 楊希枚. "Zai lun Yao-Shun 'shanrang' chuanshuo: Zhongguo gushi yanjiu fangfa lunlie" 再論堯舜禪讓傳說：中國古史研究方法論例 (Revisiting the legend of the Yao-Shun voluntary abdication, a discussion in ancient Chinese historical research methodology), part 1: *Shihuo yuekan* 食貨月刊 7, no. 7 (October 1977): 297–307; part 2: *Shihuo yuekan* 7, nos. 8–9 (November 1977): 380–407.

Yang Xumin 杨绪敏. "Lun wan Qing xuejie zongshi Yu Yue de xueshu chengjiu ji yingxiang" 论晚清学界宗师俞樾的学术成就及影响 (Discussion of the scholarship and influence of the great teacher and scholar of the late Qing, Yu Yue). *Hechi daxue xuebao* 河池大学学报 27, no. 4 (August 2007): 35–39.

Yang Yongjun 杨永俊. "Lun Yao Shun Yu shanrang de zhengzhi yuanze yu lishi xiangtai" 论尧舜禹禅让的政治原则与历史形态 (On the political principle, history, and formation of the Yao-Shun-Yu voluntary abdication). *Xinyang shifan xueyuan xuebao* 信阳师范学院学报 25, no. 4 (2005): 109–113.

Yao Ying 姚瑩. "Fu Wu Zifang shu" 復吳子方書 (Letter in response to Wu Zifang). In *Dongming wenji* 東溟文集 (Writings from the eastern sea), in *Zhongfu tang quanji* 中復堂全集 (Complete works from the Restoration Hall) (1867), vol. 1, 8a.

———. "Fu Yang Jun lun shiwen shu" 復楊君論詩文書 (Letter in response to Mr. Yang concerning literature). In *Dongming wenji* (1920), in *Zhongfu tang quanji* 中復堂文集 (Complete works from the Restoration Hall) (1867), vol. 2, 7a–b.

———. "Huang Xiangshi shi xu" 黃香石詩序 (Preface to the poetry of Huang Xiangshi). In *Dongming waiji* 東溟外集 (Supplement collection from the eastern sea), in *Zhongfu tang quanji* 中復堂全集 (Complete works from the Restoration Hall) (1867), vol. 1, 2:6a.

———. "Shi xiao lu" 識小錄 (A record of minutiae). In *Zhongfu tang quanji* 中復堂全集 (Complete works from the Restoration Hall), 13:2b: "Xibao xuan shiwen" 惜抱軒詩文 (The literary writings of Yao Nai)."

Ye Gaoshu 葉高樹. *Qing qianqi de wenhua zhengce* 清朝前期的文化政策 (Cultural policies of the first half of the Qing period). Banqiao: Daoxiang chubanshe, 2002.

Ye Gongchuo 葉恭綽. "Qingshi ying ruhe zuanxiu" 清史應如何纂修 (How a history of the Qing should be compiled). In *Youguan "Qingshi gao" bianyin jingguo ji ge fang yijian huibian* 有關清史稿編印經過及各方意見彙編 (Collection of material relating to the process of compiling and publishing *Draft history of the Qing* as well the as opinions of various parties), edited by Xu Shishen 許師慎, vol. 2, pp. 536–544. Taipei: Zhonghua Minguo shiliao yanjiu zhongxin, 1979.

Yeh, Catherine Vance. "Civilizing Our People through the Everyday Application of New Knowledge: *Everyday Cyclopedia* Riyong baike quanshu 日用百科全書." In *Chinese*

Encyclopaedias of New Global Knowledge, edited by Milena Doleželová-Velingerová and Rudolf G. Wagner, pp. 367-397. Berlin: Springer-Verlag, 2014.

Yi Peiji 易培基. "Qingshi limu zhengwu" 清史例目證誤 (Correction of mistakes in the editorial principles and table of contents of the Qing history). *Jiayin zazhi* 1, no. 6 (1915): 31-36.

Yi Qinheng 伊欽恒. *Huajing jiaozhuben* 花鏡校注本 (Annotated version of *Huajing*). Beijing: Nongye chubanshe, 1980 [1962].

Yi-geng 奕賡. "Qingyu renming yi Han" 清語人名譯漢 (Manchu names translated into Chinese). In *Jiameng Xuan congzhu* 佳夢軒叢著 (Accumulated writings from Good Dream Studio), edited by Lei Dashou 雷大受, pp. 275-346. Beijing: Beijing guji chubanshe, 1994.

Young, Ernest. *The Presidency of Yuan Shih-k'ai: Liberalism and Dictatorship in Early Republican China.* Ann Arbor: University of Michigan Press, 1977.

Yu Cuiling 于翠玲. *Yinshua wenhua de chuanbao guiji* 印刷文化的传播轨迹 (The dissemination trajectory of print culture). Beijing: Zhongguo chuanmei daxue chubanshe, 2015.

———. "Zhong-Xi zhishi jiaohui yu puji de yangben: Minguo chuqi 'riyong baike quanshu' de tezheng yu jiazhi" 中西知识交汇与普及的样本：民国初期「日用百科全書书」的特征与价值 (Specimens of the confluence and popularization of Chinese and Western knowledge: The distinctive features and value of early Republican "daily-use encyclopedias"). In *Yinshua chuban yu zhishi huanliu, shiliu shiji yihou de Dongya* 印刷出版与知识环流：十六世纪以後的东亚 (Printing, publishing, and knowledge exchange: East Asia post-sixteenth century), edited by Guanxi daxue wenhua jiaoshexue jiaoyu yanjiu zhongxin chuban bowuguan 关西大学文化交涉学教育研究中心出版博物馆, pp. 277-292. Shanghai: Shanghai renmin chubanshe, 2011.

Yu Shimei 于式枚, Miao Quansun 缪荃孙, Wu Shijian 吴士鉴, Yang Zhongxi 杨钟羲, and Tao Baolian 陶葆廉. "Kaiguan banfa jiu tiao" 开馆办法九条 (Nine points on the establishment and operation of the commission). In Zhu Shizhe 朱师辙, *Qingshi shuwen* 清史述闻 (Record of things heard regarding Qing history), pp. 82-91. Shanghai: Shanghai shudian chubanshe, 2009 [1957].

Yu, Zhu. "The Vision of New China Suggested by the Politics of Language: Liu Shipei's Interpretation of the 'Rectification of Names' and Its Utopian Moment." *Frontiers of Literary Studies in China* 8, no. 3 (2014): 468-491.

Yuan Jin 袁進. *Cong chuantong dao xianzai: Zhongguo jindai wenxue de lishi guiji* 从传统到现代：中国近代文学的历史轨迹 (From tradition to modernity: The trajectory of Chinese *jindai* literature). Shanghai: Dongfang chuban zhongxin, 2018.

Yuan Shikai 袁世凱. *Yuan Shikai quanji* 袁世凱全集 (Collected works of Yuan Shikai). Zhengzhou: Henan daxue chubanshe, 2013.

Yue Sibing 樂嗣炳. "Jiangsu sheng jiaoyuhui suo zhengji guoyu jinxing kunnan wenti de yijian" 江蘇省教育會所徵集國語進行困難問題底意見 (Opinions collected by the Jiangsu Provincial Education Association regarding the difficulties and problems of implementing the national language). *Guoyu yuekan* 國語月刊 1, no. 10 (1922): 1-11.

———. "Zenyang yanjiu guoyu de shengdiao" 怎樣研究國語的聲調 (How to research the tones of the national language). *Guoyu yuekan* 國語月刊 1, no. 8 (1922): 1-5.

Zarrow, Peter. *After Empire: The Conceptual Transformation of the Chinese State, 1885-1924.* Stanford, CA: Stanford University Press, 2012.

———. *China in War and Revolution, 1895-1949.* London: Routledge, 2005.

———. "Old Myth into New History: The Building Blocks of Liang Qichao's 'New History.'" *Historiography East and West* 1, no. 2 (2003): 204-241.

Zeng Guofan 曾國藩. *Zeng Guofan quanji* 曾國藩全集 (Complete works of Zeng Guofan). Taipei: Hanyuan chubanshe, 1976.

Zhang Guoru 张国茹 and Guo Bixuan 郭必选. "Yan'an shiqi jiceng zhengquan jianshe yanjiu" 延安時期基层政权建设研究 (Study of the grassroots construction of state power during the Yan'an period). In *Yan'an xue yanjiu* 延安学研究 (Yan'an studies), edited by Guo Bixuan, vol. 1, p. 145. Beijing: Hongqi chubanshe, 2005.

Zhang Hanmo. "From Myth to History: Historicizing a Sage for the Sake of Persuasion in the Yellow Emperor Narratives." *Journal of Chinese Humanities* 3 (2017): 91–116.

Zhang Hao 張灝 (Hao Chang). "Zhongguo jindai sixiang shi de zhuanxing shidai" 中國近代思想史的轉型時代 (The transitional period in the history of modern Chinese thought). *Ershiyi shiji shuangyuekan* 二十一世紀雙月刊 52 (April 1999): 29–39.

Zhang Juan 张娟. *Wanshi buqiuren: Jiating shiyong xiaobaike* 万事不求人：家庭实用小百科 (Myriad matters about which you don't need to ask: Small practical encyclopedia for the household). Beijing: Renmin junyi chubanshe, 2007.

Zhang Mengmeng 张濛濛. "Cong Zhang Taiyan Shuowen shouke biji kan Zhang Taiyan dui Yu Yue, Sun Yirang ershi de xueshu jicheng" 从章太炎说文授课笔记看章太炎对俞樾, 孙诒让二师的学术继承 (Research on Zhang Taiyan's academic inheritance from Yu Yue and Sun Yirang based on notes from Zhang Taiyan's lectures on *Shuowen*). *Journal of Qiqihar University* (2015): 95–98.

Zhang Shoudong 章壽棟 et al. *Guoyin xin jiaoben jiaoshou shu* 國音新教本教授書 (Pedagogical guide to the new national pronunciation primer). Shanghai: Shangwu, 1931.

Zhang Xiaohui 张晓辉 and Qin Hongfang 秦洪芳. "Feng-shan jiangjun beici an xintan" 凤山将军被刺案新探 (A new examination of the assassination of General-in-Chief Fungšan). *Jinyang xuekan* 晋阳学刊 2 (2004): 85–86.

Zhang Xueqian 張學謙. "Wuying Dian ben *Ershisi shi* jiaokan shimo kao" 武英殿本《二十四史》校刊始末考 (Examination of the editing and publication history of the Wuying Dian versions of the *Twenty-four dynastic histories*). *Wenshi* 文史, no. 1 (2014): 91–122.

Zhang Zai 張載. "Ximing" 西銘 (Western inscription). Translated by Brian W. Van Norden. http://faculty.vassar.edu/brvannor/Phil210/Translations/Western%20Inscription.pdf.

Zhang Zongxiang 张宗祥. "Chen zuanxiu Qingshi banfa" 陈纂修清史办法 (Submitted procedure for compiling a history of the Qing). In Zhu Shizhe 朱师辙, *Qingshi shuwen* 清史述闻 (Record of things heard regarding Qing history), pp. 177–194. Shanghai: Shanghai shudian chubanshe, 2009 [1957].

Zhankai fandui wushen de douzheng 展開反對巫神的鬥爭 (Conducting the Anti-Shaman Campaign). Yan'an: Shaan-Gan-Ning Bianqu zhengfu bangongting, 1944.

Zhao Chaogou 赵超构. *Yan'an yiyue* 延安一月 (One month in Yan'an). Shanghai: Shanghai shudian, 1992 [1945].

Zhao Lu. *In Pursuit of the Great Peace: Han Dynasty Classicism and the Making of Early Medieval Literati Culture*. Albany: State University of New York Press, 2020.

Zhao Wanli 趙萬裏 (Lizhou 蠡舟). "Ping Zhu Shizhe *Qingshi gao* yiwen zhi" 評朱式轍清史稿藝文志 (Review of Zhu Shizhe's bibliographical treatise in the *Draft history of the Qing*). In *Youguan "Qingshi gao" bianyin jingguo ji ge fang yijian huibian* 有關清史稿編印經過及各方意見彙編 (Collection of material relating to the process of compiling and publishing *Draft history of the Qing* as well the as opinions of various parties), edited by Xu Shishen 許師慎, vol. 2, pp. 1151–1155. Taipei: Zhonghua Minguo shiliao yanjiu zhongxin, 1979.

Zhao Yongji 趙永紀, ed. *Qingdai xueshu cidian* 清代學術辭典 (Dictionary of Qing dynasty scholarship). Beijing: Xueyuan chubanshe, 2004.

Zheng Dahua 鄭大華. *Wan-Qing xixiang shi* 晚晴思想史 (History of late-Qing thought). Changsha: Hunan shifan daxue chubanshe, 2005.

Zheng'an 正厂 (黃正厂). "Biaozhunyu yu guoyu biaozhun" 標準語與國語標準 (Standard language and standard national language). *Guoyu yuekan* 國語月刊 1, no. 12 (1923): 1–3.

Zhi-kuan 志寬 and Pei-kuan 培寬. *Dan Qingyu* 單清語 | *Gargata manju gisun* (Single Manchu words). Xylograph. Jingzhou: Jingzhou fanyi zongxue, 1891. Microfilm made from copy at Tenri University Library.

———. *Duiyin jizi* 對音輯字 | *dui yen ji dzi bithe* (Assembled characters for transcription). 2 vols. Xylograph. Jingzhou: Jingzhou fanyi zongxue, 1890. Copy held at Capital Library, Beijing.

———. *Qingwen zonghui* 清文總彙 (Comprehensive collection of Qing writing). Xylograph. Jingzhou: Jingzhou zhufang fanyi zongxue, 1897. Copy held at Peking University Library; call number: 5975.6 4414.

———. *Qingwen zonghui* 清文總彙 (Comprehensive collection of Qing writing), afterword Feng-shan 鳳山 (1897). Xylograph. Jingzhou: Jingzhou zhufang fanyi zongxue, 1911. Copy held at Capital Library, Beijing; call number 乙・一63.

Zhiwuxue dacidian 植物學大辭典 (Dictionary of botanical nomenclature). Shanghai: Shangwu yinshuguan, 1918.

Zhong, Yurou. *Chinese Grammatology: Script Revolution and Literary Modernity, 1916–1958*. New York: Columbia University Press, 2019.

"Zhonghua Minguo guoyu yanjiuhui shizhou nian jinian ge" 中華民國國語研究會十週年紀念歌 (Song commemorating the tenth anniversary of the Chinese National Language Research Association). *Quanguo guoyu yundong dahui huikan* 全國國語運動大會會刊 2 (1926): 12.

Zhou Zuoren 周作人. "Huajing" 花鏡 (*Mirror of flowers*). In *Yedu chao* 夜讀抄 (Notes from nighttime reading), edited by Zhi An 止庵, pp. 94–98. Shijiazhuang: Hebei jiaoyu chubanshe, 2002.

———. *Zhongguo xin wenxue de yuanliu* 中國新文學的源流 (The origins of the new Chinese literature). Beiping: Renwen shudian, 1934.

Zhu Huazhong 朱华忠 and Wang Jilu 王记录. "Qian Daxin zai Yuan shixue shang de gangxian ji yingxiang" 钱大昕在元史学上的贡献及影响 (Contribution and influence of Qian Daxin upon historical research into the Yuan). *Xinan shifan daxue xuebao* 西南师范大学学报 6 (1997): 103–107.

Zhu Qianzhi 朱謙之. *Zhongguo Jingjiao: Zhongguo gudai Jidujiao yanjiu* 中國景教：中國古代基督教研究 (Chinese Nestorianism: Studies in ancient Chinese Christianity). Beijing: Dongfang chubanshe, 1993.

Zhu Shi 朱軾, Cai Shiyuan 蔡世遠, and Jiang Zhang 張江, eds. *Lidai mingchen zhuan: Sanshiwu juan, xu pian: Wu juan* 歷代名臣傳：三十五卷，續編：五卷 (Biographies of famed officials over the centuries, 35 fascicles; continuation, 5 fascicles). N.p., 1729.

Zhu Shizhe 朱师辙. *Qingshi shuwen* 清史述闻 (Record of things heard regarding Qing history). Shanghai: Shanghai shudian chubanshe, 2009 [1957].

Zhu Zuyan 朱祖延, comp. and ed. *Erya gulin* 爾雅詁林 (The forest of explanations on the progress toward correctness). Wuhan: Hubei jiaoyu chubanshe, 1996. 5 vols, plus *Xulu* 敘錄 (Catalogue). 1998.

Zou Ailian 邹爱莲, Han Yongfu 韩永福, and Lu Jing 卢经. "*Qingshi gao* zuanxiu shimo yanjiu" 《清史稿》纂修始末研究 (Research on the compilation history of the *Draft history of the Qing*). *Qingshi yanjiu* 清史研究 1 (2007): 86–94.

CONTRIBUTORS

Zvi Ben-Dor Benite (PhD, UCLA) is Professor in the Departments of History and Middle Eastern and Islamic Studies at New York University. His research centers on the interaction between religions in world history and cultural exchanges across vast space and time. He is the author of *The Dao of Muhammad: A Cultural History of Muslims in Late Imperial China* (Harvard University Press) and *The Ten Lost Tribes: A World History* (Oxford University Press); and co-editor and translator of *Modern Middle Eastern Jewish Thought: Writings on Identity, Culture, and Politics* (Brandeis University Press).

Janet Chen (PhD, Yale University) is currently Professor of History and East Asian Studies at Princeton University. She is the author of *Guilty of Indigence: The Urban Poor in China, 1900–1950* (Princeton University Press).

Chu Pingyi (PhD, UCLA) is currently serving as a research fellow at the Institute of History and Philology, Academia Sinica, in Taiwan. He works on the history of science and issues related to Christianity in China during the seventeenth and eighteenth centuries.

Joshua Fogel (PhD, Columbia University) is Professor of History at York University in Toronto. His work concentrates on the cultural dimension of Sino-Japanese relations. He is the author, editor, or translator of sixty-seven books, most recently *Maiden Voyage: The Senzaimaru and the Creation of Modern Sino-Japanese Relations* (University of California Press) and *A Friend in Deed: Lu Xun, Uchiyama Kanzō, and the Intellectual World of Shanghai on the Eve of War* (Association for Asian Studies).

Theodore Huters (PhD, Stanford) is Emeritus Professor of Chinese at UCLA, and currently editor of the translation journal *Renditions*. He has devoted most of his scholarly attention to the late Qing–early Republican period of literary and intellectual history. His published work includes *Bringing the World Home: Appropriating the West in Late Qing and Early Republican China* (University of Hawai'i Press).

Joan Judge (PhD, Columbia University) is a Fellow of the Royal Society of Canada and Professor in the Department of History at York University in Toronto. She is the author most recently of *Republican Lens: Gender, Visuality, and Experience in the Early Chinese Periodical Press* (University of California Press), and *The Precious Raft of History: The Past, the West, and the Woman Question in China* (Stanford University Press). She is currently engaged in a project with the working title "China's Mundane Revolution: Cheap Print, Vernacular Knowledge, and Common Reading in the Long Republic."

Kang Xiaofei (PhD, Columbia University) is Associate Professor of Religion at the George Washington University. Her book-length work includes *The Cult of the Fox: Power, Gender, and Popular Religion in Late Imperial and Modern China* (Columbia University Press). She has published on gender, ethnicity, and Chinese religion. She is now finishing a manuscript on gender, religion, and the twentieth-century Communist Revolution in China.

Peter C. Perdue (PhD, Harvard University) is Professor of History at Yale University. He is a member of the American Academy of Arts and Sciences. His publications include *Exhausting the Earth: State and Peasant in Hunan, 1500–1850 A.D.* (Harvard University Press), *China*

Marches West: The Qing Conquest of Central Eurasia (Harvard University Press), and *Asia Inside Out* (3 vols., Harvard University Press).

Mårten Söderblom Saarela (PhD, Princeton University) is an Assistant Research Fellow, Institute of Modern History, Academia Sinica. He is the author of *The Early Modern Travels of Manchu: A Script and Its Study in East Asia and Europe* (University of Pennsylvania Press).

Ori Sela (PhD, Princeton University) is Senior Lecturer (Associate Professor) of East Asian Studies at Tel Aviv University and is currently serving as chair. He is particularly interested in the reciprocal relationship between intellectual history and sociopolitical history at various crossroads in China's past, in tandem with the history of science and technology. His 2018 book *China's Philological Turn* (Columbia University Press) was awarded Levenson Prize's honorary mention in 2020.

Peter Zarrow (PhD, Columbia University) is Professor of History at the University of Connecticut. The author most recently of *Educating China: Knowledge, Society and Textbooks in a Modernizing World* (Cambridge University Press) and *Abolishing Boundaries: Global Utopias in the Formation of Modern Chinese Political Thought* (SUNY Press), his research focuses on Chinese intellectual and cultural history, and he is now exploring national heritage in East Asia.

INDEX

abdication: of Emperor Xian of Han, 81–82, 83, 84; of last Qing emperor, 52, 70, 81, 84; legend of Yao and Shun, 80–83, 84, 85–86, 87, 88; *shanrang* and *yirang*, 85–86, 87, 88, 91n52, 91n55
Adam and Eve, 36
aesthetics, 125–127, 131, 138n29
agnotology, 142, 153
Akahata Incident of June 1908, 55
Alekseev, V. M., 193
almanacs (*lao huangli*), 144
American Eugenics Society, 159
Analects, 94, 116n37, 121, 135n8, 135n10, 137n15
ancient style prose (*guwen*), 97, 100, 105, 115n18
anti-Christian sentiment, 37
anti-Japanese sentiment, 58–59, 61, 64
antiquity: debates on, 212–13; invention of, 75–76; "restoration of," 75–77, 87, 88; *Shuowen jiezi* and, 206, 207–208, 212–13, 218n3
Anti-Shaman Campaign (1944–1945), 12, 220–221, 223, 230–232, 234, 238nn39–40; propaganda for, 224, 234, 235
Arabjur, 18
area studies, 1
Aristotle, 36–37
assimilation, 78, 192
Ayuki Khan, 18, 20, 28

Babylon, 39, 41
Bai Conghai, confession of, 224, 226, 229
baike quanshu, 143, 145, 155n12, 156n24
bannermen: as clerks, 187; works by, 184–185, 193, 194, 196
Bao Yuwan, 198
Bao Zheng, 233–234
Barmé, Geremie, 10
Barthes, Roland, "readerly" and "writerly" texts, 114
beauty and the sublime, 127–128, 129

Beida Geyao xuehui (Peking University Folksong Study Society), 156n36
Beijinghua (Beiping pronunciation), 162, 172, 173–174
Bell, John, 18, 28–29
Bellamy, Edward, *Looking Backward*, 139n42
Belt and Road Initiative, 17
Berlin, Isaiah, positive and negative liberty, 122
Bible, 36, 39–40, 41, 43, 46, 49n27
blind storytellers, 228
Boxer indemnity funds, 195
Boxer Rebellion, 119, 129, 141, 196
Brahmanism, 40, 41–42
Brokaw, Cynthia, 154n5
Brook, Timothy, 74
Buddhism: banned in Tang, 43; Cai Yuanpei and, 118, 120, 124–125, 128, 129, 135n1; concept of self, 128, 138–139n33; confession, 233; denounced by Christians, 32, 37; in the early twentieth century, 222; *seng* (monks), 35, 44; Shinshū sect, 129; terminology, 44, 45; Yang Rongzhi's views on, 40, 42

Cai Hesen, 177n25
Cai Yuanpei: on aesthetics and aesthetics education, 125–129, 130–131, 134, 139n41; and China's educational system, 119–120, 123, 130; on civic morality as liberty, equality, and fraternity, 120–123; classical citations explaining Western concepts, 120–122, 138n20; as Kantian, 118, 119, 124, 128–129, 131, 132; life and career, 118–119, 130; on "militant citizenship," 119–120; on phenomenal and noumenal, 123–128, 130, 131; political views and activities, 118, 119, 132–133, 135n4, 140n49; as president of Peking University, 118, 130; "Replacing Religion with Aesthetics," 127, 138n29; on

Cai Yuanpei (cont.)
  "scientific personal cultivation," 131–132; as transitional figure, 11–12, 132–134; views on Confucianism, 12, 122–123, 129, 133, 134; views on education, 118, 119–120, 123, 125–126, 129, 138n23; views on evolution, 129, 130, 133; views on religion, 124, 127, 129, 130, 131; views shaped by Buddhism, 118, 120, 124–125, 128, 129, 130, 135n1; warning to students, 130; works of, 118, 119
Cambridge History of China, 204
Canon of Yao, 86
Cao Cao, 81–82
Cao Pi, 81–82, 84, 91n60, 91n62
cartography, 22–23
caste system (India), 41
Catholicism, 32, 36, 40, 43. See also Diaz, Emmanuel Jr.; Jesuit missionaries
celibacy, 43–44
Central Asia, 17, 42, 86; Nestorianism and, 38, 40; Tulišen's travel account, 18, 23, 26, 27–28, 29
"century of humiliation," 3, 5
Chambers, Robert E., 38
Chambers's Information for the People, 145, 155n23
Chang family of Yan'an, 220
changran zhenji (unchanged and still), 44
Chao Yuen Ren, 162, 165, 175, 176n9, 178n42, 179n57; "Wusheng de biaozhun," 163*fig.*, 177n19
Chau, Adam, 237n28
Chen Changzhi, 218
Chen Duxiu, 6
Chen Guoqiu, 111
Chen Haozi (Chen Fuyao), 157n47; *Huajing* (Mirror of flowers), 142–143, 148–153, 157n44, 157n46, 157n57, 157n67, 158n62; "Wondrous Methods for Grafting Plants," 149–150
Chen Jingxi, 147
Chen Mei, 155n17
Chen Shou, 81–82
Chen Yan, 106–107, 112
Chen Yinque (Yinke), 194, 195
Chen Zhan, *Shuowen jiezi zhengyi*, 218n2
Cheng, King, of Zhou, 91n53
Cheng Peiyuan, 217, 218

Chengdu garrison, 185
Cheng-Zhu tradition, 108, 208, 209. See also Song Learning
Chiang Kai-shek, 171
chihua/sekka (becoming red), 59, 60, 61, 62, 65–66
Chinese civilization: crisis of, in *jindai* era, 95; as descendants of the dragon, 8; "5,000 years of," 4–7, 73, 74, 76, 88; origins of, 41, 47, 48; *Shuowen* and, 206, 213, 214; and Western technology, 211; and the Yellow Emperor, 7, 8, 76. See also national essence
Chinese Communist Party (CCP): anti-shaman campaign, 220–221, 223, 230–232, 238nn39–40; campaigns, 229–230, 231, 232, 235; class struggle, 235; as custodian of a 5,000-year-old civilization, 4; failures, 62, 66; founding of, 58; land policies resembling Taipings', 66; language use, 12, 221, 227–228, 234; Long March, 66, 222–223; and modernization, 235; as political party in capitalist country, 66; pre-1927, 61; Rectification Movement, 223, 229–230, 231, 232, 234–235, 238n38; rhetoric and policies on religion, 222–223, 224
Chinese history and world history, 8–9
Chinese humanities, 181, 182
Chinese language, 6, 9–10, 12; written, 9–10, 214. See also *guanhua*; *guoyu*; national language standardization; *Shuowen jiezi*; vernacular writing
"Chinese learning as essence, Western learning for function," 112
Chinese national character, 57–58, 60
"Chinese origins" theory, 8, 122
Chongzhen emperor, 37
Christianity: arrival in China, 33, 35; Cai Yuanpei's contempt for, 129; and Confucianism, 33; in Ming, 32, 33; of the Taipings, 52, 56; in Tang, 33, 36–37, 47. See also Catholicism; Jesuit missionaries; *Jingjiao*; Nestorian stele; Protestantism
"civilizational state" versus "nation-state," 5
Cixi, 184
classical Chinese: and the Chinese renaissance of Hu Shi, 182; and New Sinology, 13; poetry, 113; in schools,

167–168, 169, 170–171; and *Shuowen jiezi*, 205; Staunton on, 24
Classic of Poetry, 103, 105, 136n12, 137n15
Classics: on liberty, equality, and fraternity, 120–122; rejection of, 207, 213; relationship of writing to, 103, 104, 108; in school curriculum, 169; and textual research, 105–106, 208
Commercial Press, 150
common people, 109, 175; terms for, 142, 154n3
communism: and the Taipings, 52, 56; terms for, 53–54, 59, 60, 61, 62, 65–66
Communist Manifesto, 55; translations of, 55–56, 67nn9–10
community compacts, 232
Conference on the National Language Movement (1925), 175
Conference to Unify Pronunciation (1913), 161
confession, 224, 230, 232–233, 235; of shamans, 220, 221, 224, 226, 229, 231–232, 235, 238n40
Confucianism: Cai Yuanpei's views on, 12, 122–123, 129, 133, 134; and Christianity, 32, 33, 39, 43, 44, 47, 48; community compacts, 232; moral rehabilitation, 232–233, 238n48; reinvention of, through new vocabulary, 120; rejection of, 62, 207; in schools, 123; and shamans, 234; theory of *li* and *qi*, 41; today, 134; and writing, 105–106. *See also* Classics; Confucius
Confucius, 106, 109, 136n12, 138n20, 210. *See also Analects*
constitutionalism, 51, 52, 186
continuity versus rupture, 2
Council of State, 80, 85
criticism and self-criticism, 230, 231, 232–233, 235
Crossley, Pamela, 29
cultural and national identities, 118
Cultural Revolution, 53, 156n30

Daehan Jeguk (Great State of Korea), 74
Dahai (Wencheng), 189
Dai Zhen, 209, 211
daily-use compendia, 144, 149–150, 152, 153, 156n30. *See also* myriad treasures

Dai Nippon Teikoku (Empire of Great Japan), 73–74
dao, 104, 124–125, 209; and writing, 105, 108, 116n64
Daoism, 32, 222, 233; terminology, 44
Da Qin, meaning of term, 39
Da Qing diguo quantu (Complete map of the great Qing state), 74
Da Qing diguo xinbian fadian (New legal code of the great Qing state), 74
Da Qin jingjiao liuxing Zhongguo bei (Stele commemorating the spread of the luminous teaching from Great Qin to China), 32. *See also* Nestorian stele
Darwinian selection, 131, 133, 140n47
datong, 123, 138n20
Deng Xiaoping, 66
Di (supreme deity), 72
Di Kui, 217
Diamond Sutra, 128, 138–139n33
Diaz, Emmanuel Jr. (Yang Manuo): on Adam and Eve, 36; commentary on Nestorian stele inscription, 34, 35–37, 44, 47–48; on date of stele, 48n2; on the emperor, 36–37; on superstition, 37; on use of *seng*, 35–36; use of term *Jingjiao*, 35, 36
Dictionary of National Pronunciation, 162, 171
diguo (state led by the Thearch), 73–75, 89; *diguozhuyi* (imperialism), 72; *Zhonghua diguo* (Empire of China), 70
Ding Fubao, 205, 213–214, 218n1
discursive argument, 104–105
divination, 82, 84, 87, 225. *See also Yijing*
Downing, Charles Toogood, 31n19
Draft History of the Qing. *See Qingshi gao*
dragons, 7, 8, 82
Duan Yucai, 210–211, 212, 214; *Jigu ge Shuowen ding*, 216; *Shuowen jiezi zhu*, 216
dynastic histories, 6, 190, 199. *See also Qingshi gao*

education: in aesthetics, 125–126; classical and vernacular language, 167–168, 169, 170–171; and local dialects, 173; in Manchu language, 13, 180–181, 185; and national language, 161–163, 166–169, 173, 177n35; Qing school system, 123, 196; vocational, 120; Western, 126. *See also* Cai Yuanpei

278 | Index

Education Ministry (Qing), 123
Education Ministry (Republic), 161, 162, 164, 165, 167; and national language standardization, 171, 173, 178n56
Eight Nation army, 196
Elder Brother Society, 223
Eliade, Mircea, 235–236n1
Elman, Benjamin, 219n8
emic and etic knowledge, 141, 151, 224
Encyclopaedia Britannica, 145, 155n23
encyclopedias: *baike quanshu*, 143, 145, 155n12, 156n24; Japanese, 145; related genres, 147; Western-derived, 143, 145, 152, 155n12. *See also* daily-use compendia; myriad treasures
Engels, Friedrich, *Communist Manifesto*, 55–56
England, Naitō Konan on, 63, 65
En-hua, 198; *Baqi yiwen bianmu*, 194, 197
Enlightenment values, 221, 222
entangled history (*histoire croisée*), 29
epigraphy, 34, 208
"equality," 121, 122
Erdeni, 189
Erya, 216, 217–218
essay writing, 151
etymology, 54, 205, 210. *See also* philological studies
eunuchs, 78, 81
evidential scholarship (*kaozhengxue*), 1, 40, 96–97, 204, 209; in Japan, 215; study of Nestorian stele, 34–35, 39, 46. *See also* Han learning
examination system, 118, 120, 187–188
exorcism, 220, 228, 233. *See also* shamans

Fairbank, John K., 15
Fan Xiangshan, 165
Fan Xizeng, 193
Fang Bao, 108
Fang Dongshu, 106, 112; *Zhaomei zhanyan*, 101
Fang Xiaoyue, "Wo zhi gailiang wenxue guan," 108–109
fangfa (conquest of arms), 81, 83, 86
Feng Guifen, 210–211, 217
Feng Wenchang, 49n5
Feng Yuxiang, 63

Feng-kuan (Bao Bian), 195–196, 198; bibliographical précis, 195–197
fengshui, 84
Fengtian clique, 63
fiction, 93, 111, 113
First Sino-Japanese War, 145, 212
Five Emperors, 72, 73, 80. *See also* Yao and Shun; sage-kings; Yellow Emperor
five phases (*wuxing*), 39, 45, 228
Five Races, 85, 86, 91n72
five virtues, 25
Fletcher, Joseph, 28
folklore studies, 147
fortune-telling, 39, 145, 222, 228
Foucault, Michel, 224
Four Books, 185
four departments (*sike*), 94
"fraternity," 121, 122–123
French Revolution, 122; liberty, equality, and fraternity, 120–123
Fu Sinian, 6, 8, 165–166, 177n26
Fuchs, Walter, 197
Fujibayashi Tadayoshi, 54
Fungšan, 185–187, 197
Futsu-Wa hōritsu ji (French-Japanese legal vocabulary; Fujibayashi and Kabuto), 54
Fuxi, 41

Gaubil, Father Antoine, translation of Tulišen's travel account, 19, 22–23, 29
Geddes, Patrick, 131, 139n42
geomancy, 39, 84, 222
German Romanticism, 131
Goethe, Johann Wolfgang von, 131
Gojong (Korean monarch), 74
Gong Zizhen, 95, 102–103, 217
Gongsun Yan, 135n9
Goodman, Howard, 82, 91n60
Grant, Asahel, 46
Great Kantō Earthquake, 58
Great Production Movement (1943–1944), 223
"Great State," 74
Great Treason Incident of 1910, 55
Gregorian calendar, 70
Gu Jiegang, 7–8, 73, 88, 89n16; doubts on antiquity, 212; *Gouqiu Zhongguo tushu jihua shu*, 146, 156n35; study of mass culture, 146, 147, 156n32

Gu Tinglong, 146–147, 156n30
Gu Yanwu, 97, 210
Guangxu emperor, 74
Guangxu renaissance, 181–183, 189, 197
guanhua (official language), 160, 162, 163, 165, 168
Guanhua zhuyin zimu bao (Phonetically annotated newspaper of the official language), 162
Gui Youguang (Xifu), 106
Guo Houjue, 164–165
Guo Licheng, "Embarking on This Path of Folklore Studies," 147
Guo Moruo, 94
Guo Tuotuo, *Zhongshu shu* (Book on planting trees), 149
Guomin baoku quanshu (Complete treasury for citizens), 144
guoming (state destiny), 77, 78
guoyin (national pronunciation), 161–162, 172–174, 178n46. *See also* national language standardization
Guoyin changyong zihui (Commonly used vocabulary of national pronunciation), 173–174
guoyu (national language), 159, 171, 175, 198; term, 171, 176n3; tones, 164–166, 172, 174, 177n22, 177n29; two types of, 165; use in education, 161–163, 166–169, 171, 173, 175, 177n35. *See also* Li Jinxi; national language standardization
Guoyu Luomazi (Gwoyeu Romatzyh/GR), 170, 171, 172, 173, 178n42
guwen (ancient style prose), 97, 100, 105, 115n18
gu yuanfeng er sheng erqi (agitating the primordial wind and producing the two modes of *qi*), 44–45

Han Yu, 108
Han dynasty, 86–87. *See also* Han learning; Han-Wei transition
Han learning, 96, 98–99, 204, 209. *See also* evidential scholarship
Han race (*Hanzu*), 7, 73, 75, 76, 78
Han shu (Book of the Han), 190
Han-Wei transition, 81–83, 91n60
Haneda Tōru, 26, 27
Hang Shijun, 38

Hanlin Academy, 118, 184, 191
Hanyu da zidian, 94
Hao Chang, 133
Hartog, François, "regime of historicity," 5, 73, 74–75
Hauer, Erich, 198
Hayashi Jussai, 216
He Shaoji, 217
He Zhuo, 97
Heimin shinbun (The commoners' newspaper), 55
Higher School of Manchu and Mongolian Languages, 187
High Qing, 17, 204
Hinduism, 41
historical clock, 69–70, 74, 76, 88
"historical nihilism," 153
historiography, 8–9, 88, 181; Qing, 189, 192, 197, 198
history as linear, 133, 171, 234
History of the Jin, 196
Hong Xiuquan, 53
Hongxian Emperor. *See* Yuan Shikai
Hou Han shu (History of the Later Han), biography of Huangfu Gui, 77, 78
Houyi, 46
Howard, Ebenezer, 139n42
Hu Linyi, 52
Hu Shi, 6, 113, 118; notion of Chinese Renaissance, 181–182, 198
Hu Zhuo, 217
Huan, Emperor, of Han, 78
Huang Lin, 100, 101–102, 105–106, 108, 115n8, 115n18, 116n64
Huang Runhua, 186, 199n7
Huang Zheng'an, 168, 177n36
Huangchao jingshi wenbian (Collected essays on statecraft of the glorious dynasty), 209
huangdi (August Thearch), 71–72
Huangfu Gui, 77–79
Hui (Muslims), 42
Hui Dong, 97, 207, 210
Hummel, Arthur, 7, 8
Huxley, Thomas, *Evolution and Ethics*, 107
Hyakka zensho (Complete compendium of a hundred branches of knowledge), 155n23

Ichino Meian, 216
Ikeda Makoto, 67n18
Imanishi Shunjū: annotated translation of Tulišen's travel account, 18, 19, 27–28; career and publications, 26–27; on Chinese and Manchu versions, 21–22; discovery of Manchu copy of travel account, 26; and Manchu studies, 29; on significance of Tulišen's account, 28
Imperialist Time, 141, 142, 143
Indian nationalism, 215
Inoue Enryō, 129
Islam, 38, 40, 42
isolation of the writer, 106, 107, 112

Japan: anti-Japanese sentiment, 58–59, 61, 64; Christianity, 33; encyclopedias and related genres, 143, 145, 146, 155n21, 157n46; fear of Russia, 61; joint humanistic research institute, 195; philology, 17, 216
Jesuit missionaries, 15, 22, 33, 35–37. *See also* Diaz, Emmanuel Jr.; Gaubil, Father Antoine
Jesus Christ, 39–40, 98; "younger brother" of, 53
Ji (sage-king), 121, 137n16
Jia Kui, 86–87
Jia Sixie, *Qimin yaoshu* (Essential techniques for the welfare of the people), 149, 151
Jiangsu Book Bureau, 183
Jiangsu Provincial Education Association, 167
Jiangxi Soviet, 222
jiao (beliefs), 32, 34–35, 42, 43, 47, 48. *See also* religion; *zongjiao*
Jiaqing emperor, 81
Jiating baike quanshu (Household encyclopedia), 150
Jin Zhaofan, 189, 190
jindai (the modern era), 51, 95
Jingjiao, 33–34; Diaz's use of term, 35–36; Yang Rongzhi's use of term, 38–39, 43, 44
Jingjiao houxue (later followers of Nestorianism/Christianity), 34, 38, 49n5
Jingjiao tang (Nestorian/Christian churches), 34, 49n5
Jingjing (author of Nestorian stele inscription), 44

Jingjing (Bible), 40. *See also* Bible
Jingzhou garrison, 181, 184–185, 187; Comprehensive Translation School, 185
Jin-liang, 188
Judaism, 40–41, 42
judicial systems, 46, 220, 233–34, 238n48. *See also* public trials
junzheng (virtue-based rulership), 76, 77. *See also* political virtue
Juzhen Tang (Assembled Treasures Hall) print shop, 185, 200n28

Kabuto Kuninori, 54
Kaifeng, Jews of, 41
Kanda Nobuo, 27
Kang Youwei, 7; *Datongshu*, 138n20
Kangxi emperor, 20, 21, 22, 24–25
Kansai University Library, 146
Kant, Immanuel: Cai Yuanpei and, 118, 119, 128–129, 132; in China today, 134; concept of aesthetics, 128–129; notion of literary autonomy, 110; notion of noumenal world, 124, 125–126, 131, 138n32; thing-in-itself, 128, 131
kaozhengxue. See evidential scholarship
Karakhan Declaration, 61
Kariya Ekisai, 216
Katz, Paul, 233
Kawai Seiichirō, 59
Kawakami Hajime, 55, 55–56
Keevak, Michael, 34
Kinoshita Naoe, *Hi no hashira* (Pillar of fire), 54
kinsei (the modern era), 51
Kobayashi Kamin, *Atarashiki yōgo no izumi* (The source of new terms), 60
kogaku (ancient learning), 215
Kojima Seisai, 216
kokugaku, 216
Kong Yingda, 85–86
Kongzi. *See* Confucius
Koselleck, Reinhart, 7, 16, 74–75; *Sediments of Time*, 5
Kōtoku Shūsui, 55
Kropotkin, Pyotr, 131, 133
Kui-shan, "Origin of Manchu Writing," 190–192, 197
Kung Ling-wei, 194
Kushida Tamizō, 55–56

kyōsan, 56. *See also* communism
Kyoto University, 51

Lakcaha Jecende Takûraha ejehe bithe (A book describing the embassy to distant territories). *See* Tulišen's travel account; *Yiyulu*
language reform, 179n68, 206. *See also* national language standardization
Late Qing, 204
Lau, D. C., 94
"learning" (*xue*), 1. *See also* evidential scholarship; Han learning; Song Learning
Legge, James, 8, 26
leishu (category books), 144, 155n10
Lenin, Vladimir, 61
Leontiev, Alexei, 20; translation of Tulišen's travel account, 19, 20–21, 25–26
Levenson, Joseph, "museumification," 112
Li Deqi, 194–195
Li Hongzao, 211, 217
Li Hongzhang, 58, 211, 217
Li Jinxi: "Diagram Showing the Evolution of Chinese for the Last Four Millenniums," 159–161, 160*fig.*, 169–172, 174–175, 176n4; on the "Hanzi revolution," 178n45; language standardization, 159, 178n46, 179n57; on linguistic change, 175–176; lyrics for commemorative song, 175; as Mao's teacher, 159; and national language education, 169, 178n38; on tonal differentiation, 164; tour to review national language education, 167; at Zhonghua Books, 159, 177n36
Li, Leo (Li Zhizao), 33
Li Lisan, 177n25
Li Ruzhen, *Jinghua yuan* (Flowers in the mirror), 145
Li Shizhen, *Bencao gangmu* (Materia medica), 151
Li Xiucheng, 52
Li Yu, *Xianqing yuji* (Casual expressions of idle feeling), 151, 158n76
Li Yuan, 83
Liang Qichao, 8, 111, 113, 118; "New Historiography," 6–7; pamphlet against Yuan Shikai, 71; *Qingdai xuexu gailun*, 95; support for Qing dynastic history, 190, 192

Liang Size, *Yinjing fami yaojue* (Classic of revealing the secrets of silver), 147
Liberation Daily (*Jiefang ribao*), 220–221, 227; articles on shamans, 224–229
liberty, equality, and fraternity, 120–123
Liezi, 99
Liji (Record of the rites): "Great Learning" chapter, 121, 136n12; "Liyun" chapter, 123, 138n20
Lin Changyi, 97, 217
linguistic change, 5; Li Jinxi on, 159–161, 175–176
Linneaus, Carolus, 150
Li Sao, 105
literary language (*guowen*), 162, 168. *See also* classical Chinese; vernacular writing
Literary Revolution, 61, 160
literature: aesthetic dimension, 100, 101, 105, 107, 115n18; audience, 113, 114; autonomy of, 100, 108, 109, 110; didacticism in, 95–96, 102, 103; and discursive argument, 104; English term, 94, 100–101, 114n4; fiction, 93, 111, 113; national, 101; New Literature, 114; *shiwen*, 94, 101, 104, 113, 114; utilitarianism of, 101–102, 107, 108, 110; Western and Chinese, 108–109. *See also wenxue*
Liu Bei, 91n57
Liu Chengyu, 87, 88, 90n45, 92n84; "The Voluntary Yielding of the 'Hongxian Emperor,'" 87
Liu Fu (Liu Bannong), 177n23, 178n42; *Experimental Record of the Four Tones*, 165–166, 177n26, 177n29
Liu Ru, 167, 177n35
Liu Shipei: expression of *longue durée*, 7; and the Han race, 7, 76, 78–79; "On Monarchic Government and the Restoration of Antiquity," 75–77, 78–79, 88, 90n35; "On the Yellow Emperor Chronology," 76; on the Republic, 76; on the *shanrang* of Yao and Shun, 84, 87–88; and *Shuowen jiezi*, 213; and the *Wenxuan* school, 110; on writing, 113; and Yuan Shikai, 75, 77, 79, 86–87
Liu Wanyi, 226
Liu Yizheng, 212
Liuhe congtan (Collected stories from the world; comp. Wylie), 46

Liuqing ji (comp. Chen Mei), 144, 155n17
local society, 56–57
Long Xilin, 218
Long March, 66, 222–223
longue durée, 2, 7, 51
Lü Dajun, 232
Lu Shiyi, 218
Lu Xun: "Maluo shili shuo" (On the power of Mara poetry), 112; poetry of, 113–114; reference to *myriad treasures*, 145, 152; and *Shuowen jiezi*, 213; on *wenxue*, 94, 114n3
Lufei Kui, 162, 175
Luo Lin, 197
Luo Zhenyu, 189, 192
Luther, Martin, 40, 43

Ma Shouling, 217
Macartney, Lord, 23
Manchu archives, 27, 188, 189–190, 192, 196, 198
Manchu bibliography, 194–195, 196–197; bibliographical treatise of *Qingshi gao*, 192–193
Manchukuo, 74, 91n72, 189
Manchu language: as administrative language, 184, 187, 192; after the fall of the Qing, 187–189, 196; proposed treatise on, 190–192; publications, 182–186, 193, 197, 199n7; study of, 13, 180–181; terms for five virtues, 25–26; translation examination, 187–188; written language, 188, 189, 190–191, 192, 194, 198. *See also* Manchu studies
Manchu publishing, 181, 182–183, 193; linguistic works, 183–186, 199n9. *See also* Manchu bibliography
Manchu state essence (*guocui*), 186, 191, 200n31
Manchu studies: Chinese and foreign, 193; importance of Feng-kuan, 195–196; Japanese tradition, 17, 19, 26–27, 27, 29; Qing tradition, 181, 182, 197–198; Republican period, 12, 188, 197–198
Mandate of Heaven, 33, 81, 82, 83
Manichaeanism, 38, 40, 42–43
Manwen laodang (Old Manchu Archive), 27
Manzhou shilu (Manchu veritable records), 26–27

Mao Huanwen, *Zengbu wanbao quanshu* (Expanded complete compendia of myriad treasures), 142, 148, 155n19
Mao Jin, *Jigu ge Shuowen* (*Shuowen* from the Pavilion for Absorbing Antiquity), 216
Mao Yi, *Jigu ge Shuowen*, 216
Mao Zedong, 62, 66, 229; on Li Jinxi's lectures on language standardization, 176n17; "On New Democracy," 223, 237n16; "Talks on Literature and Arts at the Yan'an Forum," 223
Marxism, 55, 223
mass-line politics, 227, 228, 230, 232, 234
Masuda Wataru collection, 146, 156n29
Matsubara Iwagorō, *Saiankoku no Tōkyō* (In darkest Tokyo), 54
Matsuzaki Kōdō, 216
May 4th movements, 2, 16, 58, 96, 109, 221
May Thirtieth Movement, 63
Mei Zengliang, 97, 99–100, 101–102, 108, 111, 115n18; on isolation of the writer, 106–107; on writing for oneself, 113
Meiji Restoration, 73–74, 145
Mencius, 121, 135n9, 136n13, 137n16
Meng Sen, 188, 214
Michurin, Ivan Vladimirovich, 150
Ming, Emperor, of Han, 86
Ming shi (History of the Ming), 190
Ming shilu (Veritable records of the Ming dynasty), 26
minguo, 71, 74, 75, 76. *See also* Han race; Republic of China
"minutia learning" (*xiaoxue*), 1
minyong bianlan (brief guides for popular use), 147, 156n35
minzu (nation), 7; *minzuzhuyi* and *minzudiguozhuyi*, 72
mixin (superstition), 236n6. *See also* superstition
Mizhuan Huajing (Esoteric lore of the Mirror of flowers), 148, 157n44
Mo Youzhi, 218
modern era, 51, 95
modern medicine, 220, 221, 223
monarchy, 69, 76, 77, 79. *See also* abdication; Mandate of Heaven
Mongolian, 26, 27, 183, 187, 189, 190, 193, 195; bannermen, 185, 194

Mongyol-un üsüg-ün quriyaysan bičig (Qinding Mengwen huishu), 183–184, 185, 195, 199n11
Moore, Samuel, 55
morality: civic, 120, 122, 123; in literature, 95–96, 108, 116n64; moral rehabilitation, 232–233, 235, 238n48; and religion, 127
morality books (*shanshu*), 147
Morohashi Tetsuji, *Dai Kan-Wa jiten* (Great Sino-Japanese dictionary), 54
Moser, David, 179n68
Muhammad, 42
multilingual analysis, 17–18
museums, 127, 128, 130, 166, 206, 213; "museumification" (Levenson), 112
Musil, Robert, *The Man without Qualities*, 187
myriad treasures (*wanbao quanshu*), 142–143; contents of, 156n35; disdain for, 145–146, 147–148, 149, 152; editions of, 142–145, 146–147, 148, 153–154, 155n14, 155n19; in Japan, 145, 154–155n10, 155n21, 157n46; in libraries and archives, 146–147; in the marketplace, 143–145; supplements, 142–144, 147, 148, 149, 157n57; technical information in, 147, 149–151, 153, 157n57; woodblock and lithographed, 142, 148, 152

Naitō Konan: career of, 51; criticism of Japanese views of China, 64–65; on fall of Qing, 51–52, 57; grasp of history, 62, 66–67; and Manchu studies, 17, 26–27, 188; on "monarchical autocracy" in the modern era, 51; politics of, 55, 67n8; prediction on communism, 52–53, 58–59, 66–67; "Shakaishugi o toru," 67n8; *Shin Shina ron*, 59, 61–62, 67n18; "Shina ni kaere," 62–65; *Shina ron*, 57–58; and *Shuowen jiezi*, 216; on the Taiping Rebellion, 11, 52–53, 56–57, 66; use of terms *kyōsanshugi* and *sekka*, 53–54, 59, 60, 62, 65–66; view of republicanism, 51, 57–58; views on communism, 56–57, 60, 61, 62–63, 65
national anthem, 85–88
national essence, 186–187, 207, 211, 213; Manchu, 186, 191, 200n31
nationalism, 58, 72; and language, 174, 186, 213, 215

Nationalist Army, 63–64
Nationalist rule, 171, 195, 223, 234, 235
National Language Monthly, 177n20, 178n45
national language standardization, 12, 159; and the Manchu language, 180–181; under nationalist rule, 171–174; national pronunciation and phonetic notation, 161–162, 164–166, 167, 168, 170, 171–174, 176n9, 177n22, 178n41, 178n46; and replacement of Chinese script, 172, 175–176, 178n49; tensions and conflicts, 161–164, 167, 170–171, 172; and textbooks, 168, 171, 174. See also *guoyu*; Li Jinxi
National Language Unification Preparatory Committee, 164, 165, 171, 173, 178n46, 179n57
Nedostup, Rebecca, 234
Needham, Joseph, 151, 158n67
Neo-Confucianism, 41, 43, 131–132
Neo-Daoism, 120
Nestorianism: and Catholicism, 33, 36; celibacy in, 43–44; disappearance of, 40; in the Tang dynasty, 34, 37; in Urmia, 46; Yang Rongzhi's critique, 39–40, 44, 45–46. See also Catholicism; Nestorian stele
Nestorian stele: authenticity of, 34; authorship and content of inscription, 34, 44–45; commentaries and scholarship on, 32, 33, 34, 35–37, 44, 46–48; language of, 34, 44, 45; rubbings and printing of, 33–34; story of Noah, 45; unearthing of, 33, 48n2. See also Nestorianism; Yang Rongzhi
"New China," 6, 118, 235
New Culture Movement, 58, 61, 64, 127, 134, 139n41, 223
New Democracy, 223
"new knowledge," 143
New Learning, 95, 134
New Literature (*xin wenxue*), 114
New New China, 64
"new Qing history," 17–18, 31n24
New Sinology: approach to language of CCP state building, 221; and history of China's national language, 161; and Manchu studies, 12; and non-Sinitic languages, 17; *Shuowen jiezi* and, 12, 205;

New Sinology (cont.)
  as methodology, 2, 10, 13, 13n4; study of Chinese vernacular knowledge, 142, 153. See also philological studies; Sinology
New Testament, 40
New Text School (*jinwen pai*), 95–96, 105
Nihon kokugo daijiten (Great dictionary of the Japanese language), 54
1911 Revolution, 70, 71
Nora, Pierre, *lieux de mémoire*, 32
noumenal and phenomenal worlds, 123–126, 128, 130, 131
Nylan, Michael, 6

oath-taking rituals, 233, 235
Ogawa Yōichi, 155n10
Okamoto Kyōsai, 216
Old Testament, 39, 40, 41
opium trade, 24
Opium Wars, 3, 95, 209
original sin, 36
Ōsaka mainichi shinbun, 58, 62
Ou Fengchi, 38
outermost sphere of Heaven (*zongdongtian*), 36–37
Ouyang Xiu, 108

Pan Yantong, 217
Pāṇini, 215
Paris Commune, 54
Peace Preservation Laws (Japan, 1925), 55
Pei-kuan, 185, 186, 197, 198
Peking University, 111–112, 126, 194, 195; Folksong Study Society, 156n36. See also Cai Yuanpei
penal reform, 238n48
People's Republic of China, 3–4, 235. See also Mao Zedong
Perkins, Justin, 46
Persia, 41, 46
phenomenal and noumenal worlds, 123–126, 128, 130, 131
philological studies: and the *dao*, 209; early-twentieth-century, 8, 213; eighteenth-century "philological turn," 204, 206; Hummel on, 7; as irrelevant, 1, 15, 207; and literary writing, 108; of Manchu, 17, 191, 193, 196; and nationalism, 213; nineteenth-century, 209–212;

world philology, 1–2, 15–16, 29. See also evidential scholarship; Han learning; New Sinology; *Shuowen jiezi*; world philology
philosophy, Wang Guowei on, 109, 110
Phonetically Annotated Newspaper for the National Language (*Guoyu zhuyin zimu bao*), 176n11
phonetic notation. See national language standardization
phonology, 9, 145, 203n111, 210; and *guoyu*, 164, 167; northern Chinese, 172, 173–174, 178n46; and tones, 166, 177n29. See also *Shuowen jiezi*
Pines, Yuri, 73
pingdeng (equality), 122
Pinkney, Tony, 110
place names, 21, 22–23, 28
poetry, 97, 101, 102–107, 113
Police Affairs Bureau (Japan), 55
political virtue, 73, 76–77, 79, 80–81, 86
Pollock, Sheldon, 1, 15
popular religion, 224, 227, 234, 237n28
print culture, 143–144, 193; Manchu, 181, 182–184, 185, 193
propaganda, 227, 232, 235; language of, 221. See also *Liberation Daily*
Protestantism, 32, 40, 43–44, 47. See also Yang Rongzhi
public libraries, 184
public trials, 220, 221, 230, 232, 234, 235. See also judicial systems
Pulleyblank, Edwin, 8–9, 10–11
Pu-yi, 189; abdication of, 81, 84

Qi Zenggui, 195
Qian Daxin, 38, 209, 211
Qian Guisen, 217
Qian Qianyi, 38
Qian Xuantong, 89n16, 177n28, 178n42, 179n57; on alphabetization, 175; and *Shuowen jiezi*, 213; on tones, 164, 166
Qian Zhongshu, 93
Qiang tribes, 77, 78–79
Qianlong emperor, 81, 184, 194
Qiao Songnian, 217
Qinding Mengwen huishu (*Mongyol-un üsüg-ün quriyaysan bičig*), 183–184, 185, 195, 199n11

Qin dynasty, 71, 208
Qing archives, 198. *See also* Manchu archives
Qing dynasty: emperors, 29; fall of, 51–52, 57; last years, 187; parallels to twenty-first-century, 17; periodization, 204; State Historiography Office, 189
Qingshi gao (Draft history of the Qing): bibliographical treatise, 192–193; compilation of, 188–190; Feng-kuan's comments on, 196; lack of attention to Manchu language, 189; proposal for treatise on the dynastic language, 190–192, 196, 197
Qingwen zonghui (Comprehensive collection of Qing writing; Zhi-kuan and Pei-kuan), 185–187, 197
Qishiyi, *Xiyu wenjianlu*, 29
Qu Qiubai (Shuanglin), "Diguozhuyi de yongpu yu Zhongguo pingmin" (Servants of imperialism and the common Chinese people), 61

Rawski, Evelyn, 183
"regime of historicity" (Hartog), 5, 73, 74–75
reign eras (*jianyuan*), 70
religion, 32–33, 221–222, 235, 236n6; Cai Yuanpei's views on, 124, 127, 129, 130, 131; CCP on, 222–223, 224. *See also jiao*
religious freedom, 222
ren (humaneness), as "fraternity," 121–122
"reprint fever," 153
"Republican fever," 153
republicanism, 51, 53, 57–58. 76
Republic of China (Minguo): under Chiang Kai-shek, 171; declared by Sun Yat-sen, 70; and the Five Races, 85; national anthem, 85–88; and religion, 48; and the "restoration of antiquity," 75; under Yuan Shikai, 84. *See also* national language standardization; Yuan Shikai
Ricci, Matteo, 41; romanization system of, 172
Rice Riots (Japan, 1918), 55
Richard, Timothy, *Forty-Five Years in China*, 114n4
Riyong wanshi baoku choushi bixu (Treasure house of all daily things necessary for social relations), 144–145, 150

Romance of the Three Kingdoms, The, 81
Rome, 98
Rossokhin, Ilarion, 19, 21, 26
Ru (Confucian scholars), 207, 208, 209; used for Jesuit missionaries, 36
Ruan Yuan, 108, 110
rule by virtue and rule by heredity, 80–81, 86
Russia, 23, 28, 61, 65; Russian Sinology, 15, 19, 20–21, 25–26, 29
Russian Orthodox Church, 40
Russian Revolution, 53, 55, 58, 60

sage-kings, 6, 45, 80, 121, 169. *See also* Five Emperors
Sakai Tadao, 154–155n10
Sakai Toshihiko, 55–56
sanjiao (three schools of traditional thought), 32, 35, 38
Sanskrit language, 215
sanyi sanrang ceremony, 80, 83, 90n45
Satan, 45, 46
sati, 41
Sayišangy-a, dictionary of, 184
Schiller, Friedrich, 131
Schopenhauer, Arthur, 131
science and technology, 211, 215, 221; Chen Haozi's *Huajing*, 148–151
sekka/chihua (becoming red), 59, 60, 61, 62, 65–66; *sekka seinen* (communist youth), 59; *sekka shisō* (communist thought), 59
Selden, Mark, 238n38
self-examination, 232–233, 235
selfhood, 128, 138n32, 139nn33–34
seng (monk), 35–36, 43
Sesquicentennial International Exposition (Philadelphia, 1926), 159, 169
Shaanbei: peasant culture, 235; popular religion, 224–225, 228, 229, 237n28. *See also* Shaan-Gan-Ning Border Region
Shaan-Gan-Ning Border Region, 220, 223–224, 232, 233, 236n2, 236n14
Shajitang (Huiaitang), 38
Shakaishugi kenkyū (Studies of socialism), 55
Shakyamuni, 42
shamans: "arts of cheating," 224–227, 228, 229; case of Yang Hanzhu, 220, 229, 230, 233, 235; categories of, 225; in CCP

shamans (cont.)
    newspaper pieces, 224–229; confessions of, 220, 221, 224, 226, 229, 231–232, 235, 238n40; and Confucian elites, 234; and "Curse of the Nine Daughters," 227; distinguished from spirit mediums, 235–236n1; ghost-haunting, 233–234; healing rituals, 220–21, 224, 225–227, 228; number of, 223, 236n14; practices for protection of children, 227; and sexual corruption, 234; transformation into productive labor, 224, 228, 230, 231–232. See also Anti-Shaman Campaign
Shan, Patrick, 84, 89n1
Shanghai Library, 146, 156n30
shanrang (voluntary yielding), 81–83, 84, 90n48, 91n52, 91n55; *yirang* used for, 85–86, 87, 88; Yuan Shikai and, 83–84. See also abdication
Shen Qi, 163–164
Shen Tao, 217
Sheng-yu, 184, 193
Shennong, 41
shi (gentlemen), 36
Shi Runzhang, 97
Shibue Chūsai, 216
Shiji (Records of the Grand Historian), 6, 20. See also Sima Qian
shilu. See *Veritable Records*
shiwen (literature), 94, 101, 104, 113, 114
shu (reciprocity), as "equality," 121–122
Shujing, commentary of Kong Yingda, 85–86
Shun (sage-king), 45
Shuntian shibao, 84
Shuowen jiezi (Analysis of simple graphs as an explanation of complex characters; Xu Shen): changing use of, over time, 12, 205–207, 213; editions of, 216; in Japan, 216; in the nineteenth century, 209–212, 217–218; in the Qian-Jia period, 207–209, 210–211; as scientific tool, 211, 212, 214; from the Sino-Japanese War to the Republic, 212–215; study of, 204–205, 206–207, 208–209, 210; as "time machine," 205–206, 208, 215, 216; in twentieth century, 207, 215
Shuowen jiezi gulin (Forest of explanations on the analysis of characters and explanation of writing), 213–214, 215

Shuowen jiezi yizheng (Proofs of the meanings in the *Shuowen jiezi*), 219n12
Siberian Expedition, 60–61
Sibu beiyao (Ready essentials of the four divisions), 194
Sibu congkan (Serial printings from the four divisions), 194
Siku quanshu (Complete writings of the Four Treasuries), 21–22, 23, 73, 199n9; proposals to continue, 184, 194, 197
Sima Qian, 6, 7, 13nn20–21, 20, 109
Sino-Japanese War, 220, 223
Sinology: applied to contemporary issues, 66–67; and Chinese humanities, 180, 181, 182; convergence of traditions, 180; dialogue with historiography, 8; Japanese, 27; and multilingual analysis, 19; and non-Sinitic languages, 17, 198; old-style, 15, 13n4; Russian, 15, 19, 20–21, 29. See also Manchu studies; New Sinology; philological studies
six arts of Zhou, 126
social Darwinism, 131, 133, 140n47
social history, 15, 214
socialism, 55, 62, 67n8, 119
Society for the Diffusion of Christian and General Knowledge (Christian Literature Society), 114n4
Song Learning, 96, 98, 108, 204, 208
Souciet, Étienne, 22
Southern Society (Nanshe), 87
South Manchuria Railway Company, 28, 196
Spencer, Herbert, 129
Spring and Autumn Annals, The, 105
Stary, Giovanni, 26
statecraft, 85, 86, 98, 195, 204, 205, 209; writing and, 102, 104, 112
Staunton, Sir George, 18, 23–24, 25–26, 29, 31n24
Stein, Gunther, 236n2
Stratagems of the Warring States, 99–100
student activism, 66, 177n25
Su Dongpo, 104
Sun Xingyan, *Wenzi tang ji* (Collected writings from the Hall of Lexical Inquiries), 207–208
Sun Yat-sen, 51, 53, 58, 70, 223; on Chinese civilization, 4–5; and Yang Rongzhi, 38, 47
Sungsen, 184

superstition, 37, 149, 222, 228, 234; shamanistic healing practices, 220–221, 224, 225–227, 228; Yang on, 42, 45, 48. See also shamans
Supreme Ultimate (*taiji*), 124–125
Sutra of Perfect Enlightenment (*Yanjue jing*), 128, 139n34
Syria, 39. See also Syriac
Syriac, 34, 35, 38, 46

Taiping Rebellion, 11, 51–53, 56, 59, 66, 209
Taishang ganying pian (Treatise of Laozi on the response and return), 147
Taishō Democracy, 55
Tamura Jitsuzō, 27
Tan Sitong, 129
Tan Xian, 217
Tang, King, 86, 137n16
Tang Shaoyi, 147
Tao Zengyou, 110–111
Temple of Heaven, 79, 80, 86
thought reform, 233, 235, 238n48
Three Kingdoms period, 81–82
three teachings (*sanjiao*), 32, 35, 38
Tian Wuzhao, 218
Tian Yingsan, 226
tiangao diyuan (heaven high and the emperor far away), 57
tianxia weigong (the empire belongs to all/ the most virtuous), 80, 138n20
Tibet, 17, 22, 42, 85
Tibetan language, 190, 193
time, 2, 5, 16, 39, 118; Imperialist, 141, 142, 143; and language, 10, 13; linear, 133, 171, 234
Tokugawa period scholarship, 215–216
tonal differentiation, 163*fig.*, 164–166, 177n22, 177n29, 178n42; *rusheng*, 161, 164, 165, 172, 174
Tongcheng school of prose, 96–97, 100, 106, 107–108, 110, 113
Tongzhi restoration, 181–182, 189
Torghut Mongols, 18, 20, 30
traditional Chinese medicine, 223, 228
tradition and modernity, 11, 12, 133–134
transfer of power, 80, 81, 84, 89. See also abdication; Mandate of Heaven
transitional period, notion of, 133–134

translation, 16, 25–26, 107; of Communist Manifesto, 55–56, 67nn9–10; examination, 187–188. See also Tulišen's travel account
travel accounts, 17, 22, 23, 28, 29. See also Tulišen's travel account
Treasure House of All Daily Things Necessary for Social Relations (*Riyong wanshi baoku choushi bixu*), 144–145, 150
Trump, Donald, 4, 8
Tsinghua University, 194
tuanlian system, 57
Tulišen's travel account, 18–19, 30n5; Chinese text, 17, 21–22, 23–24, 25; comments on Russian customs, 23; European translations from Chinese, 22–23; on five basic virtues, 24–26; history of translations, 16, 18–20; Manchu text, 17–18, 20, 21, 25, 30, 31n24; prefaces, 20, 21, 24; route and place names, 22–23; Russian translation, 20–21, 25–26, 29; as source of information for Jesuit cartography, 22–23, 29; Staunton's English translation, 18, 23–24, 25–26, 29, 31n24; and transnational history, 28–29. See also *Yiyulu*
Twenty-One Demands, 3, 58

Ubukata Toshirō, *Meiji Taishō kenbun shi* (Things seen and heard in the Meiji and Taishō eras), 60
United Front, 64, 223, 224
Unkovskii (Russian envoy), 28–29
urban planning, 131, 139n42
Uyghur people (*Huihe*), 42

Vedas, 41
vegetarianism, 129, 130
Veritable Records, 26–27, 189, 195
vernacular knowledge, 141, 151–152, 153
vernacular writing (*yutiwen*): and aesthetic writing 101; and Chinese knowledge culture, 141–142; in education, 162; and fiction, 111, 113–114; in Li Jinxi's diagram of language evolution, 160; and national language standardization, 162, 165, 170, 173; neglected materials, 141, 147. See also myriad treasures; vernacular knowledge
Verne, Jules, 139n42

wakokuhon (Japanese annotated versions of Chinese texts), 155n21
Wan Zhang, 137n16
wanbao quanshu genre. *See* myriad treasures
Wanfu, 185–186, 200n28
Wang, Chaohua, 129
Wang Guowei, 7–8; "Wenxue xiaoyan" (Desultory remarks on literature), 109–110, 111, 112
Wang Hui, 72–73, 74, 75
Wang Mang, 81, 91n55
Wang Mingsheng, 207, 218n2
Wang Pu, 161, 162, 176n9
Wang Rensi, 217
Wang Shaolan, 217
Wang Shizhen, 97
Wang Shunan, 218
Wang Tao, 8, 53
Wang Xianqian, 34, 46–47, 48
Wang Yun, 217, 218
Wang Zhao, 161
Wang Zhen, *Nongsang tongjue* (Secrets of mulberry farming), 149
Wanguo gongbao (Review of the times), 114n4
wanshi buqiuren (myriad matters about which one will not need to ask), 147, 153
warlords, 63–64
Way, the, 206, 208, 209–210, 212
Wechsler, Howard, 80–81, 82, 83
Wei Yuan, 95, 102, 103, 111, 209; *Haiguo tuzhi*, 98; "On Learning," 98; preface to *Shi guwei*, 105–106; "Shi bi xing jian xu jian," 105
Wei-Jin period scholarship, 208
wen (writing), 94, 102, 169; and *bi*, 108, 110; *shiwen* (literature), 94, 101, 104, 113, 114; *wen yi zai dao* (writing is meant to convey the *dao*), 96, 103, 104, 110; *wenxian* (documentation), 114n4; *wenzhang* (refined writing), 96, 99. *See also wenxue*
Wen, King, 136n13
Weng Fanggang, 208–209
wenming, 7, 8, 76, 94. *See also* Chinese civilization
Wenxuan school, 110

wenxue (literature): as amusement, 110; in *Analects*, 94; in ancient Rome, 98; in Peking University curriculum, 111–112; and philosophy, 109–110; reconfiguration of the term, 11, 93–94, 113–114; and statecraft, 98; term in Qing, 94–95, 98–100, 107–108, 110–112; and *wenzi*, 169; Wu Rulun's concept of, 107–108. *See also* literature
Wen-zhong, 196
Western learning, 37, 109, 112, 133, 143, 204, 211. *See also* science and technology
White Lotus, 38
Whyte, Martin, 234
Wilhelm, Hellmut, 194
Williams, Raymond, 101, 110
woodblock editions and lithography, 144, 148, 152, 154n5
world philology, 1–2, 15–16
World Philology (Pollock, Elman, and Chang), 1
woxiang (self), 128, 138n32, 139n34
Wright, Mary, 181–182
Wu Huifang, 143
Wu, King, 86
Wu Meng, 168
Wu Rulun, 107–108, 109, 113
Wu Shijian, 190
Wu You, 49n5
Wu Zhihui, 161, 168, 171, 175, 177n25, 179n57; and *Shuowen jiezi*, 213, 214; on tones, 164, 166
Wuchang rebels, 51
wushen (shamans), 225. *See also* shamans
Wuti Qingwenjian, 27
Wuxi County Education Association, 168, 177n35
wuxing (five phases), 39, 45, 228
Wuzong, Emperor, 43
wuzu gonghe (five races under one union), 85, 86
Wylie, Alexander, 46, 149

Xi Jinping, 4–5, 7, 8, 9, 153
Xia Xie, 38
Xian, Emperor, of Han, 81, 82
Xiang-li-ting, 185
xiangtuan/kyōdan, 57
Xiao Yifei, 147–148

xiaoshuo (fiction), 93, 111, 113
xiaoxue (minutia learning), 1
Xie Guozhen, 195
Xie Zhangting, 218
Xinbian Riyong wanquan xinshu (Newly edited, completely thorough new book for daily use), 150
Xinjiang, 17, 194
Xin qiannian (*La Jeunesse*), 108
Xiongnu, 86
Xu Han, 217
Xu Hao, 217
Xu Ji, 49n5
Xu, Paul (Xu Guangqi), 33, 48n2
Xu Shen. See *Shuowen jiezi*
Xu Xuan, 216
Xu Zhi, 82
Xuanyuan. *See* Yellow Emperor
Xun Qing, 105
Xun Hua yirang (abdication of Yao to Shun), 85–86
Xuxiu "Siku quanshu" zongmu tiyao (Bibliographical précis for a continuation of the *Complete Writings of the Four Repositories*), 195–197, 203n111

Yamanashi Tōsen, 216
Yan Fu, 107
Yan Hui, 137n16
Yan Ruoju, 97
Yan Zhangfu, 218
Yan'an, 220–221, 223, 232–233, 236n2.
  See also Anti-Shaman Campaign
Yang Hanzhu, 220, 229, 230, 233, 235
Yang Rongzhi, 38; and the Bible, 38, 39, 43, 44, 45; commentary on Nestorian stele inscription, 34, 38, 39, 39–47; on Confucianism, 44, 47; conversion to Christianity, 38; criticism of Nestorian thinking, 39–40, 44, 45–46; explanation of *Jingjiao*, 39, 43; promotion of Protestantism, 40, 43–44, 47; refutation of Qing essays on the stele, 38–39; on religious faiths, 40–43; on Satan and evil, 36, 45; on superstition, 45, 48; on use of *seng*, 43; view that Chinese civilization originated in the Middle East, 41, 47, 48. *See also* Wang Xianqian
Yang Zhongxi, *Baqi wenjing* (Literary canon of the eight banners), 184

Yao Nai, 96–97, 98, 102, 104, 108, 115n18; disciples of, 97, 101, 103, 108, 115n18.
  See also Mei Zengliang
Yao Ying, 103–104, 105, 106, 108
Yao Yongpu, *Wenxue yanjiu fa* (The method of studying writing), 100
Yao and Shun: abdication legend, 80–83, 84, 85–86, 87; and *diguo*, 73; Gu Jiegang on, 88; in Mencius and *Analects* passages, 121, 137n15, 137n16; reference to, in national anthem, 85, 87–88
yaoran lingxu (numinous existence), 44
Ye Gongchuo, 192
Ye Huixin, 217
Yellow Emperor (Xuanyuan): and the origins of Chinese writing, 41, 214; Sima Qian on, 7, 13n21; as symbol for Chinese civilization, 7, 8, 70, 73, 75, 76
Yesujiao (teaching of Jesus), 40
yi (righteousness), as "liberty," 120–122
Yi Peiji, 192
Yi Qinheng, 151
Yi Yin, 121, 137n16
Yi-geng, *Qingyu renming yi Han* (Manchu names translated into Chinese), 196, 203n104
Yijing (Classic of changes), 41, 44, 225; and dragon sightings, 7, 8, 82, 91n57; and legitimacy, 82–83, 84; use of *wenming*, 7, 8
yili (principle), 96, 98, 102, 103, 108, 115n18, 116n64
yin and *yang*, 39, 44, 45, 228
Yiyulu (A record of alien regions; Tulišen): inclusion in *Siku quanshu*, 21–22, 23; prefaces, 21, 22, 24; publication of, 18; Staunton's view of, 23–24. *See also* Tulišen's travel account
Yu Shimei, 189, 192
Yu Yue, 209–210, 218, 219n8
Yu the Great, 80, 81, 86, 121, 126, 137n16
Yuan Jin, 95
Yuan Keding, 84
Yuan Shikai: attempt to reestablish monarchy, 11, 69–70, 72, 88–89; compared with Cao Pi, 84; denounced by Liang Qichao, 71; described as turning back the historical clock, 69–70, 74, 89n1; Hongxian monarchy, 70, 86, 87,

Yuan Shikai (cont.)
88–89, 92n84; invocation of *shanrang* model, 80, 83–86, 87, 88; letters of support, 71; and Liu Shipei, 75–79, 86–87; Naitō's view of, 57, 59; and the national anthem, 85–88; preparations for monarchy, 70–71, 79–80, 83–84, 85, 90n45; presidency, 70, 89n4; project to compile a Qing history, 188; reign title, 70; use of imperial vocabulary, 71–72; use of term *diguo*, 72–75, 89
Yue Sibing, 165, 177n20
yutiwen. *See* vernacular writing
Yuxia ji (Record of the jade casket), 147

Zarrow, Peter, 6, 69, 73, 75
Zeng Guofan, 52, 57, 58, 109, 112, 211; divisions of learning, 98–99, 100, 102; on inseparability of *dao* and writing, 105, 108, 116n64
Zhang Binglin (Taiyan), 209, 212
Zhang, Emperor, of Han, 86, 87
Zhang Guotai, 150
Zhang Mu, 218
Zhang Qingtian (Blue-Sky Zhang), 233–234
Zhang Shizhao, 169, 178n37
Zhang Yi, 135n9
Zhang Yuquan, 195
Zhang Zai, 121, 136n14
Zhang Zhidong, 111–112, 210, 219n12
Zhang Zongxiang, 190, 192, 196
Zhao Chaogou, 236n2
Zhao Erxun, 188
Zhao Shixian, 231
Zhao Wanli (pseud. Lizhou), 193, 194, 197
zhen (vitality), 76–77, 78
Zheng Dahua, 95
Zheng, King, of Qin, 71–72
Zhi-kuan, 185, 186, 197, 198
Zhili clique, 63
Zhiwuxue dacidian (Dictionary of botanical nomenclature), 150, 152
zhiyong (utility of learning), 111
Zhong Gong, 135n10
"Zhongguo" in Manchu texts, 31n24
Zhonghua Books, 159, 164, 177n36
Zhonghua diguo (Empire of China), 70
Zhongyong (Doctrine of the mean), 44; phrase *xiudao zhiwei jiao*, 43, 47
Zhou, Duke of, 91n53
Zhou Yunqing, 214
Zhou Zuoren, 96, 102, 151–152
Zhou li (Rites of Zhou), 80
Zhu Di (Yongle emperor), 91n53
Zhu Junsheng, 217
Zhu Shiduan, 218
Zhu Shizhe, 192–193, 201–202n76
Zhu Xi, 43, 96, 108, 216
Zhu Xuedan, 217
Zhu Yizun, 97
Zhu Yun, 210
Zhuangzi, 99
zhuyin zimu phonetic alphabet, 161, 162, 166, 167, 170, 171–174; name changed to *zhuyin fuhao*, 172; street signs, 179n66
zongjiao (religion), 32–33, 222, 236n6. *See also jiao*; religion
zongtong (president), 71
Zoroastrianism, 41, 46
Zunghar Mongols, 18, 28
Zuozhuan, 86–87, 191